AFRICA AND THE AMERICAS

Interconnections during the Slave Trade

Edited by
José C. Curto and Renée Soulodre-La France

Africa World Press, Inc.

P.O. Box 1892
Trenton, NJ 08607

P.O. Box 48
Asmara, ERITREA

Africa World Press, Inc.

First Printing 2005

Book design: Sam Saverance
Cover design: Dapo Ojo-Ade

Library of Congress Cataloging-in-Publication Data

Africa and the Americas : interconnections during the slave trade / edited by José C. Curto and Renée Soulodre-La France.
p. cm.
"A collection of essays from a conference held at York University, October 12-15th, 2000"--Pref.
Includes bibliographical references and index.
ISBN 1-59221-271-9 (hardcover) -- ISBN 1-59221-272-7 (pbk.)
1. Slave trade--Africa--History--Congresses. 2. Slave trade--America--History--Congresses. 3. Africa--Relations--America--Congresses. 4. America--Relations--Africa--Congresses. 5. Blacks--America--Social conditions--Congresses. 6. Brazil--Relations--Africa--Congresses. 7. Africa--Relations--Brazil--Congresses. I. Curto, José C. II. Soulodre-La France, Renée.

HT1321.A38 2005
306.3'62'096--dc22

2004030710

To Paul E. Lovejoy,
for the intellectual stimulation and the many *jeitinhos* over the years.

Table of Contents

LIST OF ILLUSTRATIONS

Preface

This volume contains a collection of essays from a conference held at York University, October 12-15th, 2000. The conference was organized by a committee consisting of José C. Curto, who served as chair; Ivana Elbl, Department of History, Trent University; Gregory Guy, at the time a member of the Department of Languages, Literatures & Linguistics at York University and now in the Department of Luinguistics at New York University; Ibrahim Hamza, a Ph.D. student in the Department of History at York University; Paul E. Lovejoy, Canada Research Chair in African Diaspora History at York University; David V. Trotman, a member of the Department of History and the Division of Humanities at York University; and Renée Soulodre-La France, at the time Coordinator of Research for the York/UNESCO Nigerian Hinterland Project and now a member of the Department of History, King's College, University of Western Ontario. The conference was made possible by grants from the Social Sciences and Humanities Research Council of Canada, Fundação Calouste Gulbenkian, Portugal, Serviço da Cooperação para o Desenvolvimento, Instituto Camões e Fundação para a Ciência e Tecnologia, Portugal, Programa Lusitânia, Departamento da Cultura, Ministério das Relações Exteriores, Brasil, and Consulado Geral de Portugal, Toronto. At York University, we wish to thank the Department of History, the York/UNESCO Nigerian Hinterland Project, the Office of the Vice-President Academic, the Office of the Dean of Arts, Founders College, and the African Studies Programme for their support. Finally, our thanks to Eugene Onutan, Webmaster of the Harriet Tubman Centre on the African Diaspora, York University, for his work on the maps and illustrations.

José C. Curto
Renée Soulodre-La France
London and Toronto, Ontario
15, December 2004

Introduction: Interconnections between Africa and the Americas during the Era of the Slave Trade

José C. Curto and Renée Soulodre-La France

In 1996, Bernard Bailyn documented a growing trend toward the study of the Atlantic World as a coherent historical unit, where historians of Europe and of North and South America had broadened their scope of analysis to include "the entire Atlantic basin, not simply descriptively but conceptually." In evidencing the rise of this phenomenon, he persistently drew upon reference works that essentially equate Atlantic history with European or western civilization. Bailyn acknowledged Africa as part of this new history by referring *en passant* to the "dark continent" as a supplier of servile labor. The slave trade was, in his view, "the great chain that joined Africa and [the] America[s]" and "fundamental to the whole of Atlantic commerce." But Bailyn highlighted none of the links in this great chain. As a result, he significantly underestimated the role of Africa and Africans in molding the history and culture of the Atlantic World.[1]

Such a conception of the Atlantic World is, of course, reminiscent of an older Eurocentric view that barely, if at all, recognized the role of Africa and Africans in its making. It was also, by the mid-1990s, myopic, insofar as a growing body of scholarly literature was already pointing to the opposite. In 1992, John K. Thornton published his revisionist monograph on the contribution of Africa and Africans in the making of the Atlantic community.[2] In contradistinction to the then current view that the Africans and their descendents in the Americas were merely victims suffocating under the oppressive control of their slave masters, Thornton carefully explained and documented exactly how they were important historical agents, in spite of their predicament. Not only did they recreate much of Africa within radically new social, political, spiritual, demographic, and physical environments throughout the Americas but, in so doing, also fundamentally affected the development of the Atlantic World. The following year, Paul Gilroy published his equally important monograph on the black Atlantic community, a world that was "continuously crisscrossed by movements of black people---not only as commodities but engaged in various struggles towards emancipation, autonomy, and citizenship."[3] In his view, blacks were also historical agents in their own right, on an equal footing with whites, and instrumental in the making of a "black Atlantic" identity. Yet, neither of these studies found their way into the bibliography that Bailyn drew upon to conceive his peculiar idea of the new Atlantic History.[4]

The contributions by Thornton and Gilroy in the early 1990s represented radically different counterpoints to Bailyn's subsequent conception of the Atlantic World and the role of Africans and their descendents in its making. But they were not problem free. Thornton portrayed the roles of Africa and Africans in the making of the Atlantic World as uni-directional, with millions of individuals taken through the slave trade out of Africa and forced to relocate in the Americas, where their recreated lives under bondage became central to the development of the Atlantic community. Gilroy provided a more complex concept in pointing to a black Atlantic world constantly interconnected through movements of black peoples. But the evidence underlying his model was both specific to the post-1850 era and approached from a northern Diasporic perspective that concentrated exclusively on the Anglophone world, especially black intellectuals. Gilroy thus completely missed the links of the previous 400 years, the crisscrossing of African diplomats, merchants, and sailors (not all of whom were bondsmen), the removal of nearly 12 million Africans to the Americas as servile laborers (most of whom were not destined to spend their lives as slaves in Anglophone landscapes), the return of some of the slaves and even larger numbers of their freed descendents back to Africa, and everything associated with these movements. Although important in their own right, the models of Africans in the making of the Atlantic World as conceptualized by Thornton and Gilroy provided but a partial picture since neither captured the interactive linkages between Africa and the Americas during the era of slavery.

It did not take long, however, for those complex interconnections to become the object of increased scholarly scrutiny. First, a number of conferences specifically dealing with these linkages were successively mounted, beginning with "A Dimensão Atlântica da África: II Reunião Internacional de História da África," late in 1996 in Rio de Janeiro, Brazil, and "West Africa and the Americas: Repercussions of the Slave Trade," at the University of the West Indies, Mona, Jamaica, early in 1997. The summer of 1997 saw Paul E. Lovejoy organize a massive conference at York University designed to "Identify Enslaved Africans" not only throughout the Atlantic, but beyond as well.[5] Other conferences followed: "Rethinking the African Diaspora: The making of a Black Atlantic World in the Bight of Benin and Brazil," held at Emory University, Atlanta, Georgia, in the spring of 1998; and "Enslaving Connections: Africa and Brazil during the Era of the Slave Trade," at York University, in the autumn of 2000. From these conferences, not to mention other venues, emerged a growing body of literature on the Atlantic world not only as an integrated unit of analysis, with Africa and Africans as equal partners in the making of this community,[6] but also as an interconnected world, with the slave trade between Africa and the Americas resulting in series of interactive linkages whose complex and multifaceted effects permeated through either shore.[7] A re-conceptualization of Atlantic history was in the making.

One of the earliest scholars to point the way was Alberto da Costa e Silva, a tireless proponent of things African in Brazil. In 1997, he boldly stated:

> There is a whole history of the Atlantic. A history, evidently, of commercial and political disputes, navigational developments, and voluntary and forced migrations. But there is also a long and important history that is becoming, little by little, less discrete. That of freed Africans and their descendents, that of mulattos, *cafuzos* (persons of Amerindian and African descent), *caboclos* (individuals of Amerindian and European background) and whites who set up shop in the African continent, returned to Brazil, and then moved back to Africa or spent their lives between both shores. That of slave ships which also operated as post-office and embassy. That brought instructions from Sultans, Emirs, Kings and other African polities to their subjects in slavery. That brought messages from Queen-Mothers and exiled Princes -since slavery also served as political banishment- to their partisans who continued to conspire in Africa. News of developments there (in Africa) arrived in the *senzalas* (slave residential areas), *cantos* (urban groups of incidental workers), and *quilombos* (communities of escaped slaves), and could thus quicken the pace of *alforrias* (manumissions) and returns.[8]

A few years later, Robin Law and Kristin Mann published an influential article in which they argued that the slave trade did more than simply foster the development of commercial links between West Africa and the Atlantic basin. Inspired by the work of Pierre Verger on the interconnections between the Bight of Benin and Bahia, in northeastern Brazil, both during and following the era of slavery,[9] they showed that the slave trade along the coast of West Africa generated a series of transatlantic cultural, demographic, and social exchanges that shaped both the history of the region and those of the world connected by it.[10] In 2001, Kristin Mann and Edna Bay went even further. In a collection of essays under their editorship, they demonstrated the reciprocal exchanges between the Bight of Benin and Bahia, during and following the era of slavery, to have been more profound than Verger had portrayed three decades earlier.[11] Both complex and multifaceted, these exchanges involved enslaved, freed, and free peoples of all stripes, commodities, various religious and other traditions, as well as changing identities that were central to the history of the two regions they connected. Then, in 2004, José C. Curto and Paul E. Lovejoy pushed the paradigm further still. In an edited volume that expanded the geographical scope of analysis to include Brazil and western Africa as a whole, they argued that the "forced migrants who went to Brazil helped to shape the demographic, linguistic, cultural, economic, political, and religious formation of both colonial and post-independence Brazil, while returning "Brazilians, whether of African or European background and often mixed, also affected the demographic, economic, political, religious and cultural composition of the coastal ports of the Bight of Benin and the towns and commercial centers of Angola."[12]

With *Africa and the Americas: Interconnections during the Slave Trade*, the new paradigm begins to reach its logical conclusion. This volume examines the interactive linkages created between Africa and the Americas during the era of the trans-Atlantic slave trade (c. 1600-1850). Its focus remains western Africa and its interconnections through slavery with Brazil. From about 1600 to 1850, some 4.5 million enslaved Africans went to Brazil, ten times as many as went to North America and far more than the total number of Africans who went to all of the Caribbean and North America combined.[13] Most came from Angola and other parts of West Central Africa, including speakers of Kimbundu, Kikongo and Umbundu, closely related Bantu languages: often referred to as Kongo or Angola in Brazil, these people constituted perhaps the greatest concentration of individuals of similar ethnic and linguistic background anywhere in the Americas. Large numbers of enslaved Africans arriving in Brazil also came from the Bight of Benin, the notorious "Slave Coast" of European accounts, including speakers of the various Gbe languages (Ewe, Fon, Allada), as well as Yoruba and at least one identifiable Muslim population from the far interior: these people, were variously known in Brazil as Gege or Mina, in the case of the Gbe group of languages, and the Brazilian term for the Yoruba was "Nago," while Muslims from the Central Sudan of West Africa were known as Malês. In each case, they constituted significant concentrations of Africans within Brazil's massive slave population, with enslaved individuals originating from West Africa concentrated in the northeastern regions of Brazil, particularly Bahia, while their more numerous West Central African counterparts predominantly relocated further south in and around Rio de Janeiro.

But *Africa and the Americas: Interconnections during the Slave Trade* also goes beyond western Africa and Brazil to include other historical agents and landscapes. First, it captures a third group of enslaved Africans arriving in Brazil, not to mention other parts of the Americas, that has rarely received scholarly attention. Mozambique also supplied significant numbers of Africans for the Brazilian market, particularly during the last decades of the eighteenth and the first few decades of the nineteenth centuries. Most commonly known as "Moçambiques," these enslaved individuals originating from East Africa also formed an identifiable population of significant proportions in Brazil. Second, this collection also concentrates upon the circum-Caribbean within a comparative perspective. Because of the particular characteristics of this region, the tentacles of the Atlantic slave trade were here as pervasive as they were in Brazil. By bringing the circum-Caribbean into the discussion, two things become much clearer: one is that the African migrants who were forcibly removed to the Americas had a tremendous impact upon the cultural, demographic, economic, linguistic, political, and religious formation of colonial and post-independence societies; and the other is that the Americas, whether through its slave merchants, commodities, and enslaved, freed, and free Africans or people of African descent who moved eastward back across the Atlantic similarly had a profound effect upon the political, religious, economic, demographic and cultural composition of African societies involved in the Atlantic slave trade. In other words, the linkages forged through this commerce produced a high rate of contact, back and forth, between

Africa and the Americas. The slave trade not only facilitated the creation of one Atlantic World out of many but, in doing so, also interconnected it through various circuitous exchanges. Moreover, by including Mozambique and Moçambiques in our discussion, it also becomes evident that the Atlantic community was far from confined to the ocean that delineated it. Indeed, the tentacles of the Atlantic slave trade spread far beyond the South Atlantic. They stretched into the Atlantic as conceptualized by Bailyn, spilled into eastern Africa and, from there, all the way to Asia.

Africa and the Americas: Interconnections during the Slave Trade is a collection of recent scholarly work by leading scholars from Africa, Brazil, Europe, and North America using innovative approaches and methodologies within a comparative and inter-disciplinary perspective. Its organization reflects an important structural feature of the slave trade itself. That is its circular nature, departing from Africa, coming to America, and then returning to Africa. Thus the volume is separated into three parts.

First of all, David Eltis, Stephen Behrendt and David Richardson analyze the slave trade along its national lines and determine that the Portuguese were critically important in the carrying of slaves. Basing their analysis on the extensive data they have collected for the Transatlantic Slave Trade Database these authors test notions of a Portuguese slave trade that was "based on two continents and was effectively fused with that of Brazil." While this analysis sharpens our image of the importance of the Portuguese trade, it also reflects the historical structures that were created through that commerce. The authors thus set the context for the next several chapters that deal with questions of ethnic identity, religion and creolization, but specifically within Brazil.

The first of these chapters is Alpers' discussion of "Mozambiques" as an ethnic group in which he focuses on the question of enslaved East Africans brought to Brazil at specific moments in the slave trade and the process of identity formation that they created through these experiences. Alpers traces out the differentiation between 'nations' that is evident in 19th century Brazilian sources and demonstrates how the "Atlantic" must be expanded conceptually to accommodate the impact of East Africans on that world. Luis Nicolau's analysis of *Candomblé* and its African roots in *Vodun*, explores the persistence of "African cognitive orientations of worldviews in the Americas." Through a multi-faceted approach, he analyses the existence of multi-divinity and serial performance characteristics as integral to the *vodun* religious system. Nicolau concludes that the way in which these characteristics of an African religious form were translated through slavery in Brazil provided the structure necessary to regroup multi-ethnic cults into a cohesive religious institution recognized as *candomblé*. Next, Elizabeth Kiddy's comparison of various black lay religious brotherhoods provides a roadmap to the complex patterns of African ethnic and creole interrelations, as well as gender distinctions, in different regions of Brazil. This work highlights the ways in which Africans and their descendants adapted their own hierarchical structures to their American reality and how these structures facilitated the expression of African collectivities and their participation in a larger Brazilian society through the brotherhoods. In the following chapter, Dale Graden investigates the relationship between African responses to the end of the transatlantic slave trade and abolitionist initiatives in Bahia. He focuses upon how Africans actively and consciously participated in the campaigns for abolition by making the continuation of the trade a dangerous proposition for Brazilian society. The end of this section is rounded out by João Reis' study of urban labor in Bahia prior to abolition. This detailed analysis of ethnically organized work groups (*cantos)* allows the author to examine the transitional phases between enslavement and freedom and the "ethnic characteristics of a free working class on the eve of abolition." Reis concludes that among this group of street workers (*ganhadores*) racial politics were gradually being mediated by notions of class identity.

From this initial section, the collection then moves into other areas of the Americas providing comparative essays by Landers, Schuler and Rey. Landers focuses on the material traditions of various maroon settlements in Spanish America and Brazil. She explores "questions about the leadership and social and political organization of maroon settlements" in the Americas. Landers suggests that these communities drew on a variety of African cultural models as they struggled for survival and the leaders of the maroon settlements adopted and adapted a wide range of African and American legitimizing strategies to solidify their leadership. The creation of maroon communities was not the only way that enslaved Africans sought to escape. Monica Schuler analyzes deliverance narratives drawn from the Caribbean to fit these into the framework of a world view shaped by the slave voyage and African beliefs. She argues that this discourse of the Diaspora provides us with a "deeper meaning of enslavement, exile, and exploitation and the possibility of reunification in a blissful African homeland." This chapter explains the ways in which actors caught up in the Atlantic world made sense of the dynamics of that world both in Africa and in America. Finally Rey's discussion of "root experiences" in West Central Africa leads him to conclude that these directly affected the nature of religious beliefs and resistance to slavery in Saint-Domingue. The importance of Kongolese religious and ideological experiences are emphasized in his analysis of revolutionary Saint-Domingue leadership.

Completing the loop, the third section brings us back to Africa with Soumonni's comparative analysis of Afro-Brazilian communities in Ouidah and Lagos during the mid-19th century. The existence of these Afro-Brazilian communities or Aguda are testimony to the multilateral linkages created through the slave trade. Soumonni shows how the establishments of returnees were shaped by local African contexts and how their essential hybridity enabled them to accommodate to the diverse situations that they confronted within Africa while retaining their Afro-Brazilian identity. That loop back to Africa is reinforced by Capela's study of the Brazilian impact on Mozambique politics and ideology, with special reference to the slave trade. In this investigation of the historical trajectory that brought Brazil and Mozambique together, the author examines the political relationships as well as the economic linkages between the two areas. He sets these relations within the context of international events and the development of political ideologies and traces out the impact that Brazilians had on such processes in Mozambique. Finally Kriger provides a conclusion with her discussion of the challenges facing historians studying culture in the Atlantic world, the innovative methods and sources that can provide a wealth of information and the need to keep addressing the issue of cultural transferals and influences from different angles.

Africa and the Americas: Interconnections during the Slave Trade thus represents a well-balanced volume on the circuitous linkages between Africa and the Americas during the era of the slave trade. It is addressed to a wide public that is increasingly fascinated with the interactions resulting from African slavery throughout the Atlantic world over the last several hundred years. Based upon a variety of theoretical foundations and widely differing sources, from archaeological digs, to texts from songs, dances, police reports and official legislation, this volume presents cutting-edge research and analysis as a contribution to our understanding of slavery and the development of African cultures throughout the broad Atlantic world. Moving beyond an exclusionist conception of the Atlantic and pushing the boundaries of scholarship beyond the now overstudied "transfer of survivals" of African cultures under the context of New World slavery, this collection not only demonstrates a variety of circuitous linkages permeating the major groups involved in Atlantic slavery, but also evidences Africans as equal partners in this process. As such, these essays provide a refreshing statement on the state of the scholarship in the field, a road map for future research, and an integrative model for studying the Atlantic world in all of its complexity and fluidity.

ENDNOTES

1. Bernard Bailyn, "The Idea of Atlantic History," *Itinerario* 20 (1996): 19-44, especially pp. 33-34.
2. John K. Thornton, *Africa and Africans in the Making of the Atlantic World, 1400-1680* (New York: Cambridge University Press, 1992). A second edition, which extends the chronological coverage to 1800, appeared in 1998.
3. Paul Gilroy, *The Black Atlantic: Modernity and Double Consciousness* (Cambridge, Mass.: Harvard University Press, 1993), especially pp. 6 and 15-16.
4. Neither did an even longer list of other works on the South Atlantic already then available, including: Lorenzo D. Turner, "Some Contacts of Brazilian Ex-Slaves with Nigeria, West Africa," *Journal of Negro History* 27 (1942): pp. 55-67; Pierre Verger, "Influence du Brésil au Golfe du Bénin," *Les Afro-Americains, Memoires de l'IFAN* 27 (1953): 11-101; idem, "Retour des 'Bresiliens' au Golfe du Benin au XIXeme Siecle," *Études Dahoméennes* 8 (1966): 5-28; idem, *Flux et Reflux de la traite des Nègres entre le Golfe de Bénin et Bahia de Todos os Santos, du XVIIe au XIXe siècle* (Paris: Mouton, 1968); J. F. de Almeida Prado, "Les Relations de Bahia (Brésil) avec le Dahomey," *Revue d'Histoire des Colonies* 16 (1954): 167-226; Norberto Francisco de Souza, "Contribution a l'histoire de la famille de Souza," *Études Dahoméennes* 15 (1955): 17-21; José H. Rodrigues, *Brasil e África: outro horizonte* (Rio de Janeiro:

Civilização Brasileira, 1961); idem, "The Influence of Africa on Brazil and of Brazil on Africa," *Journal of African History* 3 (1962): 49-67; Anthony B. Laotan, "Brazilian Influence on Lagos," *Nigerian Magazine* 69 (1964): 156-165; David A. Ross, "The Career of Domingo Martinez in the Bight of Benin 1833-64," *Journal of African History* 6 (1965): 79-90; idem, "The First Chacha of Whydah: Francisco Felix da Souza," *Odu* New Series 2 (1969): 19-28; D. E. K. Amenumey, "Geraldo da Lima: A Reappraisal," *Transactions of the Historical Society of Ghana* 9 (1968): 65-78; Richard D. Ralston, "The Return of Brazilian Freedmen to West Africa in the 18th and 19th Centuries," *Canadian Journal of African Studies* 3 (1969): 577-592; Júlio Santanna Braga, "Notas Sobre o 'Quartier Bresil' no Daomé," *Afro-Ásia* 6-7 (1968): 56-62; Manuel dos Anjos da Silva Rebelo, *Relações entre Angola e Brasil (1808-1830)* (Lisbon: Agencia Geral do Ultramar, 1970); Jerry Michael Turner, "Les Brésiliens: The Impact of Former Brazilian Slaves upon Dahomey," Unpublished Ph. D. Dissertation, Boston University, 1974; idem, "Cultura afro-brasileira na África Ocidental,"*Estudos Afro-Asiáticos* 1 (1978): 19-25; idem, "Africans, Afro-Brazilians and Europeans: 19th Century Politics on the Benin Gulf," *África* (Universidade de São Paulo) 4 (1981): 3-31; idem, "Identidade étnica na África Ocidental: o caso especial dos afro-brasileiros no Benin, na Nigéria, no Togo e em Ghana nos séculos XIX e XX," *Estudos Afro-Asiáticos* 28 (1995): 85-99; Corcino M. dos Santos, "Relações de Angola com o Rio de Janeiro (1736-1808)," *Estudos Históricos* 12 (1973): 7-68; idem, *Relações Comerciais do Rio de Janeiro com Lisboa (1763-1808)* (Rio de Janeiro: Tempo Brasileiro, 1980); idem, *O Rio de Janeiro e a Conjuntura Atlântica* (Rio de Janeiro: Expressão e Cultura, 1993); Manuela Carneiro da Cunha, "Religião, Comércio e Etnicidade: Uma Interpretação Preliminar do Catolicismo Brasileiro em Lagos, no Século XIX," *Religião e Sociedade* 1 (1977): 51-60; idem, *Negros, Estrangeiros: Os Escravos Libertos e Sua Volta à África* (São Paulo: Brasilience, 1985); Marianno Carneiro da Cunha, *Da Senzala ao Sobrado: A Arquitectura Brasileira na África Ocidental* (São Paulo: Nobel, 1985); Nicolás del Castillo, *Esclavos negros en Cartagena y sus aportes léxicos* (Bogotá: Insituto Caro y Cuervo, 1982); Frédéric Mauro, *Le Portugal, le Brésil, et l'Atlantique au XVII Siècle (1570-1670)* (Paris: Fondation Calouste Gulbenkian / Centre Culturel Portugais, 1983); Joseph C. Miller, *Way of Death: Merchant Capitalism and the Angolan Slave Trade, 1730-1830* (Madison: University of Wisconsin Press, 1988); John K. Thornton, "The African Experience of '20. and Odd Negroes' Arriving in Virginia in 1619," *William and Mary Quarterly* 3rd Series 55/3 (1988): 421-434; idem "African Dimensions of the Stono Rebellion," *American Historical Review* 96/4 (1991):1101-1113; idem, "African Soldiers in the Haitian Revolution," *Journal of Caribbean History* 25/1-2 (1991): 58-80; idem, "'I am the Subject of the King of Congo': African Political Ideology and the Haitian Revolution," *Journal of World History* 4/2 (1993): 181-214; Nina S. de Friedemann, "Cabildos de Negros: Refugios de Africanía en Colombia," *Caribbean Studies* 23/1-2 (1990): 82-97; S. Y. Boadi-Siaw, "Brazilian Returnees of West Africa," in Joseph E. Harris (ed.), *Global Dimensions of the African Diaspora* (Wash. D.C.: Howard University Press, 1993, 2nd edition), pp. 421-439; Lisa A. Lindsay, "To Return to the Bosom of their Fatherland: Brazilian Immigrants in Nineteenth-Century Lagos," *Slavery and Abolition* 15 (1994): 22-50; and Paul E. Lovejoy, "Background to Rebellion: The Origins of Muslim Slaves in Bahia," in Paul E. Lovejoy and Nicholas Rogers (eds.), *Unfree Labour in the Development of the Atlantic World* (London: F. Cass, 1994), pp. 151-82.

5. This event laid the foundation of the Nigerian Hinterland Project (NHP), based at York University and funded originally by the Social Sciences and Humanities Research Council of Canada and UNESCO. A major international collaborative research effort designed to explore the linkages between two regions from which large numbers of slaves were exported, the Bights of Benin and Biafra and their respective hinterlands, and the places in the Americas, North Africa, and the Middle East where they were forcibly relocated, the NHP has subsequently developed into the Harriet Tubman Resource Centre on the African Diaspora, also based at York University, to examine the interactive connections between Africans throughout Africa and in the Diaspora via the slave trade route. See <http://www.yorku.ca/nhp>.
6. See, for example: Ira Berlin, "From Creole to African: Atlantic Creoles and the Origins of African-American Society in Mainland North America," *William and Mary Quarterly* 53/2 (1996): 251-288; James H. Sweet, "Male Homosexuality and Spiritism in the African Diaspora: The Legacies of a Link," *Journal of the History of Sexuality* 7/2 (1996): 184-202; Douglas Chambers, "'My own nation': Igbo Exiles in the Diaspora," *Slavery and Abolition* 18/1 (1997): 72-97; Robin Law (ed.), *Source Material for studying the Slave Trade and the African Diaspora* (Stirling: Centre of Commonwealth Studies, University of Stirling: Occasional Paper No. 5, 1997); Allen D. Austin, *African Muslims in antebellum America: transatlantic stories and spiritual struggles* (New York: Routledge, 1997); Ira Berlin, *Many Thousand Gone: The First Two Centuries of Slavery in North America* (New York: Oxford University Press, 1998); Michael A. Gomez, *Exchanging our Country Marks: The Transformation of African Identities in the Colonial and Antebellum South* (Chapel Hill: University of North Carolina, 1998); Martin Lienhard, *O Mare e o Mato: Histórias da Escravidão (Congo-Angola, Brasil, Caribe)* (Bahia: EDUFBA, 1998); Sylviane Diouf, *Servants of Allah: African Muslims enslaved in the Americas* (New York: New York University Press, 1998); Robin Law and Silke Strickrodt (eds.), *The Ports of the Slave Trade (Bights of Benin and Biafra)*. (Stirling: Centre of Commonwealth Studies, University of Stirling, Occasional Paper No. 6, 1999); *The Americas* 57/2 (2000), special issue on "The African Experience in Early Spanish America," edited by Matthew Restall and Jane Landers; Rina Cáceres (ed.), *Rutas de la Esclavitud en África y América Latina* (San José, Costa Rica: Editorial de la Universidad de Costa Rica, 2001); Judith A. Carney, *Black Rice: The African Origins of Rice Cultivation in the Americas* (Cambridge: Harvard University Press, 2001); Robin Law and Paul E. Lovejoy (eds.), *The Biography of Mahommah Gardo Baquaqua: His Passage from Slavery to Freedom in Africa and America* (Princeton: Markus Wiener, Publisher, 2001); Manolo Garcia Florentino, *Em Costas Negras: Uma Historia do Trafico Atlantico de Escravos entre a Africa e o Rio de Janeiro (secs. XVIII e XIX)* (São Paulo: Companhia das Letras, 2002, 2nd edition); Linda M. Heywood (ed.), *Central Africans and Cultural Transformations in the American Diaspora* (New York: Cambridge University Press, 2002); Sweet, James H. *Recreating Africa: Culture, Kinship and Religion in the African-Portuguese World, 1441-1770*. Chapel Hill: University of North Carolina Press, 2003; and Herman L. Bennett, *Africans in Colonial Mexico: Absolutism, Christianity, and Afro-Creole Consciousness, 1570-1640* (Indiana University Press, 2003).
7. See, for example: Robin Law, "Ethnicity and the slave trade: 'Lucumi' and 'Nago' as ethnonyms in West Africa," *History in Africa* 24 (1997): 205-219; Jerome S. Handler, "Life Histories of Enslaved Africans in Barbados," *Slavery and Abolition* 19 (1998):

129-141; Bellarmin C. Codo, "Les Afro-brésiliens de retour," in Doudou Diene (ed.), *La Chaine et le lien: une vision de la traite negrière* (Paris: Unesco, 1998), pp. 95-105; Alcione M. Amos, "Afro-Brasileiros no Togo: a história da família Olympio, 1882-1945," *Afro-Ásia* 23 (1999): 175-197; Milton Guran, *Agudás: os "brasileiros" do Benim* (Rio de Janeiro: Editora Nova Fronteira, 1999); Selma Pantoja and José Flávio Sombra Saraiva (eds.), *Angola e Brasil nas Rotas do Atlântico Sul* (Rio de Janeiro: Bertrand Brasil, 1999); Paul E. Lovejoy, and David Richardson, "Trust, Pawnship and Atlantic History: The Institutional Foundations of the Old Calabar Slave Trade," *American Historical Review* 104/2 (1999): 332-355; J. Lorand Matory,, "The English Professors of Brazil: On the Diasporic Roots of the Yorùbá Nation," *Comparative Studies in Society and History* 41/1 (1999): 72-103; José C. Curto, "The Anatomy of a Demographic Explosion: Luanda, 1844-1850," *International Journal of African Historical Studies* 32 (1999): 381-405; Vincent Carretta, "Olaudah Equiano or Gustavus Vassa? New Light on an Eighteenth Century Question of Identity," *Slavery and Abolition* 20 (1999): 96-105; Linda M. Heywood, "The Angolan-Afro-Brazilian Cultural Connections," *Slavery and Abolition* 20 (1999): 9-23; Paul E. Lovejoy (ed.), *Identity in the Shadow of Slavery* (London: Continuum, 2000); Luiz-Felipe de Alencastro, *O Trato dos Viventes: Formação do Brasil no Atlântico Sul* (São Paulo: Companhia das Letras, 2000); Paul E. Lovejoy and David Richardson, "Letters of the Old Calabar Slave Trade, 1760-89," in Vincent Carretta and Philip Gould (eds.), *Genius in Bondage Literature of the Early Black Atlantic* (Louisville: University of Kentucky Press, 2000), pp. 89-115; David Northrup, "Igbo and Myth Igbo: Culture and Ethnicity in the Atlantic World, 1600-1850," *Slavery and Abolition* 21/3 (2000): 1-20; José C. Curto, and Raymond R. Gervais, "The Population History of Luanda During the Late Atlantic Slave Trade, 1781-1844," *African Economic History* 29 (2001): 83-121; Renée Soulodre-La France and Paul E. Lovejoy, "Intercambios transatlánticos, sociedad esclavista e inquisición en la Cartagena del siglo XVII," in Claudia Mosquera, Mauricio Pardo and Odile Hoffmann (eds.), *Afrodescendientes en las Américas. Trayectorias sociales e identitarias. 150 años de la abolición de la esclavitud en Colombia* (Bogotá: Universidad Nacional de Colombia, ICANH, IRD, ILSA, 2002), pp. 195-211; Isabel Castro Henriques and Louis Sala-Molins (eds.), *Déraison, esclavage ideologiques et juridiques de la traite négrière et de l'esclavage* (Paris: Éditions UNESCO, 2002); Jerome S. Handler, "Survivors of the Middle Passage: Life Stories of Enslaved Africans in British America," *Slavery and Abolition* 23/1 (2002): 25-56; Mariza de Carvalho Soares, "Descobrindo a Guiné no Brasil Colonial," *Revista do Instituto Histórico e Geográfico Brasileiro* 161/407 (2002): 71-94; José C. Curto, *Alcoól e Escravos: O comércio luso-brasileiro do alcoól em Mpinda, Luanda e Benguela durante o tráfico atlântico de escravos (c. 1480-1830) e o seu impacto nas sociedades da África Central Ocidental* (Lisbon: Editora Vulgata, 2002); Paul E. Lovejoy and David V. Trotman (eds.), *Trans-Atlantic Dimensions of Ethnicity in the African Diaspora* (London: Continuum, 2003); Paul E. Lovejoy, "The Black Atlantic in the Development of the 'Western' World: Alternative Approaches to the 'Europeanization' of the Americas," in Dirk Hoerder (ed.), *Diversity in History: Transcultural Interactions from the Early Modern Mediterranean World to the Twentieth-Century Postcolonial World* (New York: Berghahn Books, 2003), pp.109-133; Randy J. Sparks, *The Two Princes of Calabar: An Eighteenth-Century Atlantic Odyssey* (Cambridge, Mass.: Harvard University Press, 2004); Paul E. Lovejoy, "Methodology through the Ethnic Lens: The Study of Atlantic Africa," in Toyin Falola and Christian Jennings (eds.), *African Historical Research: Sources and Methods* (Rochester: University of Rochester Press, 2004), pp. 105-117; and the works listed in the subsequent notes.

8. Alberto da Costa e Silva, "Os Estudos de História de África e sua importância para o Brasil," in *A dimensão atlântica da África: II Reunião Internacional de História de África* (São Paulo: CEA-USP/SDG-Marinha/CAPES, 1997), pp. 17-18.
9. See Verger's monograph cited above in n. 4. This volume was subsequently published in English as *Trade Relations between the Bight of Benin and Bahia, 17th -19th Century* trans. by Evelyn Crawford (Ibadan: Ibadan University Press, 1976), and then in Portuguese as *Fluxo e Refluxo do Tráfico de Escravos entre o Golfo de Benin e a Bahia de Todos os Santos, dos Séculos XVII ao XIX* trans. by Tasso Gadzanis (São Paulo: Corrupio, 1987). Neither of these translations is part of the bibliography drawn upon by Bailyn.
10. Robin Law and Kristin Mann, "West Africa in the Atlantic Community: The Case of the Slave Coast," *William and Mary Quarterly* 46 (1999): 306-334.
11. *Slavery and Abolition* 22/1 (2001), special issue on "Rethinking the African Diaspora: The Making of a Black Atlantic World in the Bight of Benin and Brazil," edited by Kristin Mann and Edna G. Bay. This was subsequently published as Kristin Mann and Edna G. Bay (eds.), *Rethinking the African Diaspora: The Making of a Black Atlantic World in the Bight of Benin and Brazil* (London: Frank Cass, 2001).
12. José C. Curto and Paul E. Lovejoy, "Introduction: Enslaving Connections and the Changing Cultures of Africa and Brazil during the Era of Slavery," in José C. Curto and Paul E. Lovejoy (eds.), *Enslaving Connections: Changing Cultures of Africa and Brazil during the Era of Slavery* (Amherst, NY: Humanity Books, 2004), pp. 11-18.
13. David Eltis, Stephen Behrendt, David Richardson and Herbert Klein, *The Transatlantic Slave Trade: A Database on CD-ROM* (New York: Cambridge University Press, 1999).

1

National Participation in the Transatlantic Slave Trade: New Evidence[1]

David Eltis, Stephen D. Behrendt and David Richardson

Portuguese ships – defined as vessels owned by Portuguese nationals living mainly in Brazil – were among the first to carry slaves from Africa to the Americas, probably in 1519, as well as among the last to do so nearly three and one half centuries later as British and American warships patrolled the African and Cuban coasts. In addition, while the peak years of forced departures from Africa – the long eighteenth century – saw three-fifths of slaves entering the slave trade on non-Portuguese vessels, the Brazilian slave trade nevertheless expanded strongly after 1695. Yet Portuguese importance is not reflected in the surviving sources, with the result that the Portuguese, indeed the Iberian, trade is not as well represented in the new Transatlantic Slave Trade Data Set as most other national trades.[2] While we may not be able to compute new totals for Spanish, Portuguese and Brazilian participation in the transatlantic slave trade in any direct sense, the relative completeness of the data for some other national trades, especially the English and the Dutch, does allow us to make new assessments of the Iberian traffic on the basis of analogy.[3] In addition, on most other issues in trade – the transatlantic links, the fluctuations over time, the age and sex composition of those on board to mention only a few – we can offer much more precision than hitherto possible. What follows is based in part on some new Portuguese, Spanish and Brazilian archival material, but mainly on commodity export and slave population data in the Americas and inferences from the better known North European slave trade. We look first at the existing consensus in the literature on the volume of the transatlantic slave trade, with particular attention to its potential weaknesses, and second at the implications of the new data set for this consensus with particular reference to the trade carried on under Portuguese, Spanish and Brazilian flags. Readers should note that 90 percent or more of this trade was based in the Americas, not Europe.

The consensus figure in the literature as represented in Paul Lovejoy's last review of the work on this topic in 1989 was 11,863,000 Africans entering the Atlantic slave trade. This implied that "9.6-10.8 million would have been imported into the Americas," depending on the mortality rate chosen to convert departures from Africa into arrivals in the Americas. Elsewhere, Lovejoy prefers an estimate of 15 percent losses in the middle passage, so that we might take 10.2 million as his preferred estimate of arrivals. A more recent reassessment increases Lovejoy's estimates by about 5 percent.[4] These compare with Curtin's 1969 estimate of 9,566,000 arriving in the Americas and the Old World with a 20 percent margin of error either way. This estimate implied departures from Africa of 11.2 million.[5] While the revisions to Curtin's work do not appear extensive at the aggregate level, there have been some important changes in how this total is distributed on both sides of the Atlantic, but particularly in the Americas. In re-examining these estimates, we will assess both arrivals, upon which Curtin concentrated, and departures from Africa, which have attracted most attention from those reassessing Curtin. We rely on shipping records between 1660 and 1811 – a period which accounts for close to 60 percent of the transatlantic trade – and, where these are inadequate, on analogies drawn from these shipping records. Before 1660 and after 1811, we fall back on the consensus figures referred to above with some minor modifications.

We begin with a preliminary breakdown of voyages by national flag. The data set identifies the national affiliations of 23,302 or 86 percent of the voyages in the set. For a further 2,450, the context of the voyage and the name of the ship, owner, or captain make inferences about place of registration possible, and thus we created an imputed variable of national flag which contains affiliations for 25,767 voyages (or 24,823 of those ships that made it to Africa and embarked slaves). For some ships, this step is not possible. From 1839, the British allowed their cruisers to detain slave ships flying the Portuguese flag and carry them into British Vice-Admiralty courts for adjudication under British law. In response to this development (and to similar legislation in 1845 that extended the provision to the Brazilian flag), many slave ships abandoned ship registration papers altogether. In addition, there are undoubtedly some voyages which registered in one country, but which belonged to nationals of another, and others that sailed under false papers. Some British ships flying the French flag in the late eighteenth century are examples of the first, and both British and US owners sailing under Portuguese and Spanish papers after 1807 – sometimes fraudulent, sometimes not – are examples of the second. Overall, these cases probably account for less than one percent of the ships included in the set. It is also difficult to separate out voyages made by ships owned in Britain from those owned in the British Americas and later the US. Some ships identified as British were likely registered in the British Americas, and a similar problem arises with Portuguese and Brazilian ships in the nineteenth century. For a few voyages, even before 1839, there is no indication of any kind of the flag of the vessel. Given the fact that most slave ship owners in nineteenth century Brazil were in reality Portuguese nationals, Brazilian and Portuguese vessels may be lumped together as a single nation. Further, the vessels of unknown flag sailing after 1807 were much more likely to be Portuguese than not. Whereas the Portuguese flag was common in the trade to Cuba, the Spanish flag was almost never used in the much larger traffic to

Brazil. The assumption is accordingly made that all post-1807 voyages in the set were Portuguese. Before 1808, the problem of unknowns is much smaller. Given the solid sources available for French and Dutch ships before 1800, almost all of these 372 voyages are British, US or British colonial. As information on British registration is much more complete than its British colonial and US counterpart, then all pre-1808 voyages of unknown flag are taken to have been British colonial if sailing before 1776, and US if sailing after 1775 (effectively after 1782, for there were almost no slaving voyages from North America between 1776 and 1782). These assumptions give us the distribution shown in Table 1. The British and the Portuguese, particularly the former, dominate this preliminary breakdown accounting between them for seven out of ten transatlantic slaving voyages.

Given the national basis on which records were made, it makes sense to examine each of the European and American (40 percent of all slave voyages left the Americas) national trades more closely. We begin with the British, who entered the slave trade late – a century after it began, except for the odd voyage – and left it early, but who nevertheless carried more slaves across the Atlantic than any other nation except the Portuguese. English slave ships went mainly to English colonies, overwhelmingly so before 1714. The large numbers of slaves that the English sold or carried to the Spanish Americas passed through the English Caribbean first. An estimate of the number of slave arrivals in the English Americas is thus the same as the size of the British slave trade. Before 1662, English slave traders sold no more than 40,000 slaves in the Americas, almost all at Barbados. Between 1661 and 1713, the number was 399,800. Departures from Africa are estimated at 50,000 before 1661 and 500,400 between 1661 and 1713.[6] For the last 28 years of the British slave trade, an exhaustive database created by Stephen D. Behrendt, subsequently integrated into the new data set, provides the basis of an estimate of 924,500 slaves leaving Africa on 3,088 voyages. Table 2 (b) summarizes this information and, where necessary, derives from it slaves arrived in the Americas on the basis of voyage mortality estimates.

These three sets of estimates, two before 1714 and one after 1779 – leave the period 1714-1779 to be addressed. The British trade for these years originated overwhelmingly in the three ports of London, Liverpool and Bristol. It is likely that almost all the slave ships leaving Bristol are included in the new CD-ROM set. We are only slightly less confident about the completeness of our data for voyages leaving Liverpool. For London and the remaining British outports the proportion of slaving voyages included in the set is slightly lower than for Bristol and Liverpool, but still not less than 90 percent.[7] The basis for these assessments is simply our continuing research into eighteenth century newspapers on both sides of the Atlantic and the likelihood of any voyage that comes to our attention in these sources already appearing in the data set. Overall, the data set probably contains some record of 95 percent of the voyages that sailed from Britain between 1714 and 1779. The estimates of departures and arrivals from individual ports shown in Table 2 (a) derived directly from the data set include an allowance to accommodate missing vessels. Slave departures on Liverpool ships are increased by 1 percent, and on London ships and those operating from the minor outports by 10 percent. Bristol vessels are left unmodified. The sum of the amended values is entered in row 3 of Table 2 (b). There remains the problem of getting information on the outcome of the voyage. The main basis of Stephen Behrendt's recent reduction of previous estimates of the British slave trade after 1779 was his finding that a relatively large number of vessels set out on a slaving voyage and then failed to complete it. For the 1714-79 period, it is more difficult to discover the fate of voyages than it is in the later period. The strategy adopted here is to assume that all voyages without known outcomes, did in fact carry slaves to the Americas. Other things being equal, such a strategy produces upper-bound estimates of the British trade.[8] Table 2 (b) shows that British ships carried just over 3.1 million slaves from Africa and landed just under 2.7 million in the Americas.

The French traffic spanned a similar length of time to its English counterpart though it began and finished later. After 1700, the Mettas-Daget catalogues of voyages together with some small additions of our own are close to complete. There are two empirical tests that support this assessment. One involves tracking the sightings made of other ships during the slave voyages and reported in the Mettas-Daget. Ninety percent of the sightings in which the name of the other ship or captain is reported are included as full voyage entries somewhere else in the catalogue, and some of the remainder may have been coastal vessels or produce traders.[9] The second test developed as the new database was in preparation. In the last six months of the project, the editors added *Lloyd's List*, a shipping gazette, to the set. This publication is the most comprehensive information source on shipping movements in the eighteenth century, containing some reports on non-English shipping as well as movements of English vessels. *Lloyd's* generated only two voyages that were not already in the Mettas-Daget catalogues (and only six new voyages from Dutch ports discussed below). The few French voyages we have found that are not in Mettas-Daget ended prematurely because of capture or natural disaster, and therefore had more chance of slipping through the reporting systems that all European imperial slave systems maintained. Assuming once more that all slave voyages with unknown outcomes did, in fact, take on board slaves, and again imputing an average number of slaves carried whenever this value is not reported, the data set shows that French vessels bore away 1,035,900 people for the Americas between 1707 to 1793, the period covered by the Mettas-Daget catalogues. It is unlikely that this figure accounts for all French slave ships in this period, but given non-French sources we have consulted, and the above discussion, it is reasonable to estimate that the data set contains 95 percent of French vessels that made the crossing. Dividing 1,035,900 by 0.95 to reflect this assessment, yields an additional 54,500 slaves if the missing vessels were of similar size to those included in the set. Both these estimates are entered in Table 3.

The Mettas-Daget catalogues covers the years 1707 to 1793. On either side of this period the information on French slave shipments is less complete. For the first years of the eighteenth century we have added voyages from various sources, especially the *Asiento* ships (licensed by the Spanish Government to trade in slaves) which began to operate from France after 1701, but from 1701 to 1707, there is no reason to believe that the data are as complete as the years covered by Mettas-Daget. For 1706 and 1707 we use an annual average of 2,000, the mean of slaves carried between 1708 and 1710, and for 1701 to 1705, we use an annual average of 1,400, which is the mid point of average departures in the seventeenth century and the average for 1708 to 1710. This yields an estimate of 17,000 slaves embarked between 1701 and 1710. Of these, 6,300 are already included in the 1707-1793 estimate so that 10,700 are added to 54,500, yielding 65,200 slave exports to be allowed for missing French voyages during 1701-1793 (Table 3, row 3).

In the seventeenth century proper, our set contains only 40 records of French slave voyages disembarking 10,500 slaves, all in the French West Indies. The French slave trade was clearly larger than these figures suggest, but anyone who reads the voluminous English and Dutch correspondence from West Africa which reported the activities of all national groups knows that it was much smaller than its English and Dutch counterparts.[10] French government attempts to stimulate a slave trade from Colbert's reorganization down to the beginning of the French *Asiento* in 1701 were largely unsuccessful. The *Compagnie du Sénégal* managed a semblance of regular slaving activity, but the West India, Guinea Coast and Africa Companies never managed more than a multi-ship expedition every few years beginning with that commanded by Henrik Caroloff in 1669. There was no continuous French presence in Africa south of Senegambia. Even Senegal yielded the French only a few hundred slaves a year at this period, some of them to French galleys in Europe, and there is little evidence of an extensive French private slave trading sector before 1700. Some of the early arrivals on French ships were likely to have been captured from Portuguese vessels and would be included in the Portuguese estimates. Moreover, the Dutch dominated the small slave trade to the French Americas before Colbert's 1664 prohibition on slaves arriving in Dutch ships. Between the early 1660s and 1700, Clarence Munford's combing of the sources is consistent with no more than 1,000 slaves a year carried to the Americas in French ships, though he himself eschews any estimate. The English and Dutch documentation from Africa would suggest that this is an upper-bound figure.[11] Total arrivals in the Americas on French ships before 1700 are not likely to have been more than 32,000, or 800 a year, which implies 40,000 departures.

After 1792, there is a hiatus until the Peace of Amiens when the French trade revived briefly, this time centered on Bordeaux rather than Nantes. For this interlude we rely on Eric Saugera's work supplemented by *Lloyd's List*.[12] Saugera suggests 65 slaving voyages from metropolitan France, but about one third of these headed for the Mascarene Islands. These vessels carried on average 321 slaves. French vessels sailing to the Americas between 1800 and 1805 are thus estimated to have carried 14,000 slaves (two-thirds of 65 multiplied by 295). Mortality on board was about 3 percent and this suggests arrivals (assuming all these ships did disembark slaves) of 13,550. As Saugera suggests this is "*un ordre de grandeur*" or order of magnitude. The French trade disappeared once more when hostilities began again, and for post-1810 the volume is calculated separately below, though it is entered in Table 3. This Table pulls these various estimates together, and presents them in terms of both arrivals and departures.

The slave trade of The Netherlands was almost as well documented as its French counterpart. Table 4 summarizes current knowledge, and most of it derives from the work of Johannes Postma (whose data on the bulk of the Dutch slave trade are included in the data set), Franz Binder, Pieter Emmer and Ernst van den Boogart. Estimates derived from the work of these scholars appear in Table 4, but they do not in fact cover all the ground, at least prior to 1658.[13] The first recorded transatlantic shipment in a Dutch ship was to Trinidad in 1606, and there was the well-known small group that arrived in Virginia in 1619, although the latter had almost certainly been removed from a captured Portuguese *Asient*o vessel. Indeed, several other arrivals in Dutch ships in this early period began their voyages in Portuguese vessels that the Dutch subsequently captured, in an era when the Portuguese and Spanish crowns were joined. For the Dutch traffic to Brazil we use the van den Boogart and Emmer series totalling 31,000 departures, after an allowance for mortality is made to derive departures for those years where only information on numbers arrived is available. In the rest of the Americas in the first half of the seventeenth century, the Dutch sold slaves in Barbados and the French possessions from the moment those island began to turn to Africa for labor, but there is no indication of a regular trade to the Spanish Main at this early period. The slave trade to French and British colonies before 1650 was much smaller than the traffic to Brazil, and it is clear that the Dutch were much less important than the English in supplying Barbados, the most important – if still small – Caribbean market of the 1640s. We allow a speculative 17,000 departures from Africa in Dutch ships before 1651 to arrive at a total of 48,000 departures in Dutch ships by 1650 (Table 4, Rows 1 and 2).

From early in the 1650s, Curaçao, in Dutch hands since 1634, began its historic role as an entrepôt for Spanish America and the French islands, but it seems unlikely that more than a thousand slaves a year passed though the island between 1651 and 1657.[14] We have no precise estimates of Dutch slave supplies to Barbados and the French and Spanish Americas before 1658, but the recent literature has tended to see these branches of the Dutch slave trade as being smaller than scholars believed to be the case a few years ago.[15] If we allow one thousand a year leaving Africa for Curaçao, 1651-57, and add to this Postma's series of 44,500 arrivals (implying departures of 54,200), then the Dutch traffic, 1651-74 would total 61,200.

From 1675, we rely heavily on Postma's data. We have, however, edited them slightly by adding a few voyages, and using our own computations of imputed numbers of slaves (thus filling gaps in the data) where required. Procedures for imputed estimates are outlined in the Introduction to the data set, but for those familiar with the set itself, we have used more refined versions of the variables SLAXIMP to compute slave departures and SLAMIMP to compute slave arrivals. These estimates include an allowance for Dutch ships that disappeared from the historical record in the course of the voyage, so that in effect we assume such voyages delivered slaves. They do not include the few ships that sailed under the Dutch flag during the illegal phase of the slave trade, after the Anglo-Dutch treaty of 1818, though none of these voyages appeared to have been owned by Dutch nationals. How complete are these data? As noted above, *Lloyd's List* added little to Postma's data, but this source is available only from 1741, and even then some years are missing. Postma's sources for the 1730s – the period when the Company trade began to wind down and before the free trade companies were fully operational – are more likely to contain gaps. Moreover, during the Company era, 1674-1738, interlopers (illegal private voyages) are not as well documented as company voyages, especially in the 1670s and 1680s. Most such vessels sought gold rather than slaves, and Postma believes he has included most slaves from interloping ships in his data, but the possibility of missing voyages remains. It seems appropriate to make a small allowance for such voyages, and row 5 of Table 4 does this by adding 1 percent of our estimates for the 1676-1803 period to our overall total. From 1606 to 1829, we estimate that 452,000 arrived in the Americas under the Dutch flag, the survivors of 527,700 who left the coast of Africa.

The small Danish trade, taken up next, is well documented, and has received considerable attention in recent years. Svend Holsoe and Per Hernaes working independently of each other have collected what they consider to be close to comprehensive data on this branch of the traffic. Encouragingly their estimates are similar.[16] Per Hernaes estimates 97,850 slaves leaving Africa, but this includes 8,700 leaving Christiansborg on non-Danish ships, almost all of which are likely counted under the flags of other nations in the present exercise. Deducting these leaves 89,150 departures which likely account for all Danish transatlantic slaving voyages made in the years 1660-1806. Voyage mortality appears to have been relatively high on Danish vessels at 16.2 percent (n=86, sd=13.9) and this implies arrivals numbering 74,700. The other powers involved played a much smaller role again. Brandenburg and then the Hanse towns sent out a few voyages. There are records of 16 ventures under these flags, mainly during the era when the Electors of Brandenburg controlled Gross-Friedrichsburg just west of Cape Three Points on the Gold Coast between 1683 and 1721.[17] The Swedes may have sent a few more. We allow 5,000 departures for Brandenburg and Swedes together and 4,000 arrivals. Rows 8 and 9 of Table 6 incorporate these assessments.

The Portuguese and Spanish slave trades, unlike their British and Dutch counterparts, were largely synonymous with slave arrivals in particular areas of the Americas. The wind system of the South Atlantic ensured that the slave trade to Brazil was the preserve of traders based in the major Brazilian ports. These were mainly Portuguese even after Brazil became independent. Spanish slavers traded only to the Spanish Americas, but except at the very outset accounted for a small proportion of this trade. From early in the sixteenth century down to the second half of the eighteenth century, the Spanish chose to issue licences or *Asientos* which allowed mostly non-Spaniards to bring slaves to their territory rather than to carry slaves themselves. The licenses often changed hands several times before coming into the possession of the actual shippers of slaves. In the early days the latter could be Spanish, Genoese or Portuguese, but by the late sixteenth century were normally Portuguese. As it is difficult to separate out these different groups, all Iberian shippers before 1700 are labeled Portuguese here, but given the small scale of the early trade, the upward bias this imparts to the Portuguese trade is minor. The Spanish – mostly Cuban-based – moved into the traffic in a big way after 1807, but there is confusion arising from the fact that they often used the Portuguese flag, especially after the 1835 Anglo-Spanish treaty allowed British cruisers wider powers over Spanish slavers. In summary, from 1640, the Portuguese slave trade is virtually synonymous with the traffic to Brazil until the nineteenth century when the Portuguese flag began to appear once more in the Cuban, and to a lesser extent, the Rio de la Plata trade. Of all major national groups, the Portuguese were the least affected by war. The south Atlantic wind-system kept potential rivals at arms length.[18] The thorny problem of the number of slave arrivals in the Spanish Americas, a preoccupation of earlier work on the volume issue, is thereby largely finessed here.

Although the Portuguese trade is the most under represented in the data set, it nevertheless constitutes over a quarter of the voyages in the latter, and if the estimates of the Luso-Brazilian traffic below are correct, then well over half of all Portuguese slaving voyages are included. All transatlantic vessels, except for the very few identified under other flags, are assumed to have been Portuguese until 1640. For the very earliest period – before 1600 – Curtin's estimate of 50,000 arrivals in Brazil still holds. For the Spanish Americas of the same period, however, a major adjustment is required to his estimate of 75,000 arrivals. Bullion exports to Spain expanded rapidly at the end of the sixteenth century and peaked shortly after 1600. The best recent estimate of slave arrivals in Spanish Americas between 1595 and 1640 is 268,200, and no less than 30 percent of these arrived in the six years 1595-1600.[19] This end-of-century bulge, that bought 80,500 Africans to Spanish America – easily the largest annual average to any major national jurisdiction in the Americas before the explosive growth of the British sugar sector – is the basis of doubling Curtin's estimate for the Spanish Americas from 75,000 to 150,000. This implies a total of 200,000 arrivals in the Americas in the sixteenth century. Average voyage mortality for 1595-1640 for 66 Portuguese vessels was 25.6 percent (20 percent estimated for the shorter route to Brazil), and supports an estimate of departures from Africa of 264,100 between 1519 and 1600.

For the seventeenth century, the trade to Spanish America switched from Portuguese to Dutch and English control in mid-century, and thereafter the Portuguese slave trade is virtually synonymous with the traffic to Brazil, except for a short renewal of the *Asiento* between 1696 and 1701, this time on the part of the Portuguese Cacheu Company.[20] From 1601 to 1640, arrivals on Portuguese vessels in the Spanish Americas totaled 187,700 (the survivors of 252,000 departures). For Brazil, older estimates posited 200,000 arrivals in Brazil between 1600 and 1650 – or 173,700 after deducting those coming on Dutch ships – and 325,000 between 1650 and 1700.[21] Analogies with better-documented branches of the slave traffic suggest both earlier estimates are too high. The major buyers of African slaves in Brazil before 1700 were sugar planters. The expansion of their sugar sector in the second half of the sixteenth century was probably similar to that of its later English counterpart. Both sectors changed their supply of labor to predominantly African slaves, the first from indigenous and the second from a European indentured servant regime. The growth of the English plantation system was likely more explosive, and its focus on African labor at the end of the transition greater. At some point around 1675, exports of sugar from the English Caribbean surpassed the volume of Brazilian sugar exports just prior to the 1624 Dutch attack. The 100,000 slave arrivals in Brazil between 1600 and 1625 (half the 200,000 currently projected for 1601-50) compares well with the better documented 140,000 that arrived in the British Caribbean between 1640 and 1675, even after allowing for the Indian labor that Brazilian planters used. After 1625, however, the disruptions of the Dutch invasion and stagnation in the Bahian sugar sector suggest that 100,000 slave arrivals in the second quarter of the seventeenth century are unlikely, even allowing for arrivals on Dutch vessels. Pernambuco had accounted for well over half of Brazilian sugar output before occupation by the Dutch. Total arrivals in Portuguese vessels in the second quarter of the seventeenth century should probably be halved to 50,000. Thus, 150,000 is allowed for the Portuguese traffic to Brazil between 1600 and 1650 (making 187,500 departures, on the basis of an estimate of mortality of 20 percent on the shorter south Atlantic route). The addition of 252,000 departures for the Spanish Americas and 187,500 for Brazil yields 439,500, the total volume of slaves carried to the Americas in Portuguese vessels during 1601-1650.

For 1650 to 1700, the estimate of 325,000 arrivals in Brazil in the older literature is also in need of revision.[22] The English sugar sector absorbed 177,000 enslaved Africans yet Barbados and the English Leewards together likely produced more plantation produce than the whole of Brazil in 1700.[23] At the end of a century of slave arrivals, and a plantation economy that grew very slowly between 1650 and 1700, why would Brazil have taken in more slaves than the English Caribbean? It is of course possible that slaves were used more extensively in non-export sectors in Brazil than in the Caribbean, but African slaves were purchased, one way or another, with Brazilian exports, and export trends provide some guide to the potential for obtaining slaves. An estimate for Brazil of 177,000 is accepted for this half-century. An allowance of 12.5 percent voyage mortality yields 202,300 departures from Africa.[24] Including the illegal Portuguese traffic to Spanish America and the activities of the Cacheu Company (10,000 arrivals), then the total Portuguese trade for 1651-1700 becomes 187,000 arrivals in the Americas implying 214,800 for departures (Table 5, row 4). As the Brazilian sugar sector began to expand once more in the final quarter of the century, when the Bahian-Bight of Benin slave route began, three quarters of these departures (161,100) are assigned to 1676-1700 and the rest to 1651-1675.

For the long eighteenth century, the Portuguese slave trade is synonymous with the slave trade to Brazil, and fortunately, the sources are stronger here than for the previous century. The series of Bahia tobacco licenses continues well into the nineteenth century, but in addition there are summaries of slave departures from Angolan ports for most years made by government officials – several made by different officials in some years – as well as voyage based records which are included in our data set. Vessels sailed from Angola to all importing regions in Brazil, with the busiest transatlantic slave trade linking Luanda and Rio de Janeiro.[25] There are also some data available for the small but durable traffic between Portuguese Upper Guinea, on the one hand, and Pará and Maranhão, on the other. We take up each of these in turn.

Pierre Verger published in 1968 a count of Bahian vessels granted licenses to carry tobacco to the African coast.[26] Because it is likely that all these vessels intended to obtain slaves, and that few vessels left Bahia for Africa without tobacco in this period, the slave trade data base includes all these vessels for which documentation survived in 1994. The series of ships trading from Bahia to Africa in our data base differs from Verger's count for three reasons. First, Verger's archival work probably dates from the 1950s since when the documents have deteriorated. This makes it impossible to record all the information that was available to Verger.[27] Second, our series includes some years that Verger apparently overlooked, and for some of the vessels common to both Verger's work and our data base it has been possible to add data from other sources. Third, it has been possible to fill some of the gaps in the Bahian archival series from other sources. For 1715 and the first three months of 1716 tobacco licenses for ships leaving Bahia were published by the Brazilian National Library – shortly before the originals were lost.[28] In addition, as Verger himself pointed out, while the Bahian archives contain no records for the years 1734 to 1737, the Rijksarchief at The Hague contains records of Portuguese ships carrying tobacco to the West African coast in these years. As a result of Luso-Dutch treaties in 1641 and 1661, tobacco vessels were required to leave 10 percent of their cargo at Elmina before they proceeded to the Slave Coast.[29] By combining the data base material, Verger's cryptic annual counts, the *Documentos Históricos*, and the Dutch archival records, we are left with just twelve years between 1678 and 1810 with no information on slave ship movements from the port of Bahia. Nine of these are between 1717 and 1725 and it seems fairly clear that the reason for the gaps is because of the destruction of historical records not because there was no slave trading activity to record.

To convert what are for the most part records of possible ship departures into a series of slaves leaving Africa, two steps are required. The first is computing a mean for slaves carried on each ship from data from ships leaving the Slave Coast with known numbers on board. Such data are readily available from the data set.[30] The second is to make allowance for the years for which data are missing. For three of the twelve missing years, quinquennial averages are assigned, and for the nine-year block, the figures are estimated on the basis of a simple linear interpolation between five-year averages on either side of the gap. These procedures generate an estimate of 656,000 slave departures between 1701 and 1810. As noted, shipboard mortality data for this route are scarce before 1810, but if we use the rate from the Angola to Brazil route between 1701 and 1810 (8.81 percent, n=326, sd=7.2), then 598,200 would have arrived (Table 5, row 5).

How complete is the resulting series? There are two independent checks, one for the years 1726 to 1733 and the other after 1790. The first of these is the aforementioned annual count of Bahian ships leaving tobacco at Elmina the records of which are in The Hague. In these years 129 vessels received licenses in Bahia, and 107 reached Elmina. Given that some licensed vessels would not have sailed, or else may have fallen to the normal hazards of the Atlantic, and a very few others may have gone to Angola, then we can regard these two series as broadly supporting each other. Unlicensed vessels may have sailed from Bahia to the Slave Coast, but their chances of escaping the Dutch could not have been very great, and their numbers thus were likely inconsiderable. A second check emerges from the British records. Between 1793 and 1807, an intermittent series of journals exists of ships passing by Cape Coast Castle. It was not uncommon for ships of all nations heading to the Slave Coast to pass by, or call at, Cape Coast Castle in the process of seeking supplies, obtaining information, or in the case of Bahian vessels selling tobacco. We have extracted names of 71 vessels sailing from Bahia from this source.[31] Of these, 54 are also to be found in the Bahia tobacco series. Thus, slightly more than three out of four of the Bahian vessels reported in non-Portuguese sources also appear in the Bahia series. Some of the Portuguese vessels in the Cape Coast Castle records would have been plying the intra-African trade, and thus based on the islands of São Tomé or Princípe, and a few others may have belonged to the small trade between West Africa and Pernambuco discussed below, so that once more the tobacco license series receives support.

For the trade from Portuguese ports in Angola we have data on departures of slaves as opposed to data on ships setting out from a port with the intention of trading for slaves. For Luanda, Birmingham, Klein, Goulart and more recently José C. Curto, who has produced a useful synthesis of all earlier archival work, have between them created an almost complete annual series of departures from Luanda for 1710 to 1810.[32] Data are missing for just four years – 1715-17 and 1732 – and we have interpolated our estimates from what are available for the surrounding years. In addition we have added to the series for the period 1701-1709, by assuming that departures in these years were the same as the annual average for the period 1710-1714. These procedures yield total departures for 1701-1810 of 959,300. Mean voyage mortality (as a percent of those embarked) was 8.81 percent between Angola and Rio between 1701 and 1810 (n=326, sd=7.2). Arrivals, therefore, may be estimated at 874,800 (Table 5, row 6).

For Benguela, the other major Portuguese port, annual totals exist for all but ten years between 1730 and 1810.[33] All of the years that lack data fall in the 15 years after the annual series begins and it is possible that lack of data simply reflects a lack of slave trading. There is no evidence of slave trading activity before 1730, and prior to 1745, just over 1,000 slaves a year are recorded as departing for the Americas. We have assumed, however, that some activity did occur and have assigned 5,000 departures from Benguela in each of the quinquennia 1725-30 and 1731-35. Slave departures for the quinquennia 1736-40 and 1741-45 are inferred from the data for 1738, 1740-1742, and 1744, for which data have survived. In other words, we assume the slave trade was continuous from 1725. These procedures yield departures of 362,700 and (using the Rio-Angola voyage mortality rate of 8.81 percent), arrivals of 333,300.

Two questions naturally arise. First how many slaves were smuggled out of these ports and thereby eluded the estimates of officials upon which the above data draw? Second, how many slaves left from ports in Angola other than Luanda and Benguela? We are concerned here only with the Portuguese trade. French, British and Dutch vessels were all active in Angola from the 1670s through to 1807, and given mercantilist restrictions, Portuguese officials would not report slaves leaving on such ships that came within their knowledge. However, the voyage counts already discussed, which form the basis for estimates of these national trades, already include slaves obtained in Portuguese territory. For Portuguese vessels our data set offers some check on smuggling in that it includes some ships arriving in Rio de Janeiro that had declared they had sailed from Luanda and Benguela. Between 1796 and 1810, it is possible to match two sets of annual estimates of slaves leaving Luanda and Benguela on Portuguese ships, one made on the African side of the Atlantic, the other on the Brazilian side.[34] In sum, Rio records report 81,200 slaves leaving the two African ports, while Angolan records report the departure of 88,700. Given that Pernambuco and Bahia also drew slaves from Angola at this time – about one fifth of the vessels arriving in Luanda between 1796 and 1810 originated in Pernambuco and Bahia[35] – these totals are quite similar. Large scale smuggling in this later period at least, if it existed at all, must have circumvented officials on both sides of the Atlantic.[36] The evidence presented here is thus consistent with a relatively modest allowance of 10 percent to cover illegal slaves on Portuguese ships (and illegal Portuguese ships). The 10 percent adjustment, yielding 95,900 for Luanda and 36,300 for Benguela, are included in rows 7 and 9 of Table 5.

The second question is the extent of Portuguese slave trading in ports other than Luanda and Benguela. Once more the data set may be called into service. The northern Angola coast – that is points in and north of the Congo River – was dominated by north-western European nations. We know the African destinations of 356 slave vessels arriving at Rio between 1795 and 1810. Of these, 21 reported from Africa north of Luanda, 11 from the Congo River and Loango coast. The key point, however, is that all but one of these voyages occurred after 1807 – in other words after the British, Dutch and French had moved out of the trade.[37] Elsewhere, Portuguese ships began to obtain slaves in south-east Africa from the mid-1790s. The Rio de Janeiro records indicate 14 ships carrying 5,300 slaves from Mozambique between 1796 and 1809, and 4,100 arrivals.[38] Again, however, the Portuguese moved in only after the St. Domingue slaves and European war had diverted the attention of the French. In addition, the *Companhia Geral de Pernambuco e Paraíba* carried 9,500 slaves from the Slave Coast mainly to Pernambuco between 1760 and 1782 (8,600 estimated arrivals).[39] The next question is the extent of the free trader activity from 1778 to 1810 in these regions, about which little is known. We allow an estimate of 30,000 departures and 27,000 arrivals for this minor branch of the traffic for these years. Pulling these disparate trades together and assuming little Portuguese slaving on the northern Angola coast before British, French and Dutch withdrawal, yields totals of 44,700 departures and 39,700 arrivals. These are included in row 10 of Table 5.

Finally, in Upper Guinea Portuguese ships obtained slaves at Cacheu and Bissau in small vessels from the fifteenth to the nineteenth centuries. Much of the early trade was to off-shore islands which sometimes acted as entrepôts for the transatlantic trade and the slaves passing through these are included in the estimates of sixteenth and seventeenth century trade discussed above. Indeed, the Portuguese had established a presence in this area that ensured that Portuguese was the lingua franca long after the English had become the dominant slave traders in Upper Guinea. For several decades after Portuguese transatlantic traders dropped out of the traffic to the Spanish Americas, Portuguese traders in Upper Guinea acted primarily as intermediaries for slavers from other nations. However, a small trade to Amazonia (Belém do Pará and São Luis do Maranhão) developed from the region in the early eighteenth century which down to 1750 "could not have exceeded a few thousand."[40] Rising demand for cacao and rice from Pará and cotton and rice from Maranhão led to a strong increase in the trade. Between 1756 and 1778 the Pombaline *Companhia do Grão-Pará e Maranhão*, and then free traders between 1778 and 1788 embarked 21,000 adults (perhaps 22,000 slaves in all) from Cacheu and Bissau (20,900 arrivals estimated). The scholars who have put together these estimates offer the usual caveats on their use, but it is striking how well the data on arrivals collected in the Americas correspond with the data on departures collected independently in Africa.[41] From 1789 to 1801, there are records of a further 22,127 arrivals in Pará and Maranhão, with perhaps 16,600 of these coming from Upper Guinea. There is no corroboration from the African side for these years, but assuming voyage mortality of 7 percent (this was shortest of all transatlantic crossings), we estimate departures at 17,800. Between 1802 and 1810 we have little data, but by the 1810s and 1820s the trade was quite minor, probably reflecting the ability of the US south to squeeze out competing cotton-producing areas and thereby reduce demand for slaves.[42] It is highly unlikely that more than 1,500 slaves per year on average left from Upper Guinea to Amazonia between 1802 and 1810. If we allow 4,000 departures before 1756, 22,000 during 1756-1778, 17,500 in 1778-1801, and 13,500 during 1802-1810, then we have a total of 57,000 departures and 53,000 arrivals for row 11 of Table 5.

For the nineteenth century, the nationality of the vessel is a complicated issue. Ships changed flags frequently in response to a long series of British-initiated treaties proscribing the trade that eventually encompassed almost every maritime nation. Ships flew flags and carried registration papers that were often bogus, and sometimes they carried several sets at once. Thus the data set contains records of 259 US registered slave ships between 1811 and 1861, but in almost every case these were ships owned by Cuban or Portuguese slave traders that were under the US flag up to the moment the slaves came on board, and then reverted to either another flag or sailed without a nationality. This group have been distributed proportionally between Portuguese and Spanish registrations. The execution of Nathaniel Gordon in New York in 1862 put an end to this practice. It is clear that between 1811 and 1866, owners of slave ventures were Portuguese, Spanish, French, and to a much lesser extent, Brazilian, and that after 1832, except for a few expatriates such as the firm Gantois and Martin of Bahia, the French no longer participated. A breakdown of imputed nationality suggests that 11 percent of slave ships in the set were French, and after reallocation of the US registered ships, 18 percent were Spanish and 71 percent Portuguese-registered or Portuguese-owned. Brazilians are included in this category on the basis that most Brazilian-registered slave ships were owned by Portuguese nationals. Estimates of the volume of the slave trade already exist for 1811-1866: they are not much affected by the new data set. These comprise departures from Africa of 2,738,900, and arrivals in the Americas of 2,383,800.[43] Applying shares of national groups calculated from the data set to these estimates of departures and arrivals yields for French ships, 301,300 carried from Africa and 262,200 disembarked in the Americas (entered in Table 3); for Portuguese 1,944,600 departures and 1,692,500 disembarked (entered in row 13 of Table 5); and for the Spanish, 493,000 departures and 429,100 arrivals.

We can now complete our estimates of the Spanish slave trade. As noted above, Spanish ships were plying their trade well before 1811. Down to 1640, we have lumped such ships with the Portuguese trade. There was little Spanish transatlantic slave shipping activity for a century thereafter. In the second half of the eighteenth century, there were occasional Spanish voyages as Spain tried to break into the trade. Indeed, under the 1778 Treaty of Pardo, Spain acquired the island of Annabon in the Bight of Biafra from Portugal for the express purpose of establishing a slaving base. But subsequent Spanish slave trading activity was highly unsuccessful, and a substantial transatlantic Spanish traffic did not develop until the British and Americans pulled out of the trade in 1807.[44] Thus, while the data set contains records of Spanish ships that could have carried 16,000 slaves before 1811, two-thirds of these were on vessels sailing to Cuba between 1800 and 1810. Only a few Spanish vessels appear to have been active before 1790. We have increased this small number by half to account for missing Spanish vessels before 1811, and thus project a Spanish trade of 24,000 for 1700-1810. A small sample of shipboard mortality on Spanish vessels before 1811 suggests 13.7 percent of those taken on board failed to reach the Americas. If such a figure were typical, then 24,000 departures would have meant 20,700 arrivals.[45] Thus our total for Spanish slavers during 1641-1867 is 517,000 carried from Africa, and 449,800 disembarked in the Americas. These totals are entered directly in row 7 of Table 6.

Our assessment of the trade based in North America – the Caribbean as well as the mainland – moves the discussion toward the less well-known branches of the transatlantic slave trade. Boston may well have sent out the first North American-based transatlantic slave voyage in 1644, but between the 1640s and about 1730, Caribbean ports sent out many more voyages than did their mainland counterparts. This is particularly the case after 1680 when Caribbean shippers discovered how well rum sold in parts of West Africa and sent hundreds of small sloops from the islands to the Gold Coast.[46] Later Rhode Island slave traders simply followed a well-established pattern. Before 1714, all voyages setting out from North America are included in the estimates of the English slave trade presented in Tables 1 and 2. This means that while we do not have a record of every North American slave voyage in this era, our estimates nevertheless allow for the gaps in the records. We assume that no French, Dutch or Danish voyages set out from the Americas before 1714.

From 1714 to 1811, our data set contains records of 1,500 voyages setting out from North America, or at least that could have set out from North America in the sense that we know they reached Africa or the Americas and are reasonably certain about port of departure. For about 150 of these we do not know whether the voyage was based in Britain or English-speaking North America, but because British records are fairly complete (so that if these ships had been English they would have been identified as such), all 150 are assumed to have been North American. Our data include the 921 Rhode Island ventures that Coughtry listed. Indeed, because of Coughtry's work, the Rhode Island trade is far better documented than that from any other port in the Americas.[47] There are two central questions for those interested in the overall volume of the trade. The first is how complete are Coughtry's data? And the second is how big was the rest of the North American slave trade relative to that based in Rhode Island ports?

Answers to both these questions are possible. The new data set incorporates some little-used sources that are not specific to any single port, and which appear not to favor one port in the English-speaking Americas over another. The largest

European presence in Africa for most of the eighteenth century was to be found at Cape Coast Castle. Probably more than 80 percent of slave ships from the English Americas and Bahia called at or sailed past this Gold Coast fort, and for some years the journals which recorded such shipping movements have survived in the PRO, T70 series. *Lloyd's List*, a shipping gazette based in London, has similar characteristics as far as North American slavers are concerned, though information on the latter is not as complete as it is for English-based voyages. Finally, in the CO28 series in the PRO, there is a continuous series of Barbados Treasurer's reports of duties paid on slaves disembarked in the island for the 1740s to 1760s. We have created a sub-sample of 598 voyages from these three sources that had sailed from or were registered at North American ports for the period 1730-1807. We know the place of registration for only 407 of these vessels, but it is possible to identify the probable national flag or regional origins of the remainder from the comments of observers or the history of the ship or captain. English ships making return voyages direct to Africa from the Americas were excluded, as were the several hundred ships which were obviously from English-language regions, but for which no registration information could be inferred.

What do these new sources tell us? Initially, we should note that they have added little to Coughtry's compilation of voyages from the ports of Rhode Island. Apart from the corrections noted above, only 28 additional Rhode Island voyages emerge from these and other sources upon which the new data set has drawn. These comprise about 3 percent of Coughtry's total. We do not claim that every Rhode Island voyage is included in the set, but given the *Lloyd's List* and especially the new T70 volumes, it seems to us highly unlikely that the real total for Rhode Island exceeded Coughtry's edited voyage set plus 5 percent – in other words, 921 plus the 28 additional voyages multiplied by 1.05, or about 1,000 voyages between 1714 and 1807. A disproportionate number of these missing voyages would fall in the period 1714-30, years that precede availability of the new sources. A further set of results with implications for the volume estimates emerge from breakdowns of the T70-*Lloyd's List*-CO28 sample. First, in almost the reverse of the pre-1730 situation, voyages associated with the North-American mainland are five times more numerous than voyages based in the Caribbean (497 to 101). Second, voyages from Rhode Island make up about half of the sub-group associated with the North American mainland (49.3 percent).[48] Rhode Island was thus clearly not "synonymous with the North American mainland slave trade," as Coughtry has suggested. Third, most of the non-Rhode Island voyages are identified only as ships belonging to the USA or the mainland British colonies, but for those vessels with specified places of registration, there is an even distribution between ports of registration, with Massachusetts' ports being the most numerous followed by New York, Charleston, the Chesapeake, and Philadelphia. Rhode Island was easily the largest single center for the slave trade in North America, but any port open to transoceanic business could be involved.[49]

We can now develop our estimate of the North American carrying trade. If Rhode Island ports were responsible for approximately 1,000 slaving voyages between 1714 and 1807, and the other North American mainland ports sent out about the same number, then not all these ventures actually carried slaves to the Americas. Of these voyages, 86 percent bought slaves in Africa, and most of the rest could have done so in the sense that the ship concerned disappears from the historical record before it reaches Africa. Generally, loss ratios for ships sailing from the Americas seem to have been below those of vessels sailing from Europe, so that whereas between 5 and 10 percent of English voyages failed to deliver slaves to the Americas, the proportion of North American ships lost was closer to 3 percent.[50] Those Rhode Island ships that did reach the Americas disembarked on average 103 slaves (n = 323; sd = 49.7). The scattered data for other ports suggest similar mean numbers landed except in the case of Charleston vessels which disembarked on average one third more slaves than their Rhode Island counterparts (mean = 135; n = 34; sd = 99.7). With Charleston vessels accounting for perhaps one in ten of mainland voyages, North American mainlanders may be estimated to have brought 205,500 slaves to the Americas (after allowing for 3 percent of voyages which failed to reach the Americas), and to have left Africa with 220,600.[51] These estimates are in row 2 of Table 6.

A rough estimate of the traffic based in the English Caribbean after 1713 (earlier voyages are included in the estimate of the English slave trade) is also possible from the above ratios. The *Lloyd's List* and T70 sub-sample suggests that between 1730 and 1807 one transatlantic slaving voyage was based in the English Caribbean for every four on the North American mainland. Given the 2,000 mainland voyages derived above, an estimate of 500 Caribbean slaving voyages is thus projected. However, we require a figure for the years 1714 to 1807, rather than the 1730-1807 period from which the four to one ratio is derived, and, as already noted the Caribbean based trade declined in relative terms in the course of the eighteenth century. During the years 1714-30, there are actually more Caribbean-based than North American mainland-based voyages in our data set, and this warrants a small increment of 50 to our estimate of 500. Overall, then we thus project 550 Caribbean-based voyages between 1714 and 1807. Applying the same loss ratios as those estimated for Rhode Island ships means that 550 voyages obtained slaves in Africa, while 533 voyages reached the Americas with slaves. Average numbers disembarked from these Caribbean-based vessels were 96.2 (n= 167; sd = 65.3) and because the sample size was inadequate for the calculation of numbers taken on board we estimate the numbers carried from Africa at 110.5 (assuming a shipboard mortality loss ratio of 13 percent).[52] Finally, we have to take account of voyages based in the non-English Caribbean. These appear to have been very few in number. Several voyages from the French Antilles are already included in the French estimates in Table 2 and may be inspected in the second volume of Mettas-Daget. Transatlantic ventures owned in St. Croix and St. Thomas before 1807 are included in the Per Hernaes set of Danish voyages discussed earlier. We have found no evidence of any, and therefore have assumed no slaving voyages were actually owned in the Dutch Americas. Our estimate of slaves carried by British Caribbean vessels is the product of number of slaves carried and the number of estimated voyages. This yields 51,300 for slaves arrived and 59,400 for slaves carried from Africa, and these estimates are entered directly into row 3 of Table 6. Table 7 uses large samples from the data set to rework the estimates of national participation into quarter century intervals after 1650, half century for 1601 to 1650, and century-long before 1601.

The aggregate estimates of the volume of the transatlantic slave trade are simply the sum of individual national groups taken from Tables 2 to 6. Overall the estimates have more checks and balances, and less guesses than previous attempts to derive aggregate figures for the slave trade. At just over 11 million departures from Africa, our aggregate is about 8 percent below that of the current scholarly consensus referred to above. After allowing for the traffic to Europe, the Mascarene Islands, and the offshore Atlantic islands, not included in the present assessment, our estimates are quite similar to Curtin's figures from the late 1960s – the first in fact to accord with his estimates since they appeared. Our distribution is, however, rather different from his. Moreover, we can, we believe, offer a little more certainty than earlier estimates. Specifically, we are prepared to cut Curtin's confidence interval from plus or minus 20 percent to perhaps half that range. Given our search of sources on the slave trade in the past five years, we think it highly unlikely that another million or more slaves could have been removed from Africa beyond what we have allowed for here – even in the poorly documented Portuguese trade. We have a rough idea about how much was being produced in the major plantation areas of the Americas, including Brazil, and we have a good idea of how many slaves were carried into some areas, such as the British and French Caribbean islands. New research on the Luso-Brazilian slave trade is not likely to support quantum increases in the estimates developed here, although it will certainly fill in some of the gaps which we have noted. Indeed, as suggested above, further detailed work is more likely to lower than to increase estimates of the volume of the traffic. Whatever the nature of these changes, the framework of voyage statistics makes it easy to test and correct the totals.

Table 7 highlights the dominance of the British in the 150 years before 1807 and the massive importance of the Portuguese traffic. The Portuguese trade was based on two continents and was effectively fused with that of Brazil. A strict comparison with the British would involve adding the British Americas to the British total, but even if this were done, a large gap would still remain. Two warnings need be sounded. First, the strongest advances in the unearthing of information on slave trade activity in the last ten years have been for the British trade. There can be little doubt that the effect of increasing knowledge has been to reduce our estimates of slaves carried in British vessels from Africa.[53] We now know more about ships going to Africa that were not seeking slaves as well as about ships that set out but did not complete the voyage. It is reasonable to expect that as knowledge of the Portuguese trade increases, the volume of this trade also may be reduced. Second, it is clear that in the seventeenth century, even after our downward adjustment of the Portuguese slave trade between 1650 and 1700, more slaves arrived in Brazil than can be strictly accounted for by produce exports – at least in comparison with the English Caribbean. A comparison between Brazil and St. Domingue during 1701-92 indicates that the differential between slaves and produce exports was even more pronounced. Brazil took half as many slaves again as its French counterpart, yet export values, including gold, cannot have approached those of the French island. Perhaps the closeness of Brazil to Africa and the resulting low price of slaves meant that slave use was much more extensive in Brazil than has been appreciated. Equally, perhaps the reduced estimates of the Portuguese trade presented here are still too high. Even so, more than seven out of every ten slaves carried across the Atlantic likely found themselves on either a British or a Portuguese vessel.

Table 1: Imputed Nationalities of Slave Voyages Departing Africa, 1527-1866

	Number	Percent
Portugal/Brazil	7310	26.8
Spain	1116	4.1
France	4035	14.8
United States	1711	6.3
The Netherlands	1219	4.5
Scandinavia (mainly Denmark)	228	0.8
Great Britain	11632	42.7
	27251	100.0

Source: Calculated from the *CD-ROM.*

Table 2 (a): Slaves Carried across the Atlantic on British Ships, 1714-79, by Ship's Port of Origin (in thousands)

	Departures (Africa)
Liverpool	609.1
London	358.0
Bristol	467.6
Lancaster	23.1
Whitehaven	15.1
All other outports	12.3
Overseas port of departure	45.1
Unknown port of departure	107.0
Total	1637.3

Source: Calculated from the *CD-ROM.*

Table 2 (b): Slaves Carried into the Atlantic Trade by British Ships, 1569-1807 (in thousands)

	Departures	Arrivals
1569-1660	50.0*	40.0
1661-1713	500.5	399.8
1714-1779	1637.3	1364.8
1780-1807	924.5	862.6
1569-1807	3112.3	2667.0

Notes: *Estimate based on voyage mortality of 0.2.

Sources:

Row 1, see text.

Row 2, Eltis, "Volume and African Origins," with adjustments for shipboard mortality.

Row 3, total from row 9 of Table 2 (a) with adjustments. For latter see text.

Row 4, Calculated from the *CD-ROM.* For more detail see Behrendt, "Annual Volume."

Table 3: Slaves Carried into the Atlantic Trade by French Ships, 1699-1833 (in thousands)

	Departures	Arrivals
1669-1700	40.0*	32.0
1707-1793	1035.9	908.1
Allowance for missing voyages, 1701-1793	65.2	57.2
1794-1810	13.9	13.6
1811-1833	301.3	262.2
1669-1833	1456.3	1273.1

Notes: *Estimate based on voyage mortality of 0.2. Voyage mortality on early French voyages was not much different from that on English ships. A sample of 9 French voyages, before 1705 yielded a mean mortality of 0.193 (sd = .173).

Sources: see text.

Table 4: Slaves Carried Across the Atlantic by Dutch Ships, 1606-1829 (in thousands)

	Departures	Arrivals
Americas, other than Brazil, 1606-1650	17.0	13.6
Dutch Brazil, 1630-1650*	31.0**	26.3
Americas, 1651-1674	61.2***	53.3
Americas, 1675-1810	418.5	358.8
Americas, 1606-1829	527.7	452

Notes:

* Includes one slave vessel that arrived in 1651.

** Calculated from Boogart and Emmer, "The Dutch Participation in the Atlantic Slave Trade, 1596-1650," in Gemery and Hogendorn, *Uncommon Market*, p. 369, with an allowance for voyage mortality for the years 1630, 1636, 1646-51, during which data on arrivals only are available. Voyage mortality of 17.87 percent of those embarked is calculated from the same source. It should be noted that mortality includes some deaths which occurred after slaves disembarked and prior to sale in the Americas.

*** Voyage mortality used to estimate arrivals calculated from idem.

Sources: Row 1, see text. Row 2, Boogart and Emmer, "The Dutch Participation in the Atlantic Slave Trade, 1596-1650," in Gemery and Hogendorn, *Uncommon Market*, 353-75. Row 3, Postma, *Dutch in the Atlantic Slave Trade*, p. 35, with an allowance for voyage mortality (see note). Row 4, Calculated from the *CD-ROM.*

Table 5: Africans Carried into the Atlantic Slave Trade on Portuguese Vessels, 1519-1866 (in thousands)

	Departures (Africa)	Arrived (Americas)
1519-1600	264.1	200.0
1601-1650 (to Spanish Americas)	252.0	187.7
1601-1650 (to Brazil)	187.5	150.0
1651-1700	214.8	187.0
1701-1810 (Bahia/Slave Coast)	656.0	598.2
1701-1810 (from Luanda)	959.3	874.8
1701-1810 (from Luanda) additional	95.9	87.5
1701-1810 (from Benguela)	362.7	330.8
1701-1810 (from Benguela) additional	36.3	33.1
1701-1810 (Mina-Pernamb, Mozambique-Rio)	44.7	40.8
1701-1810 (Upper Guinea to Amazonia)	57.0	53.0
1811-1866	1944.6	1692.5
Total, 1519-1866	5074.9	4435.4

Sources:
Row 1, Curtin, *Atlantic Slave Trade.*
Row 5, Calculated from the *CD-ROM.*
All other rows, see text.

Table 6: Africans Carried into the Atlantic Slave Trade by Nationality of Carrier, 1519-1866 (in thousands)

	Departures (Africa)	Arrived (Americas)
British	3112.3	2667.2
Post 1713 Brit Mainland North America/US	220.6	205.5
Post 1713 British Caribbean	59.4	51.3
Portuguese	5074.9	4430.9
French	1456.4	1263.7
Dutch	527.7	452.0
Spanish	517.0	449.8
Danish	89.2	74.7
All others	5.0	4.0
Total	11062.5	9599.1

Sources: Tables 2-5 and text.

Table 7: Volume of the Transatlantic Slave Trade from Africa by Nationality of Carrier 1519-1866 (in thousands)

	Portuguese	British	French	Dutch	Spain	USA/Br Ca	Danish*	All nations
1519-1600	264.1	2.0						266.1
1601-1650	439.5	23.0		41.0				503.5
1651-1675	53.7	115.2	5.9	64.8			0.2	239.8
1676-1700	161.1	243.3	34.1	56.1			15.4	510.0
1701-1725	378.3	380.9	106.3	65.5		11.0	16.7	958.6
1726-1750	405.6	490.5	253.9	109.2		44.5	7.6	1311.3
1751-1775	472.9	859.1	321.5	148.0	1.0	89.1	13.4	1905.2
1776-1800	626.2	741.3	419.5	40.8	8.6	54.3	30.4	1921.1
1801-1825	871.6	257.0	217.9	2.3	204.8	81.1	10.5	1645.1
1826-1850	1247.7		94.1		279.2	0	0	1621.0
1851-1866	154.2		3.2		23.4	0	0	180.7
All years	5074.9	3112.3	1456.4	527.7	517	280.0	94.2	11062.4
% of Trade	45.9	28.3	13.2	4.8	4.7	2.5	0.9	100.0

Notes: *Danish includes a few other Scandinavian and German vessels.

Source: Calculated from the *CD-ROM* and adjusted according to text.

ENDNOTES

1. This paper overlaps with David Eltis, "The Volume and Direction of the Transatlantic Slave Trade: A Reassessment," *William and Mary Quarterly* 58 (2001): 17-46. Its main thrust is to explain the estimates of national participation which form the starting point of the *WMQ* paper and it may properly be viewed as a prequel of that publication.
2. David Eltis, et al, *The Transatlantic Slave Trade: A Database on CD-ROM* (New York: Cambridge University Press, 1999). Readers should note that the computations on which this paper are based were carried out on a slightly expanded post-publication version of the data.
3. Johannes Postma, *The Dutch and the Atlantic Slave Trade* (Cambridge: Cambridge University Press, 1990); David Eltis, "The British Transatlantic Slave Trade Before 1714: Annual Estimates of Volume and Direction," in Robert L. Paquette and Stanley L. Engerman (eds.), *The Lesser Antilles in the Age of European Expansion* (Gainesville: Florida University Press, 1996), pp. 182-205.
4. Per O. Hernaes, *Slaves, Danes, and African Coast Society: The Danish Slave Trade from West Africa and Afro-Danish Relations on the Eighteenth Century Gold Coast* (Trondheim: Department of History, University of Trondheim, 1995), pp. 140-171, offers new global estimates of *imports* of 10,869,594 to which he adds 55,889 *libertos* (freed persons) to São Tomé and Princípe for 1876 to 1900. He then converts to exports by adding 15 percent mortality and gets 12,787,758.
5. The overall estimate is actually for arrivals in the Americas *and* the Old World. For these estimates see Philip D. Curtin, *The Atlantic Slave Trade: A Census* (Madison: University of Wisconsin Press, 1969), p. 268; Paul E. Lovejoy, "The Volume of the Atlantic Slave Trade: A Synthesis," *Journal of African History* 23 (1982): 473-501; idem, "The Impact of the Atlantic Slave Trade on Africa: A Review of the Literature," Ibid 30 (1989): 365-394. The quote is from p. 373.
6. The 1661-1713 estimate differs slightly from the figure derived in David Eltis, "Volume and African Origins of the Seventeenth Century English Transatlantic Slave Trade," *Cahiers d'Études Africaines* 138 (1996): 620 on account of more refined shipboard mortality estimates. The temporal breakdown used here is 2,000 before 1601, 23,000 between 1601 and 1650, and 25,000 between 1651 and 1660.
7. Table 2 (a) shows 234,000 slaves carried on vessels coming from unknown British ports. Most of these sailed from Bristol, London or Liverpool. Thus, when we say that we are confident that the data set includes almost all ships leaving these ports, we do not mean that we are able to assign ports of departure to all these vessels.
8. For 10 percent of these voyages, a port was assigned on the basis of voyage history or captains' names.
9. For a full description of this test see David Eltis, "The Volume, Age/Sex Ratios and African Impact of the Slave Trade: Some Refinements of Paul Lovejoy's Review of the Literature," *Journal of African History* 31 (1990): 550-567.
10. For Dutch sales to the French Caribbean see Postma, *Dutch and the Atlantic Slave Trade*, p. 35; Clarence J. Munford, *The Black Ordeal of Slavery and Slave Trading in the French West Indies, 1625-1715* (Lewiston: Edward Mellen Press, 1991), p. 147. Pirates tended to be interested in gold rather than slaves (Bodleian Library, Oxford, Rawlinson Ms., C 745, fls. 195, 198, 209-11, 216), but during the war years French letters of marque captured all cargoes, including outbound which would be traded

for slaves (John Wortley to Royal African Company [hereafter RAC], September 23, 1690, Public Record Office (hereafter PRO), T70/11, fl. 104).

11. Munford, *Black Ordeal*, pp. 127-199. Munford states that "Between 1671 and 1692 at least 44 ships put out from La Rochelle (the chief French slaving port at the time) to buy captives," p. 162. Some of these carried slaves to France. There was no great activity at other French ports before 1690. See also Awnsham Churchill and John Churchill, *A Collection of Voyages and Travels* 6 vols. (London: H. Lintot, 1744-1746) VI, p. 238; William Cross, Comenda, March 3, 1686, Rawlinson, Ms. C745, fl. 337, 338; Humphreys, Wright and Boylston, Cape Coast Castle, to RAC, January 5, 1688, PRO, T70/11, fl. 31; Albert van Dantzig (ed.), *The Dutch and the Guinea Coast, 1674-1742: A Collection of Documents at the General State Archive at The Hague* (Accra: GAAS, 1978), pp. 46, 49, 64.
12. Eric Saugera, "Pour une histoire de la traite française sous le Consulat et l'Empire," *Revue française d'histoire d'outre-mer* 56 (1989): 203-229.
13. Ernst van den Boogart and Pieter Emmer, "The Dutch Participation in the Atlantic Slave Trade, 1596-1650," in Henry A. Gemery and Jan S. Hogendorn (eds.), *The Uncommon Market: Essays in the Economic History of the Atlantic Slave Trade* (New York: Academic Press, 1979), pp. 353-375.
14. Postma, *Dutch Slave Trade*, pp. 27-29.
15. Pieter Emmer, "Jesus Christ was Good, but Trade was Better:' An Overview of the Transit Trade of the Dutch Antilles, 1634-1795," in Paquette and Engerman, *Lesser Antilles in the Age of European Expansion*, p. 216; Wim Klooster, "Dutch Trade, Capital and Technology in the Atlantic World, 1595-1667," Unpublished paper presented to the American Historical Association Annual Meeting, 1998.
16. Hernaes, *Slaves, Danes, and African Coast Society*, pp. 170-233; Svend Holsoe, personal communication.
17. Adam Jones, *Brandenburg Sources for West African History, 1680-1700* (Stuttgart: F. Steiner, Verlag and Wiesbaden, 1985), pp. 1-11. The fort was virtually moribund for the first two decades of the eighteenth century before the Dutch took it over.
18. Between 1640 and 1807, British, Danish, Dutch, US and French slave traders supplied the Spanish Americas, often from entrepôts in the Americas, rather than direct from Africa. This means that we may safely ignore the *Asiento* contracts after 1640 – as long as we have confidence in our estimates of the size of the slave trades of other major carriers. See Georges Scelle, "The Slave Trade in the Spanish Colonies of America: The Asiento," *American Journal of International Law* 4 (1910): 614-661.
19. All data in the set, as well as the estimate, are from Enriqueta Vila Vilar, *Hispanoamerica y el comercio de esclavos: Los Asientos Portugueses* (Sevilla: Escuela de Estudios Hispano-Americanos, 1977). The *CD-ROM* has 83,200 arrivals – 29,800 in 1595-1600.
20. Under the new contract perhaps 5,000 slaves entered Spanish America. See Scelle, "Slave Trade in the Spanish Colonies of America".
21. For a fuller discussion of previous estimates of the seventeenth century Portuguese traffic, see Eltis, "Volume and Direction of the Transatlantic Slave Trade".
22. More recent estimates imply an even larger volume (see ibid).
23. Eltis, "British Atlantic Slave Trade," pp. 196-198. The Leewards received slaves from Dutch-held St. Eustatius that are not included here. More than off-setting this inflow were sales from Barbados to the Spanish Americas and French Windwards. On sugar

output, Barbados and the English Leewards exported produce worth an estimated £684,800 in 1700. Bahia exported an estimated £227,400 and Brazil as a whole, an estimated 568,500. See David Eltis, *The Rise of African Slavery in the Americas* (Cambridge: Cambridge University Press, 2000), pp. 197-198.

24. Shipboard mortality on vessels sailing the shorter passage between the Slave Coast and Bahia was below that for the West African-Caribbean route. A proposal to establish a Portuguese company at Corisco Island about 1724, intended to displace or reduce Portuguese slave trading on the Slave Coast, stated 10 percent loss as "*etant la computation ordinaire*" (Huntington Library, California, Stowe Ms., ST 28, p. 7). When data for the Bahian trade become available in the early nineteenth century, mortality loss was about half that on other routes. Mortality on ships arriving in Bahia from the Bight of Benin, mainly from 1810-1814, was 4.6 percent (n=101, sd=7.5).
25. For trading routes see Joseph C. Miller, "The Numbers, Destinations and Origins of Slaves in the Eighteenth-Century Angolan Slave Trade," in Joseph E. Inikori and Stanley L. Engerman (eds.), *The Atlantic Slave Trade: Effects on Economies, Societies and Peoples in Africa, the Americas, and Europe* (Durham, NC: Duke University Press. 1992), pp. 78-89.
26. Pierre Verger, "Mouvement des navires entre Bahia et le Golfe du Bénin (XVIIe-XIXe siècle)," *Revue française d'histoire d'outre-mer* 55 (1968): 10-12.
27. Arquivo Público do Estado da Bahia (Salvador), Passaportes de Embarcações, Series 439, 440, 443, 447, 449, 456.
28. Biblioteca Nacional do Rio de Janeiro, *Documentos Históricos da Biblioteca Nacional do Rio de Janeiro*, 110 vols. (Rio de Janeiro: Government of Brazil, 1929-55), vols. 61, 62.
29. Verger, "Mouvement des navires," p.12; idem, *Trade Relations Between the Bight of Benin and Bahia, 17th to 19th Century* trans. Evelyn Crawford (Ibadan: Ibadan University Press, 1976), pp. 24-26.
30. The mean number of slaves carried from the Bight of Benin by ships of all nations, 1701-1810, was 329.5 (n=2323, sd=104.8), but the estimates used here are for 25 year periods and exclude the smaller slave vessels based in North America.
31. The lists are located in PRO, T70/1565, pt. 2, 1566, 1568, 1569, 1570, 1571, 1572, 1573, 1574, 1579, 1580, 1581, and 1587, pt. 2. Two references to Portuguese ships in *Lloyd's List* and Jean Mettas, *Répertoire des Expéditions Nègriers Françaises au XVIIIe Siècle* 2 vols. (Paris, Société française d'histoire d'outre-mer, 1978-1984) are also included.
32. David Birmingham, *Trade and Conflict in Angola: The Mbundu and Their Neighbours Under the Influence of the Portuguese, 1483-1790* (Oxford: Clarendon Press, 1966), pp. 137, 141, 154-155; Herbert S. Klein, "The Portuguese Slave Trade from Angola in the Eighteenth Century," *Journal of Economic History* 32 (1972): 898, 917; idem, *The Middle Passage: Comparative Studies in the Atlantic Slave Trade* (Princeton: Princeton University Press, 1978), pp. 254-255; Mauricio Goulart, *Escravidão africana no Brasil (das orignes à extinção do tráfico)* (São Paulo: Editora Alfa-Ômega, 1975), pp. 203-205; José C. Curto, "A Quantitative Reassessment of the Legal Portuguese Slave Trade from Luanda, Angola," *African Economic History* 20 (1992): 1-25; idem, "The Legal Portuguese Slave Trade from Benguela: A Quantitative Re-Appraisal," *África* (Revista do Centro de Estudos Africanos, Universidade de São Paulo) 16-17 (1993-1994): 101-116.

33. Sources are Klein, "Portuguese Slave Trade," p. 918, for 1738-1741, 1744, 1747-1800, and Curto, "Slave Trade from Benguela," for 1730, 1742, and 1801-1810. Also Joseph C. Miller, "Legal Portuguese Slave Trading from Angola: Some Preliminary Indications of Volume and Direction," *Revue française d'histoire d'outre-mer*, 62 (1975): 135-176, and idem, "The Number, Origins, and Destinations of Slaves," for 1780-1783 and 1785-1810.
34. The Angolan data are reported by Miller in "The Number, Origins, and Destinations of Slaves," pp. 92, 100-101, and the Rio data in the set were collected by Herbert S. Klein.
35. See Graph 3 in Miller, "The Number, Origins, and Destinations of Slaves," p. 150.
36. Smuggling is never costless. Ports exist because they offer facilities for importing and exporting goods. Avoiding such facilities is always expensive. If established ports are used, then officials must be bribed. See the discussion in John J. McCusker, *Rum and the American Revolution: The Rum Trade and the Balance of Payments of the Thirteen Continental Colonies, 1650-1775* (New York: Arno Press, 1989), that concludes that scholars generally exaggerate the problem of smuggling in eighteenth century Atlantic ports.
37. Lisbon vessels attempted to slave there in the 1790s, but obtained few slaves and had to complete their complement in Luanda; Joseph C. Miller, *Way of Death: Merchant Capitalism and the Angolan Slave Trade, 1730-1830* (Madison: University of Wisconsin Press, 1988), p. 623. See also the discussion in idem, "The Number, Origins, and Destinations of Slaves," p. 92.
38. For the Rio de Janeiro end of this activity, see Klein, *Middle Passage*, p. 56, and Manolo G. Florentino, *Em Costas Negras: Uma História do Tráfico Atlântico de Escravos entre a África e o Rio de Janeiro (Séculos XVIII e XIX)* (São Paulo: Civilização Brasileira, 1997), pp. 78-84, 234. For the Mozambique records of this activity see Edward A. Alpers, *Ivory and Slaves in East-Central Africa* (Berkeley: University of California Press, 1975), pp. 185-193.
39. António Carreira, *As Companhias Pombalinas* 2nd ed. (Lisbon: Editorial Presença, 1983), pp. 247-249.
40. Colin M. MacLachlan, "African Slave Trade and Economic Development in Amazonia, 1700-1800," in Robert B. Toplin (ed.), *Slavery and Race Relations in Latin America* (Westport: Greenwood Press, 1974), p. 118. See also Jean Mettas, "La traite Portugaise en Haute-Guinée, 1758-1797," *Journal of African History* 16 (1975): 343-363.
41. Carreira, *Companhias Pombalinas*, p. 89. Compare Carreira's data to the series of arrivals in Pará and Maranhão in MacLachlan, "African Slave Trade," pp. 137, 139. Note that some of MacLachlan's totals include *peças de India* rather than slaves and that about one quarter of arrivals in Amazonia came from Angola.
42. Edmundo Armenío Correia Lopes, *A escravatura (subsídios para a sua história)* (Lisbon: Agencia Geral das Colónias, 1944), pp. 139-142; David Eltis, *Economic Growth and the Ending of the Transatlantic Slave Trade* (New York: Oxford University Press, 1989), pp. 241-247.
43. Eltis, *Economic Growth*, pp. 250-254. Note that we have excluded the French *engagés* (individuals who were slaves when they left Africa, but technically free upon arrival on French islands) taken during the 1850s and 1860s from present estimates. Hence the slight discrepancy between these and the estimates from the mid-1980s. Also

note that the difference between total departures from Africa and total arrivals in the Americas is not just voyage mortality, but includes nearly 200,000 slaves diverted to European colonies in Africa by the various naval squadrons charged with suppressing the slave trade.

44. See the memo dated February 26, 1841 in PRO, FO84/383, fl. 262, and the documents in FO84/299, fls. 19-25, the latter removed from the Spanish archives, for a summary of this activity.
45. N=11, S.D.= 0.166.
46. The first documented "rum ship" owned by a private trader (an interloper) made the voyage from Barbados in 1683. Its success was immediately noticed by the agent of the Royal African Company who quickly got the assent of the Company to send its own ships direct to Africa. Antigua merchants followed suit from 1698 by which time the RAC's monopoly had been effectively breached. See PRO, T70/116, fl. 49.
47. Jay Coughtry, *The Notorious Triangle: Rhode Island and the African Slave Trade, 1700-1807* (Philadelphia: Temple University Press, 1981), pp. 241-284, lists 930 voyages. By using sources unavailable to Coughtry we have edited his list, eliminating in the process some voyages that had been counted twice and adding others. Overall, we reduced Coughtry's list to 922 voyages.
48. This ratio is almost identical to that estimated by David Richardson from a Senate document for the years 1804-1807. See his "Slave Exports From West and West-Central Africa, 1700-1810: New Estimates of Volume and Distribution," *Journal of African History* 30 (1989): 8-9.
49. A breakdown of North American registrations in the full set, instead of just the *Lloyd's List* and PRO, T70 sub-sample, yields the following: Massachusetts ports 69 voyages, Chesapeake 34, New York, 49, Philadelphia, 16, Charleston, 85. Thus ports servicing the plantation areas, such as Charleston and the Chesapeake were the home ports for almost as many voyages as Boston, New York, and Philadelphia, a feature of the trade that does not get much attention in the literature. If we include the 130 voyages registered in the Caribbean as well, then except for Rhode Island, the plantation regions sent out far more voyages than did the "commercial" north.
50. Our hypothesis for this is that the hazards of sailing out and back from the Americas were below those of the triangular voyage. Sailing in and out of the English channel, the Irish Sea, or Baltic ports for example, and skirting hostile shores during the extended period of warfare entailed much higher risks than a return voyage from Charleston, Newport or New York to Africa. North American shipping must have incurred lower insurance costs through the slave trade era, though we have yet to examine this issue systematically.
51. Rhode Island ships left Africa with 112.7 slaves on average (n = 566; sd = 50.4). Charleston vessels embarked an average of 148.8, based on shipboard mortality of 8.5 percent of those taken on board (this figure estimated from a sample of ships based in mainland North America ports other than Charleston, because the sample size for Charleston ships is inadequate). The estimate of 220,600 in US vessels is 6 percent greater than that developed by Richardson from independent sources (though beginning with Coughtry's data) in an earlier publication. See Richardson, "Slave Exports from West and West-Central Africa," pp. 7-9.
52. These estimates of the number of vessels differ little from those of Inikori for the British Caribbean, though exact comparisons are difficult because our estimates are

calculated for a different grouping of years. However, Inikori estimates the mean numbers of slaves on board these vessels to be about 28 percent greater than the figure computed here from the data set. See Joseph E. Inikori, "The Volume of the British Slave Trade, 1655-1807," *Cahiers d'Études Africaines* 32 (1992): 669-676.

53. Compare, for example, the estimates of David Richardson, "The Eighteenth-Century British Slave Trade: Estimates of its Volume and Coastal Distribution in Africa," *Research in Economic History* 12 (1989): 170, 185-195, with those in Table 2 above.

Plate 1: The Atlantic Slave Trade

Source: Adapted from John P. McKay, Bennett D. Hill, and John Buckler, *A History of World Societies* (Boston: Houghton Mifflin, 1992), Map 18.5

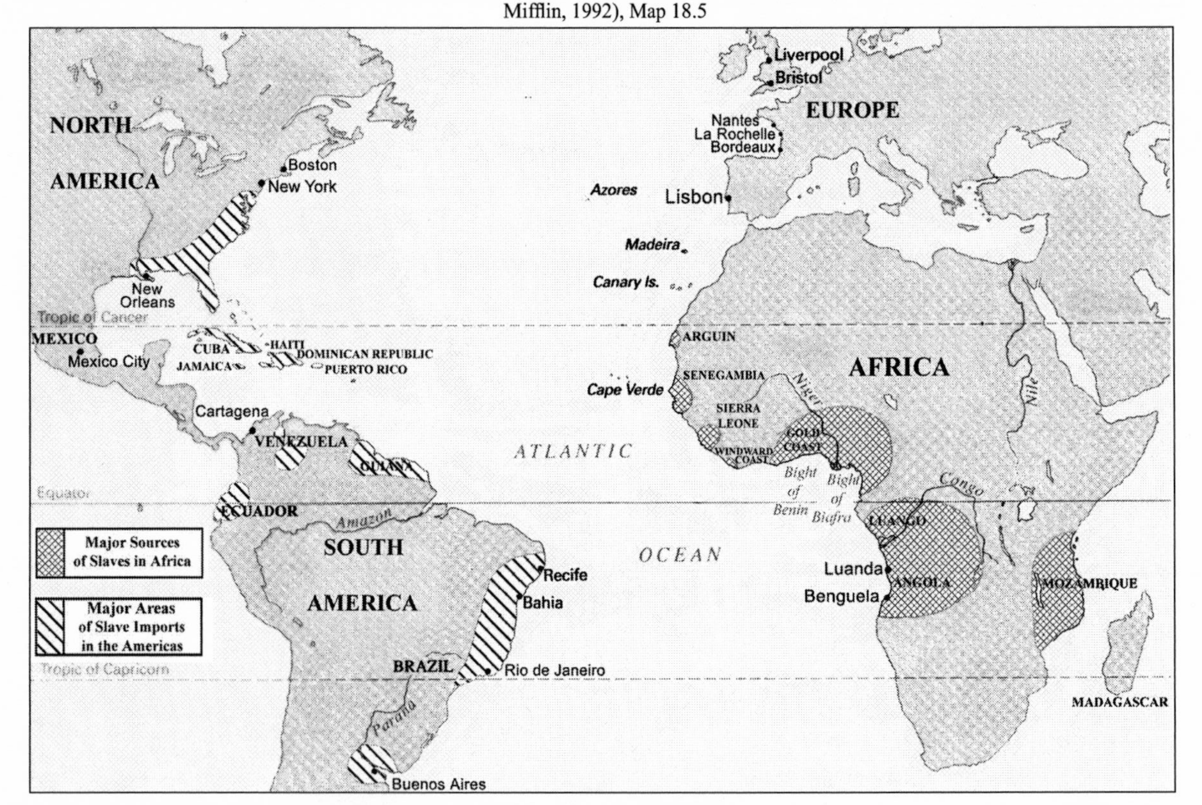

2

"Moçambiques" in Brazil: Another Dimension of the African Diaspora in the Atlantic World

Edward A. Alpers

In the continuing debate about the relative significance of West vs. West Central African origins in the history of diaspora Africans in Brazil (and, more generally, the Americas as a whole), very little attention has been paid to the place of East Africans in the Atlantic world. This is not surprising, of course, considering that relatively few peoples of East African origin were caught up in the Atlantic slave trade. But some did appear at specific moments in the history of the trade when for one reason or another the usual sources in West and West Central Africa were less able to meet rising or continuing demand for bonded labor. Thus, for example, a trade in captives from East Africa to Saint Domingue enjoyed a brief heyday from 1786 to 1791 as profit-seeking French slavers sought to exploit the low price of slaves at Kilwa and Mozambique Island.[1] Some of these found their way to French Louisiana, as well.[2] A second, final, and more sustained period of activity occurred in the first half of the nineteenth century, when the abolition movement progressively restricted the slave trade from West Africa and forced slavers to focus increasingly on sources from south of the Equator in West Central and East Africa. It is during this period that "Moçambiques" - the most widely used categorization for slaves of East African origin - began to make their presence felt in Brazil (see Plate 2) and Cuba. Here, too, with the single exception of Brazilian anthropologist and philosopher João Lupi, no one has addressed the presence of these East Africans in Brazil as a separate topic of inquiry. Lupi was the grandson of Eduardo do Couto Lupi, who served as Governor of Quelimane District in Mozambique during the first decade of the twentieth century and was himself a notable amateur ethnographer and historian. Inspired by his family connections to Mozambique and to the region of Zambesia, he also lived there for three years during the 1960s. While he succeeded in raising a number of interesting questions and making some provocative suggestions about how to understand the "Moçambiques", he did not provide very much in detail about them.[3] This chapter seeks to go beyond Lupi in raising awareness of the "Moçambique" presence in Brazil during the era of the slave trade and to suggest possible lines of research for scholars to follow up on in the archives of Brazil and among the descendants of "Moçambiques" themselves.

Although the first license to trade slaves from Mozambique to Brazil was granted in 1645, meaningful trade only dates to the eighteenth century when Portuguese imperial restrictions were gradually lifted on direct commerce between the two colonies. Even then, however, these contacts remained fitful until the end of the century.[4] Nevertheless, there is evidence from the obituary records of the *Santa Casa de Misericórdia* that includes 270 "Moçambiques" or 1.4 percent of all recorded African deaths (a total of 19,280) at Salvador de Bahia between 1741 and 1799.[5] But it is from 1795 on that East African slaves or "Moçambiques" began to make their presence felt in Brazil.

Thanks to the pioneering research of Herbert Klein, Mary Karasch, and Manolo Florentino we have a good idea of the numerical significance of "Moçambiques" at Rio de Janeiro in the first half of the nineteenth century. They demonstrate on the basis of the available evidence that from about 2.3 percent of all captives imported at Rio between 1795-1811, East Africans comprised as many as one-fifth of all enslaved Africans disembarked at Rio in the period between 1811-1830 and declining only slightly to almost 18 percent for the period from 1830 to 1852.[6] As Klein notes, "Mozambique was the third largest supplier of slaves in the nineteenth century – ahead of Biafra and just behind Benin – accounting for 14 percent of those shipped [to the Americas] in the nineteenth century from anywhere in Africa."[7] On the Mozambican side, we have valuable complementary studies by José Capela (see his chapter in this volume) and Aurélio Rocha on the central place of the slave trade in relations between Mozambique and Brazil in the nineteenth century. Although each focuses much of his analysis on the radical French political influences, including Free Masonry, which connected these colonial societies through the activities of the slave traders themselves, each also explores the details of the slave trade, the role of Brazilian slave traders in promoting it, and the rise of Quelimane under Brazilian influence as the major slaving port for Zambesia, then known as the Rivers of Sena, in the nineteenth century.[8] Although there is no question that Rio was the principal port of disembarkation for East African slaves in Brazil, scholars have paid little attention to the regional distribution of slaves of East African origin in Brazil. Indeed, the only other meaningful quantitative data we have come from Pernambuco, where "Moçambiques" are noted as rising from a low of 1 percent of all Pernambucan slaves in the decade 1811-1820 to a high of 3.2 percent for 1851-1860 and Minas Gerais, where Moçambiques constituted 2.5 percent of all slaves whose origins were known from 1715 to 1888.[9] Nevertheless, there exists a diverse assortment of historical, ethnographic and linguistic evidence that suggests that "Moçambiques" were both more widespread in Brazil than these data indicate and represent a more complex "nation" than first meets the eye.

It goes without saying that "Moçambique" itself is a highly problematic designation. First, it reflects the application of a geographical toponym to a wide variety of different enslaved Africans from a broad sub-region of the continent. Thus, the British chaplain Walsh writes in 1830, "The people of Mozambique include generally all those of Southern Africa."[10] The French artist Debret, who spent fifteen years in Brazil from 1816 to 1831, similarly comments about designations such as Cabinda, Congo, and Moçambique, "These include a certain number of nations sold at the same point on the coast . . .".[11] Second, and most importantly, this naming of the Other involves the arbitrary designation of different African people – in this case all of them Bantu-speakers from East Africa – by Europeans involved in the slave trade and the colonial slave society of Brazil, for whom it also represents an invented ethnonym that conformed to the Brazilian grouping of bonded Africans into "nations". These designations quickly became fixed into ethnic stereotypes that allowed Europeans in Brazil to classify Africans by their alleged characteristics. For example, British traveler Henry Koster wrote in the second decade of the nineteenth century: "The Mozambique Negroes are a poor and ugly race of beings, languid and inactive, and subject to despondency. Their color inclines to brown, but still they have completely the Negro features."[12] A decade later the German soldier Carlos Seidler wrote in similarly derogatory terms:

> The Moçambique black is the most repulsive. He has a small body, thickset and strong; his head ordinarily planted almost on his chest, is very large in proportion to his body.
>
> Always withdrawn, his eyes fixed on the ground, his movements are awkward, his pace is slow and gangling.
>
> He endures blows and bad treatment with stoicism, the most horrific floggings rarely wrench him from a sound of pain.[13]

Yet despite the low regard in which it appears that Europeans held "Moçambiques" in nineteenth-century Brazil, they obviously continued to import them as slaves and to exploit their labor.

I have previously argued for "Mozambiques" in Mauritius that the entire trajectory of enslavement involved a process of creolization that began from the moment of capture on the continent of Africa through transportation to the coast, holding at the coast until embarkation, oceanic passage, and finally adjustment to the conditions of slavery in the diaspora.[14] As enslaved Africans made their way to the coast, a journey that for some involved only weeks but for others often years, they learned new languages and customs, perhaps assumed new identities, from those into which they were born and raised. For example, an approximately ten-year old Nyasa boy, who would have spoken Chewa (or Mang'anja/Nyanja, as the language was known in the nineteenth century), recounts that after being captured and sold twice, he spent two years in a Yao village. "I learnt the Yao language there, and forgot my own." Later, after he had reached the coast and been sold to an Arab, "I remember selling mangos in Kilwa, and I remember trying to know the Swahili language."[15] Upon arrival at the coast, where slaves were often held for many weeks, they might repeat this process. During their harsh seaborne voyage, they again learned new ways of reconstructing themselves and formed bonds that endured in the new lands where they were forcibly settled. In Brazil, these comrades were known as *malungos*.[16] Finally, when they reached Brazil, quite apart from having to learn some Portuguese and perhaps Roman Catholic rituals, they now had to adjust to life as working slaves. Part of this final process was their coming to grips with the formation of Africans into "nations". That is, they now were faced with deciding to what extent they were willing to embrace the designations imposed on them by the slave owners and, then, to which "nation" they would ultimately belong among the possibilities open to them. To the extent that they embraced the idea of belonging to a Brazilian African "nation", this was still a further example of cultural reinvention. Thus, while we can trace certain specific cultural and linguistic practices from Africa to Brazil, it is clear that the "Moçambique" in Brazil had traveled a considerable distance from her or his natal cultural identity in East Africa, whatever that may have been. Eduardo Medeiros takes a similar view of this phenomenon that "inscribes a construction of identities," although he suggests that the process only "begins to take place on the beaches of the western Indian Ocean, between the Ruvuma and the Incomati" rivers.[17]

What I am suggesting here departs significantly from prevailing debates in the study of the African diaspora in the Atlantic world, where creolization in the Americas has generally been counterpoised to the search for African origins and retentions.[18] Instead, I am building on the position adopted by Robert Slenes that

> The making of a common "Bantu identity" in Brazil, if indeed it occurred, could only have been the result of a complex process. I suggested that for many Africans this process was initiated, not in the shared experience of the terrible crossing to the Americas, but before this, during the immense suffering of the journey to the coast; and it began with the discovery that communication with one's companions on this trip was not impossible. The continuation or rupture of this process, however, would have depended on the slaves' experience in the New World and on their chances of finding other affinities amongst themselves, beyond the community of the word.[19]

For "Moçambiques" the reality is that under slavery this designation, like those of other Brazilian "nations", was transformed into a category of self identification that assumed a life of its own independent from that originally imposed on Africans by boundary-making slave traders and owners who sought to control the slave population by applying the method of divide and rule. Indeed, according to Schlichthorst, writing in the mid-1820s,

> Almost all the blacks born in Africa bring to Brazil a great pride in their natal land that they do not leave behind even after many years of slavery. Their favorite words are: my country and my nation. They take pride in their origins and when they quarrel, the cause is almost always some ancient national rivalry. The black exclaims: I am Congo! with the same pride that the English praise British freedom, beating with an open hand on his chest.[20]

As we have seen, however, this form of social identity was not entirely out of Africa.

That these agglomerations had the desired effect may be seen from the observation by Brazilian historian Emília Viotti da Costa that "Rivalries divided the blacks into nations: the Moçambique did not tolerate the Congo, nor the Mina the Koromatum; and the police were frequently called to break up disturbances between them."[21] Contemporary observers, such as Walsh, confirm this assessment and emphasize the way in which these divisions were encouraged by the ruling class of Brazilian society.

> The Negro population [at Rio] consists of eight or nine different castes, having no common language, and actuated by no sympathetic tie; insomuch so, that they frequently engage in feuds and combats, where one, or even two hundred of a nation on each side are engaged. This animosity the whites cherish, and endeavour to keep alive, as intimately connected with their own safety.[22]

Such designations were also used to help Brazilian authorities identify slave rebels and "criminals". For example, the slave Joaquim Moçambique was imprisoned in Rio "for practicing capoeira and causing a disturbance with the black Domingos." Another example of disturbing public order is the case of the "Slave João Moçambique of Thomé Faria for loitering around eleven o'clock at night with a rock in his hand, leaning against a tree . . . and having said in a tavern in the Pedregulho that he'd throw it at the patrol if they laid a hand on him."[23] Similarly, two individuals indicted in the 1833 slave uprising in Carrancas (Minas Gerais) were identified as "Moçambiques".[24] This was, no doubt, part of the pathological need for the colonial ruling class to identify Africans by their attributed characters and to inform themselves about especially dangerous categories of slaves.

Reflecting the general habit of designating Africans by "nations", "Moçambiques" occur regularly in the literature on slavery in Brazil. For example, according to a late nineteenth-century French observer of plantation life, one area in which enslaved Africans identified themselves by "nation" was in performance of *batuques*.

> These national dances excite to such a degree these poor slaves, that they have been prohibited to them in the city. In spite of all this, however, they take place. At the risk of being cruelly beaten, the Negroes go at night, when the whites are asleep, to dance on the beach in the moonlight. They assemble in groups of the same nationality, either Congo or Mozambique, or Minas; then, in dancing and singing, they forget their ills and servitude, and only remember their native country and the time that they were free.[25]

Similarly, Karasch quotes Robertson's description from 1808 of a great public celebration that provided an occasion for different African groups to come together in dance:

> Onward pressed the groups of the various African nations, to the Campo de Sant'Ana, the destined theatre of revelry and din. Here was the native of Mosambique, and Quilumana, of Cabinda, Luanda, Benguela, and Angola....
>
> The dense population of the Campo de Sant'Ana was subdivided into capacious circles, formed each of from three to four hundred blacks, male and female... the welkin rang with the wild enthusiasm of the Negro clans....[26]

These divisions also operated in other spheres of public life in Rio, so that "Moçambiques" were kept separate from "Minas" on the board of the Black Brotherhood of Nossa Senhora da Lampadosa.[27] There is, however, some evidence that they may not have been quite so impermeable as these sources suggest. At the beginning of the century, Koster noted that during the dancing that accompanied celebration of the coronation of the King and Queen of Congo, Africans of other "nations" joined in and danced the same dances.[28] A century later there is similar testimony from Goiânia that Moçambiques, among other African "nations", were invited to join in the dance celebration of a *congada*.[29]

Still a further example of such "national" divisions seems to have involved life cycle ceremonies, particularly funerals. In the 1840s, the American Daniel Kidder remarked on the funeral of an African child that he observed at Engenho Velho, then the principal suburb of Rio de Janeiro, that it "illustrates the continuance of heathen customs among the Africans in Brazil. Great numbers of slaves are brought together at the Emperor's country seat, where they are permitted to follow the customs they prefer." The funeral procession that he witnessed involved women and children festooned with red, white and yellow strips of cloth, in front of which he observed a man "bearing on his head a wooden tray, on which was the corpse of a child, covered with a white cloth, decorated with flowers, a bunch of them fastened to its hand." Indicating that they were probably not singing in Portuguese he concluded, "They were all chanting some Ethiopian dirge, to which they kept time by a slow trot; the bearer of the deceased child pausing, once in one or two rods, and whirling around on his toes like a dancer."[30] Debret provides a fascinating insight into the funeral of a Moçambique woman in his text to accompany his Plate No. 16, "*Enterrement d'une femme nègre*". With the exception of the bearers, a master of ceremonies, who carried a staff in his hand and wore a tunic of colored handkerchiefs and a twisted cloth pad (*rodilha*) on his head, and a drummer, the cortege was composed exclusively of women, something that is strikingly similar to what Kidder saw at Engenho Velho. The drummer carried a medium-sized wooden drum under his arm on which he beat a soft rhythm with the palms of his hands when he squatted on his haunches and placed it on his knees. In between this style of playing at intervals, the women sang their funeral dirges, "whose magical lamentations caused many of their compatriots to join them at the burial." These "compatriots" were also expected to contribute to the cost of the funeral for the generally impoverished deceased. Debret then goes on to say:

> Among the *Moçambiques* the words of the funeral song are especially notable because of their completely Christian sentiment, whereas among the others they limit themselves to lamentations about slavery, although these are expressed crudely.
>
> I give here the Moçambique text in Portuguese: *we are crying for our relative, whom we never more will see; rest beneath the ground until the Day of Judgment, for ever and ever Amen.*[31]

Although we can do no more than speculate, the fact that Debret makes a point of providing this Moçambique funeral text in Portuguese suggests that possibility that the original may have been chanted in a Mozambican language, as apparently was the "Ethiopian dirge" overheard by Kidder. Finally, upon reaching the church, in this case the very same Nossa Senhora da Lampadosa mentioned above, the procession stopped, the doors were opened, the drummer beat his instrument, and people laid down their loads so that they could accompany the funeral songs with hand-clapping.[32]

Not all slaves from East Africa or even from Portuguese East Africa were known as "Mozambiques" in Brazil, as we have already seen from Robertson's identification of Africans from Quilumana (Quelimane, which I have previously indicated was a major source of slaves for the Brazilian trade in the nineteenth century). A valuable source for the variety of names by which East African slaves were known in nineteenth century Brazil is Gilberto Freyre's meticulous compilation of information from runaway slave notices in Brazilian newspapers. Of the eighteen slaves of East African origin whom he names, it is true that fourteen were designated as "Mozambiques", but the others were identified as "Quilimane" or "Quilhimane" (two), "Inhambane", the most significant southern Mozambique port for the slave trade, and "Mombaça", the major port of the northern Swahili coast in what is today Kenya (one each).[33] Similarly, Rugendas identifies one of the African subjects of his portraiture as a "Quiloa"(see Plate 3), Kilwa being the most important mainland slaving port of the Swahili coast, in what is today southern mainland Tanzania.[34] Quilimane and Inhambane also appear in Karasch's data from burials at the *Santa Casa da Misericórdia* at Rio as "national" designations, as do Lourenço Marques (now Maputo), the most southerly port controlled by the Portuguese in East Africa, and Mougão, which suggests to me the Swahili settlement of Mongalo, a small port lying between Kilwa and the mouth of the Ruvuma River in what is today southern mainland Tanzania, although this may also have been a mistaken rendering for Mujao, as contemporary Portuguese sources called the Yao of what is today northwestern Mozambique.[35] Like "Moçambique", all of these designations derive their names from an East African port and the acquisition of such an identity in Brazil would have reflected the same process of creolization as operated for "Moçambiques".[36]

Nevertheless, there are published sources that do enable us to approach the specific East African origins of these bonded Brazilians with greater accuracy. In addition to the port designations noted by Karasch, her data indicate the presence of "Macua" (Makua), the largest ethnic group of northern Mozambique, Mucena (Sena), a grouping of disparate yet related Zambezi valley people who take their name from the town of Sena (or the broader Portuguese regional designation of Rios de Sena, i.e. Zambesia), and Yao.[37] These identifications, which on the surface reflect modern ethnic identitites in Mozambique, may have been especially significant in the nineteenth century as transitional "national" designations before individuals either embraced the broader designation of "Moçambique" or sought to become Brazilian and, consequently, "negros" or "pretos."

Better still is evidence from the American traveler Ewbank of so-called "country marks" that can be used to identify the likely origins of individuals beyond the broad rubric of "Moçambiques" by which he identifies them. Always a keen observer of detail, if equally a creature of his times, Ewbank writes:

> We crossed the Bay [of Todos os Santos] in a small steamer, whose pilot was a Mozambique slave, and landed at San Domingo, where the gate-keeper or ferry-master was, or had been, another. Both were tall, middle-aged, and as finely formed men as I ever saw, the latter particularly. He had no more of the Negro lineaments than had Mark Antony or Cato, but both had indelible marks of their barbaric origin – one a double, the other a single row of pimples, the size of peas, down the middle of the forehead, and along the ridge of the nose to its very tip – the signs of their native tribes. . . . A gentleman who crossed the Bay with us had witnessed, while on a visit to the eastern coast of South Africa, the process of producing the fleshy beads. At one time he saw forty or fifty young men lying on the ground suffering from the operation. A minute incision is made through the skin for each pimple; the lips of the wound then are pulled up and tied by a thread, and in time the protuberances become permanently globose, smooth, and shining.[38]

Two decades earlier, Walsh described the cook at the home of his host in Rio, as

> a little black woman, christened Luzia, who was twenty years old, and four feet high. She was tattooed in a singular manner. The flesh of her forehead and nose was curiously raised up into protuberances the size of peas; these formed a line across her forehead, and another from that down to the tip of her nose, like two strings of large black beads; and, to make the resemblance more complete, a similar bead-like ring went round her neck. These curious protuberances were as hard and consistent as warts, and must have been attended with considerable pain in the operation; but it was performed when she was so young, that she had no recollection of it.[39]

These very same single row cicatrizations appear in a mid-nineteenth century lithograph of a liberated "yambane" man whose image was drawn at the French island of La Réunion in the southwest Indian Ocean.[40] This style of cicatrization (see Plate 4), which gave the Tsonga the derogatory nickname of *Knobneusen* among the Afrikaners of northern South Africa, continued to be the fashion among Tsonga women into the twentieth century, although it had generally disappeared among men by the end of the nineteenth.[41] In the case of Ewbank's individual, we may have a case of an "Inhambane" who was first carried to Mozambique Island, where he was then re-embarked on a slave ship bound for Brazil, thus becoming a "Moçambique". In a word, the process of naming and re-naming that masks the larger, more complex process of creolization involved in the East African slave trade to and slavery in Brazil is never quite what it seems.

Other contemporary observers correctly identified the characteristic half moon forehead tattoos of the Makua. Ebel, a German traveler to Brazil in 1824, noted of black women in Rio, "Many are tattooed or marked on the face with moons, stars and other characteristic signs." In addition, he mentions that others knocked out their upper incisor teeth, which was not a custom of any Mozambican people, or "filed them to a point, those processes of African beautification that frankly make them monstrous in the eyes of a European."[42] Debret's engravings provide further evidence for the importance of cicatrization as a means of identifying the origins of "Moçambiques" in Brazil. In the explanatory text to his Plate 22, "*Escravas de differentes nações* (Female slaves of different nations)", he identifies number 9 and 13, both of whom are tattooed, as "Moçambique". In his commentary to Plate 36, "*Negros de differentes nações* (Blacks of different nations)", he describes number 3 as "a handsome *moçambique do sertão* (Moçambique from the interior), he is an elite black employed in the warehouses of the Customs House; he is recognizable not only because of the pierced upper lip and ears, but also by the type of half moon on his forehead, a mark made with a hot iron on the blacks sold on the Mozambique coast." Here Debret was mistaken, of course, as this characteristic sign of being Makua was indigenous and not a slave brand. Of number 4 he observes only that he is tattooed in a blue-black color, and has a clearer, lighter complexion, which Debret regards as an indication that "he is from the coast." He calls number 7 a "*calava* black sold on the Mozambique coast", whose color he defines as "reddish copper" with "blue-black" cicatrizations. Finally, Debret adds that "He does not have his upper lip pierced, however he reveals an elongated lower lip, an operation that begins in infancy and is achieved by placing the lip between two small tightly compressed pieces of board."[43] Rugendas is another important source of iconographic evidence, and his full plate of five men whom he identifies only as "Mozambique" includes two clear examples of Makua with half-moon cicatrization and one of an "Inhambane" with a row of raised pimples running from his hairline down to the tip of his nose.[44] While not all of these forms of beautification are specific to the Makua, it is not surprising that the striking Makua cicatrizations and the more generalized custom of lip-piercing among slaves from northern and central Mozambique should have been noticed by European observers, since we know that many of these peoples were caught up by the trade.

Further specific evidence of broadly defined ethnic origins of slaves from East Africa may be found among the published lists of emancipated slaves from captured slave ships that were carried to Brazil.[45] Two of these were slavers from East Africa. Although one of these notes only that its cargo was composed of "Quillimanes" and "Moçambiques", the other includes a wide variety of ethnic names, although often in garbled form. What is an especially important source for trying to establish the ethnic identity of these individuals is the recording of "marks" in the registers for all of these liberated slaves. Unfortunately, not all recorded marks are African in origin; for example, those from the Brig *Asseiceira* are brands of different Brazilian slave traders.[46] Those from the Brig *Ganges*, however, include genuine "country marks", some of which, such as the characteristic semicircular or half-moon scarification on the forehead, can certainly be identified as Makua and are indicated as such under the heading of "Nação." Others will take much more research to identify, if such identification can ever be firmly established, considering the changing fashion of body art among many East African people.[47] In addition to "Macua", there are a wide variety of "nations" recorded for the 379 emancipated slaves from the *Ganges*. Many of these cannot immediately be identified, but in addition to those listed simply as "Moçambique," "Quelimane," and "Inhambane," we can certainly identify "Mucena" (Sena), "Magange" (Manganja, from the northern bank of the Zambezi River), "Ozimba" (Zimba, from the Zambezi valley), "Machibeta" or "Chipeta" (Chipeta, also from the Zambezi valley), "Mojau" (Yao), "Umbiza" (Bisa, from modern eastern Zambia), and "Cutumbuca" (Tumbuka, from the western side of Lake Malawi). Considering the disparate origins of these individuals, it is not surprising that in Brazil they would have probably come to accept their new identity as belonging to one or another of the familiar, greater "nations" such as "Moçambique" or, to a lesser extent, "Quelimane".

Yet another kind of evidence for identifying the specific origins of "Moçambiques" in Brazil is language. Schneider includes some forty to fifty words of likely East African origin in his impressive compilation of some 2500 words of possible sub-Saharan African origin in Brazilian Portuguese. Some of these are part of a broadly shared Bantu lexicon, and so have possible West Central as well as East African derivations. One such example is the adoption of the widespread Bantu term *marimba* (African keyboard percussion instrument consisting of tuned wooden bars) in Brazil, which may have been influenced by Bantu-speakers from eastern as from West Central Africa as is suggested by Gerhard Kubik's discussion of the *marimba* of São Paulo.[48] *Engoma*, which Schneider lists as "a type of drum", is a similar word associated with music and dance that is widespread throughout Bantu-speaking Africa, appearing in Makua, as well as the languages that Schneider mentions (Umbundu, Kikongo, Nyanja).[49] A good example of the way in which a widely distributed Bantu root took on different related meanings in Brazil is *mulungu*, which appears in many different East African Bantu languages as the word for "supreme being" and has variant meanings from a drum used in *candomblé* (in Bahia) to "an African idol worshipped in *macumba* cults" (in Rio).[50] *Minhoca*, with a basic meaning of "worm" in Brazilian Portuguese, but with many related colloquial meanings, similarly derives from the widespread Bantu root, *nyoka*, "snake".[51] Others include *aliamba* (variants include *diamba*, *liamba*, and *riamba*), a widespread Brazilian word for marijuana, which appears in Nyanja, Yao, and Makonde, as well as in Kimbundu; the second meaning for *dengue*, an acute infectious disease, or a fever, which Schneider traces to both Kimbundu and Tsonga; and *cachimbo*, a smoking pipe, which again can be traced to Kimbundu and Mang'anja/Nyanja.[52]

A handful of words appear to have exclusively East Africans origins, such as *aringa*, which Schneider defines as "a fortified retreat for African chiefs" but for which he provides no etymology. In fact, this is a word meaning "stockade" that appears in both Mang'anja and Yao and was incorporated into regular Portuguese discourse in nineteenth-century Mozambique, as well.[53] Kubik also has an interesting side comment in which he maintains that the late Donald Kachamba, the distinguished Malawian musician, "was able to establish a convincing identity between the distilled molasses called *cachaça* in Brazil and the stuff known in Malawi and northern Mozambique called *kachasu*," adding that the origin of this term had long been considered to be unknown.[54] A particular type of small rattle used to engage the attention of babies, the *caracaxá*, has specific origins among the Chirima sub-group of the Makua.[55] Another word may be *fimbo*, meaning "wooden lance or spear used by the *cafres* [i.e. southern Africans]", which Mendonça attributes incorrectly on the evidence he provides to a Zambezi language, but which has wide distribution in East African Bantu languages with the meaning of "stick".[56] A final example reminds us, however, that not every Africanism in Brazilian Portuguese can be traced to the era of the slave trade. Schneider includes the word *gungunhana*, meaning "an individual of the black race", and correctly notes that it owes its origin to the last great king of the Gaza Nguni in southern Mozambique, Ngungunyane Nqumayo, who after his defeat by the Portuguese in 1895 was exiled to the Azores Islands, where he died in 1906.[57] No doubt Ngungunyane's notoriety as one of the last great resistance leaders to Portuguese imperialism in Africa and possibly the dissemination of several famous photographs of him in captivity gave rise to the incorporation of his name in this way into Brazilian Portuguese. For all these tantalizing snippets, however, there is no reason to believe that historical linguistic investigation will reveal anything like the traces of Kimbundu and other Angolan languages "discovered" in the "secret language" of Cafundó in Salto de Pirapora, in the interior of São Paulo state in 1978, as well as at São João de Chapada and Patrocínio in Minas Gerais, but the fact remains that there is evidence of East African borrowings that "Moçambiques" unquestionably introduced into the lexicon of Brazilian Portuguese.[58]

Contemporary verification for the use of East African languages in nineteenth-century Brazil are not abundant, but they do exist. Nina Rodrigues writes:

> Regarding Makua, we find evidence in the criminal case records against the new blacks Umpapullea and Lauriano who in April 1823 rose up and killed the crew of the ship that carried them from Africa. The interpreters of the Makua language were native-born blacks from Mozambique. But even from Mozambique other dominant languages, such as *quimovia, ioba, quingoge*, etc., must have been spoken by the numerous slaves from that source.[59]

Indeed, they were. According to Slenes, Rugendas reported word lists from the "Tzchoambo" [Chuabo] and "Matibani" to the French geographer, Adrien Balbi, who published them in 1826.[60] Although Rugendas was mistaken in his location of the latter near to Inhambane when it is actually a small port on the coast just to the north of Mozambique Island, he correctly placed the Chuabo, a mixed people in the hinterland of Quelimane, near to the Makua.

During the visit of the United States Exploring Expedition to Rio de Janeiro a decade or so later, its official ethnographer and philologist, Horatio Hale, obtained "from the natives of Africa, who are to be found there, vocabularies of several languages spoken in the southern part of that continent." These he grouped together into two major subdivisions of a "family of cognate languages", one being "Congo-Makua", the other "Caffrarian". Holt remarks:

> The *Makua* are, on the eastern side, what the Congo nation is on the west, - the most numerous and powerful people known to us; and their name has therefore been used, in the same manner, to designate all the tribes speaking cognate languages, from the Sowaiel or Sowauli, near the equator, to the Sofala, in latitude 21° south. The principal of these are (1) the *Makua* proper, who occupy an extensive region between the latitudes 10° and 20° south; (2) the *Mudjana* [Yao], who are spread over the interior of the continent, to the north and northwest of the Makua; (3) the *Makonde*, also an interior tribe, whose country stretches towards the territory of the Bengera on the western coast. The *Takwani*, *Musena*, and *Sofala* dialects, of which vocabularies are given, are spoken by tribes of the southern Makua, who inhabit the region watered by the great river Zambeze.[61]

Holt continues to tell us about the so-called Caffres, some of whose languages were already known from travelers' accounts. But "we hitherto have had no account" of those people who inhabited the coast between Delagoa Bay and Sofala. "They are called *Nyambana*, or, as the Portuguese write it, *Inhambane*, and it is of their language that a specimen is now given. A vocabulary of several hundred words was obtained, - but, for the reasons mentioned [space constraints and the belief that missionary works would soon supercede his own], it is omitted."[62] Holt then proceeds to present a comparative list of almost sixty words from each of these languages, including body parts, common objects and phenomena, and cardinal numbers. Among these, "God" is rendered as *mulungu* or a variant in Makua, Yao, Makonde, Takwani, and Sofala, while "snake" is given as *nyoka* or a variant in Makua, Yao, Makonde, Sena, and Nyambana.[63] Not only does Holt's testimony confirm what Nina Rodrigues correctly assumed, but it explicitly drives home my earlier point abut the way in which a very generous nomenclature was used by which to identify African peoples in Brazil, indeed throughout the African diaspora. At the same time, Holt astutely recognizes the differences between the broad belt of Central Bantu languages and those of Southern Bantu.

While Rio was the major port of entry for slaves from Mozambique, it is clear that not all of them remained there. As Karasch and others point out, the internal slave trade of Brazil significantly redistributed bonded labor during the course of the nineteenth century. In particular, the demand for labor on coffee plantations in the interior of Rio and São Paulo, and in the mines of Minas Gerais, removed many slaves from the capital city. According to Karasch, 51 of 146 or 38.4 percent of the slaves dispatched to Minas Gerais in 1831-1832 were originally from East Africa, appearing in the documentation as "Moçambique" (37), "Inhambane" (12), or "Quilimane".[64] The local regional dialect of Minas Gerais bears further witness to their presence in the word "*Maçambique*" for a special kind of belt made of glass (*cinta de vidro*), as well as the names of Moçambique and Landim, the latter being a broadly applied name for the Tsonga peoples of southern Mozambique, including the hinterland of Inhambane.[65] Among the identities of slave marriages analyzed by Florentino and Goés for rural Rio in the early nineteenth century are included "Macua", "Mozambican", and "Quilimane".[66] Other evidence, indirect in this instance, that the internal slave trade involved slaves from East Africa may be suggested by the place name of Praia de Moçambique on the Atlantic coast of Florianópolis, the Ilha de Santa Catarina.[67]

It is the place of slaves of East African origin in this interior dispersal that accounts, no doubt, for the presence of a popular folk dance called "Moçambique" that is closely associated with Roman Catholic feast days. It is or was popular well into the twentieth century in São Paulo, where it seems to have originated, and then diffused to Goiás, Minas Gerais, Rio de Janeiro, Mato Grosso and Rio Grande do Sul.[68] According to the detailed research of folklorist Alceu Araújo in the mid-1940s, the center of the dance in São Paulo was São Luís do Paraitanga.[69] The Moçambique is especially associated with the day of Saint Benedict (1524-1589, beatified 1763), the Franciscan son of Ethiopian slaves, who is remembered in myth by those who perform the dance to have created it as a diversion from work:

> 'He was neapolitan, white, and went to evangelize the blacks of Africa. Being poorly received, he sought to become black and thereby facilitate his work. He also worked in clearing the land, say the dancers of Moçambique (*moçambiqueiros*), and, in order to relieve and divert the blacks, invented the Moçambique dance.'[70]

The dance that Araújo observed half a century ago was almost completely devoid of its African origins, resembling what he describes as a Morris Dance that was possibly influenced by Moorish-influenced immigrants from northern Portugal. One of its remaining African elements, the king, is apparently derived from or at least shared with the better known and more widely spread *congada*. Thus, according to a Moçambique song he collected,

> This dance is moçambique
> People say that it's congada
> With permission from Saint Benedict
> It will dance up your steps.
>
> Esta dança é moçambique
> Gente diz que é congada
> Com licência de São Benidito
> Serená a sua escada [71]

Neither the dance steps nor the instrumentation, with the important exception of leg bells (*paiá*), are African.[72] Araújo makes a clear distinction between this modern dance and "the former dance of the Moçambiques that were performed before the balls of the aristocrats of rural Brazil . . . ."[73] Based on conversations with older members of the troops of *moçambiqueiros* Araújo studied, he learned that

> The old Moçambique was a dance performed by slaves, patronized by the master, by the plantation owner, at night, in the salons, immediately after dinner, as the first part of the festivities; to follow, after the dance of the

> Moçambiques, the ball in which all the local gentry, the members of the rural aristocracy began to dance until dawn.
>
> The dance was not like the current version, informants hastened to add; the blacks, ten or twelve, entered the ball-room singing in an African language and marching in step, emphasizing the rhythm with the beats of the ankle-bells strapped to their wrists and ankles.[74]

The abolition of slavery put an end to this kind of display and over time the dance incorporated many new elements and assumed the character of a religious brotherhood.

As fascinating as Araújo's reconstruction of the slave dance is, I find it hard to believe that Moçambique was danced only at the command of a master or that it was performed only for the amusement of the plantocracy. A suggestion of what its true origins may have been, however, comes from A. Americano do Brasil, who provided the following explanation for its origins in 1925: "African dance, as explains the name which characterizes it, *moçambique*. It was known and used in the interior by the first mining slaves who were brought for the extraction of gold."[75] Here I would like to urge historians of Brazil to rescue the history of this important Brazilian dance performance from the folklorists by looking for the contemporary documentation that will reveal more concrete evidence of its "Moçambique" and probably other African origins.

Carnival is another institutionalized form of cultural expression in which Brazilians of all backgrounds engaged. In what can only be called an example of performing Africa, Nina Rodrigues quotes a local newspaper description from around 1900 or slightly earlier of the float of one of the richest Bahian clubs, the *Pândegos de África* (Revelers of Africa): "it represents the bank of the Zambeze, on whose summit, reclining in an immense shell, rests the king Labossi, surrounded by his ministers Auá, Oman, Abato, the last holding the standard of the club in his fist."[76] Whatever else may have been represented in this particular float, a collective memory of Zambesia, however contrived, was apparently at play here.

One other tantalizing piece of information that merits further historical investigation is suggested by Ramos' undocumented assertion that

> The blacks from Angola, the Congo and Mozambique were responsible for the development of wood sculpture, especially *iteques* or tiny figurines for religious purposes. Iron was worked particularly by the Mozambican Negroes, who were able craftsmen in this art.[77]

While there may not be a significant corpus of contemporary documentation against which to check this bold assertion, it seems worth the effort to consider undertaking research among current artists and artisans in these crafts.

Different testimony to the fact that these various possibilities for tracing the presence and influence of "Moçambiques" in Brazil may not be the province only of folklorists and archival historians comes from the surprising news item that the 2000-2002 Executive Secretary of the Comunidade de Países de Língua Portuguesa (CPLP), the Brazilian Dulce Maria Pereira, is a "descendante de moçambicanos" and that during her opening address to the Third Summit Meeting at Maputo in July 2000 she is reported to "have invoked yesterday [18 July 2000] her Mozambican origins."[78] If this former Executive Secretary of the CPLP knows that her origins are "Moçambique", then surely there are other Brazilians who share such knowledge and whose genealogies ought to be reconstructed. Finally, recent genetic research on Brazilian mitochondrial DNA lineages reveals that a specific haplogroup of Southeast African provenance exists, not surprisingly to the historian, in the Brazilian population.[79]

Although it is evident that Brazilian scholars and scholars of Brazil have for many years paid some attention to the presence of people of East African origins, the so-called "Moçambiques", in Brazil, they have with the single exception of João Lupi not considered them to be significant actors in the shaping of Brazilian society. In the total scheme of things, they may be right. But I believe that the evidence I have assembled in this paper suggests that they may, in fact, have been more of a factor than many would recognize. I want to conclude, however, by emphasizing with Lupi that "Moçambiques" in Brazil were not simply people from Mozambique in Brazil.[80] Like all Africans in the diaspora, they were African peoples of different origins who shared the traumatic experience of being victims of the slave trade and, in this case, being enslaved in Brazil. They carried different elements of their African heritage with them – their language, music, dance, life ways – but always filtered through a constant process of compromise and reinvention, some of which was imposed on them by others, some of which they embraced as their own. This historical process of creolization is what marks the passage of these men, women, and children, as well as their descendants, from East Africa to Brazil.

ENDNOTES

1. Edward A. Alpers, *Ivory and Slaves in East Central Africa* (Berkeley: University of California Press, 1975), pp. 185, 187-188.
2. See Gwendoyn Midlo Hall (ed.), *Databases for the Study of Afro-Louisiana, 1699-1860* (Baton Rouge: Louisiana State University Press, 2000), File://D/HallCollection/cdfiles/HallSlave&FreeDatabases/slavecals/FrequentAfricans/FrequentAfricans.HTM, which indicates that a total of 102 or 1.2 percent of all slaves in Louisiana over the period 1780-1810 were "Makwa", i.e. from Mozambique.
3. João Eduardo Pinto Basto Lupi, *Moçambique, moçambiques: Itinerario de um povo afro-brasileiro* (Santa Maria: Edições UFSM, 1988). For an example of the grandfather's writings, see especially Eduardo do Couto Lupi, *Angoche* (Lisboa: Typographia do Annuario Commercial, 1907).
4. For these early contacts, see José Capela, "O Tráfico da Escravatura nas Relações Moçambique-Brasil," *História: Questões e Debates* (Curitiba) 9/16 (1988): 187-192; Aurélio Rocha, "Contribuição para o estudo das relações entre Moçambique e Brasil no séc. XIX (Tráfico de escravos e relações políticas e culturais)," *Estudos Afro-Asiáticos* 21 (1991): 200-204.

5. William W. Megenney, *A Bahian Heritage: An Ethnolinguistic Study of African Influences on Bahian Portuguese* (Chapel Hill: North Carolina Studies in the Romance Languages and Linguistics, 1978), pp. 81-82 and Table 4. For reference to the probable death of a "Moçambique" soldier in 1754 at Porto Alegre, Rio Grande do Sul, see Cláudio Moreira Bento, *O Negro e Descendentes na Sociedade do Rio Grande do Sul (1635-1975)* (Porto Alegre: Grafosul and Instituto Estadual do Livro, 1976), p. 189.
6. Herbert S. Klein, "The Trade in African Slaves to Rio de Janeiro, 1795-1811: Estimates of Mortality and Patterns of Voyages," *Journal of African History* 10 (1969): 540, Table 4; Manolo G. Florentino, *Em Costas Negras: Uma História do Tráfico Atlântico de Escravos entre a África e o Rio de Janeiro (Séculos XVIII e XIX)* (São Paulo: Civilização Brasileira, 1997), p. 234, Apêndice 13; Mary C. Karasch, *Slave Life in Rio de Janeiro 1808-1850* (Princeton: Princeton University Press, 1987), p. 12, Table 1.2 and Appendix A, p. 15, Table 1.6.
7. Herbert S. Klein, *The Atlantic Slave Trade* (Cambridge and New York: Cambridge University Press, 1999), p. 71.
8. Capela, "O Tráfico," pp. 199-233. For an earlier discussion that focuses on numbers of slaves exported from Mozambique to Brazil, see Alpers, *Ivory and Slaves*, pp. 210-218. For a recent, tentative reassessment of the numbers, see Alpers, "Mozambique and 'Mozambiques': a global perspective," Unpublished paper presented at the UNESCO Slave Route Conference, Maputo, Mozambique, 17-19 March 2004.
9. José Raimundo Oliveira Vergolino, "A Demografia escrava no nordeste do Brasil: O caso de Pernambuco – 1800/1888," Texto para Discussão Nº.383, Departamento de Economia, Universidade Federal de Pernambuco, March 1997, p. 20, Tabela 10; Laird W. Bergad, *Slavery and the Demographic and Economic History of Minas Gerais, Brazil, 1720-1888* (Cambridge; Cambridge University Press, 1999), p. 151, Table 4.2. For references to Moçambiques in Pernambuco, see also Henry Koster, *Travels in Brazil* (London: Hurst, Reese, Orme, and Brown, 1816), p. 481 and Marcus J. M. de Carvalho, *Liberdade: Rotinas e Rupturas do Escravismo no Recife, 1822-1850* (Recife: Editora Universitária da UFPE, 1998), pp. 112, n. 33, and 159.
10. R. Walsh, *Notices of Brazil in 1828 and 1829* (London: Frederick Westley and A.H. Davis, 1830), II, p. 333.
11. Jean Baptiste Debret, *Viagem Pitoresca e Histórica ao Brasil* trans. Sergio Milliet (São Paulo: Livraria Martins, 1940 [1834-1839]), I, p. 186.
12. Koster, *Travels*, p. 420.
13. Carlos Seidler, *Dez Anos de Brasil* (São Paulo: Livraria Martins, 1941), quoted in Bento, *O Negro*, p. 39: "O Negro de Moçambique é o mais feio. É de corpo pequeno, atarracado e forte; sua cabeça ordinariamente implantada quase no peito, é muito grande em proporção com o corpo. Seu olhar agudo busca, sempre arredio, o chão, seus movimentos são desajeitados, seu andar é lento e desongonçado. Suporta com estoicismo pancadas e maus tratos, as mais pavorosas surras raramente lhe arrancam un som de dor."
14. Edward A. Alpers, "Becoming 'Mozambique': Diaspora and Identity in Mauritius," in Vijaya Teelock and Edward A. Alpers (eds.), *History, Memory and Identity.* (Port-Louis: Nelson Mandela Centre for African Culture and the University of Mauritius, 2001), pp. 117-155.

15. A. C. Madan, *Kiungani* (London: George Bell and Sons, 1887), pp. 24, 25. There are many other stories in this collection that bear witness to this process, including some that specifically discuss language. A similar phenomenon occurred in Angola, where according to an early nineteenth-century source, enslaved people from the Lunda empire, deep in central Africa, were held at the major slave market at Kassanje, where they learned to speak Kimbundu, which they all spoke fluently by the time they reached the coast at Luanda. Robert W. Slenes, "Malungu, Ngoma's Coming!" Africa Hidden and Discovered in Brazil," in Nelson Aguilar (ed.), *Mostra de redescobrimento: Negro de Corpo e Alma, Black in Body and Soul* (São Paulo: Associação Brasil 500 Anos Artes Visuais, 2000), pp. 222-223 and n. 5; See also C. Schlichthorst, *O Rio de Janeiro como é 1824-1826 (Huma vez e nunca mais)* (Rio de Janeiro: Editora Getulio Costa, 1943), pp. 139-140.
16. Walsh, *Notices*, II, p. 334; for variant meanings, see John T. Schneider, *Dictionary of African Borrowings in Brazilian Portuguese* (Hamburg: Helmut Buske Verlag, 1991), p. 192. For an extended analysis, see Slenes, "Malungu, Ngoma's Coming!," p. 222.
17. Eduardo Medeiros, "Moçambicanização dos escravos saídos pelos portos de Moçambique," Unpublished paper presented at the conference Enslaving Connections: Africa and Brazil during the Age of the Slave Trade, York University, Toronto, 12-15 October 2000, last sentence. In an important appendix to this paper, "Notas para o estudo da formação das entidades étnicas dos povos de lingual(s) emakhuwa e elómwè e advento da etnicidade macua e lómuè," Medeiros emphasizes the complex historical process whereby these people became recognized as a major ethnic grouping within Mozambique itself.
18. See Melville Herskovits, *The Myth of the Negro Past* (New York: Harper and Brothers, 1941), who argues for a broad African cultural heritage that was carried to the New World, and Sidney Mintz and Richard Price, *The Birth of African-American Culture: An Anthropological Perspective* (Boston: Beacon Press, 1992 [1976]), who contend that Africans were from such diverse backgrounds and so individualized that they created new "American" or "Creole" cultures that owed virtually nothing to Africa. Recent contributions that modify this dichotomy while disagreeing over the extent to which it is possible to trace African origins and roots in the Americas, include John K. Thornton, *Africa and Africans in the Making of the Atlantic World, 1400-1800* (Cambridge: Cambridge University Press, 1998 [1992]); Philip Morgan, "The Cultural Implications of the Atlantic Slave Trade: African Regional Origins, American Destinations and New World Developments," *Slavery and Abolition* 18/1 (1997): 122-145.
19. Slenes, "Malungu, Ngoma's Coming!," p. 223.
20. Schlichthorst, *O Rio de Janeiro*, p. 140.
21. Emília Viotti da Costa, *Da Senzala à Colônia* (São Paulo: Difusão Européia do Livro, 1966), p. 240: "As rivalidades dividiam os negros em nações: o de Moçambique não supportava o do Congo, o da Mina ao do Koromatum; e a polícia era freqüentemente chamada para apartar desordens entre eles."
22. Walsh, *Notices*, II, p. 330.
23. Leila Mezan Algranti, *O Feitor Ausente: Estudo sobre a escravidão urbana no Rio de Janeiro* (Petrópolis: Vozes, 1988), pp. 141: "por capoeira e estar provocando desordens com o preto Domingos," and 168-169: "Escravo João Moçambique de Thomé Faria por ser encontrado despois das onze horas da noite com uma pedra

na mão, encostado a uma árvore . . . e ter dito em uma taberna no Pedregulho que a mesma pedra haveria de dar na patrulha que lhe pusesse a mão." Algranti provides data to show that 5.8 percent of individuals imprisoned by the police in Rio during 1810-1821 gave "Moçambique" as their place of birth: ibid., p. 211.

24. Marcos Ferreira de Andrade, "Rebelião escrava na Comarca do Rio das Mortes, Minas Gerais: o caso Carracas," *Afro-Ásia* 21-22 (1998-1999): 81-82, Quadro 1.
25. Adèle Toussaint-Samson, *A Parisian in Brazil* (Boston: James H. Earle, 1891), quoted in Robert Edgar Conrad, *Children of God's Fire; A Documentary History of Black Slavery in Brazil* (Princeton: Princeton University Press, 1983), p. 86.
26. John Parish and William Parish Robertson, *Letters on Paraguay: Comprising an Account of a Four Years's Residence in that Republic under the Government of the Dictator Francia* (London: J. Murray, 1838) in Karasch, *Slave Life*, p. 242. See the similar description of different African peoples dancing at the end of Ramadhan (Id al-Fitr) at Muscat by Joseph B. F. Osgood, *Notes of Travel or Recollections of Majunga, Zanzibar, Muscat, Aden, Mocha, and other Eastern Ports* (Salem: G. Creamer, 1854), pp. 106-108.
27. Karasch, *Slave Life*, pp. 83-85.
28. Koster, *Travels*, p. 441.
29. Nei Lopes, *Bantos, Malês e Identidade Negra* (Rio de Janeiro: Forense Universitária, 1988), p. 152.
30. Daniel P. Kidder, *Sketches of a Residence and Travels in Brazil* (Philadelphia: Sorin & Ball and London: Wiley & Putnam, 1845), I, p. 177. A rod was equal to 5½ yards.
31. Debret, *Viagem Pitoresca*, I, p. 184. The Portuguese text provided by Debret reads "nós estamos chorando o nosso parente, não enxerguemos mais; vai em baixo da terra até o dia do juizo, hei de século seculorum amem."
32. Ibid., pp. 184-185. See also Melo Morais Filho, *Festas e Tradições Populares do Brasil* 3rd ed. (Rio de Janeiro: F. Briguiet & Cia., 1946), pp. 413-417, "Um Funeral Moçambique em 1830," which reads like a loose, unattributed version of Debret's description.
33. Gilberto Freyre, *O Escravo nos Anúncios de Jornais Brasileiros do Século XIX* (Recife: Imprensa Universitária, 1963), pp. 102, 130, 136, 142, 144, 148, 151, 155, 157, 159, 166, 167, 170 (Moçambique), 117 and 157 (Quilimane), 87 (Mombaça), and 101 (Inhambane). Schlichthorst, *O Rio de Janeiro*, p. 138, also mentions Mombaça as a source of slaves, while Renato Mendoça, *A Influência Africana no Português do Brasil* 3rd ed. (Porto: Livraria Figueirinhas, 1948), p. 140, quotes a song in which it appears. See Karasch, *Slave Life*, p. 313, for a newspaper notice about three "Moçambiques" captured in a *quilombo* in the Tijuca, and Bento, *O Negro*, p. 258, for an 1827 notice of a "Moçambique" runaway slave in Porto Alegre. For an account of a slaving voyage and shipboard revolt from Inhambane, see Conrad, *Children*, pp. 39-42.
34. João Mauricio Rugendas, *Viagem Pitoresca Através do Brasil* (Rio de Janeiro/São Paulo/Brasília: A Casa do Livro, 1972 [1835]). The plates are not paginated.
35. Karasch, *Slave Life*, pp. 11-15. For Mongalo, see Alpers, *Ivory and Slaves*, references indicated in index; for Mujau as Yao, see Karasch, *Slave Life*, pp. 22, 23
36. I also discuss the designation of "Inhambanes" at Réunion in Alpers, "Becoming 'Mozambique.'"

37. Karasch, *Slave Life*, pp. 22-24.
38. Ewbank, *Life*, p. 257.
39. Walsh, *Notices*, II, p. 22.
40. See the 1853 lithograph by Adolphe Martial Potémont of a liberated "yambane" reproduced in Benoît Jullien, et al, *Île de La Réunion, Regards croisés sur l'esclavage 1794-1848* (Saint-Denis: CNH and Paris: Somogy éditions d'art, 1998), p. 247, Plate 370. On the general topic, see Michael A. Gomez, *Exchanging Our Country Marks: The Transformation of African Identities in the Colonial and Antebellum South* (Chapel Hill and London: University of North Calorina Press, 1998).
41. Henri A. Junod, *The Life of a South African Tribe* (New Hyde Park, New York: University Books Inc.: 1962 [1926]), I, pp. 178-181. Ewbank's second-hand description of a mass operation superficially reminds one of Junod's equally second-hand description of a Tsonga male circumcision operation, but these were held in great secrecy and there is no evidence that cicatrization among men was ever a part of puberty rites of passage. See ibid., I, p. 73-76.
42. Ernst Ebel, *O Rio de Janeiro e seus arredores em 1824* (São Paulo: Editora Nacional, 1972), p. 46; on this very point, see Slenes, "Malungu, Ngoma's Coming!," p. 228.
43. Debret, *Viagem Pitoresca*, I, pp. 187 and 233: "Estas últimas compreendem um certo número de nações vendidas num mesmo ponto da costa, como a *astre*, etc." and "N°.7, Negro *calava* vendido na costa de Moçambique; tem côr de cobre avermelhado e as cicatrizes são de um preto azulado; . . . Não tem o lábio superior furado, porém mostra um lábio inferior alongado, operação a que se procede na infância, comprimindo-se o lábio entre dois pedacinhos de tábua fortemente apertadas." I am unable at the moment to identify the meaning of *calava* and of *astre*.
44. Rugendas, *Viagem Pitoresca*, Plate entitled "Mozambique".
45. Luciano Raposo, *Marcas de Escravos – Listas de escravos emancipados vindos a bordo de navios negreiros (1839-1841)* (Rio de Janeiro: Arquivo Nacional, Publicações Históricas 90, 1989/1990).
46. Ibid., facsimile register and commentary at p. 24. For a discussion of the major Portuguese slave traders to Brazil at Mozambique Island, see José Capela, "Apontamento sobre os negreiros da Ilha de Moçambique, 1900-1920 [*sic*], *Arquivo – Boletim do Arquivo Histórico de Moçambique* 4 (1988): 83-90.
47. I discuss this aspect of cicatrization in Alpers, "Becoming 'Mozambique'". For a particularly insightful discussion of the gendered nature of this form of bodily decoration, including the significance of changing fashions over time, see Heidi Gengenbach, "Boundaries of Beauty: Tattooed Secrets of Women's History in Magude, Southern Mozambique," *Journal of Women's History* 14/4 (2003): 106-141.
48. Gerhard Kubik, *Angolan Traits in Black Music, Games and Dances of Brazil: A study of African cultural extensions overseas* (Lisboa: Junta de Investigações Científicas do Ultramar, Centro de Estudos de Antropologia Cultural, 1979), pp. 36-39. See also Karasch, *Slave Life*, pp. 233-235
49. Schneider, *Dictionary*, p. 142; P. Prata, *Dicionário Português-Macua* (Cucujães: Edição da Sociedade Missionária Portuguesa [1986]), where *ekoma* is listed under the entries for *batuque*, *dança*, and *tambor*, i.e. dance, African dance, and drum.
50. Ibid., pp. 224-225. *Macumba* is the "umbrella" term used for two principle forms of African spirit worship in Brazil, *Candomblé* and *Umbanda*.

51. Ibid., p. 206.
52. Ibid., pp. 8, 131.
53. Ibid., p. 16; David Clement Scott, *A Cyclopaedic Dictionary of the Mang'anja Language spoken in British Central Africa* (Farnsborough: Gregg International Publishers Limited, 1968 [1892]), p. 253: "*Linga*, II, a stockade"; G. Meredith Sanderson, *A Dictionary of the Yao Language* (Zomba: The Government Printer, 1954), p. 115: "Lînga, a stockade; a wooden fence". For its variant in Makua, see Prata, *Dicionário*, p. 163: "Fortaleza, *eringa*, *erinka*, *erika*". For the *aringa* system in Zambesia, see M.D.D. Newitt, *Portuguese Settlement on the Zambesi* (London: Longman, 1973), pp. 226-229.
54. Kubik, *Angolan Traits*, pp. 12-13; also Schneider, *Dictionary*, p. 62.
55. Schneider, *Dictionary*, pp.105-106.
56. Mendonça, *Influência Africana*, p. 226. See for example, Sanderson, *Dictionary*, p. 241, for its Yao variant: "*Simbo*, a staff. (2) a walking stick". According to Harold W. Fehderau, *Dictionnaire Kituba (Kiongo ya Leta)-Anglais-Français et Vocabulaire Français-Kituba* (Kinshasa: Editions Cedi, 1992), p. 46, *Fímbu*, *mfimbu* appears in Kituba, the colonial lingua franca of northern Democratic Republic of the Congo and the southern Congo Republic. I am grateful to my colleagues Christopher Ehret and Thomas Hinnebusch for advice on this word and for explaining the relevant sound shifts that operate in the different Bantu languages.
57. Schneider, *Dictionary*, pp. 159-160. For the career of this African leader, see Gerhard Liesegang, *Ngungunyane: A figura de Ngungunyane Nqumayo, Rei de Gaza 1884-1895 e o desaparecimento do seu Estado* Colecção Embondeiro Nº.8 (Maputo: ARPAC, 1986).
58. Carlos Vogt and Peter Fry, *Cafundó - A África no Brasil: Linguagem e sociedade* (São Paulo: Editora da UNICAMP, 1996); Lopes, *Bantos*, pp. 172-178. I am grateful to Roquinaldo Amaral Ferreira for bringing the first reference to my attention.
59. Raymundo Nina Rodrigues, *Os Africanos no Brasil* 3rd ed. (São Paulo: Companhia Editora Nacional, 1945), p. 248: "Do Macua, encontramos provas nos autos de um processo-crime contra os negros novos Umpapullea e Lauriano que em abril de 1823 se sublevaram e mataram a tripulação do navio que os trazia da África. Os interpretes da lingua macua eram negros ladinos de Moçambique. Mas mesmo de Moçambique outras linguas que ali dominam como o quimovia, o ioba, o quinoge, etc., deviam ter sido falados pelos numerosos escravos desta procedência." *Quimovia* probably refers to Mavia, or lowland Makonde, which would have been spoken by slaves purchased at the Kerimba islands and perhaps at Kilwa. I cannot identify *Ioba*. *Quingoge* perhaps indicates the language spoken by slaves exported from Angoche, in which case it would have been either a dialect of Makua or possibly even Koti, the language spoken at and around Angoche itself. For details on the shipboard slave revolt of 1823, see Clovis Moura, *Rebeliões da Senzala: Quilombos-Insurreições-Guerrilhas* (Rio de Janeiro: Conquista, 1972), pp. 142-143.
60. Slenes, "Malungu, Ngoma's Coming!," p.222 and n. 7.
61. Horatio Hale, *Ethnography & Philology*, a separate volume in Charles Wilkes, *United States Exploring Expedition. During the Years 1838, 1839, 1840, 184, 1842. Under the Command of Charles Wilkes, U.S.N.* (Philadelphia: Lea and Blanchard, 1846), pp. 657, 658.

62. Ibid., p. 658. I hope to locate Holt's raw notes among the complete papers of this curious expedition in the Library of Congress.
63. Ibid., pp. 659-666.
64. Karasch, *Slave Life*, p. 53, Table 2.6.
65. Aires de Mata Machado Filho, *O Negro e o Garimpo em Minas Gerais* (Rio de Janeiro: Livraria José Olympio Editora, 1943), pp. 136, 138. In his discussion of the popular mining songs known as *vissungo*, which he recorded in 1928 and contained many words and grammar from southern Angola ("lingua de benguela"), Machado Filho notes that one *vissungo* melody was like that of the "*achicundas* of Angola." But the Achikunda were, in fact, a people from Zambesia. Ibid., pp. 7, 66. Schneider, *Dictionary*, p. 184, gives a completely different definition for "*maçambique*" as "a bivalve mollusk" in the dialect of São Paulo.
66. Manolo G. Florentino and José R. Góes, "Slavery, Marriage and Kinship in Rural Rio de Janeiro, 1790-1830," in Paul E. Lovejoy (ed.), *Identity in the Shadow of Slavery* (London and New York: Continuum, 2000), pp. 155-156. The authors argue that depending on fluctuations in the level of slave importations to Rio marriage practices shifted either to reinforce ethnic boundaries or to break them down through ethnic intermarriage.
67. Marcos Cherinda, "Praia de Moçambique no Brasil," *Tempo* (Maputo) 119 (29 March, 1992): 38-43. My thanks to Kathie Sheldon for bringing this article to my attention.
68. For short references, see Luís da Câmara Cascudo, *Dicionário do Folclore Brasileiro* 4th ed., revised and enlarged (São Paulo: Edições Melhoramentos e Instituto Nacional do Livro, 1979), p. 498; Alaôr Eduardo Scisínio, *Dicionário da Escravidão* (Rio de Janeiro: Léo Christiano Editorial Ltda., 1997), pp. 253-254; Lopes, *Bantos*, pp. 156-157.
69. Alceu Maynard Araújo, *Folclore Nacional, I: Festas, Bailados, Mitos e Lendas* (São Paulo: Melhoramentos, 1964), p. 354.
70. Ibid., pp. 191-192: "'Era napolitano, branco, e foi evangelizar os prêtos da África. Sendo mal recebido, pediu para ficar prêto e assim facilitou o seu trabalho. Também êle trabalhava na roça, dizem os moçambiqueiros, arrando a terra e, para descançar e divertir os prêtos, inventou o bailado do Moçambique'"; other versions appear at pp. 201 and 352.
71. Ibid., p. 374, from n. 68 beginning on p. 373.
72. For details on leg bells, see ibid., pp. 363, 365, 366. Lupi, *Moçambique, moçambiques*, p. 86, suggests that there may be a link between the crossed batons (*bastões*) around which the *moçambiqueiros* dance and a knife dance noted in the late nineteenth century for coastal Mozambique, but this seems highly unlikely to me, as Indian Ocean sword dances were strictly an Arab form of cultural expression. Few enslaved East Africans would have recognized such a dance or have brought any memory of it with them to Brazil.
73. Ibid., p. 351: "*a antiga dança dos moçambiques, realizada antes dos bailes da aristocracia rural brasileira* . . . . "
74. Ibid., p. 380, Apêndice Nº.10, "A Antiga Dança de Moçambique": "O moçambique antigo era uma dança realizada pela escravaria, patrocinadada pelo senhor, pelo fazendeiro, à noite, nos salões, logo depois do jantar, como primeira parte dos festejos; a seguir, após a dança dos moçambiques, o baile em que tôdas as pessoas gradas (*sic*), os membros da aristocracia rural iriam dançar até amanhecer. . . . A dança não era

como as aruais, adiantam os informantes, os prêtos, dez ou doze, entravam no salão, cantando em lingual africana, dando passos de marcha, ressaltando o ritmo com as batidas dos paiás presos nos pulsos e tornazelos." In the modern dance, the *paiás* are worn around the leg at the top of the calf at the knee like a garter: see photograph facing p. 368 and p. 381. Similar ankle bells are still used in dances by southern Mozambican peoples.

75. Quoted in Cascudo, *Dicionário*, p. 498: "Dança africana, como explica a palavra que a caracteriza, moçambique. Foi conhecida e usada nos sertões pelos primeiros escravos mineiros trazidos para o trabalho da extração de ouro."
76. Rodrigues, *Os Africanos*, p, 291: "representa a margem do Zambeze, em cuja riba, reclinando em imensa concha, descansa o rei Labossi, cercado dos seus ministros Auá, Oman, Abato, empunhando o último o estandarte do clube." Although Rodrigues provides no date for this newspaper account, he died in Paris in 1906: Homero Pires, "Prefácio" to ibid., p. 9. See the contemporary description in Manuel Querino, *Costumes Africanos no Brasil* 2nd ed. (Recife: Fundação Joaquim Nabuco-Editora Massangana, 1988), pp. 62-63, which does not mention the Zambezi.
77. Artur Ramos, *The Negro in Brazil* trans. Richard Pattee (Washington, DC: The Associated Publishers, Inc., 1951), pp. 131-132.
78. Eunice Lourenço, "III Cimeira da CPLP terminou ontem em Maputo" in *O Público* (Lisboa), 19 July 2000, distributed electronically by António Teixeira to curry-lusoafrica@virginia.edu, 19 July 2000: "invocou ontem essas suas origens."
79. Juliana Alves-Silva, et al, "The Ancestry of Brazilian mtDNA Lineages," *American Journal of Human Genetics* 76 (2000): 444-461; H.-J. Bandelt, et al, "Phylogeography of the human mitochondrial haplogroup L3e: a snapshot of African prehistory and Atlantic slave trade," *Annals of Human Genetics* 65 (2001): 549-563. I am indebted to Professor Sérgio D.J. Pena, Universidade Federal de Minas Gerais, for these references.
80. Lupi, *Moçambique, moçambiques*, pp. 71, 89-94.

Plate 2: Mozambiques in Brazil

Source: João Mauricio Rugendas, *Viagem Pitoresca Através do Brasil* (Rio de Janeiro/São Paulo/Brasilia: A Casa do Livro, 1972 [1835]), plates unpaginated.

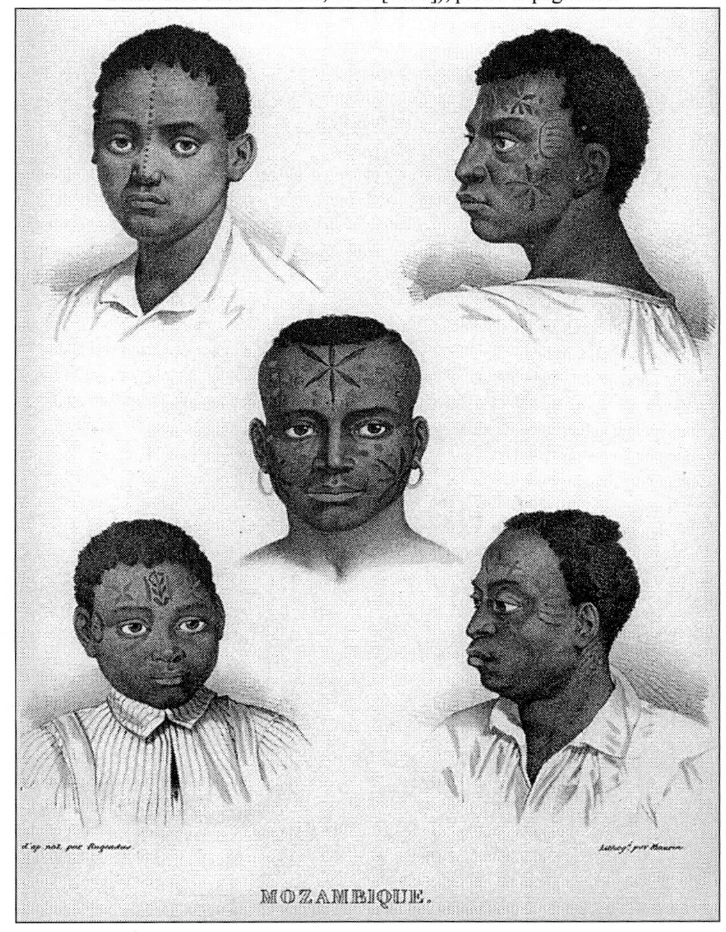

Plate 3: Kilwa Man in Brazil

Source: João Mauricio Rugendas, *Viagem Pitoresca Através do Brasil* (Rio de Janeiro/São Paulo/ Brasilia: A Casa do Livro, 1972 [1835]), plates unpaginated.

Plate 4: Nyambane Man in Brazil

Source: João Mauricio Rugendas, *Viagem Pitoresca Através do Brasil* (Rio de Janeiro/São Paulo/ Brasilia: A Casa do Livro, 1972 [1835]), plates unpaginated.

Plate 5: Map, Mozambique

Source: Adapted from Edward A. Alpers, *Ivory and Slaves in East Central Africa* (Berkeley: University of California Press, 1975), p. xx.

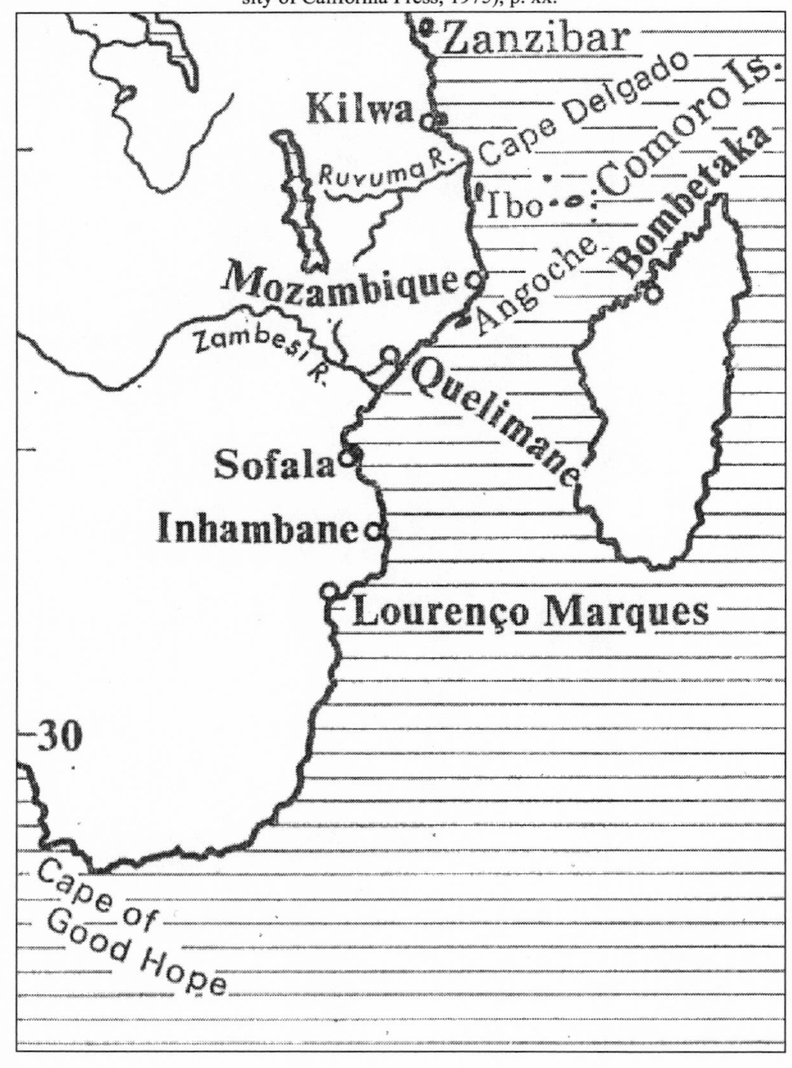

3

Transformations of the Sea and Thunder Voduns in the Gbe-Speaking Area and in the Bahian Jeje Candomblé[1]

Luis Nicolau Parés

The debate over processes of cultural continuity and discontinuity that were operative during the slave trade has lately shifted from a focus on identifying "africanisms" to an emphasis on examining the persistence of African cognitive orientations of worldviews in the Americas. It has also been suggested that it was the ability of Africans and their descendants to adapt and develop new social institutions that allowed them to define and maintain a differentiated identity. In Brazil, for example, religious values and practices of African origin were instrumental in the progressive creation of a particular religious institution, *Candomblé*, which became of critical importance in the reinvention a new Creole culture.[2]

In Brazil, religious activity of African origin dates back to the early times of slavery, but the religious institution of *Candomblé* as we know it today finds its historical antecedents in the first decades of the nineteenth century. Before that, the eighteenth century colonial "calundus" involved mainly healing and oracular activities for the service of individual clients, usually performed by a single religious expert, sometimes helped by one or two assistants. These activities could be held in domestic spaces and did not require a permanent site or "temple". Africans and their descendants also gathered in drumming-dancing celebrations known as "batuques", which often were timed to coincide with Catholic brotherhood feasts, but again these rituals seem to have been unsystematic, and some were not even necessarily of a religious nature.

It is not until the nineteenth century that the record shows the appearance of more stable and complex systems of religious organization, comprising, (1) a relatively permanent sacred space with shrines devoted to a plurality of deities, (2) a complex hierarchical organization of the religious group based on initiation processes, and (3) a relatively stable calendar of ceremonies going beyond the healing and oracular functions. This sort of extra-domestic religious institution, what I call *Candomblé* as opposed to "*calundú*", was only achieved when freed African slaves, mainly in the urban context, succeeded in organizing a social network that could guarantee the necessary resources, such as the possibility of land ownership. In that sense, *Candomblé* cannot be said to have emerged until the first decades of the nineteenth century and logically, if we want to understand the African elements that intervened in this formative period, we should look at the religious values and practices being imported to Brazil from Africa at that time.[3]

It has been well documented by historians that in early nineteenth century Bahia there was a huge increase of slaves from West Africa, mainly Nagô, Hausa, Tapa and Jeje. During the second half of the eighteenth century in Bahia, the Jeje from the Gbe-speaking area are likely to have been the largest African "nation", but in the 1820s they were surpassed by the Nagô. The demographic majority of the Nagô among the black population in the first half of the nineteenth century has been considered one of the main reasons for the eventual hegemony of the *orisha* (generic designation for the deities of the Yoruba pantheon) cult in the organization of the *Candomblé* institution. As I argue elsewhere, the demographic factor might have been critical only as far as it increased the probability of the presence of a higher number of religious experts. Other reasons, related to the "complexity" of the religious institutions operating in West African societies, may have been more important in determining the success of their replication or adaptation in the New World.[4] I contend that in this process the Jeje vodun tradition may have played a more significant role in the development of *Candomblé* than has been usually acknowledged.

"PANTHEONS," HIERARCHIES AND MULTI-DIVINITY CULTS

Although Brazilianists have repeatedly noted the importance of the Jeje linguistic contribution to the ritual terminology of *Candomblé*, the overall influence of the vodun tradition in the *Candomblé*'s organizational model has not been fully recognized.[5] In this section I look at a structural element of the vodun religion, namely the conceptualisation of the spiritual world into *constellations* or *groups of deities* with the corresponding multi-divinity cult and serial form of performance, which, when compared with the more "*monotheistic*" Yoruba *orisha* cults, supports the view that the *Candomblé* formative process was primarily inspired by the vodun tradition.

Along with deified ancestors or "lineage gods" and "personal gods and forces" like Legba or Fa, Herskovits divides the Dahomean "public" or "great gods" into four main groups: the Mawu-Lisa or sky pantheon, the Sakpata or earth pantheon, the Dan or snake pantheon and the Hevioso or thunder pantheon. Herskovits notes that "the Dahomean does not conceive of a single deity as performing all the functions of each of the elements. He rather envisages *groups of deities*, with each group forming a pantheon ruled by a *pantheon head* [my emphasis]."[6] As stated by Maupoil, "le tonnerre, la terre, tous les grands voudu possèdent un ensemble de *satellites* entre qui se répartissent les devoirs de leur charge."[7] What I want to emphasize is the idea that voduns are conceived as forming *groups*, sometimes with genealogical ties, and that their respective shrines are aggregated within a given temple according to a logic of religious efficacy and accumulation of spiritual power (*acè*).

As Olabiyi Yai notes, to call these groups of deities "pantheons" may be misleading since the word pantheon "surreptitiously introduces the new and potentially subversive twin concepts of verticality and hierarchy as definitional dimensions/features of divinity in the world view of the people of the region" - features that may not have always existed.[8] However, we must concede that ideas of verticality and hierarchy were not alien to the vodun religion, and this in a variety of ways.

Already in the seventeenth century, Bosman noted in Ouidah the supremacy of the snake cult over cults of the tree and sea deities, suggesting a corresponding hierarchy among its priesthood. However, the Fon kings were the ones reputed to have established, beginning in the eighteenth century, a highly centralised and hierarchical religious system in Dahomey. Maupoil talks of a "plan d'assujettissement des autels au trône" and Maurice Glele of a "contrôle de police administrative" by the state over the vodun congregations.[9] This political control of religious life resulted in the centralization and hierarchical organization of the vodun priesthood. Tegbesu's mother, Na Hwanjile, is credited with having introduced the Mawu-Lisa cult into Abomey, transforming this couple into the supreme creator gods, occupying the apex of an increasingly vertical and hierarchical "pantheon". At the same time, the introduction of the male-dominated Fa divination system, and the promotion of the Nesuhue royal cult into a "national cult" - with precedence over the rest of "public" cults - contributed to the pyramidal structure of the religious system.[10]

The progressive establishment of an "official pantheon" in Abomey during the eighteenth and nineteenth centuries was accompanied by the development of conceptual and ritual bonds between its constituent parts, the "public" or "state deities". The otherwise independent Mawu, Hevioso and Dan cults were variously related through myths, in attempts to establish coherent cosmologies. Yet these efforts toward cohesiveness were mainly restricted to Abomey and its area of influence.[11] Although we should not underestimate the impact of these efforts outside Abomey, what seems to have prevailed in the region is what Peel, speaking of Yorubaland, calls a series of "local cult complexes", each defined as "an ensemble of cults which is likely to include both a good many of the *orisa* [vodun] found widely (…) and others of more local currency, perhaps even unique to that place."[12] Therefore, it is useful as an analytical tool to distinguish between, on the one hand, a "national cult complex" established by Abomey promoting a highly hierarchical vertical pantheon, and, on the other, various "local cult complexes" which could assimilate but also shift from the official model.

In general terms each vodun congregation had a relative autonomy in installing its own shrines. Even if the voduns worshipped in a temple tended to belong to the same generic category (*hunve* or red vodun like Hevioso, *atimevodun* or tree vodun, Dan, Sakpata, Nesuhue etc.), new voduns, for a variety of reasons, could be "acquired" or "bought" and aggregated to the existing ones as "satellites". Eventually, a temple could host voduns from various categories. This resulted in a continuous movement and transformation of the "pantheon" or "pantheons" of any given temple, and consequently of any "local cult complex". Comparison of the vodun lists provided in different regions of the Gbe-speaking area, both within and outside of Dahomey, shows recurrent contradictions in the number, identity, gender, attributes, function or relative kinship position of the deities of any particular "pantheon". This clearly indicates that, despite Abomey's centralised religious organization, the "pantheons" were never static or homogeneous. The examination of this dynamic in relation to sea and thunder voduns will be the subject of the next section.

Regardless of this variability, within each vodun temple, one deity is usually indicated as the ruling head of the spiritual gathering. This minimal hierarchical element is often, although not always, expressed in genealogical terms. The father figure or the original genitor couple will often express the pre-eminence of particular voduns over the rest of the group. As I shall argue below, in some cases hierarchies among deities may reflect corresponding hierarchies among their priesthood. Narratives stressing particular hierarchies are often developed in order to legitimate a deity or group of deities, normally those to whom the narrator is connected, against those of concurrent religious congregations.[13] In summary, the concept of *groups* or "families" of interrelated deities ruled by a leading figure and worshipped in a single temple under the centralized supervision of a male-female pair of *vodunons* (priests, literally "owners" of the vodun) are fundamental features of the vodun religion. The logical consequence of this is a serial form of ritual performance, in which the various spiritual entities are praised sequentially in a collective celebration.

These features of the vodun cult in the Gbe-speaking area seem to contrast, to a certain extent, with the *orisha* practice in Yorubaland, where the interconnectivity between *orishas* is apparently less strong. According to Verger each *orisha* cult constitutes an independent institution resulting in what he has called a series of "juxtaposed monotheisms". In other words, each religious congregation, or even each village, would be consecrated to the veneration of a single autonomous deity. Although in Yorubaland we find ensembles of various cults in any given town, and in some cases even the worship of more than one *orisha* within the same religious congregation, Verger's hypothesis of a certain independence of the *orisha* cults seems to be confirmed in a study by Mckenzie. Based on an analysis of *orisha orikis* or praise songs and Ifa verses, Mckenzie concludes that, with the exception of Shango, Obatalá and the "Ifá triad" (Exu, Orunmila and Olodumaré), the *orisha* cults present few if any verbal allusions to other deities, suggesting a relative "separatism" between them and an absence of a fixed pantheon. Mckenzie, who criticizes previous unitary models of the Yoruba pantheon, is less radical than Verger and adopts a conciliatory middle term, talking of *constellations* of *orishas* around a few prominent ones, existing among them "partial uniformities, but without ever completing a cosmological whole."[14]

Verger's hypothesis leads to the conclusion that the juxtaposition of a plurality of individual cults within the same religious congregation, found in Brazilian *Candomblé*, Haitian Vodou and Cuban Santeria, (what he calls "polytheism" as opposed to the "juxtaposed monotheisms") was a fundamentally New World creation resulting from the new socio-cultural conditions of slavery, where limited human and material resources would have encouraged the merging of otherwise separated cults. This phenomenon would thus constitute a critical difference between *Candomblé* and West African *orisha* traditions. Verger's Nagô-centric interpretation has been uncritically accepted and reproduced by most of the Afro-Brazilian literature, most notably by Bastide.[15] It does not take into account however the ample evidence collected in the Gbe-speaking area (some of it by Verger himself) showing a long established tradition of multi-divinity cultivation.[16]

Furthermore, as documented by Andrew Apter in the kingdom of Ayede, in the Ekiti Yoruba Highlands, and Margaret Thompson Drewal in Igbogila, a village in the Egabado region, multi-divinity *orisha* cults and serial forms of performance are also found in Yorubaland. Apter concludes that the merging of *orisha* cults may well be a common characteristic throughout Yorubaland, and also questions Verger's hypothesis, suggesting that *Candomblé*'s multi-divinity cultivation may find its antecedents in West African *orisha* traditions. Yet, in Ayede, the clustering of deities around the cult of a central *orisha* only appeared after 1845, hence with little if any influence on the *Candomblé*'s genesis, while in the Igbogila case, as Drewal suggests, multi-divinity *orisha* cultivation may have been a vodun practice in origin, appropriated by the Ahori from the Gun of Porto Novo, and subsequently replicated by their Egbado neighbors.[17]

It is also worth noting that in these Yoruba cases of multi-divinity cultivation, the ritual is conducted by a plurality of specialised religious experts, each one responsible for an *orisha*, while in the vodun temples we find a centralised leadership, often a male-female pair of *vodunon*, heading the whole group of deities. According to Nina Rodrigues, in late nineteenth-century Bahia, there were no specialised priests; each *iyalorixá* or *babalorixá* directed the worship of all deities installed in the temple, except on special occasions when several priests would gather together for important festivals.[18] This additional structural element reinforces the hypothesis that the vodun cult tradition may have been instrumental in the constitution of nineteenth-century *Candomblé*.

To think in terms of a polarization between a vertical "polytheistic" Dahomean system of religious organization and a horizontal "multi-monotheistic" Yoruba one is certainly reductionist and analytically misleading. Religious hierarchy and centralization are not unique to the Fon, and evidence from the historical and ethnographic records proves that centralized forms of religious organization were also common among the Yoruba groups.[19] Similarly, as I have shown, multi-

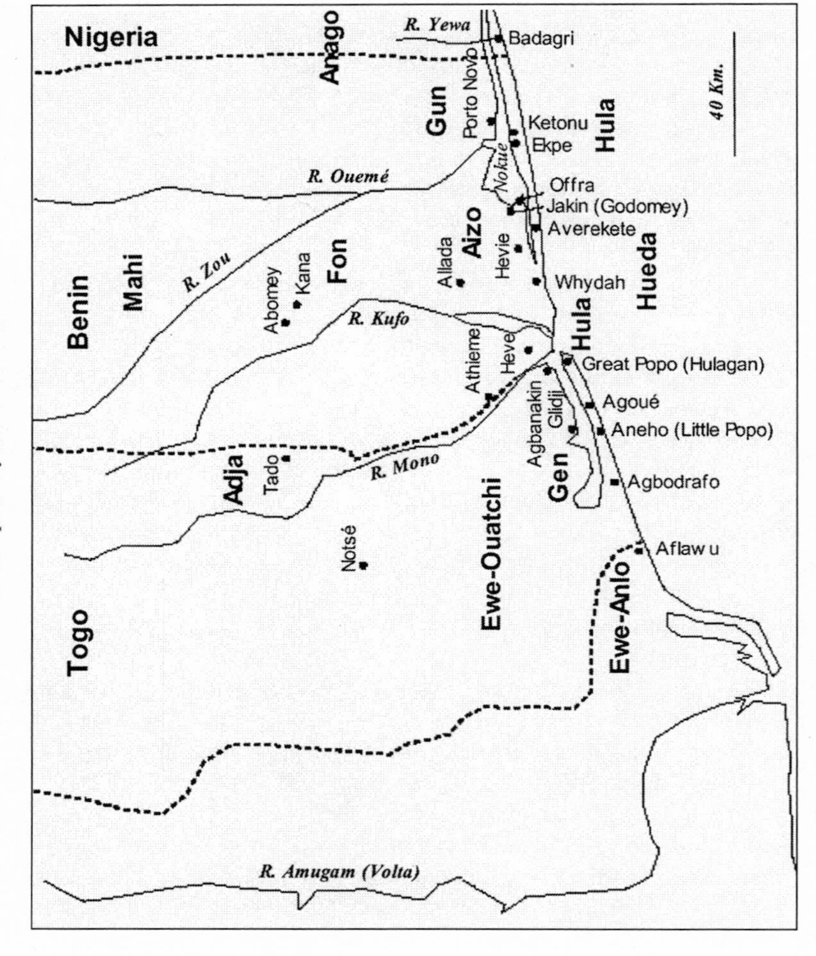

Plate 6: Map, Gbe-Speaking Area

Source: Composite by Luis Nicolau Parés

divinity cultivation and serial form of performance are not exclusive to the vodun cults. Yet, the available data suggests that these practices were a long established tradition in the Gbe area, while they would be only a relatively recent tendency in Yorubaland. My hypothesis is that what I call the "aggregation principle" operating in the Gbe vodun religious system, in which the dynamic of adding new deities within an existing ritual complex is the rule rather than the exception, persisted as a critical Jeje structural orientation in the formative process of *Candomblé*.

THE SEA AND THUNDER "PANTHEONS": A CASE STUDY

I have attempted to show that the conceptualization of the spiritual world into "pantheons" and the inclusion of multiple deities within the same rituals and temples are fundamental features of the vodun religious system. In order to show how this "aggregation principle" operates I present a historical analysis of the internal dynamic of the sea and thunder vodun "pantheons" both in the Gbe-speaking area and in the Bahian Jeje *candomblés*. This case study shows how these deities were progressively inserted in increasingly wider multi-ethnic "pantheons" and also suggests that this dynamic of change occurring at the level of spiritual entities, which add new deities and "forget" others by differentially relating them in hierarchies, may reflect distinct social and ethnic interactions as well as changes in the corresponding priesthood organizations. In other words, the organization of the spiritual world mirrors certain aspects of the social dynamic.

A simplified scheme of this case study can be divided into four stages. (1) At one point, the sea and thunder vodun cults were independent religious institutions ascribed to particular ethnic groups or lineages, namely the Hula and the Aïzo-Seto respectively. (2) Later, the sea and thunder cults were progressively appropriated by other ethnic groups, spreading throughout the Gbe-speaking area and becoming "public" or "popular" vodun cults. In this process the two vodun groups became conceptually and ritually related in various degrees, depending on the region. Yet, in many cases, the sea and thunder voduns were integrated into a single "pantheon" and worshipped in the same temples. (3) In Brazilian Jeje *terreiros*, at least in Bahia and Maranhão, the already-integrated thunder-sea group of voduns, known as Kaviono or Hevioso, became an inclusive "pantheon" incorporating a series of deities which in the Gbe-speaking area belonged to separate groups. (4) In the Bahian Jeje-Mahi *terreiros* the Kaviono family (also known as Mundubi), although identified as a distinct group of voduns, is ritually juxtaposed to other groups of Mahi voduns and Nagô *orishas*, like the snake vodun Dan, the earth vodun Sakpata and the *yabas* (female *orishas*) Oyá and Oxum, among others.

The first problem we face in confronting this variable multi-ethnic progressive aggregation of deities is that of locating all this movement in time and space. The historical analysis of any group of voduns in the Gbe speaking area, and in particular the sea and thunder voduns, certainly presents serious problems due to the absence of detailed data until the second half of the nineteenth century. This creates serious methodological difficulties which can only be surmounted by resorting to linguistic analysis, oral tradition and the projection into the past of twentieth century ethnographic data. Yet, the cautious combination of these indirect forms of evidence, together with the sparse available written documentation, allows us to sketch a reasonably plausible chronological and geographical outline.

The ancient cult of sea worship, widespread throughout the Bight of Benin, has been documented since the second half of the seventeenth century. Dapper mentions offerings and sacrifices to the sea in the Benin kingdom, Barbot reports that priests from the Popo region "pray to the fetishes to make the sea favourable", and Bosman mentions the sea as the third deity of the Ouidah kingdom.[20] In many cases, sea offerings were made invoking the arrival of European boats or to appease its fury so that goods and slaves could be shipped, hence sea worship appears to be associated with European commerce and its economic advantages. Yet, there are also indications that the veneration of the sea was rooted in previous autochthonous beliefs, since in various landlocked kingdoms, such as Allada, Oyó and Dahomey, there were explicit religious prohibitions about seeing the sea.[21]

In the Gbe-speaking area, sea worship seems to have been originally a Hula prerogative; significantly, the sea voduns are known as *Hulahun* and today the Hula claim to be their original "owners". The Hula, known in different periods and by different people as Popo, Fulao, Pla, Flà or Afla, were mainly lagoon fishermen and salt producers, with their political capital in Agbanankin, in the Mono delta. Given their navigational skills and the lagoon's commercial importance as a local trade route, they quickly expanded along the coast. The available data suggests that at least by 1630 they were already established in various coastal settlements from Aflawu to Jakin, if not further east until Apa (Badagry).[22] Therefore, despite the absence of written documentation, it is probable that the sea cult was also spread over this region since that period.

Thunder worship is less well documented and the earliest sources, from the seventeenth century, relate mostly to the Gold Coast. Barbot, probably following information by Marees and Villaut, documents the Akan association between the thunder and a sky divinity variously spelt as Jean Goeman or Jankomé [*Onyankome*]. Bosman, referring to the same region, mentions that "the Negroes [are] of the opinion that the force of the thunder is contained in a certain stone" and suggests its association with "super-natural things".[23] Although these comments do not allow us to make inferences about the existence any sort of organized cult, they do imply an ancient deification of the thunder phenomenon in the region. In the Gbe speaking area, the first reference to the thunder cult appears in the kingdom of Ouidah in an anonymous French manuscript dated between 1708 and 1724. It refers to worship of thunder, which was believed to kill thieves with thunderbolts.[24]

However, only in the mid-nineteenth century do we find evidence of a named thunder cult in the Gbe-speaking area. Frederick Forbes, who visited Ouidah and Abomey in 1849-50, provides the first reference to "Soh", the thunder and lightning "fetish". In April 1863, the barrack where the priests from the *Missions Catholiques* were lodging in the Portuguese Fort in Ouidah was stricken by lightning. Father Borghero, who refused to pay the fee asked by the Hevioso priests, was imprisoned. Borghero wrote "Dans la langue Gegi, le Dieu foudre s'appelle Kevioso. C'est le même que le Schango des Nangos." Richard Burton, who was in Ouidah in 1863-64, probably informed by Borghero, mentions "So or Khevioso, the thunder fetish, worshipped at Ouidah, in a So Agbajyí, or thunder closet." Burton also suggests that Hevioso was an "adaptation" of the Yoruba thunder *orisha* Shango.[25]

In the Gbe-speaking area, according to Le Herissé, a variety of Sô or thunder cults (sô = thunder) coexisted. There was the Djisô (the thunder from the sky) worshipped by the Djetovi, presumably a proto-Yoruba group living in the Abomey plateau. And there was the Hevieso or Hevioso, the Sô from Hevie, which at least from the nineteenth century onwards seems to have been the most popular form of thunder cult in the region. In Hevie, a village in the Aïzo region, between Allada and Ouidah, the Hevioso voduns are also called *Setohun*, or deities of the Seto. According to Serpos Tidjani, the Seto were an ethnic group from Athiemé on the Mono river bank who migrated to Hevie in the seventeenth century. Yet, according to Pazzi, the diffusion of the So cult from Hevie into the neighboring regions only occurred in the nineteenth century.[26]

Although this twentieth-century information based on oral tradition should be treated with caution, what emerges from this brief sketch is that the thunder and sea vodun cults were originally independent ethnically-bound religious institutions. In other words, they were *hennu* or *ako* voduns, whose worship was the exclusive responsibility of a particular lineage. Besides the linguistic evidence – the sea voduns are called *Hulahun* and the thunder voduns *Setohun* - contemporary ethnographic documentation seems to corroborate this. Verger collected lists of voduns worshipped in Hevie and various eastern Hula villages. In Hevie he did not found any trace of the sea deities (except for Ahuangan who is identified either as a thunder or sea vodun), while in the Hula villages of Ketonou, Godomey and Avlekete, the vodun Hevioso is absent or only incidental, apparently as a late borrowing associated with other public voduns like Lisa or Sakpata. In Allada, in Aïzo territory, Herskovits also documented the presence of Hevioso gods and only a single independent shrine for the sea vodun Agbé. This data strongly suggests that the Hula sea cult and the Aïzo-Seto thunder cult, at some point in the past, were distinct separate religious institutions.[27]

REGIONAL VARIATIONS AND DYNAMIC OF CHANGE OF SEA-THUNDER "PANTHEONS"

Over time, however, the sea and thunder cults were progressively appropriated by other ethnic groups, such as the Hueda, Fon, Gen, Ewe or Anlo, spreading throughout most of the Gbe-speaking area and becoming "public" or "popular" vodun cults. In this process the two vodun groups became conceptually and ritually related in various degrees in various regions. In many cases, following the above mentioned aggregation principle, the sea and thunder voduns were integrated into a single "pantheon" and worshipped in the same temples.

In Ouidah, although the Hevioso presence is found in some Hueda temples, its most important site is the temple of Hunon Dagbo, the sea high priest. The Hunon kinship collectivity is Hula in origin, but its presence in Hueda territory may predate the Dahomean arrival in the 1720s. The Hunon Dagbo is said to "own personally" the Hevioso voduns, but their late juxtaposition to his lineage sea voduns suggests that the Hevioso voduns were from the start subordinated to the sea deities. This was effectively sanctioned when the Hunon Dagbo was promoted by the Fon kings as Ouidah's supreme religious authority, and all the Hevioso cults were hierarchically dependent on him. This situation is conceptually expressed when the Hunon states that all the Hevioso voduns are sea voduns, children of Agbé.[28]

The opposite seems to have happened in Abomey, where the sea voduns appear under the religious jurisdiction of the thunder priests. Le Herissé, in 1911, is the first author to note that the sea pantheon was integrated into and implicitly subordinated to the thunder pantheon: "Dans le choeur de Hébyoso sont compris Hou, la mer et sa famille. Hou, ou Agbé ou Houalahoun, est comme son dernier nom l'indique, originaire Houala [Gd. Popo] (...) Hou est le mari de Na-èté, dont il a eu Avrekete, cette trinité est honorée dans les temples du tonnerre et a les sept mêmes plantes sacrées a lui." In the thunder temples, the couple Agbé and Naeté are considered to be Sogbo's progeny.[29]

In Agbanakin and Heve, in Hula territory, home of Agbé and the sea voduns we also find the Hevioso cult, but apparently in independent temples. In the Hevioso congregations from Heve, the thunder voduns are called *yehwe*, suggesting an interpenetration with the Togoland *Yehwe* cults. As Herskovits notes, "the Yehwe cult is in terms of Dahomean culture but vodu worship with particular regional emphasis on the gods of thunder and the sea and less separatism in the worship of other affiliated deities" [like Gbade, Loko or Dan].[30]

Indeed, in Togoland, probably among the Anlo or Ewe, Spieth reports the leadership of the Yehwe pantheon composed by the male vodun So, imported from Hevie, and his wife the female vodun Agbui [Agbé], imported from Avlekete (a Hula village). We see how outside the Hula territory, Agbé may become a female deity, symbolically subordinated to her husband, the thunder vodun. Despite variations in gender and kinship links, like in Abomey, the integrated thunder-sea voduns present an apparent dominance of the thunder side.[31]

Finally, in Aneho (Petit Popo) and Glidji, in Gen territory, we find a mixed couple of thunder and sea voduns, the male Hevioso and the female Tokpadoun, giving birth to a mixed progeny of sea voduns (Avlekete, Agboe or Anatê) and thunder voduns like Gbede [Gbadé] and Aklobè [Akolombé], the latter considered the father of other thunder voduns like Sogbo and Da Ahwanga. According to Fio Agbonon II, a first So (Monta-So) was imported into Glidji from Hueda territory in the early eighteenth century, while the So from Hevie (Heviesso) was imported later, probably in the nineteenth century. According to Verger, the Hevioso from Aneho came from Heve, suggesting a transfer of the Hevioso cult to Togoland through the Hula.[32]

The evidence gathered in Ouidah, Abomey, the Mono delta and Togoland clearly demonstrates the mobility of the vodun values and practices across ethnic and geographical boundaries and the myriad regional variations resulting from this movement. In Ketonu, capital of a Hula royal lineage, the sea cult is paramount and there is no evidence of the Hevioso, while in Gen territory we find a mixed sea-thunder couple with an equally mixed progeny. As we move westward, from Ketonu to Togoland, there seems to be more connection, as if the integration of both groups of deities became easier outside the home area of each cult. It is also important to note, for future reflections on Brazil, that the sea-thunder interpenetration extended beyond the borders of the Dahomey kingdom.

Commenting on a similar dynamic in the *orisha* cult, Peel observes: "The mobility of *orisa*, whether as a consequence of the migration of their ordinary adherents or through the promotional zeal of their priests, also promotes shifts in the character of the orisa. An incoming orisa may find its special niche already occupied, or it may seek to carve out a new niche for itself."[33] The gender, kinship and hierarchical shifts noted in relation to the sea-thunder voduns may follow a similar principle. The male Agbé, for instance, can suffer a change of gender or kinship position where it is a latecomer to communities that already had a dominant male thunder deity. Many other examples of vodun attributes regional shifts are available in the ethnographic data, some of which may be caused by other reasons difficult to systematize.

As regards the time when this sea-thunder aggregation and its movement across ethnic and geographical boundaries occurred, much can be speculated but very little can be said with certainty. It was indeed an asystematic process that occurred in successive moments in different areas. The same vodun may even have been imported into different temples in the same village by different families in different periods. Since in Brazil the sea and thunder voduns always appear juxtaposed, one can assume that such aggregation was already established in some places in the late eighteenth century or early nineteenth century.

The hierarchical relationships expressed in genealogical terms at the level of spiritual entities can reflect processes of appropriation of the cults and shrines by violent as well as by peaceful means. The hierarchical status inversion between thunder and sea voduns in Ouidah and Abomey could be explained in chronological terms: the incoming group of deities would always be subordinated to the pre-existing one. This is clear in Ouidah where the Hevioso voduns were the latecomers, since the sea voduns were the Hula lineage deities. It would also imply that the sea voduns were imported into Abomey once the Hevioso cult was already established there.

According to Merlo, the presence of the Hevioso voduns in the Hula sea temple in Ouidah predated Agadja's invasion of Savi in 1727. Although the first indirect evidence can only be found in Burton's work, the Hueda-Hula assimilation of the Hevioso voduns must be an old one, since the Hevioso devotees, in Abomey and elsewhere, at the end of their initiation period, are called Huedanu (inhabitants of Hueda), for their secret ritual language is the Hueda. This religious terminology, which varies according to the different vodun cults, may indicate sometimes the place of origin of the cult, but in this case indicates one of its points of diffusion.[34]

As suggested above, the installation of the Hevioso cult in Abomey and Kana must have occurred in different periods. Oral traditions in different Hevioso temples date the cult's arrival variously to Agadja's, Tegbesu's or Agonglo's reigns.[35] Over time Hevioso became the most important "public" deity in Abomey and as a warrior god of justice became somehow associated with the Dahomean domination. The importance granted in Abomey to Hevioso -who was also known as Agbohun, or "deity of Abomey" – is comparable to the importance granted to Shango in Oyó.

The late arrival of the sea vodun may have occurred any time after the conquest of Savi and there is some evidence of it already during Agaja's reign. In 1727, Snelgrave reports that, during the first visit of a Dahomean military chief to the Jakin beach, a human sacrifice to the sea was performed by local priests. The sacrifice was ordered by Agaja's "Great Captain", or by the king himself, although it is unclear whether the Dahomean patronage of the sea cult was an occasional practice or already an "officialised" one, with sea shrines installed in Allada (where the king was established at the time). According to Le Herissé, the sea voduns were imported into Abomey, and aggregated within the thunder temples, during Tegbesu's reign. By mid nineteenth century, the Dahomean royal appropriation of the sea cult was already institutionalized.[36]

Oral tradition is also contradictory about the place from where the Hevioso cult was imported into Abomey. Although Ouidah is a possibility, Hevie is the village more often reported. Yet other versions mention Heve, Ahla Heve, Djekin (Jakin) and Agbanankin.[37] Except for Hevie, these are all Hula settlements, indicating that, as in Ouidah, an early Hula appropriation of the Aïzo-Seto voduns may have occurred, especially among populations in the Mono river area such as Heve, which seems to have been another point of diffusion of the Hevioso cult.

The coastal Hula and the Hueda are likely to be the ethnic groups that first integrated the two "pantheons", becoming responsible for their subsequent diffusion. Yet, by the mid-eighteenth century, when the trans-Atlantic transfer of the cult may have begun, and certainly in the early nineteenth century, when it is more likely to have contributed to the formative process of *Candomblé*, the thunder-sea cult was spread all along the coast from the Volta to Badagry, and practised by a number of groups including Hula, Hueda, Fon, Aïzo, Tori, Dovi, Gen, Ewe and Anlo. Yet in Brazil the thunder-sea vodun worshippers are known as Mundubi, an ethnic denomination for which no clear trace can be found in the Gbe-speaking area.

THE MUNDUBI AND THE NINETEENTH CENTURY JEJE TERREIROS

Mundubi – variously spelt as Mandubi, Mondubi, Mondobi, Mendobi, Mudubi, or Modobê – was used in the early-middle nineteenth century by Bahian slave owners as a denomination of African origin. To my knowledge, the first documented use of this "ethnonym" occurs in 1812, and although quite rare, it seems to be more widely used from 1830 onwards.[38] After the end of the trans-Atlantic slave trade in 1850, like most African ethnic denominations, it progressively disappears from the written record. Yet, Mundubi continued to be used by the African population and their descendants, especially within the Jeje religious context. Like other ethnonyms such as Mahi or Agome, Mundubi became the name of a "province" or "land" of the Jeje "nation of *candomblé*". More precisely, Mundubi came to designate a particular rite or liturgy with characteristic drum rhythms and dances, and - more importantly for our analysis - associated with a specific group of voduns: the Kaviono or Hevioso family. As stated by a reputable Jeje religious expert, "Mundubi is Kaviono, and they sing: *ooo, ooo, ooo, Daomé, o Kavieceli vodun daome*."[39] The strong link of the ethnonym with the Jeje liturgy indicates that the similarity between Mundubi and Mundómbe (Ndombe), a Bantu ethnic group occupying the hinterland of Benguela, may be a case of phonetic convergence, and that Mundubi should relate to a group from the Gbe-speaking area.[40] Verger identifies them with the Hueda and Hula, although other groups who by the early nineteenth century were also worshipping the Hevioso deities (i.e. Aïzo, Tori, Dovi, Gen, Anlo, Fon) should not be discounted.[41]

While the origin and etymology of Mundubi remains unclear, we should keep in mind that in Brazil, both in Bahia and Maranhão, wherever the designation is preserved, it always relates to the integrated sea-thunder voduns, with a hierarchical predominance of the thunder group. This is evident in different ways. To start with, the name given to this group or "family" of voduns is Kaviono or Hevioso. Its leading figure is the thunder vodun Sogbo, followed by his progeny (Bade, Akolombé etc.), while the sea voduns, Averekete, Abé (Agbé) or Naté (Naeté) are less well known and usually relegated to secondary positions. This hegemony of the thunder voduns reproduces the pattern found in Abomey, not the one prevailing in Ouidah. This could lead us to identify the Mundubi with the ethnic groups that in the Gbe speaking area presented the same hierarchical relationship (i.e. the Fon in Abomey or more likely the Gen and Ewe groups in Togoland).

Before I continue with the examination of the Kaviono family it may be useful to provide a brief outline of the nineteenth century Jeje *terreiros* in Bahia. We have evidence of a Jeje *terreiro* in Salvador dating back to 1829, when the police report of a raid on a cult house in the Brotas neighborhood mentions the worship of a "Deus Vodum" (vodun god).[42] Three decades later, in the 1860s, the local satirical paper *O Alabama* provides evidence of at least four Jeje *candomblés* in Salvador: the Bogum, the Agome, the Campina and the Querebetan.[43] The Agome, Campina and Querebetan are already extinct and there is no information about which groups of vodun they worshipped. The Bogum, after a long period of transition following the death of its late high priestess in 1994, is still active. Its members identify it as belonging to the Jeje-Mahi "nation". Yet, the Sogbo group (i.e. Hevioso) is considered the "royal family" who hosts the other groups of voduns and *orishas*. This pre-eminence of the Hevioso group in a Mahi *terreiro* is significant and I shall come back to it later on.

Oral tradition tells of the existence of a fifth *terreiro*, the Kpo Zerrem, located beside the Bogum in Salvador and functioning from the second half of the nineteenth century until the 1940s. The Kpo Zerrem is sometimes identified as belonging to the Jeje-Mundubi "nation", where the worship of Sogbo and other sea voduns like Averekete was central. Both the Kpo Zerrem and the Bogum maintained strong religious ties to another Jeje-Mahi *terreiro* in the neighbouring city of Cachoeira, the Seja Hunde, which is still active. Founded around the 1890s, the Seja Hunde, was started by members of another Cachoeira *terreiro*, popularly known as the Roça de Cima, which was headed by Africans and had been in existence at least since the 1860's. The Roça de Cima is also said to have been Jeje-Mundubi.

This expressive presence of the Jeje *terreiros* both in Salvador and Cachoeira in the second half of the nineteenth century reinforces the initial hypothesis of significant contributions by the vodun tradition during the formative period of *Candomblé*. Yet, in order to know something about their "pantheons" we are forced to rely on very few elements: a few names of deities appearing in *O Alabama* in the 1860's; a list of voduns collected in Salvador at the end of the nineteenth century by Nina Rodrigues; oral testimonies of actual witnesses of Jeje rituals in the first two decades of the twentieth century; and contemporary ethnographic evidence mainly from the Bogum and the Seja Hunde. How far back into the past we can project this data is uncertain, but the combination of these sources allows us to infer some general ideas.

THE TRANSFORMATIONS OF THE NAGÔ-VODUN "PANTHEON"

A further stage of the aggregation principle can be traced in Brazil. On the one hand, the Hevioso or Kaviono group became in the Jeje *terreiros* of Bahia and Maranhão an inclusive niche or conceptual category incorporating a series of deities, like the panther vodun Kpo or the tree vodun Loko (also Lisa and Nana in Maranhão), which in the Gbe-speaking area did not belong to this group.[44] On the other hand, the Kaviono or Mundubi family, although identified as a distinct group of voduns, was ritually juxtaposed to other groups of Jeje-Mahi voduns and Nagô *orishas*.

This is expressed for instance in the order in which deities are praised in ritual songs during contemporary Jeje-Mahi ceremonies: (1) the openers of the way Legba, Averekete and Ogun Xoroqué; (2) the war *orisha* Ogun; (3) the hunter voduns Agué and Odé; (4) the earth-smallpox voduns Sakpata-Azonsu; (5) the *yabas* or female *orishas* Oxum-Yemanja-Oyá; (6) the thunder voduns Sogbo-Badé-Loko-Kpo; (7) Nana; (8) Olissa-Oxalá; and (9) the snake vodun Dan-Bessem. The latter, considered to be the "owner" or "king" of the Jeje-Mahi nation, closes the sequence as a sign of distinction. This complex multi-ethnic process of aggregation, which resulted in what the Jeje adherents call the Nagô-vodun "pantheon", can be represented as follows.

Jeje-Nagô and Mundubi-Mahi aggregation processes in the Jeje-Mahi terreiros

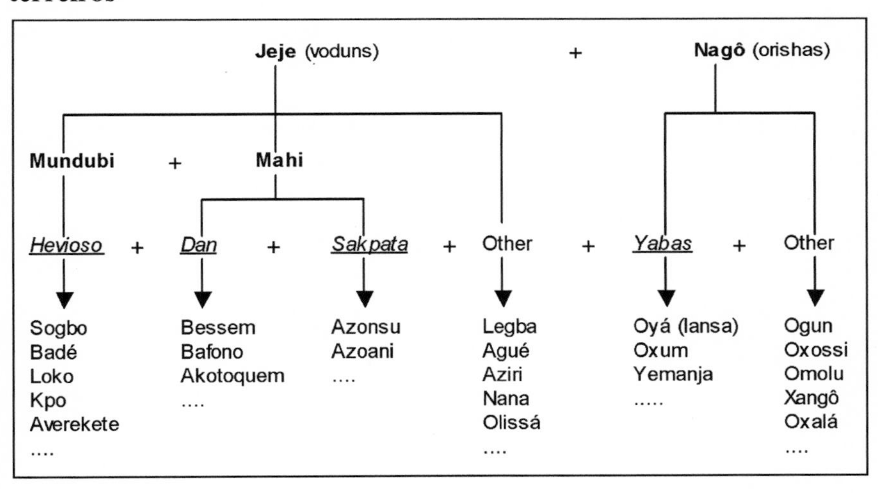

The first noticeable aspect is the ritual juxtaposition of the coastal Mundubi Hevioso group with the Mahi vodun groups like the earth vodun Sakpata and the snake vodun Dan. This juxtaposition of groups of voduns, which in the Gbe-speaking area belonged to separate cults, most probably resulted from the gathering of religious experts from different Gbe ethnic groups due to the management of limited resources imposed by the oppression of slavery. Again my suggestion is that this process was undoubtedly favored by the aggregation principle already intrinsic to the vodun religious system. In fact, it could be understood as just a wider application of the principles of multi-divinity cultivation and serial form of performance operative at a smaller and more restrictive scale in African vodun cults.

Together with this Jeje multi-ethnic inclusive process, we observe a wider inter-ethnic interpenetration between the Jeje voduns and the Nagô *orishas*. Despite the fact that in public ceremonies praises for certain Nagô *orishas* can be heard within the corresponding vodun song segments, the most remarkable borrowing from the Nagô is the inclusion of the *yabas* or female *orishas*, especially Oyá and Oxum, which have no counterpart in vodun.

It is uncertain whether the juxtaposition of the Mahi-Mundubi predated or was contemporary of the Jeje-Nagô one, but it is clear that the heterogeneous aggregation of deities observed today was already latent in mid-nineteenth century, and was certainly consolidated by the end of the century.[45] In the 1860's, the newspaper *O Alabama* explicitly documented the names of Sogbo, Legba and Loko, indirectly those of Agué and Nana, and made a reference to the cult of the "snake" and the "smallpox," suggesting that the essence of the Jeje pantheon was already configured at that time. Moreover, in the description of a feast headed by a famous Jeje priestess in 1869, we are told that they were singing in praise of Oyá, implying that the *yabas* were already worshiped in the Jeje houses. Not only this, but in a footnote Oyá is referred as "the wife of the greatest saint - Sogbo." Replicating the Nagô myth that considers Oyá the wife of Xangô, in the Jeje houses she is identified as the wife of Sogbo.[46]

At the end of the century, Nina Rodrigues registered in Salvador the names of several voduns that we can safely assume to be some of the deities worshipped in the above mentioned Jeje-Mahi and Jeje-Mundubi *candomblés*.

> Besides Mawu, Khêbiosô, Legba, Anyi-ewo, Loko, Hoho, Saponan and Wu (the sea), confused with the corresponding Nagô orixás Olorum, Xangô, Elegbá, Oxumarê, Irôco, Ibeji, Xaponã and Olokum, there exist a great number of voduns or Jeje deities less well known such as Dsô, the fire, Nati and Avrikiti, marine deities; Bá, god of the warriors, and animals like the crocodile, the leopard, etc.[47]

The mention of Hevioso, Anyi-ewo (Aido-hwedo or Dan) and Saponan (a Yoruba name for Sakpata) suggests their simultaneous veneration in the Jeje *terreiros* of that period. The "confusion" with the Nagô *orishas* also suggests their inclusion – at least of some of them – in the Jeje cults. What Nina Rodrigues interpreted as "confusion" may have arisen from his familiarity with the Nagô deities and his Jeje informants' efforts to speak in terms that he would understand, although it could also reflect a predominance of the Nagô referents in the wider *Candomblé* community. Still, within the Jeje congregations, vodun worship persisted, differentiated yet juxtaposed, with the *orisha* cult.

The degree of persistence of a particular vodun in the religion can be measured by different indexes, from the lowest to the highest: it can be remembered only by name, it can be praised in the ritual songs, it can have a shrine, or it can have devotees consecrated to it. The latter, which is inclusive of all the rest, expresses the highest level of actuality of a deity in the religious community.

Between 1913 and 1920, in the Seja Hunde *terreiro* of Cachoeira, there were some 26 dancers (20 of these were initiated in the same period).[48] Seven of them, more than a quarter of the total, were consecrated to voduns belonging to the Kaviono family (two Sogbos, three Badés, one Kpo and one Akorombé). At the same time, an equal number of initiates were consecrated to the female *orishas*

Oxum and Oyá, a fact that indicates a clear ritual penetration of the *yaba* cult in the Jeje cult. This state of affairs is also reproduced in the Bogum of the post-abolition period where, significantly enough, two of its four high priestess were Sogbo devotees, and the presence of Oyá and Oxum devotees is also remarkable.

Despite the fact that during the nineteenth century the majority of *Candomblé* participants were women and, as the importation of Africans stopped, increasingly creole, we know that *Candomblé* leadership was predominantly male and African. Women constitute a majority in the *Candomblé* leadership today, but probably only achieved this supremacy around the turn of the century, coinciding with the post-abolition period.[49] My suggestion is that the inclusion of Nagô *orishas* in the Jeje *terreiros*, especially the *yabas* Oyá and Oxum, although it may have dated from early times, was perhaps increased and reinforced by the shift favoring women as high priestesses of the religious congregations. In this case, shifting patterns of gender in the priesthood, rather than ethnic interactions, would have been reflected in the "pantheon" configuration.

The increasing importance of female *orishas* in the Jeje spiritual world may also be due to complementary conceptual factors. In the Nagô mythology, Oyá and Oxum are the wives of the thunder *orisha* Xangô, and by association, as we have seen in relation to Oyá, in the Jeje *terreiros* they are also the wives of the vodun Sogbo. Despite the central role played by the snake vodun Dan and the earth-smallpox vodun Sakpata, the hegemony of Xangô prevailing in the more numerous Nagô *candomblés* and in the wider religious community may have contributed to the pre-eminence of the thunder vodun Sogbo in the Jeje-Mahi houses and the consequent assimilation of its female counterparts.

The dynamic of the aggregation principle in the multi-divinity cults is complemented by a parallel principle of selectivity or exclusion which would account for the progressive forgetfulness of certain deities. The decreasing importance of the Jeje sea voduns in Bahia may be an example of this (see appendix). Nina Rodrigues mentions at least four sea voduns: Hu, Naeté, Averekete and Tokpodun (the crocodile, usually included within the sea pantheon in the Gbe-speaking area). Yet, in the list of dancers at the Seja Hunde, there is a noticeable absence of devotees of any of these sea voduns. Hu (Agbé) and Tokpodun are completely forgotten; Naeté is vaguely remembered by name but is hardly recalled in ritual songs. Averekete is the only vodun praised in songs and with shrines, although the ritual knowledge to prepare new initiates seems to have been lost.[50] Even the male *orisha* Olokum, the traditional Nagô sea deity from the Ijebu Awori and Egbado, somehow lost standing to the female Yemanjá, a deity of the Ogun river, originally worshipped by the Egba from Abeokuta, who gradually became the main sea *orisha* in Bahia. In the Jeje-Mahi *terreiros*, the female Aziri Tobosi, originally a river spirit worshipped by the Mahi-Agonli, became associated with Yemanjá and as such persisted as the main Jeje water deity.

These interrelated transformations, such as in the case of Oxum and Oyá, suggest that there was an increasing "feminization" of the *orisha*-vodun "pantheon", in which male sea deities such as Agbé and Olokum were progressively replaced by female river water deities. In the same way that in eighteenth century Dahomey the juxtaposition of sea and thunder voduns reflected processes of appropriation of foreign cults, and that in mid-nineteenth century Bahia the Mundubi and Mahi vodun ritual juxtaposition reflected the gathering of religious experts from various Gbe ethnic origins, we have reason to think that the late-nineteenth-century "feminization" of the *orisha*-vodun "pantheon" was a response to the increasing importance of women in the *Candomblé* leadership.

CONCLUSION

To summarize, I have tried to show that the formative process of the *Candomblé* institution, despite its being a genuine New World creation resulting from the socio-cultural conditions of slavery, reproduced and adapted the basic principle of multi-divinity cultivation and serial form of performance characteristic of the vodun religious system. These principles have persisted in the Americas as essential features which provided the structural means to aggregate a plurality of multi-ethnic fragmented cults into a relatively cohesive religious institution. I have also tried to show, through the historical analysis of the internal dynamic of a particular group of deities in the Gbe-speaking area and the Bahian Jeje *terreiros*, that the transformation of any given "pantheon" is always based on simultaneous integrative-cumulative as well as selective-discriminatory processes. I have further attempted to demonstrate that these processes occurring at the conceptual level of spiritual entities may reflect specific ethnic interactions and changes in corresponding priesthood organizations. It is furthermore possible that such historical analyses of the internal dynamics of "pantheons" might reveal aspects of the socio-political organization of their worshippers, and particularly of their sacerdotal officials. Further research on other groups of voduns, such as the Dan and Sakpata "pantheons", would help determine whether this hypothesis suggested in relation to the Hevioso group holds for other related case studies.

APPENDIX: SEA AND THUNDER VODUNS IN DAHOMEY AND BRAZIL

	Gbe-speaking area			Brazil	
	Burton	**Herissé a)**	**Rodri.**	**C.M.**	**Jeje-Mahi**
Thunder voduns					
Hevioso b)	x	x	x	x	x
Sogbo (So)	x	x	-	x	x
Badé	-	x	-	x	x
Akolombé	-	x	-	-	x
Aden (Adaen)	-	x	-	-	x
Djakata	-	x	-	-	-
Besu	-	x	-	-	-
Kunte	-	x	-	-	-
Zo Ogodo	-	-	x	-	x
Bossu	-	-	-	x	x
Jogorobossu	-	-	-	-	x
Betá Yoyo	-	-	-	-	x
Jokolatin	-	-	-	-	x
Sogbo Baba Guidi	-	-	-	-	x
Sea voduns					
Naeté (Naté)	x	x	x	x	x
Averekete	x	x	x	x	x
Agbé (Hu)	x	x	x	x	-
Tokpodun	x	x	x	-	-
Gbengbo	-	x	-	-	-
Ahuangan	-	x	-	-	-
Saho	-	x	-	-	-
Bago c)	-	-	-	-	x
Other vodun d)					
Nana	-	x	x	x	x
Lissa	x	x	x	x	x
Loco	x	x	x	x	x
Kpo	x	x	x	-	x
Ajanutoe	-	-	-	x	-

Note: In the first two columns, I indicate thunder and sea voduns in the Gbe-speaking area, as reported in Ouidah to Burton in 1863-4 and in Abomey to Le Herissé in 1911. In the third one, I show the sea-thunder *voduns* known in Bahia by the turn of the century and mentioned by Nina Rodrigues. The remaining two columns include the voduns known in contemporary Jeje *terreiros* founded in the nineteenth century in Maranhão (*Casa das Minas* or House of the Mina, identified as CM) and Bahia (Seja Hunde and Bogum, identified as Jeje-Mahi). In the Brazilian Jeje *terreiros* I mark with a bold "**x**" the voduns considered to belong to the Hevioso or Kaviono group. The list of voduns is not comprehensive and only records the names more often quoted.

a) The voduns Aden and Besu are mentioned by Verger, *Notas sobre o culto*, p. 525; and Herskovits, *Dahomey*, II, p. 152.

b) Hevioso is a generic name for the thunder voduns rather than a particular deity.

c) Only known in the Cachoeira extinct *terreiro* Roça de Cima.

d) In the *Casa das Minas*, Nana manifests through the Hevioso "linha", but does not belong properly to this family. Vo Missa, Ajahuto de Alada and his son Afrejo are also included in this family, but I have not listed them, since in most Tambor de Mina cult houses Vo Missa is the same Nana, while Ajahuto and Afrejo are just friends who do not belong properly to the Hevioso family: Sérgio Figueiredo Ferretti, *Querebentan de Zomadonu. Etnografia da Casa das Minas do Maranhão* (São Luis: EDUFMA, 1996 [1985]), pp. 120-126.

ENDNOTES

1. I would like to thank Louis Brenner, Robin Law, Liza Earl Castillo, Peter Cohen and Roger Sansi for their comments and suggestions on earlier versions of this chapter. Following H. B. C. Capo, *Comparative Phonology of Gbe* (Berlin and New York: Foris Publications, 1991), I use the term *Gbe-speaking area* to refer to the southern regions of modern Togo and Republique du Benin, occupied by the linguistically related Fon, Gun, Aïzo, Mahi, Hueda, Hula, Ouatchi, Adja, Ouemenu, Agonli, Ewe, Gen and affiliated peoples, usually referred in the literature as Adja-Ewe. Jeje is the ethnonym by which the enslaved people from the Gbe-speaking area were known in Brazil from the eighteenth century onwards.
2. Sidney W. Mintz and Richard Price, *An Anthropological Approach to the Afro-American Past: A Caribbean Perspective* (Philadelphia: ISHI, 1976), pp. 5-7; idem and idem, *The Birth of Afro-American Culture: An anthropological perspective* (Boston: Beacon Press, 1992), pp. 18-19; Sandra T. Barnes, "The Many Faces of Ogun: Introduction to the First Edition," in Sandra T. Barnes (ed.), *Africa's Ogun: Old World and New* (Bloomington: Indiana University Press, 1997), pp. 9-10.
3. Luiz Mott, "Acotundá - raízes setecentistas do sincretismo religioso afro-brasileiro," *Revista do Museu Paulista* New Series 3 (1986): 124-147, documents a ritual in Minas Gerais (ca. 1747) suggesting the existence of "complex" forms of religious organization already in eighteenth century Brazil. Yet, in the absence of further evidence, this seems to have been an exceptional isolated case.
4. The "complexity" of West African religious institutions can be characterized by the features associated with "*candomblé*" as described above, as opposed to those of colonial "calundus" more characteristic of the Bantu societies. The higher "complexity" of West African religious institutions should not be interpreted as "cultural superiority" as suggested by Raymundo Nina Rodrigues in relation to the Nagô: *Os Africanos no Brasil* (São Paulo: Companhia Editora Nacional, 1977 [1906]), pp. 230-231. For a comparative analysis of the West African and Bantu religious institutions, see Luis Nicolau Parés, "The phenomenology of spirit possession in the Tambor de Mina:

An ethnographic and audiovisual study," Ph D dissertation, School of Oriental and African Studies (London), 1997, pp. 14-18. For a demographic analysis of the Jeje in Bahia, see idem, *Do Lado do Jeje: História e Ritual do Vodun na Bahia* (Rio de Janeiro: Pallas, forthcoming 2005).

5. For the Jeje linguistic contribution to the ritual terminology of *Candomblé*, see: Vivaldo da Costa Lima, "A família-de-santo nos Candomblés Jeje-Nagôs da Bahia: um estudo de relações intra-grupais," M. A. thesis, Universidade Federal da Bahia, 1977, pp. 72-73; Yeda Pessoa de Castro, "Língua e nação de candomblé," *África* (Revista do Centro de Estudos Africanos, Universidade de São Paulo) 4 (1981): 75; Julio Braga, *Na Gamela do Feitiço. Repressão e Resistência nos Candomblés da Bahia* (Salvador: EDUFBA,1995), pp. 39, 56.
6. Melville J. Herskovits and Frances S. Herskovits, *An Outline of Dahomean Religious Belief*, Memoirs of the American Anthropological Association 41 (Menasha WI: American Anthropological Association, 1933), pp. 9-10; Bernard Maupoil, *La Géomancie a l'Ancienne Côte des Esclaves* (Paris: Institut d'Ethnologie, 1988 [1946]), p. 56.
7. Maupoil, *La Géomancie*, p. 56.
8. Olabiyi B. Yai, "From Vodun to Mahu: Monotheism and history in the Fon cultural area," in Jean-Pierre Chrétien (ed.), *L'invention religieuse en Afrique: histoire et religion en Afrique Noire* (Paris: Karthala, 1992), p. 246.
9. William Bosman, *A New and Accurate Description of the Coast of Guinea* (London: Frank Cass & Co. Ltd., 1967 [1704]), p. 368a; Maupoil, *La Géomancie*, p. 64; Maurice Ahanhanzo Glélé, *Le Daxomé: Du pouvoir Ajá à la nation Fon* (Cotonou: Nubia, 1974), p. 75.
10. A. Le Herissé, *L'Ancièn Royaume du Dahomey: Moeurs, Religion, Histoire* (Paris: Emile Larose Ed., 1911), pp. 126-127; Melville J. Herskovits, *Dahomey, an ancient West African kingdom* (New York: J.J. Augustin Publisher, 1938), II, pp. 103-105; Yai, pp. 254, 256; Edna G. Bay, *Wives of the Leopard: Gender, Politics, and Culture in the Kingdom of Dahomey* (Charlottesville: University of Virginia Press, 1998), pp. 92-96.
11. Herskovits, *Dahomey*, II, pp. 150-151, 163.
12. John Peel, "A comparative Analysis of Ogun in Precolonial Yorubaland," in Barnes, *Africa's Ogun*, pp. 275-276.
13. See for instance Herskovits, *Dahomey*, II, p. 159.
14. Pierre Verger, *Notas sobre o culto aos Orixás e Voduns na Bahia de Todos os Santos, no Brasil, e na antiga Costa dos Escravos, na África* trans. Carlos Eugenio Marcondes de Moura (São Paulo: Edusp, 1999 [1957]), pp. 15, 39; idem, "The Yoruba high god – a review of the sources," *Odu* 2 (1966): 24; P. R. Mckenzie, "O culto aos òrìsà entre os yoruba: algumas notas marginais relativas a sua cosmologia e seus conceitos de divindade," in C. E. M. de Moura (ed.), *Candomblé, Desvendando Identidades* (São Paulo: EMW Editores, 1987), pp. 134-135, 137, 139.
15. Roger Bastide, *Sociologia de la Religion* [*Les religions africaines au Brésil*] (Gijón: Ediciones Jucar, 1986 [1960]), pp. 113, 316; Pierre Verger, *Notícias da Bahia-1850* (Salvador: Corrupio, 1981), pp. 228-229.
16. See for instance, Christian Merlo, "Hiérarchie fétichiste de Ouidah," *Bulletin de l'IFAN* 2/1-2 (1940): 1-84; Herskovits, *Dahomey*, II, p. 304.

17. Margaret Thompson Drewal, "Dancing for Ògún in Yorubaland and Brazil," in Barnes, *Africa's Ogun*, pp. 211, 230-231; Andrew Apter, "Notes on Orisha Cults in the Ekiti Yoruba Highlands," *Cahiers d'Études Africaines* 35/138-139 (1995): 373, 392-393, 396-397. Although further historical research would be necessary to date the Igbogila's *orisha* serial form of performance, the circular choreography (a form characteristic of the *orisha* dances) and the order in which the *orishas* are praised (Elegba, Ogun, Eyinle, Iroko, Ondo, and Omolu) are strikingly similar to the *xiré* or starting song-praise sequence practised in Bahian Ketu *candomblé*, suggesting that the Egbado people may have been important agents in the formative process of the *Candomblé* institution.
18. Rodrigues, *Os Africanos no Brasil*, p. 236.
19. For instance, in relation to the thunder *orisha* Shango in Oyó: J. Lorand Matory, *Sex and the Empire that is No More: Gender and the Politics of Metaphor in Òyó Yoruba Religion* (Minneapolis: University of Minnesota Press, 1994), pp. 13–22.
20. Olfert Dapper *Naukeurige Beschrijvinge der Afrikaensche Gewesten* (Amsterdam: J. van Meurs, 1668 [1676]), quoted by Verger, *Notas sobre o culto*, p. 50; Paul E. H. Hair, Adam Jones, and Robin Law (eds.), *Barbot on Guinea: the writings of Jean Barbot on West Africa 1678-1712* (London: Hakluyt Society, 1992 [1688]), II, pp. 620-621; Bosman, *New and Accurate Description*, p. 383. For the sea worship in the Gold Coast see also: ibid., p. 153; Paul Erdman Isert, *Voyage en Guinée et dans les îles Caraïbes en Amérique* (Nicoué Lodjou Gayibor, ed.) (Paris: Karthala, 1989 [1793]), p. 45.
21. In relation to Great Ardra: Bosman *New and Accurate Description*, p. 383. In relation to the Oyo (J-oes): William Snelgrave, *A New Account of Some Parts of Guinea and the Slave Trade* (London: Frank Cass & Co. Ltd., 1971 [1734]), p. 59. In relation to the Fon: Francesco Borghero, *Journal de Francesco Borghero, premier missionnaire du Dahomey (1861-1865)* (Renzo Mandirola and Yves Morel, eds.) (Paris: Karthala, 1997 [1865]), p. 123. See also Isert, *Voyage en Guinée*, p. 123.
22. Roberto Pazzi, "Aperçu sur l'implantation actuelle et les migrations anciennes des peuples de l'aire culturelle Aja-Tado," in François de Medeiros (ed.), *Peuples du Golfe du Bénin (Aja-Ewé)* (Paris: Éditions Karthala, 1984), pp. 13-14; idem, *Introduction à l'histoire de l'aïre culturelle ajatado* (Lomé: Université du Benin, Institut National des Sciences Humaines, 1979), pp. 172-174, 199-200; Thomas Mouléro, "Histoire et légendes des Djêkens," in *Études Dahoméennes* New Series 3 (1964): 43-45; Robin Law, *The Kingdom of Allada* (Leiden: Research School CNWS, CNWS publications, 1997), pp. 5-6, 42; Nicoué Lodjou Gayibor, *Les Peuples et Royaumes du Golfe du Bénin* (Lomé: Université du Benin, 1986), pp. 29-30.
23. Hair, Jones, and Law, *Barbot on Guinea*, II, pp. 581, 589; Bosman, *New and Accurate Description,* p. 113. Richard Burton, *A mission to Gelélé King of Dahomey* (London: Routledge & Kegan Paul, 1966 [1864]), p. 78, reports that in Ouidah the "tall thunder fetish shrub" is called *Ayyan* or *Soyan*. Paul Baudin, *Fetichism and Fetish Worshippers* (New York: Benziger Bros., 1885 [1884]). p. 23, reports that *Ayan* is the tree where according to the Yoruba legend Shango hanged himself. In Hair, Jones and Law, *Barbot on Guinea*, II, pp. 582-583, Adam Jones notes that Jean Goeman or Jankomé corresponds to the Akan term *Onyankome*. If the root of this term, *Onyan*, was an Akan phonetic evolution of *Ayyan* or *Soyan*, we would have indirect evidence

of a thunder cult spread from Yorubaland to the Gold Coast already in the seventeenth century, since it is usually assumed that the cult spread from east to west.

24. Anonymous, "Relation du royaume de Judas en Guinee, de son gouvernement, des moeurs de ses habitants, de leur religion, et du négoce qui s'y fait," Archives d'Outre-Mer, Aix-en-Provence: Dépôt des Fortifications des Colonies, Côte d'Afrique ms 104, undated, (certainly post-1708, and pre-1727), p. 52. Also cited in Robin Law, *The Slave Coast of West Africa 1550-1750: The impact of the Atlantic Slave Trade on an African society* (Oxford: Oxford University Press, 1991), p. 111. My thanks to Robin Law for drawing my attention to this document.
25. Frederick E. Forbes, *Dahomey and the Dahomeans* (London: Longman, Brown, Green, and Longmans, 1851), I, p. 171. Forbes (ibid., pp. 102-104) also refers to an incident at Agoue in February 1850, when the flagstaff of the 'English factory' (presumably that of the firm of Thomas Hutton) was struck by lightning, and the 'fetish people' demanded admittance, in order to carry off the flagstaff, and demanded payment - and the agent gave them $200 worth of goods; Borghero, *Journal*, pp. 129-134; Burton, *A mission to Gelélé,* p. 295. The first explicit record of Shango in Yorubaland is provided by T. J. Bowen, *A Grammar and Dictionary of the Yoruba Language* (Washington: Smithsonian Institution, 1858); see also Verger, *Notas sobre o culto*, p. 343. Le Herissé, *Anciѐn Royaume du Dahomey*, p. 115, mentions Shango as the probable origin of Hevioso. A series of similitudes in their ritual performance, noted by Verger in 1957, would seem to confirm the hypothesis: Verger, *Notas sobre o culto*, p. 530.
26. Le Herissé, *Anciѐn Royaume du Dahomey*, pp. 115-116; Serpos Tidjani, "Notes sur le marriage au Dahomey," *Études Dahoméennes* 6 (1951): 35; Pazzi, *Introduction à l'histoire*, p. 123. Nowadays, the Seto are also settled in certain neighbourhoods in Porto Novo, and they speak the Seto language. R. P. B. Segurola, *Dictionnaire Fon-Français* (Cotonou: Procure de l'Archidiocèse, 1963), II, p. 482, says that the first worshippers of So were the Aïzo from Hevie.
27. For the vodun ethnic terms: Le Herissé, *Anciѐn Royaume du Dahomey*, p. 108; Herskovits, *Dahomey*, II, p. 157. For the vodun lists: Verger, *Notas sobre o culto*, pp. 521, 528-529, 542-545; Herskovits, *Dahomey*, II , p. 304. Mouléro reports Hula oral tradition according to which, in Godome, the Hevioso pantheon (Sogbo, Gbadé, Aden) are considered proper Hula voduns. This seems to contradict Verger's data. Yet, Mouléro apparently collected his information in Ouidah and this could explain the importance granted to the Hevioso in this narrative; Mouléro, "Histoire et légendes," pp. 47-49; Pazzi, *Introduction à l'histoire*, p. 163.
28. Merlo, "Hiérarchie fétichiste," pp. 6-8; Hunon Daagbo, Ouidah, interview 16 July 1995.
29. Le Herissé, *Anciѐn Royaume du Dahomey*, p. 109; Herskovits, *Dahomey*, II, pp. 151, 302.
30. For Agbanakin: Emmanuel Karl, *Traditions Orales au Dahomey-Benin.* (Niamey, Niger: Centre Regional de Documentation pour la Tradition Orale, 1974), p. 236. For Heve: Verger, *Notas sobre o culto*, pp. 529, 541. See also Herskovits, *Dahomey*, II, p. 193.
31. Jacob Spieth, *Die Religion der Eweer in Süd-Togo* (Leipzig: Dieterich'sche, 1911). p. 173; Herskovits, *Dahomey*, II, p. 193.

32. Fio Agbonon II, *Histoire de Petit Popo et du royaume Guin* (Nicoué Lodjou Gayibor, ed.) (Lomé: Université du Benin, 1984 [1934]), pp. 164, 168; Verger, *Notas sobre o culto*, p. 529.
33. Peel, "A comparative Analysis of Ogun," p. 275.
34. Verger, *Notas sobre o culto*, p. 105; Herskovits, *Dahomey*, II, p. 188; Segurola, *Dictionnaire*, p. 482. The "So Agbajyí or thunder closet" reported by Burton in Ouidah may have been located in modern Sogbadji, the neighbourhood where the Hunon Dagbo sea temple is located: Burton, *A mission to Gelélé,* p. 295.
35. Le Herissé, *Ancièn Royaume du Dahomey*, p. 108, says that Hevioso was imported into Abomey by Tegbesu, a tradition not confirmed in 1938 by Herskovits, *Dahomey*, II, p. 153. Segurola, *Dictionnaire*, p. 484, suggests that it was Agonglo who installed the Hevioso in Gbekon-Huegbo under the name of Agbohun. See also Verger, *Notas sobre o culto*, pp. 525-530.
36. Snelgrave, *A New Account,* pp. 101, 104; Le Herissé, *Anciè n Royaume du Dahomey*, p. 108. In 1849, Forbes documents a ceremony (also described by Borghero and Burton) in which soldiers planted along the road from Abomey to the beach of Ouidah successively fired their guns as "a salute to the Fetish of the Great Waters, or God of Foreign Trade": Forbes, *Dahomey and the Dahomeans*, I, p. 18. In 1860, there is evidence of human sacrifice offered by king Glele, as part of the funeral ceremonies for his father, king Ghezo. This is described by Peter Bernasko, in Ouidah: "Wednesday the 11th of July I started from this [i.e. Ouidah] for Abomey to see the Custom. I met with a man in the way, two days after my departure, nicely dressed as a cabboceer coming down to this, was riding in hammock, with a large umbrella and a cabboceer's stool, and a number of men accompanied him, and when I arrived at Cannah ... here I learned that the poor man was going to be thrown into the sea to join the two Porters of the Sea gate to open it for his father to enter in and wash himself...": Peter Bernasko, Ouidah, 29 November 1860, Archives of the Wesleyan Methodist Mission Society (SOAS). I am indebted to Robin Law for providing this reference. Burton, probably referring to the same events comments that king Glele occasionally sent human offerings to be sacrificed to the sea in Ouidah: Burton, *A mission to Gelélé,* p. 295.
37. Verger, *Notas sobre o culto*, pp. 525-30.
38. Carlos Ott, "O Negro Bahiano," in *Les Afro-Américains* (Mémoire de l'Institut Français d'Afrique Noire, No. 27. Dakar: IFAN, 1952), pp. 144-145; Maria José Souza de Andrade, "A mão-de-obra escrava em Salvador, de 1811 a 1860: um estudo de História Quantitativa," M. A. thesis, Universidade Federal da Bahia, 1975, table 4 (2); Pierre Verger, *Fluxo e Refluxo do tráfico de escravos entre o Golfo do Benin e a Bahia de todos os Santos* (São Paulo: Corrupio, 1987), p. 670; Manoel Querino, *Costumes Africanos no Brasil* (Recife: Fundação Joaquim Nabuco, Editora Massangana, 1988 [1938]), p. 72.
39. Vicente Paulo dos Santos, Salvador, interview 8 October, 1998. Kaviono is interpreted by some Jeje priests as a phonetic evolution of Hevioso or Kevioso. Would it have any relationship with *kaviecile* (or *kawo kabiyecile*), the praise name of the thunder *orishas* and voduns?
40. In Brazil, Artur Ramos, *As Culturas Negras no Novo Mundo* (São Paulo: Ed. Nacional-INL-MEC, 1979 [1937]), p. 224, refers to the *Mundombes* as belonging to the "cafres bantus em Angola." For information about the *Mundombe* or *Ndombe* in Angola see: José C. Curto, "The Story of Nbena, 1817-1820: Unlawful Enslavement

and the Concept of 'Original Freedom' in Angola," in Paul E. Lovejoy and David V. Trotman (eds.), *Trans-Atlantic Dimensions of Ethnicity in the African Diaspora* (London: Continuum, 2003), pp. 43-64.

41. Pierre Verger, *Notícias da Bahia-1850* (Salvador: Corrupio, 1981), p. 228.
42. João José Reis, "Nas Malhas do Poder Escravista: A Invasão do Candomblé do Accú," in João José Reis and Eduardo Silva (eds.), *Negociação e Conflito. A resistência negra no Brasil escravista* (São Paulo: Companhia das Letras, 1989), pp. 36, 128.
43. *O Alabama*. For the Bogum: 2 and 10 May, 1867; 14 April, 1869; 23 June, 1870. For the Querbetan: 15 May, 1867. For the Agomé: 11 November, 1871. For the Campina: 23 June, 1870. I thank João José Reis for providing copies of the Bogum references which led me to other *terreiro*'s references.
44. The Kaviono family in Bahia today includes voduns such as Zo Ogodo [the fire vodun], Sogbo Baba Guidi [or So Baguidi, may be phonetic evolution Gbaguidi, the Hueda family ruler of Savalu], Jogorobossu, Bossu [may be phonetic evolution of Besu or Bossum], Jokolatin and Betá Yoyo [or Beta Oyo]. These secondary deities, some of which might be Brazilian creations, do not have devotees consecrated to them and do not manifest in public ceremonies.
45. The first indirect evidence of multi-divinity cult in Bahia of which I have notice dates only from 1858, when in a *candomblé* at Quintas da Barra, in the Victoria district of Salvador, the police found several ritual dresses and emblematics that suggest this plural worship: Arquivo Público do Estado da Bahia (Salvador), Policia Delegados 1842-1866, Maço [bundle] 2994-1, 13 April, 1858, (document found by Alexandra Brown and João José Reis); see also Rachel Elizabeth Harding, "Candomblé and the alternative spaces of black being in nineteenth century Bahia, Brazil: a study of historical context and religious meaning," Ph. D. dissertation, University of Colorado, 1997, pp. 76, 99, 316.
46. *O Alabama*, 19 May, 1869, p. 3.
47. Rodrigues, *Os Africanos,* p. 234 (my translation).
48. Luiza Frankelina da Rocha, Cachoeira, interview 7 November, 1999.
49. Harding, "Candomblé and the alternative spaces," pp. 117-120; Jocélio Teles dos Santos, *O dono da terra (o caboclo nos candomblés da Bahia)* (Salvador: Editora Sarah Letras, 1995), p. 19.
50. As Herskovits observes, "following the usual Dahomean pattern, the youngest child, spoiled by his parent, astute, capricious, intractable, plays the most headstrong and undisciplined role of any god in the pantheon." Averekete, the youngest and most favoured child of Agbé and Naeté, follows this pattern and having the greatest cunning plays the role of trickster. Averekete always comes in the front opening the way for the other voduns, joking and making grimaces, spreading rumours and acting as messenger. Herkovits, *Dahomey*, II, pp. 155, 158. Sharing the same functionality and versatile character of Legba, Averekete is seldom praised in the Jeje-Mahi *terreiros* when singing for the thunder voduns, but never forgotten when singing for Legba. This may have contributed for his/her persistence. It must be also noted that in Maranhão Agbé, Naeté and specially Averekete are still important voduns.

4

Kings, Queens, and Judges: Hierarchy in Lay Religious Brotherhoods of Blacks, 1750-1830

Elizabeth W. Kiddy

Africans and their descendents formed brotherhoods throughout Brazil during the colonial period and the empire. Travelers' accounts, brotherhood documents, and official documents of both the church and the state all comment upon these organizations.[1] Brotherhoods of blacks existed in all of the central economic regions of the colony — Pernambuco, Bahia, Rio de Janeiro, Minas Gerais — as well as on the peripheries — Santa Catarina, Goiás, Ceará, Pará. Slave, free, and freed black populations formed brotherhoods mostly in the cities, but plenty of evidence exists to demonstrate that they also existed on plantations. Despite the institutional similarity between these lay religious brotherhoods of blacks, they manifested differently in each region and in what time period they existed. Although all the regions shared an identity as being part of the Portuguese colony in the Americas, each had distinct economic, social, geographic, and cultural characteristics. The African and African descended populations of each region also differed significantly in their backgrounds, their familiarity or not with European culture, and their own personal and collective histories. Ethnicities entered diverse regions at different times. At any given period, the population of free blacks, and/or Brazilian born blacks became significant. African and Brazilian born black women, too, became important in the demography of the black population, as well as the economic well being of the communities. This constellation of contrasts came together in the lay religious brotherhoods of blacks, and the members of those organizations had to find ways to interpret, organize, and construct effective corporations, and a corporate identity, from a foundation of difference.

The formation of collectivities demonstrates a major way in which Africans re-created an African world in the Americas — an enslaving connection. This strategy was a primary way by which Africans and their descendents combated the alienation and displacement of slavery, finding remedies against the isolation of complete displacement and the insidious witchcraft that had caused the misfortune of the slave condition.[2] Examining the process of community formation, rather than the existence of "survivals" begins to answer the challenge put forward many years ago by anthropologist Sidney W. Mintz. His thoughts on the matter are worth quoting at length:

> It is the determination of those "deeper" principles that poses for the student of Afro-American civilizations one of the most difficult problems in methodology and in theory. Surface manifestations of African origins are no less African by virtue of being obvious. But they have too often been used as the only measures of the degree of "African-ness" or as sufficient evidence in themselves that deeper-lying and more fundamental features were necessarily present. In fact, surface manifestations . . . may or may not be the "most African" of surviving features; *their absence* may distract scholars from the presence of much more fundamental, but subtler, materials of African origin.[3]

The communities formed within brotherhoods of blacks demonstrated the "deeper principles" referred to by Mintz. One of the main manifestations of this was the way in which the reformed communities organized themselves carefully along well-defined hierarchies. Vertical organization of power existed strongly in Portuguese society, yet African societies also were profoundly hierarchical. As Igor Kopytoff points out, "African societies are suffused with a sense of hierarchy in social, political, and ritual relations."[4] These hierarchies existed not only in large and small states, but in "families, kin groups, civic and 'secret' societies." In fact, "hierarchy imposed itself upon any relationship involving any degree of dependence."[5] The re-creation of hierarchies within the brotherhood collectivities points to the creation not only of cultural connections but of the reformulation of an African political culture in Brazil, infused with its own sense of power and privilege. Through this preliminary exploration I demonstrate the creation of a dynamic political culture drawn from an African past yet sensitive to the demands of the local and regional European dominated colony.

The members of the black brotherhoods formed this political culture by creating hierarchies among the disparate groups that made up that membership. The divergences within the membership ran along four main lines: *nação* (nation/ethnicity), *côr* (color), *sexo* (gender), and *condição* (legal status as slave or free).[6] Throughout history and certainly during the three hundred years of the slave trade, Africans did not identify themselves as a homogeneous group of "blacks", or even as Africans, but rather as members of distinct groups. Whatever these distinct groups were in Africa, they came to be translated into what were called *nações* (nations) in Brazil. The term nation as used by the Portuguese did not indicate allegiance to a particular state; instead it identified a person's place of birth, or origin. Although the African nations of Brazil were identities created by the dynamic of the slave trade itself, sufficient evidence exists in the documentary record to establish that blacks did self-identify with one or another particular nation, or ethnicity as these groupings are most commonly called today.[7] Those identities were often very general, such as the far-reaching general divisions of Angola (Central Africa) and Mina (West Africa, the Bight of Benin), but just as often were discreet, as in the Savaru (sometimes in the documentation as Sabaru), Ardas, DaGome, and Nagô "nations" of West Africa. *Crioulo*, a term used for

Brazilian-born blacks, can also be considered a "nation" because it indicates the place of birth of members of a group that would become an increasingly important part of the brotherhood membership, especially in Minas Gerais, towards the end of the colonial period. In all of these cases, I choose to use the "ethnic" titles that the membership themselves used, and assume that they understood the way that appellation distinguished them from the others.

The term race was never used in the brotherhoods books, or in colonial Brazil. Instead, phenotypic differences were differentiated under the rubric of color (*côr*). Documentation pertaining to the brotherhoods from late colonial Brazil identifies three main divisions by color: *preto* (black), *pardo* (mulattos, browns, or persons of mixed black and white ancestry), and *branco* (white). Less frequently used terms were *cabra* (individuals of mixed ancestry; black mother and possibly a mulatto father), and *mestiço* (persons of mixed ancestry). Despite the variety of terms used to describe people in the brotherhoods according to color, the brotherhoods under discussion here were collectively identified as brotherhoods "of the blacks" in all of their documentation. The term black, in the colonial period as today, represented a wide range of elements having to do with phenotype, economic standing, cultural/historical ties, and legal status. The interplay between these elements would serve to place the individual or group on the Brazilian color scale, yet as has been well documented, the least advantageous place to be on that scale was black and the most advantageous, white. The question of legal status tied in intimately with, and became relative to, the question of color. Some scholars have noted that in the last decades before the end of slavery in 1888 the term "black" was synonymous with slave, and that ex-slaves would self-identify as *pardos*.[8] Nevertheless, many of the members of the brotherhoods of blacks were free, yet they willingly participated and often ran the brotherhoods of blacks. The brotherhoods also usually had a number of white and *pardo* members, some who served as patrons. The "of the blacks" then, referred to the larger brotherhood structure in the society in which the brotherhood was non-white. The non-white status of the brotherhood pertained not only to the color of the members but to the cultural practices within the brotherhoods, which often included kings and queens and dances to the drums of the nations — surface manifestations that echoed and actively remembered an African paSaint

The black brotherhoods also accepted both men and women into their membership, unlike their white counterparts, and women often held high positions in the ritual hierarchy of the brotherhoods. Nevertheless, women were excluded from the important decision making roles in the brotherhoods' ruling boards. Women's inclusion in the brotherhoods can be understood as a reflection of gender as understood by both Euro-Brazilian and African sectors of the population. In many African societies, women did enjoy more economic freedom, especially when the societies were matrilineal. Women both owned their own property and engaged extensively in trade. In many regions they also participated politically in their societies.[9] Nevertheless, as Claire Robertson so cogently points out, the presence of matrilineality, and even matrifocality in African societies did not imply that those same societies were not profoundly patriarchal, and that "patriarchal authority dominated most facets of life" in Africa.[10] Therefore, the participation of women in the brotherhoods, especially in the important economic and ritual roles they played, and their simultaneous exclusion from the decision-making processes, mirrors an African past that became exacerbated by colonial Brazilian gender norms. Yet the extent to which women participated in, or were marginalized from, participation in the brotherhoods varied from place to place and from time to time, and constituted another important axis of difference in the brotherhoods.

Because identity formed around axes (nation, color, legal status, and gender) and their relation to external factors, the process of the creation of a communal identity within lay religious brotherhoods of blacks was profoundly local. An examination of the formation of communities and hierarchies within black brotherhoods, then, must be done in a comparative manner. In order to take a preliminary comparative look at some ways in which Africans and their descendents organized their world politically inside the brotherhood structure, I examine three brotherhoods in different regions in the late colonial period. The comparative approach allows the study to have greater depth not only to the substance of the organizations, but the important processes that molded the particular organizations in discreet regions. I begin the discussion by sketching out brotherhood organization in Brazilian society in a general way, and then turn to examine in more detail three black brotherhoods. I present two rosary brotherhoods of blacks, one in Recife, Pernambuco, and the other in the village of Bacalhau in the interior of Minas Gerais. The final example presents a more ethnically exclusive brotherhood of Saint Elesbão and Saint Ephigenia in Rio de Janeiro. In all of these regions the black brotherhood membership chose to restrict their membership in various ways; they also all found different ways to define and organize difference within their membership through the creation of hierarchies. The creation of a community organized in a way Africans would have understood allowed the membership to act in a unified way within the larger society. Their unity assured the success of the *work* of the brotherhood — important rituals for the dead and calling for the aid of the other-worldly beings, and service as an antidote to alienation and marginalization.

LAY RELIGIOUS BROTHERHOODS OF BLACKS, AN OVERVIEW

Black brotherhoods had to interact as corporations on a macro-societal level while organizing themselves internally in a micro-societal manner. On a macro-societal level, black brotherhoods, despite their juridical equality to and similar legal responsibilities as other brotherhoods, represented an organization on the bottom rung of the social ladder throughout Brazil, a hierarchy that mirrored Portuguese society. At the societal level the brotherhoods divided by color, social status, and occupation. The white brotherhoods of the local elite, which required purity of blood of the brother/member, his wife, and their forebears, occupied the highest place on the social ladder. The brotherhoods of blacks occupied the loweSaint In between were a range of brotherhoods that restricted membership in a variety of ways, defining and creating a space for group cohesion and social protection and support.[11] All brotherhoods competed by attempting to outdo one another in their lavish festivals and through their competition for positions in frequent processions.[12]

Black brotherhoods divided on this macro-societal level by placing restrictions on their membership. In the two largest slave-importing ports of Brazil — Salvador, Bahia and Rio de Janeiro — black brotherhoods split along ethnic lines.[13] Both Salvador and Rio de Janeiro boasted huge African and African descended slave and free populations, creating a diversity mirrored in the discreet national divisions of the brotherhood structure. Salvador and the region around the Bay of All Saints also had "sisterhoods" of blacks, divided along gender lines.[14] At times black brotherhoods distinguished themselves by legal status, excluding slaves from their membership.[15] In the frontier regions of Minas Gerais and Goiás, where Africans were one further step removed from their place of origin, brotherhoods occasionally split along the lines of color.[16] Throughout Brazil, however, the majority of black brotherhoods opened their membership to people of any nation, color, gender, and legal status, especially the ubiquitous rosary brotherhoods. Because of the inclusive nature of the organizations, their memberships had to organize a larger mosaic of diversity, and all black brotherhoods devised strategies for dealing with differences in their membership, even when that meant excluding certain groups to remain effective as corporations.

To become effective as a brotherhood, some sort of unity had to be achieved within the organization so that its work could be carried out. The work included both spiritual and temporal responsibilities. The mixing of spiritual and material goals within the brotherhoods would have been a combination that Africans recognized, for African groups did not separate material and spiritual cause and effect.[17] The Portuguese model of the internal structure of the brotherhoods was extremely hierarchical, ordered in a vast array of titles and positions of responsibility. This would also have been a type of organization that Africans recognized because of the hierarchical nature of African societies.[18] In addition, leadership positions in the brotherhoods were elected positions. Likewise, leaders in Africa, especially those in the highest positions, were elected or had their positions passed on at the time of the previous leader's death. In both cases, however, people of importance in the polity had to agree upon the selection of the new leader.[19] Often the highest position in the brotherhood, that of the king, emperor, or regent, was also responsible for heading the *folias*, or festive dances and coronations held on feast days. This role represents the ritual responsibility of that leader, whose power would derive in part from his or her ability to channel those invisible powers made available through the saints representing the brotherhoods and spirits of the dead.[20] In order to be effective, therefore, black brotherhoods recreated an African political culture built upon the knowledge of the members from West Africa and Central Africa, and their descendents, yet embedded in local Brazilian society.

In general, the internal organization of black brotherhoods followed patterns set in all brotherhoods throughout the Portuguese Empire. Elections included the administrative officers: the secretary, treasurer, and often two procurators. Sometimes the positions of secretary and treasurer were reserved for whites, in other cases color was not a prerequisite. These positions, however, were those most tied into the Portuguese church and state structures, for they were responsible for preparing, guarding, and presenting the brotherhoods' paperwork to Portuguese state and church officials. The *procuradores*, a word that does not have a good English translation, were usually responsible for informing brotherhood members of important events, illness or death of a member. The administrative positions were held exclusively by men. The brotherhood also elected a board of directors, which most often had both male and female members. The black brotherhoods had various ritual positions such as male and female judges, often one for each saint honored within the brotherhood, who were responsible for the devotion to that saint. All of these elected positions required the member to pay a higher annual fee as well as to participate in the meetings, funerals, and feast days, and be on hand to celebrate the masses of the brotherhoods. The presence of women differentiated the black brotherhoods from their white counterparts, which did not include women as members. The divergence between Portuguese and African based attitudes about the proper level of women's political and economic participation in society accounted for this difference.[21]

Black brotherhoods that included slaves within their membership also differed from other brotherhoods in that the former either elected or bequeathed positions of royalty, either kings and queens, emperors, regents, or some combination of these. These positions represent a structure outside of the traditional European brotherhood organization.[22] Often the royalty participated significantly in the *folias*, or dances, of the brotherhoods. Although Portuguese authorities were not extremely sympathetic to *folias*, they usually allowed brotherhoods to celebrate in this way, at least through the end of the colonial period, because the dances were perceived as harmless pastimes that alleviated, for a while, the sufferings of slavery. These dances and coronations of royalty were common only in brotherhoods that included slaves, signifying a closer link, perhaps, to an African tradition. Yet these brotherhoods were never exclusively slave, and in some of them slaves themselves were even prohibited from holding the positions of king and queen.

Although many of the basic structures of brotherhoods remained fairly constant between regions (and between different types of brotherhoods), local manifestations varied tremendously. Generalizing further about the internal organization of black brotherhoods, then, would begin to cloud the real diversity that existed between these organizations — not just between different types of brotherhoods but between the same brotherhood in different Brazilian regions. These political structures did not exist in a vacuum; they were profoundly affected by internal and external demographics and by the social milieu of the particular region in which they emerged. An examination of the similarities and differences between the regions will provide a background for understanding strategies of the organization of difference articulated within black brotherhoods in late colonial Brazil. These strategies bring to light how the population that participated in the brotherhoods of blacks were able to re-form communities based on African concepts within the social space of the brotherhoods, and thus serve as an antidote to and resistance against the degradation of slavery and the low social and economic status of many freed blacks and their descendents.

THE BROTHERHOOD OF THE ROSARY OF BLACKS, PARISH OF SANTO ANTÔNIO, RECIFE, PERNAMBUCO

Pernambuco was the first successful captaincy in the colony of Brazil, and along with Bahia one of the first and longest lasting sugar economies. Recife, the largest city and seaport of the captaincy, was situated at the delta of the river Capibaribe and was built on the swampy land of several islands divided by the river and its tributaries as they flowed into the sea. In the seventeenth century, the Dutch captured and held Recife for twenty-four years, and were finally thrown out by combined Brazilian and Portuguese forces in 1654. Slaves had already begun arriving in large numbers by the end of the sixteenth century to work in the growing sugar economy, and the Dutch continued to import slaves during their occupation. A Dutch observer noted the presence of Africans from a wide range of regions — Guine, Cabo Verde, Sierra Leone, Congo, Sonho, Ardra, and Calabar.[23] After the Dutch left, the Portuguese slave trade returned to more West Central African sources, in large part because of the start of the Angolan wars that generated huge numbers of captives. In the first half of the eighteenth century, an influx of West African slaves increased in the markets of Pernambuco, probably in large part because of the competition with the growing market in the newly discovered gold-mining region to the south. From the middle to the end of the eighteenth century, however, with the creation of monopolistic trading companies, the trade turned back to Central Africa.[24] At the same time, the Brazilian born and free population of color was growing.[25] By the late eighteenth century, the black population in Recife, while predominantly Central African or of Central African descent also had a significant a level of diversity that would be organized within the rosary brotherhoods.

After the defeat of the Dutch in 1654, a rosary brotherhood of blacks began in the parish of Santo Antônio, Recife, and by the 1660s the members were able to begin building their own church.[26] The incorporating statutes, or *compromisso*, opened membership to men and women, to slave and free, and to Angolan or *crioulo*, and the members would elect every year a king and queen who could only be Angolan or *crioulo*.[27] Clearly, this early brotherhood wanted to restrict its membership along ethnic lines. By the mid-eighteenth century, however, the population of Recife had grown, matured, and diversified, and the brotherhood revised its statutes to reflect those changes. Two of the most important revisions in the 1782 *compromisso* were the extreme attention to the details of hierarchy and protocol for the brotherhood, which limited the access to power positions for slaves, and the change in how different ethnicities were organized in the brotherhood.

The first twenty-seven chapters of the *compromisso* laid out the general organization and responsibilities of the brotherhood. The leadership positions for the men, from highest to least important, were judge, treasurer, secretary, two procurators, an *andador* (alms collector), twelve *mordomos* (stewards), and twelve other board members. The *compromisso* restricted these positions to free men, because "this brotherhood has plenty of free members, and the slaves are often impeded by their masters in order to fulfill their obligations by the diminution of the time of their services."[28] In addition to the requirement of being free, the judge and the secretary needed to be literate, and the treasurer an older member of the brotherhood, a man of honor and probity. Except for the position of treasurer members also elected women to fill parallel positions in the brotherhood, such as a female judge, a woman secretary, and women mordomos and members of the board. Finally, the brotherhood elected a white judge and board members to help financially with the annual festival.[29]

The careful delineation of the vast array of positions in the brotherhood demonstrates the importance of hierarchy in the brotherhood. Much of the *compromisso*, in fact, was dedicated to the exact definition of hierarchy in this brotherhood. For example, the *compromisso* strictly laid out the order of the processions, how many masses would be said, and even how many times they would ring the bell to announce the death of one or another member of the board. The position of the members around the table at the meetings serves as an example of the importance of hierarchy in this brotherhood. The judge sat at the head of the table, and had the special privilege of having a seat with a back. The chaplain sat to the right of the judge. Continuing around the table would be the secretary, the first *definidor* (a high ranking official in the organization) if he had previously been judge or secretary, then the treasurer, the second *definidor*, the two procurators, and the rest of the board.[30] Women were noticeably absent from these hierarchical orderings, demonstrating that women were given positions in order that they contribute financially, but that they did not have real power within the brotherhood administrative structure. This marginalization of women demonstrates the combination of African and European gender ideologies, in which women were still able to participate economically, as in Africa, yet almost completely excluded politically, as in Portugal and Euro-Brazil.

The 1782 *compromisso* also reflects an interesting change of emphasis on origin or nation to that of a color consciousness. It broadened the membership by dropping the ethnic restrictions and stating that blacks, *pardos*, or whites could join the brotherhood. The changes point to a reorientation of identity along color lines.[31] The last article of the statutes, however, demonstrates that the consciousness of ethnic divisions had not disappeared; it remained in the ritual division and organization of the brotherhood. This chapter lay out the responsibility of the King of Congo, and the Queen, both of whom were listed in the regular election. The King of Congo had to be from the Kingdom of Angola, free from slavery, married, and of "good customs". The king had the responsibility to name (*fazer*) a governor in each nation, who would take possession of his position in the church. The chapter also called for the governors to hand in their commissions (*patentes*) to store them in a book in the brotherhood. When the King of Congo wanted to name a governor he would give the name to the *procuradores* of the brotherhood, who would verify if the named governor would be able to occupy the position. The qualifications for the position of governor stipulated that the post should be held by the most peaceful and attentive leaders of the nation.[32]

Throughout its first twenty-seven articles, the 1782 *compromisso* seems to be a document of an organization that had moved in the direction of the acceptance of Portuguese values, with the marginalization of both slaves and women from the decision making process. This last section opens the door on a part of the brotherhood that kept it linked to an African past and hierarchy. What is remarkable, however, is that this ethnic/political structure of the brotherhoods interfaced with the larger Recifense society through the commissions mentioned in the *compromisso*. Successive governors of the captaincy of Pernambuco in the late eighteenth century issued commissions to governors of various African nations, which were then entered into an official book of government military commissions. The earliest extant commission granted to the governor of an African nation, dated 3 February 1776, named Simião da Rocha the governor of the nation of DaGome, which the document divided from the nation of Savaru with which it had been mixed.[33] According to the document, the members of the nation of DaGome had elected da Rocha to that position, and the governor of the captaincy, José Cezar de Menezes, had simply made the election official by giving a commission. Later that same year, Menezes granted a commission to a governor of the Savaru, and another to the governor of the Ardas do Botão of the Costa da Mina. According to the commission, Ventura de Souza Graces, who had been the Lieutenant Colonel of the Ardas, was elected to the position of governor because the former governor no longer wanted the position due to his advanced age.[34] The next governor of Pernambuco, Thomás José de Mello, in 1791 granted Narciso Correa de Castro the commission to be governor of the Ardas do Botão of the Costa da Mina because of the death of Ventura de Souza Gomez.[35]

These documents reveal a hierarchy both between nations and within each nation that participated in the brotherhoods. This hierarchy was articulated in the last chapter of the 1782 *compromisso* of the brotherhood and was verified and upheld by successive governors of the captaincy of Pernambuco. The *compromisso* acknowledged the difference among the members by nation of origin, and placed the members of the nations under the general stewardship of the King of Congo. The seventeenth century brotherhood reserved the position of King and Queen in the brotherhood for Angolas and *crioulos*.[36] In the late eighteenth century *compromisso*, the position of King and Queen had been modified to be "of Congo" even though the King and Queen themselves were to be from Angola.[37] The other nations were to be loyal to the King of Congo, and were all West African.

Much more prevalent than commissions granted by nation, however, were commissions granted by the governors of Pernambuco to the black leaders of certain professions. This professional structure linked to the rosary brotherhood, and closely resembled the *cantos* (groups of workers for hire) of late nineteenth century Bahia.[38] The books of commissions granted by the governors of Pernambuco between 1776 and 1802 listed thirty commissions given to members of professions to be governor of that profession (or in two of the later cases for the position of *capataz*, or foreman). The professions included canoe driver, fishermen, markers of sugar boxes, and workers of the plaza. In almost every case, the position was identified as that of the blacks — the black canoe drivers, etc. Many of the commissions, as had been the case in the naming of the governor of the Savaru, were granted because the members of that profession had elected the individual to that position. In some cases the commission stated that the holder of the office had satisfactorily held another position in the hierarchy of that profession. For example, Feliciano Gomes dos Santos became governor of the workers of the plaza because he was elected by his peers and also had successfully held the position of counselor colonel (*coronel conselheiro*) of those workers.[39] In almost every case, the commissions charged the recipients with keeping peace among members of their profession, so in some ways they could be seen as a form of external social control. In another sense, however, they represent a remarkable level of self-governance by the blacks of these professions, and an ordering of their professions in a way they recognized and respected, and over which they had some control.

Three of the commissions of workers granted women the position of governor (*governadora*) of a certain profession. The first, granted in 1788 to Bernarda Eugênia de Souza, made her the governor of the black female street vendors. She was named to this position in order to have someone maintain the peace among these workers.[40] In 1802 the commissions were granted to two other women, both freed blacks, to be governors of the *pombeiras* or female pigeon peddlers, one in the district outside of Recife, and the other in Olinda. In both of these cases, the women had held other positions in the hierarchy: Josefa Lages had been the colonel of the *pombeiras*, and Reynalda Pinta de Carvalho had been the field marshal of the *pombeiras* in Olinda, a neighboring city.[41]

Although the rosary *compromisso* did not specify a link to these professional hierarchies, evidence exists that suggests a connection. Many of the commissions mentioned the King of Congo, and commanded him to honor, esteem, and respect these office holders, signifying that the King of Congo was the ultimate leader of these different office holders — both national (ethnic) and professional. These ties certainly linked these larger populations to the brotherhood structure. Also, like the requirements in the *compromisso* for the various nations, the professions kept records in the brotherhood's archive. Historian José Antonio Gonçalves de Mello found a registration book of masses for the *capineiros* (weeders) of several neighborhoods of Recife and Olinda. The book contained registers of the masses from 1757 to 1829, and listed several of the positions in the hierarchy of the weeders of Recife. These positions included viceroy, governor, field sergeant (*mestre do campo)*, colonel, lieutenant colonel, captain, supervisor (*provedor)*, high-ranking judge (*juiz de fora*), and counselor.[42] Following one person through the ranks of the weeders, Gonçalves de Mello found that Ventura Barbosa was captain in 1768, *mestre do campo* in 1770, governor in 1773, viceroy in 1802, and King of the Congo nation when he died in 1806.[43] Ventura Barbosa's ascension to the position of King of Congo demonstrates the trajectory of one member of the brotherhood, also a member of the profession of weeders, as he ascended to the highest position in the brotherhood.

The profession of weeders never appeared in the government commissions, which offer little insight into the different ranks listed in registrations of masses found in the rosary brotherhood archive. The detailed division within the professions was noted elsewhere, however. The early nineteenth century visitor to Pernambuco, Daniel Kidder, noted the division of the canoe drivers into military ranks.[44] In 1815, the governor of Pernambuco, Caetano Pinto de Miranda Montenegro, complained that the blacks of Pernambuco divided themselves into "Kings and governors, that by their letters and commissions name secretaries of state, generals, lieutenants, sailors, brigadiers, colonels, and any other military post."[45] In fact, successive governors of Pernambuco had confirmed and sanctioned these commissions. Caetano Pinto believed that this practice of the blacks needed to be stopped, but maintained that it should be stopped slowly in order to avoid rebellion.[46] He was successful in his efforts, and by Brazilian independence in 1822, the complex structuring of life in the black community through the interfaced worlds of work and devotion, had either stopped, or been forced underground.

The complex hierarchical structure in the rosary brotherhood of Recife and its political influence in the larger community in the late colonial period demonstrate ways that Africans and their descendents chose to organize their society, through interfaced webs of hierarchies. The formal, administrative, brotherhood structure mirrored in many ways the Portuguese styled organization, and although it included women and slaves they did not wield the power in the organization. A parallel organization, which operated under the umbrella of the brotherhood, was headed by the King of Congo who had to be Angolan. The West Central African king served as the highest power, and under him were leaders of various other nations (all West African) who recognized his power, just as he recognized theirs. The "black" governors were not appointed by the King of Congo, or by the governor of Pernambuco, but rather were either chosen by the group of people who they were representing or rose into power by advancing through a clearly defined hierarchy.

Both the official positions within the brotherhood and the nations and professions identified in the commissions – linked through the figure of the King of Congo – articulate a self-conscious, vertically organized, community present in a thriving collective of blacks who were slave and free, men and women, and from many different nations. By the end of the colonial period, the brotherhood had been officially incorporated for over 175 years. Its organization demonstrates the complexity of the membership and the care taken to organize difference, reflecting both African and European conceptions of hierarchy. Recife was an old and established part of Brazil, and was known for its conservative attention to social conventions and protocol. The rosary brotherhood had also been established for a long time, and the late colonial *compromisso* demonstrates its recognition of contemporaneous social norms. Yet the brotherhood took this a step further, by organizing the ethnic differences in a vertical hierarchy. This organization kept the members of the brotherhood from simply being a mass of poor blacks on the bottom of the Euro-Brazilian social ladder, and turned them into a parallel society of their own. Such a strategy demonstrates a deeper principle of social organization drawn from a collective African paSaint It enabled the community to survive and become powerful in the society because of the social coherence it created within its own community.

THE BROTHERHOOD OF THE ROSARY OF BLACKS, ARRAIAL DE BACALHAU, DISTRICT OF MARIANA, MINAS GERAIS

The rosary brotherhoods of Minas Gerais interacted in a completely different social context than those in Recife. A distant gold mining region that emerged in the beginning of the eighteenth century, Minas Gerais prospered into a fast growing and chaotic frontier society. Far from the metropolis, it was a place in which fortunes could be made quickly: money blurred the lines of strict social stratification. This blurring of social lines occurred not only within white society, but across the lines of color categories and of free and slave. Slaves were noted as living in "licentious liberty", not respecting their position as slaves and living relatively autonomous lives.[47] The opportunities available to slaves decreased towards the end of the colonial period, as social stratification hardened. Nevertheless, the early years had an impact on the overall demographics and attitudes of the mining region, creating a semi-independent slave population with access to capital, as well as an enormous population of free blacks and people of mixed descent, and the unusual economic and social conditions that allowed the Brazilian born black population to grow.[48] The conditions also allowed for an important presence of rosary brotherhoods, and an acceptance of them, their *folias*, and their coronations by the Portuguese and church authorities that did not exist elsewhere in Brazil.

Brotherhoods thrived in the frontier atmosphere, and, as in the rest of Brazil, became one of the most important organizations in the hamlets, towns, and cities. Like Pernambuco, the brotherhoods of the rosary were the most prevalent brotherhoods for slaves and free blacks in Minas Gerais. Unlike the coastal cities of Recife, Salvador, and Rio de Janeiro, however, the rosary brotherhoods of Minas Gerais did not divide internally (Recife) or externally (Salvador, Rio de Janeiro) along ethnic lines. In the early decades of the eighteenth century, some *mineiro* brotherhoods had large populations of West African, mostly Mina, slaves.[49] In the second half of the century, the population in the brotherhoods became significantly more Central African and Brazilian born. In addition, the rosary brotherhoods in Minas Gerais, in the colonial period, never excluded slaves from positions of authority. The leadership positions rotated among all different ethnicities in the brotherhoods, and between slave and free members.[50]

The election lists from the brotherhood of the rosary in the small hamlet of Bacalhau offer insights into the inner workings of a rosary brotherhood. Bacalhau was located in the region of the seat of the diocese, Mariana, and near to the larger town (*vila*) of Guarapiranga. Faithfully recorded elections over a sixty-nine year period (1761-1830) show that the brotherhood had two full sets of administrative officers, listed as white officers (*oficiais brancos*) and black officers (*oficiais pretos*).[51] The white officers included a protector, secretary, treasurer and procurator, and the black officers repeated these, minus the protector. The other elected positions in the brotherhood were kings and queens, male and female judges dedicated to one of the saints represented in the brotherhood, brothers and sisters of the board. Other members were listed as having positions *por devoção*, meaning that the people volunteered for the position out of devotion, perhaps to fulfill a promise to one of the other saints represented in the brotherhoods — Saint Benedict and Saint Ephigenia. Over the entire period, slaves held just over fifty percent of all the positions, whereas one third of the free elected officials were *forros* (freed slaves).[52] The brotherhood in Bacalhau showed a gradual decrease in the presence of slaves and an increase in free persons in leadership positions. Also significant, was the number of forros in leadership positions through the 1820s, even though their overall population in Minas Gerais dropped off by the second half of the eighteenth century. Even in the highest leadership positions, those of king and queen, slaves remained a significant presence.

The presence of slaves in leadership positions leads to the conclusion that in Minas Gerais slaves were able to accumulate more money to be able to pay the dues expected of the position. Also, masters accepted the brotherhoods enough to allow their slaves time to participate in the funerals, processions, and *folias* that were expected of members. Yet in contrast to the rosary brotherhood in Recife, where by the end of the eighteenth century slaves no longer filled the most important roles, in Bacalhau they continued to be an important presence in leadership positions, even in the highest positions of king and queen.

Table 1: Percentage of leadership positions by region in Arraial de Bacalhau, Guarapiranga[a]

Decade	Atlantic Islands	Brazil	Central Africa	East Africa	Unknown[b]	West Africa
1760	1.81	20.65	58.70	0.00	2.54	16.30
1770	2.48	20.92	60.28	0.71	6.03	9.57
1780	2.00	56.00	32.00	0.00	4.00	6.00
1790	0.73	51.92	38.57	0.00	1.83	6.95
1800	0.94	49.34	43.50	0.19	1.69	4.33
1810	0.00	67.02	29.34	0.21	1.07	2.36
1820	0.00	59.46	35.52	0.39	0.39	4.25
1830[c]	0.00	64.29	28.57	3.57	3.57	0.00
Total	0.90	48.16	42.09	0.25	2.13	6.48

Source: Arquivo Eclesiástico da Arquidiocese de Mariana, Y12, Livro de Termos de Meza, Irmandade de Nossa Senhora do Rosário, Arraial de Bacalhau, Freguesia de Nossa Senhora da Conceição de Guarapiranga, 1758-1893.

[a] This table represents only the 2440 leadership positions for which the African nation of the person holding the position was listed. The total number of cargo holders for the years in question was 4467.

[b] Unable to identify location of African nation listed.

[c] 1830 was the last year of the election lists, so this represents only that year, not the decade.

Men and women held positions in about equal numbers, and for almost every male position, there was a corresponding female position. Because there were dues to be paid for every position held in the brotherhood, this signifies that women participated equally in supporting the brotherhood financially, just as they did in the rosary brotherhood in Recife. In fact, women who participated in leadership positions in the brotherhoods made up part of the freed population more often than the men, mirroring the general trend in the population of Minas Gerais as a whole. Women were excluded, however, from the important positions of secretary, treasurer, and *procurador* — the administrative positions in the brotherhood. In addition, women did not sign the minutes of the meetings at which important decisions were made about the brotherhood and the church. Nevertheless, the queen was present at some of the meetings, demonstrating that women were not completely closed out of the meetings and the decision making process.[53]

The list of elections included over forty African ethnic descriptors to identify the membership. Clearly, the brotherhood served as a meeting place for a heterogeneous mix of members.[54] The ethnic composition of members over the duration of the election lists demonstrates that a gradual change occurred within that population. Table 1 demonstrates that the number of Brazilian born members increased their overall representation over the period in question. The number of Central Africans, the majority of whom identified themselves as Benguelas, Angolas, and Congos respectively, decreased. But an even greater contraction

Table 2: Slave and free Kings and Queens in the Rosary Brotherhood of Bacalhau

	Free	Slave	Grand Total
No descriptor	38	4	42
Crioulo	28	9	37
Benguela	6	6	12
Mina	5	5	10
Congo/a	1	4	5
Preto/a	4		4
Angola	1	2	3
Cabo Verde	1	1	2
Bamba	1		1
Chibante		1	1
Forro	1		1
Rebollo		1	1
Songo		1	1
Grand Total	86	34	120

Source: Arquivo Eclesiástico da Arquidiocese de Mariana, Y12, Livro de Termos de Meza, Irmandade de Nossa Senhora do Rosário, Arraial de Bacalhau, Freguesia de Nossa Senhora da Conceição de Guarapiranga, 1758-1893.

took place amongst West Africans who, never constituting a large percentage of the population, mostly identified themselves as Mina.

It was not uncommon for members to hold several different positions over the course of several years. White officers tended to hold their positions for many years — for example, Second Lieutenant João Dias Braga was the white procurator from 1816 to 1827. Free blacks also held different positions for several years, for instance Caetano Gomes de Oliveira held the position of black treasurer in 1810, 1811 and 1819, was the black secretary in 1814, and a brother of the board in 1816 and 1826. Even slaves occasionally returned several times to participate in the running of the brotherhood. Antonio Angola, the slave of Antonio Correia, served as a brother of the board in 1763, 1766, and 1769, and as judge in 1768. Women slaves also returned to serve several times, for example Felipa, the crioula slave of João Ferreira de Souza, volunteered to be a Queen *por devoção* in 1810, and was elected as a sister of the board in 1815 and 1821. Most often, however, members served for only one year. Bacalhau was not a thriving commercial port like Recife, it was simply a small *arraial* (hamlet). The high number of members participating in the brotherhoods so consistently over so many years demonstrates that brotherhoods of the rosary played as important a role in the lives of blacks and people of mixed descent in many of the smaller villages as they did in the larger towns and cities. On the other hand the rotation of positions of power in the Bacalhau rosary brotherhood does not show a movement up through a hierarchy, as the example from Recife demonstrates.

The most important positions in the brotherhood, however, that of King and Queen, never were limited to one or another ethnicity. The frequent passing of the title of king and queen in the brotherhoods has led many scholars to conclude that the role of the kings and queens in the brotherhoods was politically insignificant. In the eighteenth century, however, the black kings of Minas Gerais held such power as to prompt the vicar, Padre Leonardo de Azevedo Castro of a small town near the city of Mariana, to write a petition in 1771 to the governor of Minas Gerais complaining about the abuses of kings in the rosary brotherhoods. Padre Leonardo complained that the titles of king and queen were "indecent, abominable, and incompatible" with slavery and attached a series of documents to the complaint that, in his view, proved the bad character of the blacks. In one example, the king went to the jail to order the freedom of some prisoners. When the jailer asked for the order of the judge, the king responded that he did not care what the judge ordered, that he was the king and it was he who gave the orders. In another, the king and his retinue passed by two shoemakers who did not remove their hats nor stand up when the group passed. In response, the blacks started a brawl that the chief of police had to break up. Clearly, the kings of the brotherhoods had an understanding of their temporal, local, power as the leaders of the black population. Kings also played a part in the religious/magical complex present in the brotherhoods. Padre Leonardo complained that in his city the blacks knew that the reelected king was their true king because an oracle had foretold of it. Members of the brotherhood respected the king as a fortune-teller and people came from all over seeking his advice.[55]

The title King of Congo only appeared once in the election lists of the rosary brotherhood in Bacalhau. In 1830, a list of elected officers identified the slave José Congo as the King of Congo in the same year that they listed a black king and queen who were both *crioulos*.[56] The record points to a position called the King of Congo in this brotherhood that may have differed from the position of the black king and queen, who were elected every year. The documentation does not give enough information to draw any conclusions, but does hint that perhaps a King of Congo existed slightly beneath the surface of the official documentation of the brotherhoods in Minas Gerais, hidden from the eyes of the authorities.

A picture emerges from the documentation from Bacalhau of an organization in which differences were not organized hierarchically, but rather in which a heterogeneous population shared positions of power. The one aspect of difference that the election lists of Bacalhau do not demonstrate is a division of work according to color. In fact, the black brothers and sisters had a contentious lawsuit with the white officers and the chaplain in the late eighteenth century, which led to a halt in their record keeping for a ten-year period. From this conflict in Bacalhau, and from my examination of several *compromissos* of other mineiro rosary brotherhoods I suggest that an identity based on color, rather than ethnicity, emerges in the documentation. In the black brotherhoods of Minas Gerais, positions were prescribed by color, specifically by white or black. In addition, the brotherhoods of Minas Gerais seemed incredibly free of squabbles, and again, when disagreements broke out they were generally between people of different colors rather than between nations. The disagreements and limitations to accessing services in the brotherhoods were not only limited by the three main groups usually identified in Brazilian rhetoric over color (black, *pardo*, white), but by a surprisingly polarized black/white discourse. In the macro-societal arrangement of brotherhoods, *pardos* did form brotherhoods for themselves in the villages of Minas Gerais, perhaps in order to distance themselves from that bottom ladder rung associated with slavery. Nevertheless, the rosary brotherhood membership also included a significant number of *pardos* in their membership, some of whom were slave masters.[57]

The distribution of positions in the rosary brotherhood of Bacalhau on the whole points to an organization much less concerned with hierarchy than its cousin in Recife. Although the *compromisso* of the Bacalhau brotherhood no longer exists, the other *compromissos* still extant from Minas Gerais never define so strictly the hierarchical positions within the geography of the brotherhood meetings, processions, and funerals. Two factors help explain this difference. First, the equalizing ambience of the frontier probably affected both slaves and free blacks and peoples of mixed descent. Also, slaves came into Minas Gerais not only from Africa but also from other parts of Brazil, and Minas Gerais had a growing population of *crioulos*. These factors may have allowed national and slave/free divisions to become less important than the divisions so apparent in the dominant society, those based on differences of color. It may have also been a combination of these factors that prompted the whites of Minas Gerais to accept the black brotherhoods and their coronations to the extent that they wrote them into their municipal laws at independence, an act unique in the new Brazilian Empire.[58]

THE BROTHERHOOD OF SAINT ELESBÃO AND SAINT EPHIGENIA OF RIO DE JANEIRO

The city of Rio de Janeiro rose to importance relatively late in the colonial period. It emerged in the eighteenth century as the main port of entry for slaves going to the mining regions of Minas Gerais and further west, and as the main port for the export of minerals and gems. In 1763, Rio de Janeiro became the new capital of Brazil. During the eighteenth century, sugar production suffered from competition from the Caribbean, and the economic center of the colony shifted south, making Rio de Janeiro, with its large bay and safe harbors, the natural place for the capital. Through much of the eighteenth century, the vast majority of slaves being brought into Rio de Janeiro came from Central Africa. The city's population, however, included slaves and ex-slaves from various regions of Africa, most notably from the Bight of Benin, or Mina Coast as it came to be called in Brazil.[59]

Like the African population in the large slave importing city of Salvador, Bahia, Africans and their descendents in the city of Rio de Janeiro formed several different types of brotherhoods, divided by ethnicities.[60] The earliest of those brotherhoods, that of Our Lady of the Rosary founded before 1669, opened its membership to people of any color, status, or gender, yet like most rosary brotherhoods was a brotherhood "of the blacks".[61] Another black brotherhood, the brotherhood of Lampadosa, has become well known through Mello Moraes Filhos' account of the coronations of kings and queens in that church.[62] In that case, the coronations crowned kings and queens from Central African nations, even though *pretos minas*, or Mina (nation) blacks, had created a brotherhood of Our Lady of Lampadosa in the rosary church in the 1730s.[63] Thus, in Rio de Janeiro, rather than include all of the different ethnicities under the umbrella of a Central African hierarchy within a single rosary brotherhood, as occurred in Recife, or simply mix up the ethnicities, as occurred in Bacalhau, Minas Gerais, the West African groups formed their own brotherhoods. One of the best known of these organizations was the brotherhood of Saint Elesbão and Saint Ephigenia.

In Minas Gerais and Recife, Saint Ephigenia was often venerated in the churches of the rosary. In fact, she and Saint Benedict were the two black saints regularly presented side by side with Our Lady of the Rosary (they often were placed in the lateral altars of rosary churches). In Rio, however, the two saints of Saint Elesbão and Saint Ephigenia had their own brotherhood, run by West African slaves and free blacks. The early *compromisso* of the brotherhood, written in 1740, began with a petition and response. The official response pointed out that there were already many brotherhoods of blacks in the city, and even one of *pretos minas*. Nevertheless, the church official, D. Antônio de Guadalupe, would allow for this particular brotherhood to incorporate because they had presented a list of seventy members who wanted to start this new organization.[64]

The earliest *compromisso*, dated 27 of October, 1740, which was also the feast day of the Saints, restricted its membership to all blacks, men and women, who had been born in the Mina coast, Cabo Verde, São Tomé, or Mozambique. In some cases *pardos* would be allowed to join, and the treasurer would always be white. In no cases, however, would Angolas, *crioulos*, *cabras*, or *mestiços* be allowed to join the brotherhood. The *compromisso* listed all of the positions of the brotherhood in the traditional manner of lay religious brotherhoods. They would elect a judge, a secretary, a treasurer, a procurator, and brothers of the board. Women did not appear as holders of power in the brotherhood until chapter twenty-two, when the *compromisso* mentions the positions of female judge and sisters of the board.[65]

In 1748 the members of the brotherhood added four new chapters that allowed Angolas, *crioulos*, and the other groups that had been excluded earlier, but that at least six members of the board would have to be from the "founding" group and six from the newly admitted groups. Whites and *pardos*, who had been allowed into the brotherhood in the earlier section of the *compromisso*, could also serve but as members of the newly admitted groups. This batch of new chapters also prescribed punishments for those who did not respect the elected positions in the brotherhood as being held by "superiors". In 1764 the brotherhood members once again re-wrote the *compromisso*, probably as a result of the building of their chapel. The first chapter of the new statutes included the positions of Emperor and

Empress and of prince and princess, each to be held for three years. In addition to the Imperial court, brotherhood members would elect seven kings, specifically adding that they did not need to elect queens or princes and princesses, only the kings.[66] These new positions may have been formed in response to a growing and diversifying population as well as because of the funds those positions were thought to bring in during festivities.[67] In October of 1764, these new statutes were approved by the *provedor*, Antonio Jose Corrêa. His comments were telling of the attitudes of whites towards these new positions in the brotherhood.

> And even though the word — folias — does not sound good to our ears, because this consists of an Emperor, an Empress, Prince and Princess, Kings and Queens, in order to obtain through this means more peace and more alms for this black group . . . maybe this consolation is how they mediate their unhappiness with all the work of slavery.[68]

The *compromisso* was then sent to Lisbon and confirmed in 1767, and then re-confirmed in Rio de Janeiro in 1820.

The organization of the brotherhood under an Emperor and Empress, who then had seven kings under them, echoes a similar strategy of group organization that occurred in Recife during about the same time period. Interestingly, the *compromisso* never mentioned a king before the creation of the Imperial court, nor did it mention divisions within the group of *pretos minas* in the brotherhood. A document written in the 1760s, however, does name an early king in the brotherhood of Mina blacks. The document reviews the history of the brotherhood of Saint Elesbão and Saint Ephigenia, and was written in the style of a dialogue between Francisco Alvez de Souza, the regent of the blacks from the Kingdom of Makii on the Mina coast, and Alferes Gonçalo Cordeiro, his secretary. Souza wrote that he arrived in the capital from Bahia in 1748 and found a corporation of *pretos minas* already in existence. These blacks came from various kingdoms: Dagome, Makii, Tanno, Agolin, and Sabaru, all of whom spoke a *lingua franca*.[69] He mentions that a king, Pedro da Costa Mimoxo, then already headed the organization. After Mimoxo's death, Clemente de Proença took over the position, with the same title. In comparison to the *compromisso*, which only named elected positions, this demonstrates that the kings in the brotherhood of Saint Elesbão and Saint Ephigenia held their positions for life and passed them on upon their death.

After the death of Proença, Souza mentioned the unrest within the brotherhood between the different nations from the Costa da Mina, ending in the separation of the Makii and the selection of their own king, Captain Ignacio Gonçalves do Monte in 1762. After the death of Monte in 1783, however, there ensued a struggle between Monte's ex-wife, who proclaimed herself queen, and Souza, who asserted that Monte had passed the title to him.[70] In the dialogue, the Souza and Cordeiro tell their side of the story, and the dialogue and accompanying statutes of the congregation of *almas* (souls), can be read as a justification of Souza's rule. The statutes, never confirmed by the Portuguese authorities, were included in the dialogue. They represent the formalization of a congregation of Makii, headed by Souza, within the larger brotherhood of Saint Elesbão and Saint Ephigenia of *pretos minas*.

Table 3: Positions Named by Souza

Name	Title in the lingua franca	Title in Portuguese	Job	Other Responsibilities
Gonçalo Cordeiro			Secretary	
Jose Antonio dos Santos	Jacobû de Atoqquêm	Duque	First Counselor	First key to the safe
Alexandre de Carvalho	Eceçûm valûm	Duque	Second Counselor	Second key to the safe
Marcal Soares	Acolû Belppôn Lisoto	Duque	Third Counselor	Third key to the safe
Boaventura Fernandez Braga	Acolû cocoti de Daçâ	Duque	Second Secretary and Fourth Counselor	Inside key to the safe
Jose Luis	Ajacôto Chaûl de Zá	Marques de Tal Parte	Fifth Counselor	
Luis da Silva	Ledô	Conde	Sixth Counselor	
Luis Roiz Silva	Aggau	General	Procurador	
Jose da Silva	Aggau	General	Procurador	
Luiz de Figueredo			Vice-regent	
Antonio da Costa			Second Vice-regent	

Source: Biblioteca Nacional do Rio de Janeiro, Secção Manuscritos, "Regra ou estatutos por modo de Hûm Diálogo," 9,3,11, p. 24.[73]

Souza refused the leadership position repeatedly, until important members of the congregation sent a petition to the high court saying they wanted Souza to be their king. Finally he accepted the position, but he refused to accept the title of king. Instead, he would only call himself regent, a position he had already held for several years during the Monte's illness. The group responded with alarm, saying that they gave him the same respect as they would give their father, and it had been like that since the beginning of time. Souza replied that he wanted to prevent discord within the group, and that the elimination of the title of king allowed him to do that.[71] Once he accepted the title, Souza asked what he could do for the group. They answered in unison that he should "not take away, our positions, and names that imitate the *fidalgos* [nobles] of our Kingdom of Makii, that you use for us others to distinguish the higher from the lower nobles . . . and to have respect among ourselves."[72] Souza acceded to their demands by dividing the important positions using both Portuguese titles, titles in the *lingua franca*, as well as the jobs within the congregation and responsibilities associated with them.

Souza took possession of the position of regent, and gave his own wife the position of *regenta*, actions applauded by the assembled group of supporters. Together, the leaders wrote the statutes of the Congregation of *Almas* of the Minas Makii. Chapter ten of the statutes confirmed the regent as the highest position in the organization, and that both the regent and regenta should be treated with respect as should all of the people "with names" in the organization.

These statutes demonstrated that the organization arranged itself hierarchically along lines already established among the group — along lines of ethnicity, gender, and condition. Men who were not slaves and from the nation of Minas Makii clearly organized and planned to run the Congregation of *Almas*. They would be the only members who could be elected to official posts. Other people, except Angolas, who wanted to join could become members after first being rigorously examined by the Aggau to make sure they were not heathens and did not follow superstitions.[74] In fact, the dialogue expressed antipathy towards Angolas throughout. Souza described blacks from the Mina coast as being "proud and god-fearing" in contrast to the Angolas, who participated in heathen singing and superstitions at their own funerals, which is why the whites thought all blacks behaved badly in that manner.[75] In the manner of the dances (*folias*) that occurred on feast day celebrations, the Minas Makii would only go out and participate in the rosary festival, associated more generally with Angola and *crioulo* blacks, if the newly elected king were from the Mina CoaSaint Otherwise, they would go out only in front of the house of the viceroy and then go quietly home.[76]

The dialogue, the statutes, and the earlier *compromisso* of the brotherhood of Saint Elesbão and Saint Ephigenia demonstrate that the main way in which this group of Mina blacks divided themselves was by ethnicity. The divisions come up not only between Mina and Angola, although the greatest antipathy was reserved for this last group, but between the Makii, Sabaru, and the other groups named from the Costa da Mina. The dialogue barely mentioned condition, but the question of free/slave status showed up in the statutes of the Congregation of *Almas*. In those, the seventh chapter made provisions for the brotherhood to help captive members to buy, or finish buying, their freedom, and the eleventh chapter identified different amounts to be paid by free and captive members. Nevertheless, free and freed men clearly controlled the most powerful positions in the organization. Souza himself was *forro*, as were the important men who gathered around him who received "names".

The dialogue and its accompanying statutes also expressed a great antipathy towards women, almost to the point of misogyny. The only mention of women in the statutes, for instance, called them "proud" and "upsetters of peace and tranquility".[77] The reason for this was that the widow of the recently deceased king, Monte, had declared herself the queen of the congregation upon his death. According to Souza, this strange action occurred because a *crioulo* from Bahia had enticed her into the position — putting her again into a weakened position in that she could only have acted on the impulse of a man. Souza, Cordeiro, and the others on their side, discussed two main reasons why she could not be the queen. First of all, because the position had to be approved by an election of everyone in the congregation, she did not have the votes to win. In fact, she had only four people on her side, while 113 people had signed the petition to elect Souza. Secondly, women were not able to rule over men. Their job was to govern their own homes and to look after the souls of their dead husbands.

The protagonists used several arguments in different places in the document to back up their claim. First, they affirmed that other, already established, brotherhoods never allowed women to vote on the ruling board, nor even to be members of the ruling board because of their "sex". In fact, women really only became judges in the organizations because they could contribute money. There were also religious reasons: for instance God had named Saint Peter the head of the church, when he could have named the Virgin as head.[78] Despite her denigration in the dialogue, the woman (who was never named but only referred to as "the widow") won a case in court that allowed her to keep the safe and the other symbols of leadership, and effectively forced Souza to admit defeat. Two years after the writing of the dialogue and Souza's defeat in court, he and the others involved in the creation of the dialogue wrote another statute, this time for a brotherhood of Our Lady of Remedios, with the objective of providing alms to the poor members of their nation.[79]

The example of the brotherhood of Saint Elesbão and Saint Ephigenia, and the accompanying dialogue, demonstrate both the creation of internal hierarchies in the larger brotherhood and an offshoot, and the type of power plays that could exist within these organizations. Within the Congregation of *Almas*, the leadership created a hierarchy that bridged a traditional African form and a Portuguese form, and used both titles to "name" the important and powerful men. The dialogue described the ways in which leadership positions were handed down through generations, and the power plays that occurred when those were not clear. Through its discussion of the Angolas and the rosary brotherhood, we can better understand the relationship between black brotherhoods. It also serves as an example of how both sides of the fight used the Portuguese legal system to try to achieve their own ends. Yet the brotherhoods in Rio de Janeiro were also unique in their ethnic fragmentation and infighting. Only when put together with the studies of brotherhoods in the captaincies of Pernambuco, Minas Gerais, and other regions, can definitive conclusions about black brotherhoods in Brazil begin to be drawn.

CONCLUSION

The three examples of the internal organization of lay religious brotherhoods of blacks offer a look at the way different groups of Africans and their descendents structured their worlds. Many similarities emerge from the documentation. All of the organizations distributed positions of power hierarchically. As in many African traditions, the positions of power in all of the organizations were either elected positions, or when they were hereditary they still required the approval of a majority of the group. Souza's argument against the widow repeatedly brought up the issue that he had been selected by the people and she had not. Even the commissions of black governors in Recife, given by the Portuguese governors, often stated that the recipient had been elected by his or her own peers. Although the process of electing leaders within the brotherhoods mirrored a practice of all brotherhoods, it also echoed an African tradition where there was "an awareness by the chief that his authority derives from his people."[80] Likewise, the brotherhoods as organizations embodied both temporal and spiritual responsibilities. More than any other corporation in Brazil, the combination of the sacred and the secular rang of an African tradition as well. African leaders mediated, by means of ritual action, between society and the natural environment and between the living and the dead, and had at their disposal both tangible and unseen powers.[81] Likewise, the leaders in the black brotherhoods oversaw corporations that concerned themselves with the proper care of the dead and communication with the saints.

Rather than imagining that hierarchical relations inside the brotherhoods became a source of disunity, which at times they were, as the case of Rio de Janeiro clearly demonstrates, it may be more useful to see them as leading to a greater corporate cohesiveness within the brotherhoods of blacks. Kopytoff states that "hierarchy in relations within a group was accompanied by the corporate unity in its relations without."[82] The brotherhoods found ways to distribute power within and between groups in order to avoid discord so that the collective work of the brotherhood could be accomplished. That work involved the important spiritual and social work of the brotherhood – the care of the dead and maintenance of a relationship to ancestors, the care of the poor and the needy – and the ongoing maintenance of a relationship with the larger Brazilian society. An examination of the internal workings of the black brotherhoods can not be undertaken without the acknowledgement that black brotherhoods interacted often with other brotherhoods as well as with the political structure of Portuguese Brazil. This relationship emerges in all three of the examples analyzed above. In fact, one important function of the brotherhood was to allow Africans and their descendents to enter more fully into the life of the society in which they lived. Clearly, the internal dynamic allowed for that external relationship.

The comparison of the manifestations of brotherhoods in the different regions sheds light not only on the similarities of these organizations, but importantly on the differences as well. Again, the diverse ways in which these brotherhoods of blacks developed in the captaincies of Pernambuco, Minas Gerais, and Rio de Janeiro, point to adaptive strategies used by groups of Africans and their descendents in these disparate regions. The contrast between the brotherhood in the frontier society of Minas Gerais, with its rhetoric of difference based on color, and those in Pernambuco and Rio de Janeiro, with more ethnic divisions, stand out as exceptionally striking. Clearly, this study is preliminary and there is much more work to be done to understand more fully the variations in these organizations and how those dissimilarities and similarities relate to the particular societies in which they were embedded. Nevertheless, the study demonstrates that hierarchy and the conscious definition of difference became a transnational and transcultural strategy. Through this strategy, Africans and their descendents could recreate African social structure in order to become a viable community embedded in yet separate from Euro-Brazilian society, while simultaneously becoming a part of that society on their own terms.

ENDNOTES

1. The research for this paper was made possible by a Kenyon College Faculty Advisory Committee Grant. It was first presented at the Enslaving Connections conference, October 2000, York University, Toronto, Ontario, Canada. Thanks go to Renée Soulodre-La France and José C. Curto for their helpful comments on this paper, and to all the participants at the conference for their insightful comments and criticisms.
2. Joseph C. Miller, "Retention, Reinvention, and Remembering: Restoring Identities Through Enslavement in Africa and Under Slavery in Brazil," in José C. Curto and Paul E. Lovejoy (eds.), *Enslaving Connections: Changing Cultures of Africa and Brazil during the Era of Slavery* (Amherst NY: Prometheus/Humanity Books, 2004), pp. 90-91.
3. Sidney W. Mintz, "Africa of Latin America: An Unguarded Reflection," in Manuel Moreno Fraginals (ed.), *Africa in Latin America: Essays on History, Culture, and Socialization* trans. Leonor Blum (New York: Holmes & Meier Publishers, Inc., 1984), p. 294.
4. Igor Kopytoff, "The Internal African Frontier: The Making of African Political Culture," in Igor Kopytoff (ed.), *The African Frontier: The Reproduction of Traditional African Societies* (Bloomington: Indiana University Press, 1987), p. 35.
5. Ibid., p. 36.
6. See A. J. R. Russell-Wood's discussion of the composition of social standing in colonial Brazil in "Ambivalent Authorities: The African and Afro-Brazilian Contribution to Local Governance in Colonial Brazil," *The Americas* 57/1 (2000): 15-16.
7. João José Reis, "Identidade e Diversidade Étnicas nas Irmandades Negras no Tempo da Escravidão," *Tempo* 2/3 (1997): 13; Joseph C. Miller, "Central Africa During the Era of the Slave Trade, c. 1490s-1850s," in Linda M. Heywood (ed.), *Central Africans and Cultural Transformations in the American Diaspora* (New York: Cambridge University Press, 2001), p. 42.
8. See, for instance, Hebe Maria Mattos de Castro, *Das cores do silencio: os significados da liberdade no sudeste escravista, Brasil século XIX* (Rio de Janeiro: Arquivo Nacional, 1995), pp. 102-105.
9. See Claire Robertson, "Africa into the Americas? Slavery and Women, the Family, and the Gender Division of Labor," in David Barry Gaspar and Darlene Clark Hine (eds.), *More Than Chattel: Black Women and Slavery in the Americas* (Bloomington: Indiana University Press, 1996), pp. 9-10.
10. Ibid., p. 12.
11. Manoel S. Cardozo, "The Lay Brotherhoods of Colonial Bahia," *Catholic Historical Review* 33/1 (1947): 22-23; Caio César Boschi, *Os leigos e o poder: Irmandades leigos e política colonizadora em Minas Gerais* (São Paulo: Editora Ática, 1986); A. J. R. Russell-Wood, *Fidalgos and Philanthropists: The Santa Casa da Misericórdia of Bahia, 1550-1755* (Berkeley: University of California Press, 1968), pp. 116-145; Fritz Teixeira Salles, *Associações religiosas no ciclo do ouro* (Belo Horizonte: Universidade Federal de Minas Gerais, 1963).
12. Cardozo, "The Lay Brotherhoods," p. 23.
13. Patricia Mulvey, "The Black Lay Brotherhoods of Colonial Brazil: A History," Ph. D. dissertation, City College of New York, 1976, pp. 289-303; Mary C. Karasch, *Slave*

Life in Rio de Janeiro, 1808-1850 (Princeton: Princeton University Press, 1987), p. 84; Reis, "Identidade e Diversidade."

14. E. Valerie Smith, "The Sisterhood of Nossa Senhora Da Boa Morte and the Brotherhood of Nossa Senhora Do Rosario: African-Brazilian Cultural Adaptations to Antebellum Restrictions," *Afro-Hispanic Review* 11/1-3 (1992): 64-67. Smith identifies "sisterhoods" of Boa Morte outside of Bahia, yet offers no evidence that they were exclusively for women: I have not seen any evidence to this effect elsewhere.
15. As in the case of the rosary brotherhood in Paracatu, in the interior of Minas Gerais. This was unusual for rosary brotherhoods that usually remained very open in their membership requirements. Arquivo Público Mineiro (hereafter APM), Secção Províncial (hereafter SP) 959, *Compromisso* da Irmandade de Nossa Senhora do Rosário, que fazem os pretos livres do Arraial de São Luiz e Santa Ana Minas do Paracatu, 1782.
16. See Marcos Magalhães de Aguiar, "Vila Rica dos confrades: a sociabilidade confrarial entre negros e mulatos no século XVIII," M. A. thesis, Universidade de São Paulo, 1993.
17. Wyatt MacGaffey, *Kongo Political Culture: The Conceptual Challenge of the Particular* (Bloomington: Indiana University Press, 2000), p. 2.
18. Igor Kopytoff, "The Internal African Frontier," p. 35.
19. On this type of tradition as a pan-African one see Kwame Gyekeye, *Tradition and Modernity: Philosophical Reflections on the African Experience* (Oxford: Oxford University Press, 1997), pp. 116-118.
20. On political power deriving from both sacred and material sources, see the case of Kongo political culture in MacGaffey, *Kongo Political Culture*, pp. 2-5.
21. Gender as a category of analysis has not often been used to discuss brotherhoods, especially the white brotherhoods in which women were only present as recipients of dowries or as wives and mothers. Some work has been done on women in the black brotherhoods: Smith, "The Sisterhood of Nossa Senhora"; Mieko Nishida, "From Ethnicity to Race and Gender: Transformations of Black Lay Sodalities in Salvador, Brazil," *Journal of Social History* Winter 1998: 329-348.
22. The only Portuguese feast day celebration I know of that has royalty, in this case, is that of the Divine Holy Spirit. See Martha Abreu, *O Império do Divino: Festas religiosas e cultura popular no Rio de Janeiro, 1830-1900* (Rio de Janeiro: Nova Fronteira, 1999), pp. 33-100.
23. Gaspar Barlaeus, *Historia dos feitos recentementes Praticados durante Oito Anos no Brasil* trans. Cláudio Brandão (Rio de Janeiro: Ministério de Educação, 1940), pp. 143-144.
24. Luiz Geraldo Silva, "'Sementes da Sedição': Etnia, Revolta Escrava e Controle Social na América Portuguesa (1808-1817) *Afro-Ásia* 25-26 (2001): 14-20; Joseph C. Miller, *Way of Death: Merchant Capitalism and the Angolan Slave Trade 1730-1830* (Madison: University of Wisconsin Press, 1988), pp. 458-463; Herbert S. Klein, "A Demografia do Tráfico Atlântico de Escravos para o Brasil," *Estudos Econômicos* 17/2 (1987): 137.
25. Marcus J. M. de Carvalho, *Liberdade, rotinas e rupturas do escravismo no Recife, 1822-1850* (Recife: Editora Universitária da UFPE, 1998), pp. 74, 89, 230; Henry Koster, *Travels in Brazil* (London: Longman, Hurst, Rees, Orme, and Brown, 1816), pp. 385-399.

26. See Mulvey, "The Black Brotherhoods," p. 289; Silva, "'Sementes da Sedição,'" p. 21; Marcelo MacCord, "O Rosário dos Homens Pretos de Santo Antônio: Alianças e Conflitos na História social do Recife, 1848-1872," M. A. thesis, Universidade Estadual de São Paulo, UNICAMP, 2001), p. 50.
27. "Manuscritos da Igreja de Nossa Senhora do Rosario dos Homens Pretos do Recife," *Arquivos* (ed. Diretoria de Documentação e Cultura, Prefeitura Municipal, Recife) 1-2 (1945-1951): 53-89.
28. Universidade Federal de Pernambuco, Divisão de Pesquisa Histórica; Arquivo Histórico Ultramarino (Lisbon), Pernambuco, Códice [Codex] 1293, "*Compromisso* da Irmandade de Nossa Senhora do Rozario dos homens pretos erigida nesta Villa de Santo Antonio do Recife (1782)," Capítulo [Chapter] 9.
29. Ibid., Capítulo 10.
30. Ibid., Capítulo 23.
31. A similar type of re-orientation occurred in the black brotherhoods in Minas Gerais in the late colonial period. See Elizabeth W. Kiddy, "Ethnic and Racial Identity in the Brotherhoods of the Rosary of Minas Gerais, 1700-1830," *The Americas* 56/2 (1999): 221-252.
32. "*Compromisso* da Irmandade de Nossa Senhora do Rozario dos homens pretos erigida nesta Villa de Santo Antonio do Recife (1782)," capítulo 28.
33. Arquivo Público do Estado de Pernambuco (hereafter APEPE), Patentes Provinciais (hereafter Pp) 02, Simião da Rocha, Governador dos pretos de Nação Dagome, 3 February 1776, fl. 114v. Silva, "'Sementes da Sedição'," also discusses the importance of these commissions. All of the groups listed above were from the Mina Coast — for an explanation see Pierre Verger, *Fluxo e refluxo do tráfico de escravos entre o Golfo de Benin e a Bahia de Todos os Santos dos séculos XVIII ao XIX* (São Paulo: Currupio, 1987).
34. APEPE, Pp 02, O Preto Bernardo Pereira, Governador da nação da costa denominada de Sabaru, 3 April 1776, fls. 129-129v; and ibid., Ventura de Souza Graces, Governador dos pretos Ardas da Costa da Mina, 7 April 1776, fl. 133v.
35. APEPE, Pp 07, O Preto Narciso Correa de Castro, Governador da Nação das Ardas do Botão da Costa da Mina, 10 May 1791, fl. 10.
36. Documents from the rosary brotherhood, starting in 1674, published in "Manuscritos da Igreja de Nossa Senhora do Rosario dos Homens Pretos do Recife," pp. 53-120.
37. "*Compromisso* da Irmandade de Nossa Senhora do Rozario dos homens pretos erigida nesta Villa de Santo Antonio do Recife (1782)," Capítulo 28.
38. The *cantos* were groups of "incidental workers", divided into ethnic groups that hung about the commercial districts and docks of Bahia: Kim D. Butler, *Freedoms Given, Freedoms Won: Afro-Brazilians in Post-Abolition São Paulo and Salvador* (New Brunswick, NJ: Rutgers University Press, 1998), pp. 137-138; João José Reis, "'The Revolution of the *Ganhadores*': Urban Labour, Ethnicity and the African Strike of 1857 in Bahia, Brazil," *Journal of Latin American Studies* 29 (1997): 355-393. The *cantos* are also the subject of the chapter by João José Reis in this collection.
39. APEPE, Pp 03, Feliciano Gomes dos Santos, Governador dos pretos ganhadores desta praça, 14 November 1778, fl. 158.
40. APEPE, Pp 06, Bernarda Eugenia de Souza, Governadora das pretas boceteiras e comerciantes, 30 June 1788, fl. 75v.

41. APEPE, Pp11, Josefa Lagos, Governadora das pombeiras da repartamento de fora de Portas, 12 November 1802, fl. 279; APEPE, Pp12, Reynalda Pinta de Carvalho, Governadora das Pretas Pombeiras do Recife, 1 October 1802, fl. 38.
42. The titles of *provedor* and *juiz de fora* are difficult to translate in this context. In the state hierarchy, the *provedor* was a crown official who oversaw brotherhoods, endowments, and testaments, while the *juiz de fora* was a crown appointed judge from outside of the jurisdiction. In the context presented here they were titles adopted by the weeders themselves to represent certain levels of the hierarchy within their organization.
43. José Antonio Gonçalves de Mello, "Aditamentos e correções," in F. A. Pereira da Costa (ed.), *Anais Pernambucanos* 10 vols. Recife: Fundarpe, 1983-1985.
44. See Marcus Carvalho, *Liberdade*, p. 36.
45. APEPE, Ofícios do Governo 15, Caetano Pinto de Miranda Montenegro to Desembargador Ouvidor Geral Antonio Carlos Ribeiro de Andrada, 24 December 1815, fls. 160-161.
46. Ibid.
47. See Kathleen J. Higgins, *"Licentious Liberty" in a Brazilian Gold-mining Region: Slavery, Gender, and Social Control in Eighteenth-Century Sabará, Minas Gerais* (University Park, PA: Pennsylvania State Press, 1999), pp. 66-88.
48. Laird W. Bergad, *Slavery and the Demographic and Economic History of Minas Gerais, Brazil, 1720-1888* (Cambridge: Cambridge University Press, 1999), pp. 123-159.
49. Arquivo Eclesiástico da Arquidiocese de Mariana (hereafter AEAM), P28, Assentos de Irmãos, Irmandade de Nossa Senhora do Rosário, 1750-1886, Mariana.
50. Kiddy, "Ethnic and Racial Identity," pp. 221-252.
51. There was a ten-year period from 1778-1789 during which the elections were not listed due to a conflict within the brotherhood.
52. AEAM, Y12, Livro de Termos de Meza, Irmandade de Nossa Senhora do Rosário, Arraial de Bacalhau, Freguesia de Nossa Senhora da Conceição de Guarapiranga, 1758-1893.
53. Ibid.
54. For more detailed information on the numbers of the brotherhood, see Kiddy, "Ethnic and Racial Identity," pp. 241-243.
55. Cited in Gilberto Freyre, *Sobrados e mucambos, decadência do patriarcado rural e desenvolvimento do urbano* 5th ed. (Rio de Janeiro: Livraria José Olympio Editora, 1977), II, pp. 412-415. See also Elizabeth W. Kiddy, "Who is the King of Congo? A New Look at African and African-Brazilian Kings in Brazil," in Heywood, *Central Africans and Cultural Transformations*, pp. 153-182.
56. AEAM, Y12, Livro de Termos de Meza, Irmandade de Nossa Senhora do Rosário, Arraial de Bacalhau, Freguesia de Nossa Senhora da Conceição de Guarapiranga, 1758-1893.
57. This finding is based on preliminary results from cross-checking brotherhood lists and the census of 1831 in Minas Gerais. Many of the members not listed in brotherhood documents by color were identified as *pardo* in the census: database of the 1831 Minas Gerais census, compiled and organized by the Centro de Desenvolvimento

e Planejamento Regional (CEDEPLAR), Faculdade de Ciências Econômicas, Universidade Federal de Minas Gerais.

58. AEAM, 0158, Dom Frei José da Santíssima Trindade, 1823 02-2-034, "Postura das Câmaras Municipais da Província de Minas Gerais confirmadoas pelo Conselho Geral da mesma Província," Capítulo 2, Artigo [Article] 137.
59. See Klein, "A Demografia," pp. 135-136.
60. See Mariza de Carvalho Soares, *Os Devotos da Cor: Identidade étnica, religiosidade e escravidão no Rio de Janeiro, século XVIII* (Rio de Janeiro: Civilização Brasileira, 2000), pp. 98-99; Karasch, *Slave Life*, p. 84.
61. Joaquim José da Costa, *Breve noticia da Irmandade de Nossa Senhora do Rosario e S. Benedicto dos Homens Pretos da Cidade do Rio Capital do Imperio do Brasil* (Rio de Janeiro: Typ. Economica de Jacintho J. Fonte, 1886), pp. 75-78.
62. Alexandre José de Mello Moraes Filho, *Festas e tradições populares do Brasil,* rev. and ed. Luís da Câmara Cascudo (Rio de Janeiro: Tecnoprint Gráfica S.A., 1967), pp. 396-400.
63. Soares, *Os Devotos da Cor*, p. 99.
64. Arquivo Nacional do Rio de Janeiro, SDE/Diversos Códices, NP, Códice 670. Estatutos da Irmandade de Sto. Elesbão e Sta. Effigenia, 1836. See also the analysis of this *compromisso* in Soares, *Os Devotos da Cor*, pp. 138-155.
65. Estatutos da Irmandade de Sto. Elesbão e Sta. Effigenia, 1836, Capítulos 10, 22.
66. Ibid.
67. See Soares, *Os Devotos da Cor*, pp. 148-149.
68. Estatutos da Irmandade de Sto. Elesbão e Sta. Effigenia, 1836, proviso.
69. Biblioteca Nacional do Rio de Janeiro, Secção dos Manuscritos, 9,3,11, "Regra ou estatutos por modo de Hûm Diálogo," p. 22. Although the dialogue does not specifically mention the brotherhood of Saint Elesbão and Saint Ephigenia, there are several references in the document, including meetings in the *consistório* (meeting room behind the sanctuary) of the church of those saints, which point to a connection.
70. Ibid., p. 13; Souza, *Os Devotos da Cor*, pp. 166-167.
71. "Regra ou estatutos por modo de Hûm Diálogo," p. 17.
72. Ibid., p. 22.
73. See also Soares, *Os Devotos da Cor*, pp. 169-170. Our readings of the orthography of the names are slightly different.
74. "Regra ou estatutos por modo de Hûm Diálogo," p. 31.
75. Ibid., pp. 7, 21.
76. Ibid., pp. 35, 43.
77. Ibid., p. 34.
78. Ibid., pp. 39-41.
79. Soares, *Os Devotos da Cor*, pp. 172-173.
80. Gyekye, *Tradition and Modernity*, p. 117.
81. See MacGaffey, *Kongo Political Culture*, p. 216.
82. Kopytoff, "The Internal African Frontier," p. 37.

Plate 7: Collection of Alms for the Maintenance of the Church of the Rosary (Brazil)

Source: Jean Baptiste Debret, *Viagem Pitoresca e Historica ao Brasil* trans. Sergio Milliet (São Paulo: Livraria Martins, 1940 [1834-1839]), III, p.223, Plate 30.

Plate 8: Festival of Our Lady of the Rosary (Brazil)

Source: João Mauricio Rugendas, *Viagem Pitoresca Através do Brasil* (Rio de Janeiro/São Paulo/Brasilia: A Casa do Livro, 1972 [1835]), plates unpaginated.

Plate 9: Map, Brazil

Source: Composite by Elizabeth W. Kiddy and Stephen Mech.

5

African Responses to the End of the International Slave Trade and Abolitionist Initiatives in Bahia, Brazil, 1850-1865

Dale T. Graden

In a sweeping study of the Americas at the middle of the nineteenth century, James Dunkerley writes that "whatever the subsequent interpretation by historians [with regards to the ending of the international slave trade to Brazil in 1850-51] the local economic incentives for ending the trade seemed to be growing, and they were certainly sharpened by the activity of the British warships." If the academic debate around this now seems obscure and abstruse, this is probably because "in stark contrast to the experience in the USA most of these developments took place at a great geographical distance, had few deep material roots in most sectors of civil society, and never came to the point of violent crisis."[2] This interpretation fails to include perhaps the most important variable of all in analyzing this critical historical juncture: the actions of African slaves and former slaves at various Brazilian ports. This chapter examines African responses to the ending of the slave trade in the North Eastern Brazilian province of Bahia and to abolitionist discourse that surfaced during the next fifteen years (up to 1865 when Brazil declared war on Paraguay).

THE CULMINATION OF THE SLAVE TRADE TO BRAZIL IN THE NINETEENTH CENTURY

Sailing ships carried over 4.5 million slaves to Brazil over the course of more than three centuries (1520s-1850s). During the first half of the nineteenth century, slave imports reached some of their highest annual and decadal levels. Various factors contributed to the upsurge of slave imports into Brazil. With the disappearance of sugar and coffee plantations from the French Caribbean island of St. Domingue after the Haitian Revolution (1791-1804), sugar and coffee planters in Brazil sought to supply international markets with output from their estates. Working conditions on plantations were harsh; free persons had little interest in such employment. To attain high levels of production, planters remained dependent on enslaved laborers. In Bahia, a region of expanding sugar output, slave imports reached their pinnacle in the 1820s and the 1840s. To satisfy demand for workers on the expanding coffee estates south of Bahia, ships disembarked slaves in unprecedented numbers. David Eltis has concluded that between "1821 and 1850

Table I: Volume of Imports of Slaves into Brazil, 1751-1867 (in thousands)

1751-1775	431.7
1776-1800	570.5
1801-1825	803.2
1826-1850	961.4
1851-1867	6.9

Source: David Eltis, "The Volume and Structure of the Transatlantic Slave Trade: A Reassessment," *William and Mary Quarterly* 60 (2001): 17-46.

more slaves arrived on a four-hundred-mile stretch of coast around Rio de Janeiro than in the rest of the Americas put together."[3]

Another reason for the upsurge in slave imports at this juncture can be traced to investor responses to suppression efforts by the British government. Treaties between Great Britain and Portugal (in 1815 and 1817), as well as a treaty between Great Britain and Brazil in 1826 (following Brazilian independence in 1822), placed legal restrictions on slave traders. Ratification of the latter treaty by the British Parliament (in 1827) stipulated that the slave trade to Brazil would become illegal three years later. A law passed in November 1831 by the Brazilian government confirmed the illegality of importing slaves into Brazil. It stipulated that any slave entering Brazil henceforth would be free and provided police the right to examine ships suspected of involvement in the trade. One article included in the 1831 law affirmed that African slaves could appeal to judges if they believed themselves to have been illegally transported to Brazil. With inadequate enforcement, however, and with a multitude of planters willing to pay large sums for African slaves to cultivate export crops, the 1826/27 treaty and the 1831 law proved inconsequential. In 1845, the British Parliament passed the Aberdeen Act, which allowed British cruisers to seize Brazilian slave ships wherever they were encountered. This act demonstrated the continued determination of a small group of British politicians to halt the slave trade to Brazil. But such initiatives only encouraged the major participants in the slave trade (Brazilian, Portuguese, British, and U.S. citizens) to transport as many slaves as possible to Brazil, in case such suppression efforts succeeded.[4]

The continuous arrival of thousands of African slaves into Brazilian ports and along more remote beaches to avoid detection meant that many cities and towns included large numbers of African and Afro-Brazilian inhabitants. João J. Reis has described the largest cities of Brazil at this juncture as "little Africas".[5] By 1835, for example, there were 27,500 slaves within an overall population of 65,500 in Salvador, Bahia's major port, constituting 42 percent of the total. Reis has further noted that, in the early nineteenth century, "most slaves were foreigners."[6] Indeed, the mid-1830 captive population of Salvador included no less than 17,325 African-born slaves, representing nearly two-thirds of the enslaved inhabitants. With the number of Brazilians of color, either free or manumitted, combined with freed

Table II: Volume of Imports of Slaves into three locales in the Americas (in thousands)

	1801-1825	1826-1850	1851-1867
British mainland			
North America	73.1	-----	0.3
Spanish Caribbean	268.7	297.0	152.6
Bahia	182.0	146.5	1.9

Source: David Eltis, "The Volume and Structure of the Transatlantic Slave Trade: A Reassessment," *William and Mary Quarterly* 60 (2001): 17-46.

Africans, totaling about 19,500, the white inhabitants of Salvador constituted but a minority (28.8 percent) of the city's inhabitants. Writing of Salvador in 1858, the German traveler Robert Avé-Lallemant observed that:

> if you did not know you were in Brazil, you would think, without much imagining, that you were in an African capital, the home of a powerful Negro Prince, in which the population of pure white foreigners passed completely unnoticed. Everything appears Negro: Negroes on the beach, Negroes in the city, Negroes in the lower part [of the city, near the port], Negroes in the upper barrios.[7]

A similar pattern emerged in the city of Rio de Janeiro, where slaves constituted an estimated 38.3 percent of the population by 1849. The presence of nearly 80,000 slaves made Rio de Janeiro the city with the largest slave population in the Americas. Mary Karasch estimates that African-born slaves numbered 52,341, or more than 65 percent of the slave population of Brazil's capital.[8] Significant numbers of slaves, both African-born and creole (born in the Americas) also resided in other coastal towns, including São Luis (Maranhão Province), Belém (Pará), Fortaleza (Ceará), Recife (Pernambuco), Maceió (Alagoas), Vitória (Espírito Santo), the city of São Paulo, and Santos (on the coast of São Paulo province).[9]

Africans of diverse ethnic backgrounds and Brazilian-born slaves profoundly influenced both urban and rural society in Brazil from the sixteenth to the nineteenth centuries. Slaves provided urban transport by carrying goods on their shoulders, unloaded large ships and sailed smaller vessels in the harbors, and served owners as domestic laborers in urban households. Slaves educated their own children and often raised the offspring of whites, provided architectural and construction skills, cultivated food on small plots both in cities and the countryside, and contributed to the creation of a rich popular culture. Still, the majority of the African and creole slaves across the Americas ended up enduring the harsh conditions of the plantations. Slaves played a key role in providing the labor and expertise that enabled owners to produce and export large quantities of agricultural commodities for a profit. Therefore, during the years of upsurge in the first half of the nineteenth century, rural planters joined the merchant elite in paying close attention to the slave trade. Wanting to get rich, they facilitated all aspects of the slave trade between Africa and Brazil. But, in the process, they also saw their concerns over personal and public security mount appreciably.

The rebelliousness of African-born slaves had been demonstrated repeatedly. In Bahia, more than twenty rural and urban slave revolts between 1807 and 1835 left slave owners distraught. In 1835, African slaves led the Revolt of the *Malês* (Muslims) in Salvador, the largest urban slave revolt in the history of the Americas.[10] By the 1830s, social instability caused by economic depression, slave revolts and violence, slave flight, the existence of *quilombos* (communities of escaped slaves), and repression by light-skinned elites characterized Brazil's two largest cities (Salvador and Rio de Janeiro) and their hinterlands. Other provinces in the Brazilian Empire (the term used to describe the vast nation of Brazil ruled over by the emperor Pedro II), such as Pará, Rio Grande do Sul, and Maranhão also witnessed violent outbreaks. Inspired by dissatisfaction with imperial policies, these latter provincial upheavals involved rebels from a wide range of class and color backgrounds including whites, free blacks, *mulattos* (offspring of African women and white men), *mestiços* (persons of mixed ancestry), Indians, and in some instances slaves. In the northern city of Belém, Pará, mestizo and Indian "bandits" attacked and destroyed the homes of foreigners residing in the city. The President of Pará lamented that "in every place where white or rich persons might be killed or robbed, there appeared immediately those who willingly carried out this service."[11] Such a state of insurgency has been described as "the most radical and violent rebellions in Brazilian history, before or since."[12]

The maintenance of social cohesion in the empire became an issue of paramount importance. Debates ensued over how to control rebellious slaves and what lay in store for a nation that included so many Africans and creole blacks among its inhabitants. A few intellectuals suggested ways to attract free European colonists to settle in Brazil. Even naïve observers recognized that an expanding slave trade could have dangerous consequences for the future. In particular, Brazilians asked whether or not their nation might succumb to an African-led revolt similar to what had occurred in the Haitian Revolution or face other urban revolts as had occurred in Salvador. Owners of sugar estates in the interior of Bahia asserted that knowledge of the Haitian Revolution had been passed through the port of Salvador.[13]

The presence of large numbers of recently arrived African slaves, alongside African and creole slaves with years of residence, made Bahia, and particularly Salvador, a volatile and tense environment by the late 1840s.[14] In June 1849, a British envoy summed up the situation: The Rio Janeiro slave market is glutted; "indeed it is impossible to approach this capital in any direction without meeting troops of Bozal negroes [slaves recently arrived from Africa]. They are landed openly and no measures whatever are taken by any Brazilian authority to repress the traffic. At Bahia the public sale of slaves, which was prohibited, is again in full operation and the depots are overflowing with newly-imported Negroes."[15]

AFRICAN RESPONSES TO THE ENDING OF THE INTERNATIONAL SLAVE TRADE

With the appointment of Rear-Admiral Barrington Reynolds to command Great Britain's South America squadron in October 1849, efforts to suppress the slave trade to Brazil reached a fever pitch. Moving its base of operation from Montevideo to Rio de Janeiro, the squadron carried out attacks on slaving vessels returning from Africa and departing from Brazilian ports. Partly as a result of this intensification of policy, Brazil's Foreign Minister, Paulino José Soares de Sousa, helped pass an anti-slave trade bill in the Council of State and Council of Deputies in July 1850. On September 4, it became law.[16] For African slaves in Salvador, the most visible manifestation of this major shift in British and Brazilian official policy from late 1849 was the interception of slave ships along the Bahian coast and the appearance of British cruisers in the port of Salvador.

In response to the changed political milieu, it would appear that a group of African slaves planned to revolt in early 1850. Not surprisingly, documents from the period allude to the Revolt of the *Malês* fifteen years before. The chief of police wrote:

> In January of 1850, everyone was aware of rumors of a slave insurrection that would occur in the near future. The police became convinced that one group of Africans had been conspiring, and that the main leader was a black African freedman named Lucio Jeronimo da Costa. There were arrests and searches of houses, and in some of those houses the police found iron harpoons, secret books (*livros cabalisticos*), and clothes similar to those worn in earlier insurrections. This negro Lucio had wealth and practiced a form of idolatry similar to all of the negroes, who without doubt sought to repeat the bloody scenes of 1835.[17]

To ensure that Lucio did not succeed in his plans, the police deported him to Africa in July 1850 on board the US slave ship *Bridgeton*, along with an African freedwoman named Felicidade.[18] In the months that followed, police deported many Africans, while temporary arrests of African slaves, freed persons and *africanos livres* (liberated African slaves seized from slave ships in the mid-1800s who were landed in Brazil)[19] became commonplace.

To lessen the potential of another African-led revolt, authorities focused on the port of Salvador. In 1850, the provincial government of Bahia passed legislation that prohibited some 1,000 African slaves and African freedpersons (described as *africanos livres*) from working on the small boats in the harbor of Salvador. Portrayed as an enlightened act, officials in fact sought to disband what they considered to be a disruptive and dangerous group of African sailors. Although we know little about the Africans forced out of their jobs, they certainly possessed impressive knowledge about conditions in the bay and throughout the city of Salvador. They understood well the transatlantic slave trade and the way in which traffickers carried out their business in Bahia. These Africans had seen or knew of the landing of thousands of African slaves along the Bahian coast. They witnessed first hand the actions of the British squadron along the coast, and the arrival of liberated Africans taken from slaving vessels into the city. Some had lived through the Revolt of the *Malês* in 1835 and various manifestations of individual and group slave resistance in the 1840s. Clearly cognizant of their hold over the port, these African slaves fought with free workers on several occasions in the late 1840s. In the words of one observer, extirpating the African sailors from the port had extinguished the "terrible nucleus of slave insurrections."[20]

Concern over a potential slave uprising rose dramatically again in late 1855. During the cholera epidemic of 1855-56, some 30,000 slaves died in the Bahian Recôncavo, the area surrounding the Bay of all Saints, where Salvador was (and still is) located. In spite of these huge losses, officials believed that slaves were planning yet another a revolt. In October 1855, investigators found guns and loaded cartridges in the town of Cachoeira. Inhabitants in the region claimed that "a revolution was being planned before it was aborted by the appearance of the cholera morbus [the epidemic of the previous July]."[21] As had been common since the slave revolts in Bahia from the first decade of the nineteenth century, police in Salvador reacted to aroused suspicions in the nearby Recôncavo. In November 1855, the chief of police requested that searches be carried out of the houses of African freed persons and slaves who lived independently from their owners in Salvador. Although nothing was found that might be used or related to a possible insurrection, officials arrested several Africans in whose homes were found "superstitious objects."[22]

To ensure that slaves did not disturb the peace or create any problems, police and the provincial government implemented harsh policies of intimidation and retribution. In early 1858, Salvador faced a "catastrophic situation" due to a lack of food caused by drought in the interior of Bahia.[23] The cost of basic necessities such as meat and manioc flour rose dramatically. The municipal government attempted to control the sale of these items at specific locations throughout Salvador. Infuriated by incompetent bureaucrats and the knowledge that food had been exported out of the province, a multitude of "people of the low class" congregated in front of the palace of the president in the afternoon of February 28. Military troops and police violently forced the protesters to disperse.[24]

Numerous slaves participated in this manifestation, judging by the way that African and creole slaves bore the brunt of the reprisals that followed. On March 2, police "conveniently whipped" twelve slaves, "some of whom had been part of this popular uprising." Another eight arrests followed on March 5 and several more during that month of March. The arrests and beatings reflected at least two central concerns of Bahian authorities. They wanted to make sure that slaves understood the harsh penalties they would face if they appeared in public protests. The police also sought to impede any sort of organizing between slaves residing in Salvador and lower-class free persons. Such an alliance might pose a threat to the provincial elite, which Katia Mattoso has characterized as united and well organized.[25] Not surprisingly, police focused their investigations on *Candomblé* (religious institution, sacred place, religious community and its rituals, created by Africans in Brazil, largely Yuroba in origin) during the months that followed, since these appeared as a focal point of African subversion. Such houses attracted persons of different classes and color, including slaves, former slaves, free persons, blacks, persons of mixed ancestry, and whites. Members of *Candomblé* acted in ways that challenged the interests of slave owners. This included hiding fugitive slaves who had fled from owners in Salvador, the interior of Bahia, and other provinces. Other forms of support included the creation of a sense of community and succor for persons in need. For the ruling male elite of Salvador, *Candomblé* posed a dilemma in that it flourished outside of its control. *Candomblé* represented to its enemies a place where Africans plotted how to undermine and end the slave regime.

Candomblé caused a furor among many of the free population of Salvador. Police intervened at *Candomblé* ceremonies on five occasions during the twelve months after April 1858. This number of "invasions" exceeded those carried out during any twelve-month period since the appearance of daily police records in Salvador in 1842.[26] In descriptions of their encounters with houses of *Candomblé*, officials noted the exact number of persons arrested and their status. They often depicted in detail the instruments and clothes used by the participants. On August 2, 1858, for example, police arrived at a house owned by an African in the parish of *Rio Vermelho* (Red River). There they arrested three mulattos (males), two mulattas (females), five female creoles, seven female Africans and the African male owner for "carrying out dances and *batuques* (African drumming associated with dance celebrations), what is vulgarly known as candonblé [sic]." The police removed "diverse objects and clothes used in the dances" from the house.[27] On October 29, 1858, police surrounded a house on *Rua do Paço* (Palace Road). To their amazement they encountered "more than sixty persons, among them mulattos and creoles, African freed persons and liberated Africans, and slaves of both sexes, engaged in *batuques* and prohibited dances."[28] The president of the province demanded that police destroy these houses of *Candomblé*. Such a reaction reflected elite insecurity in the face of organized gatherings and abolitionist expression.

Several well-publicized actions carried out by Bahian officials after mid-century reflected concern over the beginnings of a formal abolitionist movement. An abolitionist society coalesced at the Faculty of Medicine in 1850. Since these students did not invite slaves to participate, the president of Bahia judged it acceptable.[29] During the 1850s, the provincial government annually celebrated the November 1850 law that ousted African slaves from their small boats in the harbor in favor of free Bahians as an enlightened, abolitionist act. In December 1857, the police captured with great fanfare captain D. Benito Derezans of the slave ship *Relampago* (intercepted off the Bahian coast in 1851). Taken into custody for illegal slave trading, Derezans had been on the run from police for more than five years. Police also arrested owners accused of beating their slaves.[30] Such acts assuaged the conscience of elite Bahians and placated international criticism.

AFRICAN PROTESTS

Africans residing on the island of Itaparica, situated in the Bay of All Saints, within view of Salvador, created lots of disturbances during the 1860s. In December 1864, twenty six African slaves walked off the estate owned by Ignacio Dias de Andrade. Showing up before local police officials, they demanded an end to bad treatment. Such a dramatic initiative by a group of African slaves had few precedents. The police report did not mention the involvement of outside agitators or sympathetic abolitionists.[31] Nor do we know exactly what ensued. Nevertheless, such an act demonstrates clearly African slaves reacting to abusive owners and probing how best to use the legal system to improve their living conditions and ultimately end their enslavement. African and creole slaves paid close attention to such events and emulated this example. Escapes by groups of African slaves and groups of creole slaves occurred with frequency in the years that followed.

Similar departures occurred in other provinces. In the interior of São Paulo a year later, slaves assassinated the administrator (or manager) of an estate. A group of 31 slaves then traveled to the city of São Paulo and appeared before a judge. They acknowledged their guilt in carrying out the crime. Likewise, in March 1866, slaves killed an administrator on another Paulista estate and then presented themselves to the authorities.[32] Alienated by constant abuse, the slaves believed appeals to the police and courts their best hope to defend themselves from further bad treatment. Reflecting on these episodes, President Toledo of São Paulo wrote that he considered the potential for a slave insurrection minimal due to the severe punishments carried out by owners after the police returned the slaves. Nevertheless, he did raise questions about the availability and effectiveness of weapons used by National Guard troops and the provisional police corps in the city of São Paulo to deal with criminal elements and slaves who fled into the forests.[33]

African freed persons, estimated at some 2,500 persons in Salvador in 1848, continued to provoke Bahian authorities during the early 1860s in spite of their small number. It would appear that most African freed persons acted conservatively due to their precarious status; the threat of deportation as one form of elite coercion remained prevalent during these years. Yet, freed persons obviously did not hesitate to create disturbances and fuel discontent among slaves. In May 1862, the well-known businessman Joaquim Pereira Marinho requested that the police deport the African freedman Bendito Marinho. Formerly the owner of Bendito, Joaquim Marinho claimed that the African had become "incorrigible" and "always incited peaceful slaves to act against the interests of owners." He accused the African of organizing a thieving ring in the port composed of African freed persons and slaves. Masters inflicted harsh retribution on those slaves believed to be involved. Some were unable to return to work due to the severity of their injuries. Joaquim Marinho accused Bendito of having raised the money to purchase his freedom from the sale of stolen goods. After investigating the case, the chief of police joined with Marinho in denouncing the African. He requested that Bendito be deported, a necessary penalty for a freedman who had "planted the germ of insubordination among the slaves."[34]

In January 1865, police in Salvador arrested eighteen Africans during one sweep. This group included nine freedmen and five freedwomen, along with three male slaves and one female slave. The police report includes the Brazilianized names of each of the Africans, including Feliciano Martins Torres, Maria Rosa Perpetua Paraíso (Mary Rose Eternal Paradise) and Izabel Maria dos Santos. The record does not tell us how long these Africans remained in jail or what happened after. Nor do we know if these Africans actually had been planning a revolt in Salvador.[35] What the document does demonstrate is continued widespread distrust of African freed persons and fears that they might join with African slaves in an insurgency. As at mid-century, external threats contributed to a hardening of internal policy and increasing repression directed at Africans.

In the 1860s, protests to provincial authorities by liberated Africans mounted. Several liberated Africans appeared before the police to demand full liberty based on the November 1831 law that made free all Africans brought to Brazil after that date. In June 1864, the liberated African Samuel argued that he had been "under the tutelage" of the provincial government and therefore should be granted legal papers assuring his freedom.[36] Another liberated African known as Ismael, cited in the police documents as free African number 235, complained about poor treatment by his employer (meaning his master), the Baron of São Lourenço (Francisco Martins, former chief of police and president of the province).[37] Such accusations shed a bad light on politicians who sought to portray themselves as progressive leaders.

The provincial government and private owners considered it offensive that liberated Africans challenged their dependent status and poverty. Police carried out arrests of liberated Africans "for correction". They pointed to the "dangerous" participation of free Africans at *Candomblé* festivities. One official complained that "in general all of the liberated Africans in this province comport themselves poorly. Each extra day that they remain here their presence poisons our nation."[38] He requested that the imperial government deport all of the liberated Africans back to their African homelands.

Despite such opinions, Pedro II freed all the liberated Africans in Brazil in September 1864 by imperial decree. Not surprisingly, Bahian owners were slow in providing official emancipation cards to liberated Africans under their direction. As a result, many liberated Africans were forced to escape from the private homes where they resided. Other liberated Africans in Bahia failed to receive news about their legal emancipation and remained under the control of individuals for years after. Given that the British had made emancipation of the liberated Africans a diplomatic issue with Brazil's imperial government from May 1862, historians have focused on external pressures as the determining factor that caused this outcome.[39] Such an interpretation overlooks the many initiatives of liberated Africans themselves in protesting their despicable treatment and tenuous status.

CONCLUSION

Most Africans residing in Bahia communicated orally rather than in print. Therefore, police and court records offer small glimpses of African perspectives at mid-century in Salvador and other locales of the province, shedding light on individual leaders and diverse strategies. African and creole slaves shared information among themselves in Salvador and in the interior of the province. They gained a clear sense of which tactics worked and which did not. Africans recognized the benefits to be gained from organized confrontations, such as urban strikes.[40] They also understood well the potential benefits to be gained from other manifestations of resistance. By the early 1860s, the appearance of groups of African and creole slaves at the offices of police officials and judges presented questions not quickly resolved. *Candomblé* ceremonies became important locales to share information and discuss strategies. The diverse expressions of African resistance had a profound impact upon the Bahian elite. The latter reacted with violence and scorn to organized protests and legal challenges posed by Africans during these years. Abolitionist rhetoric espoused by Bahian officials from 1850 to 1865 sought to placate critics and stifle African dissent.

James Dunkerley's *Americana* disregards the internal dynamics of Brazil's "African cities" at mid-century. Perhaps one can agree that the "developments" in 1850-51 "had few deep material roots in most sectors of civil society." But such developments did have a profound impact on the African sector of Bahian society. Furthermore, the proposition that most of these developments "never came to the point of a violent crisis" merits closer scrutiny. The harsh and myriad forms of repression implemented by provincial and imperial authorities from 1848 to 1851 would support the view that the situation had in fact reached a crisis, with high potential for violence.[41]

The actions of Africans in Salvador made the continuation of the slave trade a most dangerous proposition. African slaves and freed persons long resident in Salvador remembered well at this juncture the Revolt of the *Malês*. Newly arrived Africans learned of that revolt and observed personally the interceptions of slaving voyages by the British squadron. Abolitionist activists in the 1850s encouraged a wide expression of resistance to enslavement of Africans and Afro-Brazilians. African slaves and freed persons along with liberated Africans played an integral role in what can be considered as the first phase of the abolitionist movement in Brazil.

ENDNOTES

1. My thanks to the Fulbright Commission of Brazil and the University of Idaho Research Office for financial support the for research in Brazil in 1999-2000 upon which this chapter is partially based and the Department of History, the University of Idaho, for travel expenses related to the dissemination of the results. Thanks to José C. Curto for editorial assistance. This chapter is part of my forthcoming book *From*

Slavery to Freedom in Brazil: Bahia, 1835-1900 (Albuquerque: University of New Mexico Press).

2. James Dunkerley, *Americana: The Americas in the World, Around 1850 (Or "Seeing the Elephant" as the Theme for an Imaginary Western)* (London: Verso, 2000), pp. 433, 435.
3. David Eltis, *Economic Growth and the Ending of the Transatlantic Slave Trade* (New York: Oxford University Press, 1987), p. 195.
4. This was similar to what occurred in the late 1820s before the 1830 deadline agreed upon went into effect. See Robert Edgar Conrad, *World of Sorrow: The African Slave Trade to Brazil* (Baton Rouge: Louisiana State University Press, 1986), pp. 68, 126-153.
5. João José Reis, "Quilombos e revoltas escravas no Brasil," *Revista USP* 28 (1995-1996): 24.
6. João José Reis, *Slave Rebellion in Brazil: The Muslim Uprising of 1835 in Bahia* trans. Arthur Brakel (Baltimore: Johns Hopkins Press, 1993), p. 6.
7. Robert Christian Berthold Avé-Lallemant, *Viagem pelo norte do Brasil, no ano de 1859* (Rio de Janeiro: Instituto Nacional do Livro, 1961), p. 20.
8. Mary C. Karasch, *Slave Life in Rio de Janeiro, 1808-1850* (Princeton: Princeton University Press, 1987), pp. 65-66.
9. Maria Idila Leite da Silva Dias, *Quotidiano e poder em São Paulo no século XIX* (São Paulo: Brasiliense, 1984); Lilia Moritz Schwarcz, *Retrato em branco e negro: Jornais, escravos e cidadãos em São Paulo no final do século xix* (São Paulo: Companhia das Letras, 1987); Maria Cristina Cortez Wissenbach, *Sonhos africanos, vivências ladinas: Escravos e forros em São Paulo (1850-1880)* (São Paulo: Editora Hucitec, 1998); Marilene Rosa Nogueira da Silva, *Negro na rua: A nova face da escravidão* (São Paulo: Editora Hucitec, 1988); Marcus J. M. de Carvalho, *Liberdade: Rotinas e rupturas do escravismo no Recife, 1822-1850* (Recife: Editora Universitária da UFPE, 1998). African slaves and their descendants labored in port cities across the Americas. See Franklin Knight and Peggy K. Liss (eds.), *Atlantic Port Cities: Economy, Culture and Society in the Atlantic World, 1650-1850* (Knoxville: University of Tennessee Press, 1991).
10. Reis, *Slave Rebellion.*
11. Arquivo Nacional in Rio de Janeiro, Secção de Poderes Executivos (hereafter ANRJ/SPE), IJJ 9 110, Francisco José de Sousa Soares d'Andrea to Minister of Empire, Belém, June 27, 1836.
12. Leslie Bethell and José Murilo de Carvalho, "Empire, 1822-1850," in Leslie Bethell (ed.), *Brazil: Empire and Republic, 1822-1930* (Cambridge: Cambridge University Press, 1989), p. 103.
13. For the legacies of the Haitian Revolution in Brazil, see Carlos Eugênio Libano Soares e Flávio Gomes, "Sedições, *Haitianismo* e conexões no Brasil: Outras margens do Atlântico Negro," *Novos Estudos CEBRAP* 63 (2002): 131-144.
14. See Dale T. Graden, " 'An Act Even of Public Security': Slave Resistance, Social Tensions and the End of the International Slave Trade to Brazil, 1835-1856," *Hispanic American Historical Review* 76/2 (1996): 249-282.
15. Hudson to Palmerston, Rio de Janeiro, June 9, 1849, *British and Foreign State Papers* 38 (1849-50): p. 461, cited in Dunkerley, *Americana*, p. 421.

16. Leslie Bethell, *The Abolition of the Brazilian Slave Trade: Britain, Brazil and the Slave Trade Questions, 1807-1869* (Cambridge: Cambridge University Press, 1970), pp. 242-63; Dunkerley, *Americana*, pp. 432-434.
17. Arquivo Público do Estado da Bahia, Secção do Arquivo Colonial e Provincial (hereafter APEB/SACP), *maço* [bundle] 5707-01, Chief of police Gama to President, Salvador, June 22, 1850.
18. APEB/SACP, *maço* 5707-01, Chief of police Gama to President, Salvador, June 22, 1850.
19. For descriptions of *Africanos livres* (liberated Africans), see: Conrad, *World of Sorrow*, 154-70; Alfonso Bandeira Florence, "Nem escravos, nem libertos: os 'africanos livres' na Bahia," *Cadernos do CEAS* (Salvador) 121 (1989): 58-69; Beatriz Galloti Mamigonian, "Do que 'o preto mina' é capaz: Etnia e resistência entre Africanos livres," *Afro-Ásia* 24 (2000): 71-95.
20. "A industria do saveiros," *O argos cachoeirano*, November 9, 1850, p. 2.
21. APEB/SACP, *maço* 5718, Chief of police Mattos to President, October 10, 1855.
22. APEB/SACP, *maço* 5718, Chief of police Mattos to President, November 5, 1855.
23. Katia M. de Queirós Mattoso, *Bahia século xix: Uma província do império* trans. Yedda de Macedo Soares (Rio de Janeiro: Editora Nova Fronteira, 1992), pp. 453-454.
24. APEB/SACP, *maço* 5723, Chief of police Madureira to President, March 1, 1858.
25. Mattoso, *Bahia: século xix*, p. 453.
26. For a description of one of the invasions see APEB/SACP, *maço* 5723, Chief of police Aragão e Mello to President, October 29, 1858.
27. APEB/SACP, *maço* 5723, Chief of police Leão to President, Salvador, August 2, 1858.
28. Ibid., Chief of police Mello to President, Salvador, October 29, 1858.
29. Luís Anselmo da Fonseca, *A escravidão, o clero e o abolicionismo* (Recife: Editora Massangana, 1988 [1887]), p. 244.
30. APEB/SACP, *maço* 5723, Chief of police Madureira to President, December 29, 1857.
31. APEB/SACP, *maço* 5782, Chief of police Bittencourt to President, Salvador, December 16, 1864.
32. ANRJ/SPE, IJ 1 522, President of São Paulo to Minister of Justice, São Paulo, March 27, 1866.
33. ANRJ/SPE, IJ 1 522, President Joaquim Floriano de Toledo to Minister of Justice, São Paulo, March 27, 1866.
34. APEB/SACP, *maço* 5753, Chief of police Lacerda to President, Salvador, March 19, 1863.
35. APEB/SACP, *maço* 5782, Chief of police Bittencourt to President, Salvador, January 16, 1865.
36. APEB/SACP, *maço* 5781, Chief of police Villaboim to President, June 14, 1864.
37. APEB/SACP, *maço* 5753, Chief of police Lacerda to President, March 9, 1863.
38. APEB/SACP, *maço* 5747, Chief of police Morães to President, Salvador, July 17, 1861.
39. Robert Edgar Conrad, *The Destruction of Brazilian Slavery 1850-1888* (Berkeley: University of California Press, 1972), pp. 41-44.

40. João José Reis, "The Revolution of the Ganhadores: Urban Labour, Ethnicity and the African Strike of 1857 in Bahia, Brazil," *Journal of Latin American Studies* 29/2 (1997): 355-393.
41. Dunkerley, *Americana*, p. 453.

Plate 10: View of São Salvador

Source: João Mauricio Rugendas, *Viagem Pitoresca Através do Brasil* (Rio de Janeiro/São Paulo/ Brasilia: A Casa do Livro, 1972 [1835]), plates unpaginated.

Plate 11: Capoeira, the Dance of War

Source: João Mauricio Rugendas, *Viagem Pitoresca Através do Brasil* (Rio de Janeiro/São Paulo/ Brasilia: A Casa do Livro, 1972 [1835]), plates unpaginated.

6

Street Labor in Bahia on the Eve of the Abolition of Slavery[1]

João José Reis
Translated by H. Sabrina Gledhill

African *ganhadores,* slaves and freedmen who worked for hire in the streets, have interested me for nearly three decades, since I began studying the 1835 Muslim-led slave rebellion in the city of Salvador. My study of that rebellion revealed that these workers, who were mostly Nagôs (Yoruba-speaking Africans), were ethnically organized in work groups called *cantos* (literally "corners") that played a central role in the uprising. Thus, in addition to religion, class and ethnicity represented important dimensions of that movement. The Bahian authorities were so sure of this that, soon after they defeated the rebels, they resolved to impose severe restrictions on the *cantos.* In the following years, slaves and freed Africans mounted a systematic, albeit peaceful, resistance to the Bahian government and eventually managed to preserve the autonomy of these work groups.[2]

In 1857, the authorities made another attempt to control the *ganhadores,* but once again they resisted with a strike that lasted over a week. They protested against the requirement of registering with the city council, paying an annual tax and wearing a metal tag bearing their registration number, and the need for freedmen to have white guarantors who would vouch for their future good behavior. This movement gained a much larger following than the revolt of 1835, possibly because it was peaceful and therefore much less risky than an armed uprising. The capital of Bahia's transportation sector nearly came to a halt, because all transportation was done on the *ganhadores*' shoulders. I also studied the 1857 strike in an article published a few years ago, in which I once again discussed the role the *cantos* played in mobilizing the strikers. Unlike the revolt of 1835, this stoppage resulted in partial gains: the annual tax was revoked, and freedmen were exempted from presenting guarantors, except for testimonials of past behavior provided by justices of the peace.[3]

Between the strike of 1857 and the official abolition of slavery in 1888, the Bahian authorities continued to pressure the *ganhadores* with attempts to restrict their freedom to work and impose taxes. All indications are that the government gradually won that war of attrition, although it made some concessions along the way. The year 1880 witnessed an innovation that was certainly a milestone in the history of street laborers. An edict titled "Police regulations on the services of workers in the commercial district" was published on October 5th of that year.[4] This document introduces the central topic of this chapter: the *cantos* on the eve of Abolition.

I am using Abolition as a point of reference because, throughout most of the nineteenth century, paid work done by slaves-for-hire was a characteristic of urban slavery. However, in the 1880s, they had nearly vanished from the scene. The new laws regulating *ganhadores* were drafted in the context of a sharp decline in slavery in Salvador, and Bahia in general. In 1872, there were somewhere between 72,000 and 81,000 slaves working on plantations in the Bahian Recôncavo (the fertile area fringing All Saints Bay), the hub of the province's slave economy. That same year, Salvador's slave population numbered approximately 12,500, or 11.6 percent of the city's 108,138 inhabitants.[5] Unfortunately, I do not have any figures for the following decade. But, just before Abolition in 1888, the number of slaves probably fell by at least 50 percent in the Recôncavo and even more in Salvador. An estimate for the entire province of Bahia suggests that the slave population dropped from 165,403 to 76,838 between 1874 and 1887 due to a high mortality rate, the sale of slaves to other provinces, manumissions and the effects of the "free womb" law.[6] Thus, if the number of slaves in the capital fell in the same proportion, there would have been roughly 6,700 in Salvador in 1887. However, because slavery was crumbling at a much faster rate in the city, the reduction in the enslaved population would have been much more dramatic than that in the rural sector, especially on sugar plantations. Therefore, a more realistic estimate would be somewhere between 3,000 and 4,000 urban slaves in 1887 in a city of 140,000. In fact, the abolitionist Luís Anselmo da Fonseca calculated that there were 3,172 slaves registered in Salvador in that year, to whom we can add a few dozen unregistered slaves.[7] In other words, between 1872 and the last year of the slave regime, Salvador's slave population declined from about 12 percent to something like 2.5 percent of the total population.

As a result, the new regulations for *ganhadores* in the 1880s would have been imposed on a category of workers made up of an increasing number of free and freed men. Since the 1850s, at the very least, there had already been a considerable number of freedmen among Salvador's street workers, although slaves still outnumbered them. Nearly forty years later, that situation had changed. If *ganhadores* were once subjected to the dual control of their masters and the government, now that their condition was less and less defined by slavery it was up to the state to regulate their work. This may explain why stronger measures were required, and why a task once performed by the municipality was transferred to the police. However, the municipal government did not leave the scene altogether. It still maintained laws regulating street labor, and the city council's officials still worked to enforce them. But as we will soon see, the most important role in enforcement was played directly by the police.

The regulations included *cantos* located in the "commercial district", which in the strictest sense basically included the parishes of Nossa Senhora da

Conceição da Praia and Nossa Senhora do Pilar on the waterfront of Salvador's lower city. This could mean that *cantos* in other areas – the Upper City or outside the urban center, for example – may not have been subject to the new regulations. The hypothesis that they could only operate in the commercial district and were prohibited elsewhere, does not hold water, because if this were the case, the regulations would have said so.

Fortunately, the voluminous *Livro de Matrícula* (Registry Book) produced in the late 1880s sheds light on the situation. The first document of its kind ever to emerge from the dust of the archives, it is the main source for this essay. For now, suffice it to say that, according to that book, although the *cantos* were concentrated in the docklands, they could be found throughout the city. I do not know precisely what led to the expansion of the area covered by the police Regulations of 1880, while the other rules were generally in effect. It could be that, as the end of slavery approached, the police decided that it would be advantageous to exercise stricter control over black street workers in general, both in and outside the commercial district. As we will see in the analysis of the registry book – where it is clear that the area originally regulated was expanded – there were very few slaves in the *cantos* in 1887, including those formed by Africans. Again, the intention was to regulate the freed and free black population, a tendency then found everywhere in Brazil, often under the pretext of combating vagrancy. The 1880 Regulations should be viewed in this broader light.[8]

The Regulations contain eleven articles and establish standards for the organization, supervision and operations of the work of porters, except those working in the customs house or for warehouses and retail establishments. These rules were intended for so-called "public workers" or hired laborers. This confirms the fact that, since the 1850s, people whose work was directly related to sea and port activities – stevedores per se – were set apart from other kinds of porters working in the city streets. But this is merely what was written down on paper. As we will see further on, there were many *cantos* on the shore and docks, in warehouses and markets. It seems that their members were not allowed to unload ships that went through customs, but they could work with coastal shipping vessels that docked in Bahia and the vast number of boats and ships that shuttled between the city and the plantation zone, or Recôncavo.

An essential aspect of the new regulations was the imposition of the *cantos*' monopoly on transportation within the commercial district. Clause 10 prohibited freelance workers and slaves-for-hire from engaging in that activity. Anyone who wanted to work as a porter would have to join a registered *canto.* This expedient not only strengthened the organization of these work groups – which included, in a way, guaranteeing them a corner on the market – but facilitated the state's policing and political control of these workers. Peer pressure and the orders of their leaders or captains would make workers less likely to break the law, including stealing merchandise.

When we compare these rules with regulatory measures attempted in 1836 and 1857, we can see some important changes. First, unlike 1836, when the government tried to replace the *canto* captains with "overseers" chosen by the police, the captains were maintained and given the authority to form and disband *cantos*. In other words, it recognized the traditional leaders of these work groups and even preserved their title of *capitão de canto*, as well as allowing them to be directly elected by their subordinates. However, the *cantos*' chosen leaders had to be approved by the chief of police, who could fire them "when he deems it convenient" (Clause 6). The state's control over these workers was strengthened by the fact that the police issued a "title of appointment" for the captain, a kind of certificate showing that the authorities officially recognized his leadership. These measures established a direct relationship between the chief of the *ganhadores* and the chief of police, unlike the regulations of 1836, which authorized junior officials – in this case, justices of the peace and, below them, their inspectors – to issue the documents legitimizing the overseers who were to replace the captains. The new system reinforced the mechanisms of control from the basis of the organization of the *ganhadores* themselves, which had once been independent. It was a masterstroke for the government, which could not risk depriving the city of the essential services that these workers provided. At the same time, although they belonged to a subordinate group, their leaders were given a previously nonexistent official legitimacy.

All *canto* members were obliged to register with the police rather than the city council, as had been done in 1857. Control over the *ganhadores* would also be exercised by obliging each of them to wear their registration number and the letter identifying their *canto* on their right sleeve. This measure revoked the requirement of wearing metal tags around their necks, a measure that led to the extension of the strike of 1857 and would be systematically ignored by the workers.

While the regulations asserted the police chief's authority over the captains, it also recognized and legalized subordination of the *canto* members to their leaders. The captains played an intermediate role between their subordinates and the police. According to Clause 8, "workers are obliged to obey their captains", and only the latter could organize working procedures in their *cantos*. At the same time, "on pain of dismissal for incompetence", the captains had to answer for their subordinates' behavior to the police chief and report any infractions or crimes, handing them over to the police for punishment. In addition to being intermediaries between the police and the *ganhadores,* the captains were theoretically allied with the police against the *ganhadores*.

The 1880 Regulations were certainly a high point of the campaign to control Salvador's street laborers, but although the police were calling the shots, we must not conclude that no concessions were made. The most important one was the maintenance of the *cantos'* structure, particularly their traditional political hierarchy. Although they were more closely subordinated to the police, the *cantos* were free to determine their internal administration. For example, no channels were open between *canto* members and the police to enable the latter to intervene with the captain on the workers' behalf. If their leaders were dictatorial, incompetent or irresponsible, the *canto* members themselves could decide how to deal with them. Whereas the captain could count on the police for help in controlling his subordinates, the latter had only themselves to rely on.

All of this was set down on paper. Unfortunately, the written regulations reveal little about the internal dynamics of the *cantos,* the mechanisms and values involved in the exercise of power, the rituals of solidarity and command, or even the organization of work procedures. At this point, I would like to explore a source that, although it does not allow us to get an in-depth look at the world of the *cantos,* does provide a detailed and truly revealing depiction of their situation on the eve of Abolition.

THE REGISTRY BOOK FOR SALVADOR'S *CANTOS*

The *Livro de Matrícula,* which underpins this contribution, was a product of the 1880 Regulations ordering captains to register the *ganhadores* working in their *cantos* with the police. Unfortunately, it does not give the dates when *ganhadores* were registered, but it does show when some *canto* captains were appointed. The appointments that are dated are broken down as follows: nine in 1880, four in 1881, one in 1882, one in 1884, one in 1886, fifty-one in 1887, one in 1888, and one in 1889. Most of the activity (74 percent of the appointments) took place in 1887, the year prior to abolition, as if the police had undertaken some kind of reorganization of the *cantos,* with a stricter requirement for registration, the creation of new *cantos,* or a combination of these factors. Whatever the circumstances, the year 1887 stands out in the document, and that is why the title of this paper refers to "the eve of abolition". I believe that the vast majority of *ganhadores* either registered or updated their registration in 1887.[9]

The book was probably filled in between 1887 and 1889, although it reports the appointment of captains in 1880, one of which is dated just thirteen days after the Regulations were published. There seems to have been little activity in the year of abolition, at least in the leadership of the *cantos,* as just one captain was appointed in 1888. I do not know if there were other books of this kind for previous years. It may have taken seven years for the regulations discussed above to be fully adhered to on this point. Given the precedents, there must have been some resistance to the new rules among workers. Furthermore, the police may have been too incompetent or inefficient to enforce the law. By 1887, slavery was rapidly expiring, and there was an urgent need to exert tighter controls over street workers. The registry book attests to this.

The *Livro de Matrícula* gives the exact location of the *cantos* in Salvador, which enables us to understand the geographic distribution of the groups of *ganhadores* in the city. It is the most detailed record of the subject so far discovered. Not only that, but it provides varied information about each member, headed by the captain and his assistant, for whom the dates when they were appointed are also given, although with several lapses. The Registry contains the following information about each *canto* member: full name; age; marital status; address (just the name of the street); place of birth; physical description, including height, skin color, type and color of hair ("nappy", "straight", "very straight", "curly", "graying", etc.); facial features (size and shape of nose, eyes, mouth, beard, mustache, goatee, etc.); body markings (scars, tattoos, ethnic marks, etc.); and physical anomalies that could be either congenital or the result of diseases, accidents and other traumatic incidents.

This was, in short, a personal police record, with the *ganhador's* number, *canto,* vital data (name, age, marital status, address etc), physical description and a variety of supplementary observations that could aid in his identification. One can visualize the worker in a room in the police department standing before a clerk who examines his body and notes down his "physical characteristics", including the state of his teeth, as though he were buying a slave. Workers were, most likely, also stripped naked for the examination. Otherwise, how should we interpret the observation made about Vitorino de Assunção Araújo, 22, whose color is described as *pardo* (light-skinned mulatto), who had a "big head and enlarged scrotum".[10] No other kind of worker was subjected to such treatment. While being so humiliated at the age of 80, the African José Bartholomeu must not have made the slightest effort to be pleasant with the police clerk, who made the following observation: "an ugly and surly black".[11]

This exercise in identification eloquently characterizes the government's view that *ganhadores* were potential criminals who belonged to the world of the streets, which was thus viewed as close to the underworld. This is yet another factor that confirmed the ruling classes' worries about the activities of the free and freed men and women who made their livings in the streets as hired workers, most of whom were black.[12] It is no accident that such detailed descriptions were once part of advertisements about escaped slaves published in the nineteenth-century press. Here we see the seigniorial method of search and capture being applied to free men in the registry book. It also, undoubtedly, reflected the influences in Bahia of "scientific" practices used by the European police at the time, the so-called "search for individual singularities" mentioned by Alain Corbin.[13]

Therefore, the *Livro de Matrícula* is a window on myriad aspects of the *ganhadores*' world. I will only discuss a few of them here, particularly the role of workers' occupations, racial backgrounds and places of birth in the formation of the *cantos*.

THE WORKING WORLD OF THE *CANTOS*

The *Livro de Matrícula* lists 89 *cantos* scattered throughout Salvador's urban area, containing 1,703 members, all of whom were freed or free, with the exception of five slaves.[14] Although some *cantos* were not registered in 1887, almost all were. Those located in the Upper City and in districts far from the docklands contained no more than 18 percent of all these workers. Most of the *cantos* and the ones with the largest membership were situated in the Lower City in what is known as the commercial district, in the parishes of Conceição da Praia and Pilar, where the largest share of the job market was found: carrying cargo as well as merchandise and personal luggage of people arriving in and leaving the harbor. Many groups gathered along the sea terminals, including 27 on the docks, totaling 646 *ganhadores* who represented 38 percent of all registered *canto* members of Salvador. There were no less than five *cantos* comprised of 70 members on Amarras Dock, four *cantos* totaling 93 members on Barroso Dock, and just two – the largest in the city, with a total of 135 porters – on New Dock. In these cases, each *canto* occupied one of the staircases of each Dock. In fact, the stairs best defined the space occupied by the groups located on each Dock.[15]

In sum, the port and the surrounding facilities – shipyards, warehouses, markets, retail establishments – were the main reason for the formation of such work groups.[16] However, the introduction of new means of cargo transportation was already expanding the geography of the *cantos*. This is the case of those established in the Calçada area, some five kilometers from the commercial district, a 23-man *canto* facing the Bahia and São Francisco Railway terminal, built by the British about twenty years earlier, and another nearby, at the Gasômetro (city gas deposit), made up of 25 workers.[17] These were relatively large groups.

At the time, *ganhadores* were mainly porters who carried cargo and baggage. Although they carried small items in baskets on their own, and heavier loads in groups with the help of poles and ropes, in the second half of the century they may also have begun using two-wheeled wagons drawn by mules or donkeys, or a type of cart with four small wheels that was pulled by the *ganhadores* themselves. On the other hand, by the late 1880s, the number of sedan chairs or litters (*cadeiras de arruar*) was rapidly declining, having once taken up the time of many *ganhadores*. They were once found in *cantos* all over the city, including exclusively residential districts such as Vitória, where there is no record of any *cantos* at all in 1887. By that time, the city had new means of passenger transport, such as streetcars drawn by donkeys. There were two lines in the early 1880s, one covering a 26.6 kilometer distance, the other 12.1 kilometers. There was also a public elevator, also known as hoisting machinery, that could carry up to twenty passengers between the upper and lower parts of the city. Whites used to move around the city on sedan chairs that blacks carried up and down the steep pathways. The decline of slavery in Salvador had helped eliminate an occupation – chair carrier – that may have been the most explicit symbol of black people's occupational subordination in the city.[18]

These chairs had not vanished completely, however. There were probably still some *ganhadores* carrying them in 1887 in the upper city and perhaps some in the lower parts as well. Nearly ten years later, at the turn of the century, Raymundo Nina Rodrigues, a Medical School professor and pioneer of black studies in Brazil, would write, "few [Africans] carry the remaining chairs or litters".[19] He added that, at this time, the only *cantos* of chair carriers were found on Ladeira de São Bento (across from the Paris Hotel) and Piedade Plaza. Unlike the others Nina Rodrigues mentions,[20] the latter *canto* and another that was once in Campo Grande plaza, at the entrance to the elegant Vitória district, were not listed in 1887. They may have been created afterwards: but another possibility might be that not all of Salvador's *cantos* were registered that year after all. However, the hypothesis that the *cantos* located outside the commercial district were not obliged to register with the police cannot be accurate because others mentioned by Nina and also registered in 1887 were all in the upper city.

The *Livro de Matrícula* of 1887 also contains information that leads one to question whether *ganhadores* then made their living exclusively as porters. This is because the registry book states that many had trades that were not typically associated with that occupation. To begin with, it should be said that none of the 822 *ganhadores* listed as being African-born was shown to have some kind of skill. Even if they plied another trade, their other occupations were not listed because the police official presumed that the Africans in the *cantos* were all bearers and nothing more. Other people might have had other jobs, but not them. However, the most likely reason for the lack of information in the registry book could be a strategic silence on the part of the Africans themselves. If they stated a trade, they would have had to pay the annual 10,000 *réis* tax owed to the province by every African "who should exercise a mechanical trade".[21] This was one of the measures used to burden the African-born with taxation.

On the other hand, half of the 869 Brazilian-born *ganhadores* who did not have to pay that tax stated 35 occupations, apart from being bearers. The most frequently mentioned "mechanical trades" were 114 masons, 69 carpenters, 40 cooks, 34 joiners, 32 blacksmiths, 32 field hands, 17 cobblers, 14 tailors, 12 caulkers, 11 butlers, 9 bakers and 7 tanners. These comprised 90 percent of all the occupations shown in the registry book. The most common trade (26.2 percent) was masonry. All told, the four activities typically associated with construction work – mason, carpenter, joiner and blacksmith – produce the considerable proportion of 57.2 percent. These data confirm that the job market for a sizeable portion of the *ganhadores* was not limited to porterage. But why were these skilled workers engaged in that activity?

According to historian Kátia Mattoso, the 1880s were not a prosperous time. For example, export revenues fell nearly 17 percent compared with the previous decade, and the trade deficit rose from 16 to 30 percent. The entire period was marked by droughts that drastically reduced farming activities, which were the basis of the regional economy. Mattoso describes the period as a stage of acute economic depression until 1887, the year when our registry book for the *cantos* was more active. Furthermore, the previous year, 1886, saw the beginning of a cycle of rising food prices that would last until the end of the century.[22] *Ganhadores* who had specific trades and other occupations must have had few opportunities to practice them in that generally unfavorable economic climate.

Simply put, there was no work. Therefore, they occasionally worked as bearers, which gave them an alternative source of income.

All of this is based on the reasonable supposition that skilled workers earned more than bearers. In addition to better pay, more skilled professions enjoyed greater prestige and had their own guilds, such as the Montepio Society of Artists.[23] Therefore, despite the attractions of working in the streets, the exhausting and socially degrading manual labor of carrying loads would not as a rule have been preferable for those who could work as nineteenth-century "artists".

But let us return to the main point. Who were these skilled laborers who were registered as *canto* members? Let us take the case of the masons, who were present in large numbers, as we have seen. According to Mattoso, their wages grew steadily in the nineteenth century, peaking at a little over 600,000 *réis* per year in the mid-1870s before falling to 500,000 *réis* and staying at that level throughout the 1880s.[24] The large number of masons found among the *ganhadores* probably reflected a difficult time for the construction industry, a period of unemployment in that sector, which would explain the drop in wages. In fact, it is amazing that these wages did not fall even further. Nonetheless, another reason for the 1887 registration was surely to regulate the number of workers entering the informal urban labor market in large numbers and for the first time, swelling the existing *cantos* and creating new ones. In addition to being a means of controlling autonomous workers, it was also a measure taken in the context of unemployment and therefore an ideal climate for increasing social tensions. Then, there was the migration to Salvador of farm workers fleeing the drought. In short, the end of slavery, drought and economic crisis were not exactly fertile soil for social harmony.

In the case of masons and workers in similar trades, many *cantos* became veritable construction gangs and their captains were like building contractors. This is the case of the *cantos* listed as P, BM, EE, RR and GG, whose members included a large number of masons, joiners, carpenters and blacksmiths.[25] For example, *Canto* P, located in an outlying district of the city, was made up of 17 members, ten of whom worked in construction-related trades, four of whom had other trades and three stated no specific trade. It is not hard to imagine that that larger group made up of five masons, two blacksmiths, two carpenters and one joiner could eventually work separately or together with the others on construction projects. It is interesting to note that the captain had once been a 47-year-old African-born freedman with no stated trade, whose registration showed that he had left the *canto*. He was probably replaced by his assistant, a 30-year-old light-skinned mulatto who worked as a carpenter.

Continuing down the list of building *cantos,* of the 31 members of *Canto* EE, thirteen had construction-related skills. In *Canto* RR, this was true for eleven of its sixteen members. The largest group working in that trade was found in *Canto* GG, on Ouro Dock, which had 29 (mostly masons, joiners, carpenters and blacksmiths) among its 37 members. No matter how small the group of workers qualified to work in construction, they could easily have trained the others to do the less specialized jobs involved in that industry. In short, *ganhadores* with some expertise in the building trade could act as small contractors who were ready to work in construction just as they joined forces to work in transportation. The intermittent nature of their construction activities made it easy to work in both areas. Not only that, but the two activities complemented each other because one of the main jobs involved in building was transporting construction materials, such as stones, bricks, tiles, sand, clay, lime, wood and iron. In the port area itself, they could occasionally find work in the construction or restoration of ships, warehouses, buildings and public works on an individual basis or as a group.

Therefore, working as a bearer did not necessarily conflict with other economic activities, whether in times of economic crisis or prosperity. Moreover, although mainly comprised of bearers (only a quarter of them stated that they had a trade), the *cantos* were also informal employment agencies for a number of occupations. For example, if someone wanted to hire a blacksmith, a joiner, cook or so forth, their best bet was to seek out a *canto.* That may be how a baker named Victor Celestino de Mattos, 26, left *Canto* CC in Preguiça street to work in a bakery.[26]

Throughout the registry book, we find notes indicating that *ganhadores* had left the *cantos,* although most do not give the reason for it. In many cases, they were simply moving from one group to another. However, one suspects that in most cases they were recruited to work outside the *cantos,* including people like the *pardo* blacksmith Jacinto Thomé de Mattos, 20, who belonged to *Canto* I, about whom we read: "Stopped being a *ganhador* at this *canto* and registered as the servant of Major Leocadio Duarte da Silva." Or another pardo, Joaquim Tavares de Passos, 25, who left *Canto* O in May 1887 to work for the *Companhia dos Trilhos Centrae*s, a streetcar company. He spent a month there before going back to being a street worker, this time in *Canto* A. Joaquim's experience could reflect the extreme instability of employment in Salvador at that time. However, it could also be an example of someone who could not get used to working full time and preferred the relative freedom of work for hire. If so, one doubts whether this behavior was typical. For example, a *pardo* from the plantation village of Santo Amaro, José Veranda, 48, left his *canto* across the street from the *Companhia Bahiana de Navegação* to work at the shipping company itself. It is easy to imagine him keeping an eye out, making inquiries and seeking more stable employment there.[27]

Apart from those commonly required by the construction industry, many skilled workers were employed in transportation as a supplementary or alternative activity. When not working as bearers, the numerous cobblers, tailors, saddlers, straw weavers, hatters and ropers – all trades listed in 1887 – could make or mend shoes, clothing, saddles, straw mats, baskets and hats at their *canto*'s gathering place.[28] Some could even refuse to carry merchandise and passengers if they were too busy with their other trades, which included meeting deadlines agreed upon with customers. On the other hand, stokers, butlers, cooks, cowherds, gardeners, farmhands and fisherman could not do that because their activities required leaving the *cantos,* if only temporarily. For them, street work was a real alternative to full unemployment. But if some could go back to their jobs in the urban labor market when times improved, others could not. The large number of farmhands and the three or four cow herders listed in the registry book could have chosen city life as a permanent move, abandoning a countryside scourged by drought and ruled by planters and political bosses. Unable to become independent farmers, the landless may have chosen a more independent work at the *cantos.*

In short, the *cantos* being analyzed here, particularly those made up of Brazilian (not African-born) workers, were established primarily, but not exclusively, to provide transportation services. It remains to be seen whether this phenomenon was specifically related to the end of the century and slavery. Although it may have existed earlier, it certainly intensified during that period and came to involve a larger occupational universe and a greater number of workers. Thus, the innovation would be linked to both structural changes in the economy – in other words, the death throes and ultimate demise of slavery – as well as to the depression of the 1880s. The innovation also points to a fundamental change: the decline of Africans as the absolute masters of Salvador's *cantos.*

AFRICAN- AND BRAZILIAN-BORN *GANHADORES*

Historically, the *cantos* were veritable African strongholds in Salvador. Unlike the bureaucratic police document that officially appointed their captains as of 1880, the latter's inaugural ceremony was an elaborate ritual of power and affirmation of African identity.[29] However, the African-born population was aging and rapidly dying out, as it had not been renewed since the trans-Atlantic slave trade was abolished in 1850. In 1896, Nina Rodrigues calculated that there were approximately 2,000 of them, possibly half as many as there had been ten years earlier, when the *Livro de Matrícula* was begun.[30]

In 1857, Africans represented virtually 100 percent of all *ganhadores* in Salvador, with the majority enslaved.[31] By 1887, nearly all were freed: representing 822 (49 percent) of the workers whose birthplace is known to us, almost all were graying or gray; only 6 percent were under 50, while 74 percent were over 60, with the majority having secured their freedom through the emancipation of 60-year-old slaves.[32] For example, *Canto* BC, which was located in Santo Antônio da Mouraria, was dying out because its membership included just four Africans aged between 68 and 73.

African-born *ganhadores* were still in the majority compared, for example, with the 368 (22 percent) born in Salvador. Natives of other Bahian towns and cities numbered 438 (26 percent) and there were 41 from other provinces of Brazil (2.5 percent). Viewed from another angle, the majority – precisely 78 percent – of those who worked as bearers were still outsiders in Salvador, from other towns and sometimes other provinces. The latter generally arrived in ships as crewmen and decided to swap the sea for dry land. João José de Jesus do Espírito Santo, 17, a curly-haired *pardo* from Pernambuco, arrived in the city aboard the steamer *Jaguaribe,* on which he worked as a servant. A year later, he joined *Canto* H. Illiterate and unskilled, he decided to try his hand at working as a *ganhador*. José Alves dos Santos, 22, described as a *cabra* (dark-skinned mulatto), also arrived in Salvador by ship. His registration in *Canto* N reads, "arrived from Maranhão 2 years ago – arrived a few days ago from Rio de Janeiro." In other words, he had continued sailing after establishing a base in the port of Bahia. Like João José, José Alves seems to have wanted to leave the seafaring life for the life of the *canto.* The native of Maranhão liked to move around: we also find a record of his transfer to *Canto* BM. But the one who traveled the farthest to reach Salvador was Belizário Fernandes de Lima, 27, a black man from Rio Grande do Sul, a province in the southern extreme of the country, who gave his occupation as a seaman.[33]

Unlike Rio de Janeiro, where European immigrants gradually replaced part of the African and Afro-Brazilian street slaves in the second half of the nineteenth century (although to a much smaller extent in the docklands), in Bahia that process did not involve newly arrived Europeans. I did not find a single white foreigner listed as a *ganhador.* In Bahia, African street workers slowly gave way to Afro-Brazilians, particularly people from other towns in the province of Bahia.[34]

The vast majority of *ganhadores* working in Bahia's capital on the eve of Abolition were primarily from the Recôncavo and Africa, having gone there willingly or under duress. Work for hire may have been a way for migrants to enter the urban job market. Among those from the sugar region, which was rapidly declining, the largest number came from Santo Amaro, São Sebastião do Passé, Cachoeira and São Francisco do Conde, municipalities of the sugar plantation zone from where 11.6 percent of the *ganhadores* originated. Like nearly all of the Africans, many were former slaves. For example, Rufino Gallo was a 50-year-old freedman born in São Sebastião do Passé, from where he probably migrated to Salvador after obtaining his manumission at an unknown date. He then joined *Canto* E on Escada da Cal Dock, where in 1887 he replaced his captain, the African Francisco Joaquim Gonçalves, who died that year. The group was made up of 14 *ganhadores,* including eight freedmen, only three of whom were born in Brazil. Rufino was not the only one who left the Recôncavo and other parts of Bahia for Salvador after gaining his freedom. Despite having a "twisted right leg", Leocádio Dionízio, 32, a dark-skinned mulatto, left Fazenda Nova in Bom Jardim, near Santo Amaro, after Abolition on May 13, 1888; Euleutério Januário, 32, and black, was from Itaparica Island; Agostinho Machado, 27, also black, and Epiphanio Machado, a dark-skinned mulatto, were both from São Gonçalo dos Campos and former slaves of José da Silva Machado; and Albino Baptista, 40, a black man who had migrated from Cruz das Almas in 1886.[35] Many other freedmen, most born in the countryside of the province, had decided to enjoy their freedom far from the environment where they had once been slaves. Seeing such people working as freelancers in the streets as the end of slavery approached was worrying for slaveholders, particularly plantation owners, who complained that the workforce was dwindling because ex-slaves refused to continue working on their land.[36]

Africans were not as worrisome because, as pointed out above, they were too old to be of any significance to the future of large-scale farming or of any other sector of the economy. But who were they? Unfortunately, the authorities were not interested in listing their ethnic backgrounds – whether they were Nagôs (Yoruba-speaking), Jejes (Gbe-speaking) or Hausas. Only two entries for Africans provide this information: Ivo Villarinho Gomes, of the Mina ethnic group (probably from Little Popo on the Slave Coast), a 40-year-old *ganhador* from *Canto* AA who wore a moustache and goatee; and Guilherme da Cunha, 50, a married Jeje registered with *Canto* M who was tall, thin and graying.[37] These two men may have insisted that their ethnic groups be recorded, perhaps because they did not want to be confused with the numerous Nagôs of Salvador. In the other entries for African-born *ganhadores*, the clerk merely stated that they were from Africa, and nothing more. If there was already a tendency to do this in documents related to the 1857 strike, imagine thirty years later. In 1857, Nagôs made up nearly 80 percent of the African-born *ganhadores* because they were the most constant victims of the last twenty years of the African slave trade. Naturally, by 1887, nearly all African *canto* workers were Nagô. When slavery ended, they were more than ever the "typical" Africans, which reinforced the stereotype held by Bahians, particularly the Bahian police officers who produced the *Livro de Matrícula.* Why should they be concerned about the details of men over 60 who no longer represented the threat they did in their youth? When the Nagôs were staging rebellions, it was important to distinguish them from other Africans. Now, for the purposes of police control, it was enough to know that the person in question was born in Africa.

Luckily for us, in the following decade Nina Rodrigues took a specific interest in ethnic differences among Africans in Bahia. In 1897, he watched a group of elderly Nagôs and Hausas embark on their return voyage to Africa, an episode that served as a pretext for reflection. He concluded that, despite spending so many years in Bahia, those men and women were still foreigners, and had retained their ethnic identities: "They set themselves apart from the general populace in whose midst they live and work, they shut themselves off or limit themselves to small circles or colonies of black nations."[38] The registration of the *cantos* undertaken in 1887 confirms Nina's observation in part, but only in part.

In fact, the 1887 registry book lists a large number of *cantos* occupied exclusively by people born in Africa: 24 *cantos* comprising 376 Africans, or 45.7 percent of all Africans registered. But this means that most of them mingled with Brazilians in other work groups. There were two kinds of integration: groups in which Africans were the majority but allowed Brazilian workers to join, and groups that were predominantly Brazilian, but accepted Africans. There were more of the first type of *canto* (sixteen) and they included the largest number of *ganhadores*, 300 Africans and 76 Brazilians. The second type included a few Africans here and there, with the exception of *Canto* H at Água de Meninos Dock, which had 17

Brazilians and 14 Africans who, despite being in the minority, elected the captain from amongst themselves.

These numbers show that Africans were not as segregated as Nina would have liked to believe. He wrote the following on this subject: "Each seeks and lives on his own land and the last remaining Africans share the sentiments and affinities of their countries in this city in small circles or societies. The nations that are still numerous have their *cantos,* sites in the city where, whether weaving straw hats or baskets or reminiscing fondly about their youth, the aged wait [to carry] cargo."[39]

Let us take a closer look at signs of the integration and separation of African and Brazilian *ganhadores*, starting with some of the *cantos* Nina mentioned as being exclusively made up of certain ethnic groups. They may be the same ones listed in the 1887 list, although the registry book does not show the *ganhadores*' ethnicity, merely identifying those who were born in Africa. Nina states that the *Gurunci* or *Grunci* (probably Gurensi from north of Ashanti in the Bight of Benin) group controlled the *canto* in Arcos de Santa Bárbara. It was probably the one listed as *Canto* SS in the 1887 registry book, and in fact almost all of its members were Africans, with the exception of two *crioulos* (blacks born in Brazil), one from Salvador, a 20-year-old caulker, and the other from Rio de Contas, aged 55, as well as a 44-year-old *pardo*. The two *crioulos* may have been related to some of the Africans in this *canto* and therefore allowed to work there, although this is unlikely in the case of the light-skinned mulatto. In any event, these three Brazilians would not have upset the absolute hegemony of the Africans (or *Gruncis*?) in this *canto*.

São Raimundo *canto,* located in Mercês, was the equivalent of *Canto* BD in our registry book. According to Nina, it was exclusively controlled by two or three blacks from the Mina ethnic group. They were probably all that were left of the ten workers registered there in 1887, all of whom were born in Africa, and aged between 44 and 70. Nina also observed that most of the other *cantos* belonged to the numerous Nagôs. There were several on Princesas Street, in the docklands. In fact, two *cantos* located on Rua Nova das Princesas – identified by the letters X and PP – were entirely African in 1887, respectively made up of 25 and 33 members. Finally, in Baixa dos Sapateiros, there were groups of "Africans of various nationalities" in Nina's time. Two *cantos* were listed there in 1887, one inside the market and another in the street outside – the first is probably AG in the registry book, with 24 African members, and the second AV, with 23 members, of whom just 7 were African-born.

Nina was actually right in most cases – the *cantos* he identified as being African were just that. The problem is that he seems to have focused exclusively on these because he was only interested in finding Africans so as better to observe them as racial and cultural types. The details in the 1887 registry book show that Africans were more integrated into the local working class than that keen but biased observer would have us think.[40] In several passages, in fact, he actually contradicts himself regarding the ethnic exclusivity of the *cantos* during that period of the nineteenth century. "At the Campo Grande *canto*", he writes, "some Nagôs were joined by three or four Jejes". In Baixa dos Sapateiros, repeating his own words, there were "Africans of various nationalities."[41] In all likelihood, the situation was not much different ten years earlier. What we have here is probably a case of minority groups being absorbed by the great Nagô majority who, because they were the majority, could have more ethnically exclusive *cantos*. This phenomenon would therefore be explained more by demographics than ethnic ideology. Of course, this does not belie the existence of a "Nagô identity" in Bahia at that time, which was expressed in the Candomblé religion through rituals that may have been performed within the *cantos* themselves.[42]

Apart from the question of the exclusivity of African ethnic groups and the grouping of Africans of different ethnicities in the *cantos,* the registry book documents the integration of Africans and Brazilians in the process of street labor in Salvador. Nina Rodrigues sidestepped this issue altogether. However, this mixture does not mean that Africans put less confidence in working with their own kind. The *cantos* certainly did not lose their characteristic as a place for the development and affirmation of ethnic identity. But something about the makeup of the ethnic situation was changing drastically during this *fin d'époque,* or had already changed due to pressures brought to bear by other alterations in the characteristics of the people that worked in the *cantos*, particularly demographic changes. I repeat: although they continued to represent a sizeable percentage of that market, the Africans who had reigned supreme over street labor in the mid-nineteenth century had to compete, by 1887, with a native-born population of equal size. Africans were rapidly leaving the market due to age, death and even the return of many to Africa.

Before they disappeared from the scene altogether, many African *ganhadores* shared their experience with Brazilian-born workmates, most of whom were probably outsiders who had recently arrived from the interior, just as the Africans had once been recent arrivals from foreign lands. One detail that demonstrates the enduring prestige of the Africans among Bahian workers is the significant number that held the post of *canto* captain. If Africans made up 49 percent of all *ganhadores,* they were 57 percent of their leadership. The origins of the other captains were as follows: 23 percent from Salvador, 17 percent from other parts of Bahia and 3 percent from other provinces. These numbers lead me to believe that experience – or the traditional control over the street labor market that Africans wielded in Salvador – led Brazilian workers who had recently entered that market to defer to their leadership. To do so, they had to set aside the prejudice that many felt towards Africans and which had once been an important limiting factor to the participation of Brazilian-born blacks and mulattoes in the world of Bahian street labor.[43]

According to the registry book, when Africans were in the majority, they usually elected their leader. However, the opposite is not true. For example, *Canto* K, located on Moreira Dock, had 16 members, just five of whom were African freedmen, including their captain, Zepherino de Moura, aged 70. However, this *canto* also had another characteristic: only three *ganhadores* were born in Salvador, and all the rest were from rural Bahia. Together with the Africans, these country folk formed a majority of "strangers" in the capital. Could it be that this was a convergence of people who were discriminated against by the locals and joined together? Is it possible that this was a recruitment strategy devised by the Africans to renew the membership of their *cantos* that was once renewed by bringing in newcomers from Africa before the slave trade was abolished? In part, that answer is yes.

When recruiting people from outside their group, Africans seem to have preferred *ganhadores* who were not from Salvador, which probably eliminates the supposition that they were mainly the children of African workers. Among the predominantly but not exclusively African *cantos,* the Brazilian minority included 39 from Salvador and 63 who were born elsewhere. Of the 16 *cantos* with that makeup, only one had a non-African leader. That was *Canto* CC, in Preguiça, which had 11 members from Africa, 5 from Salvador and a captain from Santo Amaro, Manoel do Bonfim, 41, a cobbler.

However, it was nothing like the *canto* that formed at the door of a sugar warehouse in Santo Antônio do Cabrito, an outlying district of Salvador, which was made up of 17 Bahians, nine from Salvador, and led by the group's sole African, the freedman Olympio Pedro Caetano, aged 47. Nevertheless, this man was almost a Brazilian. Relatively young compared to other Africans in 1887, he must have crossed the Atlantic in the 1840s as a child of at most 10. Therefore, he was practically raised in Bahia and may not even have spoken Portuguese with a foreign accent, unless he grew up in the isolation of some ethnic African enclave. As a result, his position in the group may have differed from that of an experienced foreigner at the head of Brazilian *ganhadores,* which may have been the case with the captain of *Canto* K mentioned above. Pedro Caetano was practically a native-born Brazilian.

While Africans allowed Brazilians into their *cantos,* the opposite was also true, but less common. Africans joined a few Brazilian *cantos* individually or in groups of two, three or four. They may have been *ganhadores* from small ethnic groups who, for some reason, had not managed to integrate themselves into the majority ethnic networks in the African community, which were dominated by the powerful Nagôs. And these African minorities adapted better by living or at least working among Afro-Brazilians. That may have been the case with Ivo Villarinho Gomes, a Mina, and Guilherme Cunha, a Jeje, the only two Africans whose ethnonyms appear in the registry book. The former belonged to *Canto* AA of Cachoeira Dock, where he was the only African-born *ganhador* among the 16 men who made up the group; the latter joined *Canto* M, where he was also the only African among its 16 *ganhadores.* Both men's captains were Bahian dark-skinned mulattoes or *cabras*, one of whom was 40 and the other just 26 years old.[44]

Nevertheless, Africans did not always live in peace with Brazilians. Daniel da Silva Freire, 50, worked in *Canto* AV with six other African freedmen as well as several Brazilians, seven blacks, six *pardos* and a *cabra*. The darkest-skinned mulatto (listed as a cabra*)* was the group's captain, Lourenço Astério Honorato, 41, with whom Daniel had a falling out that led him to exit the group and join *Canto* AU, whose members were all born in Africa. This may be an example of an African who tried and failed to work with Brazilians, although the other six Africans apparently succeeded.[45]

Rather than indicating the weakening of African exclusivity, could the integration of Africans and Brazilians in the *cantos* be a form of subordination of Brazilians to African groups? This may have been true in predominantly African *cantos,* although we should allow that Brazilians could have limited themselves to working alongside Africans and not necessarily become one of them. But many rural immigrants who joined them may have been seeking something more than a place in the job market. They may also have sought to take part in new networks of sociability and solidarity that would help them make a new life in the city. They may have been gateways to membership in Candomblés and Catholic brotherhoods frequented by their co-workers. Despite that, most would never be "truly" African (meaning, for the most part, Nagô). A single *ganhador* appears to have come close to that status and he was born in Salvador. According to an observation in the registry book, Lino Antônio, 30, the only Brazilian among the 25 members of his *canto* was "a native of this city [but] speaks with an African accent".[46] Lino lived on Nagôs Street and must have been raised in the bosom of his African family – his parents, aunts and uncles. There must have been other Brazilian-born blacks like him in and outside of the *cantos,* but the majority had weaker ties with the African community.

There were also Africans who went the other way. Once again, the evidence is found in their speech. "He speaks very clear Portuguese" – this note is found beside the name of the octogenarian African freedman Ricardo Burgos. Similarly, Faustino José Pereira, a tall, thin, beardless black man described as *fulo* (lighter skinned black person), was, according to a somewhat confused clerk, "born in Socorro Parish, I say he is a Creole but he was born in Africa and came here as a small child."[47] He was 22 when he was registered in the *Livro de Matrícula*, which does not state whether he was a slave or freedman. All indications are that he was taken to Brazil as a free child in the 1860s under circumstances unknown to us. Now he belonged to an 18-man *canto* of Brazilians. He had become a "Brazilian" himself.

Whether they were like Lino, Ricardo or Faustino, the *ganhadores*' demographic nationalization had varying impacts on the makeup of the *cantos.* That is why the arrival of Brazilian migrants was decisive. As noted above, while about 70 of them were absorbed by African-dominated *cantos*, the vast majority – nearly 500 workers all told – eventually joined predominantly Brazilian groups. Whether they banded together with people from the same towns or cities, just as the majority of Africans had done in the past by grouping according to their ethnic groups, is a question that has no clear-cut answer. In some cases there were small groups of two to four *ganhadores* from the same municipality who mixed with people from other parts of Brazil. Yet, there was nothing like the ethnic exclusivity – or near exclusivity – that seems to have characterized most African *cantos* when the transatlantic slave trade was at its height. There is no reason to believe that the nine natives of Santo Amaro found in *Canto* GG on Ouro Dock were there by chance. Even if that small grouping arose from their common roots, perhaps of people who had known each other before migrating to Salvador, they were only nine in a universe of thirty-eight *ganhadores*. The same can be said of the six men from Santo Amaro who joined *Canto* DD, established across from Companhia de Navegação Bahiana by eighteen workers. Certainly, although there was a large number of Santo Amaro-born *ganhadores*, rather than forming exclusive *cantos,* they were found in almost all the Brazilian groups and some African ones.[48]

It is also unlikely that the presence of two of the only three sons of Camamú – a coastal village in southern Bahia, 159 km from Salvador – joined the same *Canto* OO by chance. They were Tobias Manuel de Brito, 25, and Eguidumno (possibly an African name) Martins, 26, two black men who probably made the journey to the big city together in search of work. Before and after slavery was abolished, many former slaves may have traveled the same route as these young men, migrating together from plantations, farms and rural villages to seek their fortune as freedmen in the capital. Their status as former slaves would then have been yet another factor involved in their choice of certain *cantos.*

A large group of freedmen migrated from sugar plantations in São Sebastião do Passé to *Canto* XX in Salvador. They included Saturnino de Jesus, 30, a black sailor who was married to Maria Faustina de Jesus, and was the former slave of Joaquim Ignacio Bulcão, the scion of a slaveholding dynasty in the Recôncavo; José Theorodo, 25, whose color is given as *fulo*, the former slave of a no less distinguished slaveholder, the Baron de Matoim; and José Antonio Dorea, 48, a *fulo* blacksmith, freed by the late Isiquiel Antonio de Menezes Dorea. The group also included the *cabra* Pedro Celestino, 26, and José Antero, 28, also *fulo,* who were the former slaves of João Baptista Pinto Sanches.[49]

Like Pedro and José, many freedmen had left the same place and master behind. Pedro Francisco de Souza, 18, and Nilo Manoel de Souza, a 19-year-old joiner, migrated to Salvador from São Tomé de Paripe, where they were freed on May 13, 1888, after being the property of Benjamim de Souza. Now, they both lived in the capital at the same address, Larangeiras Street, and worked at *Canto* B, at the Central Sugar Warehouse. As in the case of many others, they both retained the surname of the man who had enslaved them. This habit allows us to identify more *ganhadores* who once had the same master. We find some at *Canto* PP, such as the Africans Agostinho and Vicente Baraúna, as well as Cézar, Luiz and Tobias Teixeira Gomes. *Canto* QQ's membership included Antonio, 31, born in Salvador, Severiano, 27, from Alagoinhas, and Januario, 22, a native of Pernambuco. All indications are that they were registered on the same day as members of the same *canto*, all lived in the Barbalho district and had the same surname, Ferreira Lima.[50] These and other freedman may have worked together as slaves-for-hire before their manumission, and stayed together afterwards.

The most singular example of a grouping of workers who had once been slaves of the same owner is found in *Canto* AX, located at Largo do Guadalupe. This group had sixteen members, nearly all of them freedmen. Their captain, who took office in September 1887, was named Aprigio Francisco. A relatively young *pardo* at the age of 29, with impressive fiery hair, he was born in Santo Amaro, 67 kilometers from Salvador. The only *canto* members who were born free were a 20-year-old *pardo,* also from Santo Amaro, and a black youth of 16 who was born in Salvador. Interestingly enough, thirteen of the sixteen freedmen had once belonged to Raimunda Porcina Maria de Jesus, who had died in October of the same year.[51]

Porcina must have been a remarkable woman. Her name appears just once in the registry book of *Canto* AX, where the clerk listed one of her freed slaves, Pedro Felisberto dos Santos. When the other freedmen were registered, the following observation appears: "was the slave of the Chapadista." This was her nickname because she owned a group of slave musicians who made up the Chapada Band, which was probably named for the Chapada Diamantina, a mining region in the interior of Bahia where they toured giving performances. In fact it seems that the band performed throughout the interior of the province, as well as being famous in Salvador. So much so that Porcina was known to her contemporaries as the "Chapadista".

In her 1887 will, which she wrote just before dying, Porcina declared she would leave no heir, and that upon her death she would manumit 29 slaves (25 men and 4 women) of the 34 (28 men and 6 women) that she owned. This cannot be said to have been a magnanimous gesture. In 1887 it was more than clear that the days of slavery were numbered. Furthermore, she did not have any relatives who would lose out as a result of her gesture. And she even left four slaves to render services to people she called "her protégés" and a servant, Tibério, the brother of one of the slave women she freed, Theodolina. It is clear that Porcina distributed her generosity unevenly.[52]

In light of these facts, a question arises: were all of her 28 male slaves members of the Chapada Band? Only if the answer were yes would we be able to state with assurance that the *ganhadores* in *Canto* AX were musicians. If the answer is that some were and some were not, the *canto* could have been formed by the non-musicians. The problem is that we cannot be sure. We only find thirteen of the Chapadista's former slaves in this *canto.* Apart from them, only one of her freedmen is registered. What about the other fourteen? Were they, and only they, the members of the band?

Many of the *ganhadores* in *Canto* AX had adopted Porcina's surname, which was a common practice among freed slaves. This projected something of the dependence of slavery into their freedom. Their names were Gasparino

Porcino de Jesus, 27, *fulo*, Manoel Porcino de Jesus, 19, *fulo*; José Porcino de Jesus, 60, African; Vicente Porcino de Jesus, 45, *fulo*; Cassiano Porcino de Jesus, 60, *fulo;* Manoel Porcino, 37, black. There was also a Theodolina Porcina de Jesus, who was married to the *ganhador* Pedro Felisberto dos Santos, a 30-year-old black man who had escaped from bearing his mistress's name. Pedro – who is mentioned in Porcina's will as Pedro Crioulo – and Jacintho Santos, 33, who was black and another former slave of the Chapadista, may have been purchased when they already bore the surname of another master. However, they may have chosen the name Santos (Saints) as an expression of Catholic devotion, and a sign of independence from their former mistress.

Porcina was a wealthy woman. In addition to slaves, she owned several houses and would later distribute their rents among her freed men and women, bequeathing 10,000 *réis* per month to some and 5,000 *réis* to others. At least those who lived at Fonte das Pedras occupied a two-story house she owned. Regarding the band's instruments, she wrote in her will that she was leaving them "to several people who are my friends and have always been in my company." I would like to believe that these people were her former slave musicians, but it is strange that she was not more explicit.

Porcina lived at Fonte das Pedras, where six of her freed *ganhadores* still resided. The rest lived close by, five on Independência Street and two in the Desterro district. The *canto* they formed was also located in the vicinity, on Guadalupe Plaza. The slaveholder had formed a group whose common experience of enslavement was not enough to explain their unity. Supposing that the *ganhadores* in this group were all musicians, they were probably tied by their mistress's authority and the slaves' occupation, as they all depended on each other to form the band. However, I do not believe that the slaves were exclusively devoted to music. They may have spent much of their time working as slaves-for-hire before obtaining their manumission, as the band is not likely to have played every day, and rehearsals probably did not take up all their time. I recall the barbershop bands whose members played Bumba drums and clarinets as often as they plied their scissors and razors. The *canto* registered in 1887 may have existed earlier when its members were still slaves. In that case, the group of freedmen was merely continuing an experience that began when they were slaves. There are many possibilities in this story.

One of the Chapadista's former slaves left the group, although he stayed in the neighborhood, working at *Canto* AT, also located on Guadalupe Plaza. The African-born freedman Pedro da Costa decided to join an exclusively African group where he was the captain's assistant. This may have been one of those cases in which ethnic identity spoke louder than occupational identity. Even the name he adopted alludes to West Africa (*Costa da África* in Portuguese). Conversely, José and Cassiano Porcino de Jesus, who were also Africans, remained in the first *canto*. Their very names suggest a closer association with Porcina's band.[53]

THE COLORS OF THE *CANTOS*

Let us now look at other connections that may have had some weight in the workers' choice of and/or acceptance by certain *cantos*. Having given a detailed analysis of their occupation and place of birth, I will now attempt to determine whether there was any relationship between the *cantos* and their members' racial and ethnic background.

The "racial" categories listed in the 1887 registry book are extremely varied, particularly regarding the individual's skin color. "Racial" categories are mentioned here only in the sense that skin color, in all its variety and other physical attributes, have been central elements of Brazil's historically constituted racial ideology.[54] In that sense, the categories employed by the police in 1887 are racialized without mentioning specifically the term race; a term, however, that was not absent from the political and intellectual discourse of the period.[55] Because it described the workers' physical characteristics for the purposes of identification so that police control could be more efficient, the police clerk noted down the chromatic nuances of the workers who stood before him. Such categories were most probably attributed by the police and not the *ganhadores* themselves. Thus, we have a long list of colors, the most frequent being *preto* (black), *fulo*, *pardo* (brown), mulatto, *caboclo*, and *cabra*. Here we no longer see the term *crioulo,* which dates back much earlier and persisted throughout most of the nineteenth century, when it was used to refer to black people born in Brazil to distinguish them from the African-born, who were formerly referred to merely as *preto*. This term was now used to describe black Brazilians and Africans alike, which is another indication that society was adapting to dealing with just one type of black people: those born in Brazil. Being called by the term once applied to Africans, Brazilian-born blacks underwent a kind of Africanization in the system of hegemonic racial classification. It could be said that the *crioulo* was reduced to the status of the African in the turn-of-the-century mentality: "reduced" because Africans were once viewed as being more "primitive" than Brazilian-born black people.[56]

Other terms were used because the intention was, again, to seek out unique individual traits for the purposes of identification. *Fulo* meant blacks whose skin was not dark black but rather characteristic of the Fulani, the African ethnonym from which the term derived (this does not signify that a "*preto fulo*" was literally descended from the Fulani, an ethnic group that was rarely found among the Africans shipped to Bahia). *Cabra* meant someone whose skin color is somewhere between brown and black; *caboclo* refered to people who more closely resembled Brazilian Amerindians, the offspring of an Amerindian and a white or black parent, with different types of hair depending on their ancestry.

The other categories mentioned above are not problematic, although one has to enjoy classifying colors to distinguish the subtle differences between *pardo* and mulatto, for example, or between *fulo* and *cabra*. The difference often lay in the person's type of hair, but in the *canto* established at the Ferreira refinery, for

Table I: *Ganhadores* and the population of Salvador by skin color

Color	Cantos (1887)		1872 Census	
Black	1,421	83.4 percent	27,179	22.8 percent
Mulatto	136	8.0 percent	53,779	45.0 percent
Cabra	105	6.2 percent	not included	---
Caboclo	37	2.2 percent	2,210	1.8 percent
White	4	0.2 percent	36,296	30.4 percent
Total	1,703	100.0 percent	119,464	100.0 percent

example, there were several *pardos* with "*carapinha*" (nappy) hair and one with "curled hair"; in *Canto* FF, on Forca Street, there was a *pardo* with hair described as "*corrido*" (very straight) and *Canto* S had a *pardo* tailor with "straight hair".

Historically, racial designation in Brazil has been largely situational, depending on the context and the social rank of the person doing the classifying and the person being classified. The situation is all the more complicated when miscegenation is considered.[57] In 1887, police officers probably tended to classify unskilled workers "downward". Thus, for example, unable to accept that a *ganhador* from Alagoas registered in *Canto* AL was white, the clerk classified him as being "light-skinned, almost white."[58] If he had been a professor of medicine or even a policeman, the official would probably not have hesitated to describe him as white. A mere *ganhador* could not be ranked as white that easily.

As in the case of mid to late twentieth-century surveys with open answers on racial classification, the 1887 registry book offers several other expressions referring to skin color. These include *preta escura* (dark black), *escura* (dark), *preta anêmica* (anemic black), *fulo anêmica, cabra fulo, cabra escura, parda escura, parda acaboclada* (Amerindian brown), *parda macilenta* (pale brown), *parda clara* (light brown), *parda afogueada* (reddish brown), *acaboclada* (Amerindian looks), *avermelhada* (reddish), *morena* (brownish).

At the risk of impoverishing the imagery of the time, reclassifying all of the available terms around the more common ones that best demarcated the color boundaries (*preto, pardo* or mulatto, *cabra, caboclo*, and white or "almost white") results in the following distribution of *ganhadores* in 1887: 1,421 (83.4 percent) *pretos;* 136 (8 percent) *pardos* and mulattoes; 105 (6.2 percent) *cabras;* 37 (2.2 percent) *caboclos* and 4 (0.2 percent) whites and "almost whites". Even when Africans are left out, *pretos* were by far the largest group. When Africans are included, black was the most typical skin color of Salvador's *ganhadores* in the late 1880s. Assuming that the racial distribution of the city remained the same between 1872 (a census year) and 1887, blacks found themselves over represented among the *ganhadores* by more than 50 percent. In other words, they made up 23 percent of the city's residents and 83.4 percent of *canto* workers. With the exception of *caboclos*, all of the other groups were drastically underrepresented in the *cantos* (see Table 1).[59]

However, the fact that workers from categories other than "black" entered this sector of the job market is also significant, since *cantos* were once the exclusive dominion of blacks. In addition to the replacement of Africans by Brazilians, this is another important novelty of the period in question: mulattoes, *pardos* and even whites were entering the world of the *cantos,* which had been entirely black thirty years earlier. This might be considered yet another indication of the economic difficulties of that time, which may have obliged scores of mulattoes and a handful of whites to seek employment in a sector that had, until recently, been historically stigmatized as black (African, in fact). This suggests that mulattoes were suffering a decline in social status, a very different situation from that described by Gilberto Freyre, who wrote of the rise of the mulatto in Imperial Brazil.[60] It may be that more mulattoes were descending the social ladder than climbing it.

In Salvador's *cantos,* the lighter-skinned newcomers necessarily worked with blacks, although the majority of the latter were born in Brazil. The all-African groups excepted, there is no indication of racial/ethnic segregation among the *ganhadores.* Some *cantos* were made up entirely of workers described as *pretos*, whether they were Brazilians or of mixed Brazilian and African ancestry. This was common due to the large number of black people who worked as *ganhadores*. For example, there were twenty Africans and eleven black Brazilians in *Canto* J. *Cantos* AQ, MN and RR were respectively made up of nine, four and nineteen Brazilian-born blacks. But the majority of the Brazilian *cantos* had mulattoes, *pardos*, *cabras* and *caboclos* toiling side by side with the black majority.

Pardo and *cabra* captains even headed some groups, fourteen all told, in a proportion equivalent to their share of the population of *ganhadores.* This can be seen in the table below. Seven *cabras* and six *pardos* were leaders of *cantos* in which people of their color and *caboclos* were in the minority. However, in most cases, they were not small minorities. In fact, these *cantos* had 100 pardo, cabra and caboclo members, or 36 percent of all the racially mixed workers listed in the registry book. Therefore, they were over represented in these 14 *cantos.* If they were evenly distributed, these *cantos* should only have had 43 racially mixed members. This leads to the conclusion that the latter were either joining them because they were led by men of the same color, or once there was a significant number of them in a given *canto*, they could elect their own leaders.

In nearly all of these groups, the always more numerous blacks did not elect captains of their own color. Could this be a sign that the newcomers were supplanting them in leadership positions? There is no way of telling from the basis of the synchronic nature of the registry book. To answer this question we would have to know more about the process of selecting captains other than the fact that they were elected, and whether skin color counted as much as it did in the surrounding society, where *mestiços* (persons of mixed ancestry like *pardos*, *cabras*, *caboclos*, etc.) had more opportunities for advancement than blacks.

Table 2: Racial makeup of *cantos* led by *cabras* and *pardos*.

Cantos with captains described as *cabras*	
Canto M:	10 blacks; 1 *pardo*; 1 *caboclo*; 4 *cabras*
Canto AK:	5 blacks; 1 *pardo*; 1 *caboclo*; 5 *cabras*
Canto AL:	2 blacks; 7 *pardos*; 7 *caboclos*; 2 *cabras*; 5 whites or "nearly whites"
Canto AA:	12 blacks; 1 *pardo*; 4 *cabras*
Canto BK:	10 blacks; 5 *pardos*; 4 *cabras*
Canto BR:	3 blacks; 3 *pardos*; 3 *cabras*
Canto GG:	26 blacks; 4 *pardos*; 10 *cabras*
Canto AV:	14 blacks; 6 *pardos*; 1 *cabra*
Cantos* with captains described as *pardos	
Canto C:	7 blacks; 6 *pardos*; 1 *cabra*
Canto AE:	9 blacks; 5 *pardos*
Canto F:	12 blacks; 3 *pardos*; 2 *cabras*
Canto AX:	14 blacks; 3 *pardos*
Canto BL:	18 blacks; 5 *pardos*
Canto DD:	13 blacks; 2 *pardos*; 2 *caboclos*; 1 *cabra*

It is also possible that in such a working environment, black and other Afro-Brazilians identified more closely with their social class than with their racial characteristics. (Although the latter still had some weight, as demonstrated in the penultimate paragraph.) This had implications for solidarity or cooperation based on skin color and, in the specific case of Africans, ethnicity. Compared with the surrounding society, the distance between blacks (Africans and Brazilians), *cabras, pardos* and *caboclos* was smaller in the world of the *cantos,* where non-whites were nearly all black or treated as such by the Bahian authorities. Therefore, a leader's color may not have been as important as his other attributes. Even so, it should be recalled that most *cantos* were still led by blacks, who were also the leaders of most *mestiço* workers.

One *canto* which was led by a *cabra* differed from the rest in terms of mixture. *Canto* AL, located at the Calçada railway station, is the only one whose *ganhadores* included two "nearly whites" and three "whites," the latter probably very light skinned indeed to merit that classification. These five workers displayed a "racial" *esprit de corps* by gathering in the same *canto.* As they are rare birds, they deserve a detailed introduction. João Alves Damasceno, 36, was born in Santana de Catu (Recôncavo). He was tall, had straight brown hair, wore a mustache and goatee and had tattoos. He had been a member of the Fifth Army Battalion band, a police officer, and a tinker, and was now a *ganhador.* Pedro Alves, 43, had straight, greying hair and also wore a goatee. He was born in Vila Nova da Rainha (now Bonfim) in the Bahia hinterland, and, like Damasceno, had spent some time in the army as a soldier in the Seventh Battalion. The youngest of the white group was Thomas da Silva Mendonça, still beardless at the age of 18, born in Salvador.

He and Damasceno joined the *canto* at the same time. While Damasceno wore tattoos, Thomas was covered in scars – both had working class bodies.

As for the "nearly whites", they included Eduardo Pereira Lima, 30, of Penedo, Alagoas province, who wore a moustache and had a scar on his belly. The other was Victorino de Souza, 50, the only married man in the group, who also had a moustache. Both had "curly black hair" (*cabelos pretos anelados),* which may be why they were not classified as full-fledged whites. Like Damasceno, Victorino was born in Catú. All five men lived in Calçada, the same district where their *canto* was located.

This group appears to be unique because its 23 members included just one black and one *fulo.* The rest included two *cabras,* the three whites and two "nearly whites", seven *pardos* of different hues, and seven others described as "*acaboclados*" or having an Amerindian appearance. However, their captain was not one of the lightest-skinned members: he was Victorino dos Passos Vieira, 47, listed as a *cabra*. A blacksmith, he lived in a district near the railroad station, had a beard and greying hair and a pockmarked face.[61] It may not be coincidental that this not-so-black group worked far from the harbor, in a non-traditional area in the geography of the *cantos,* taking in *ganhadores* whose skin color (white and "nearly white") was also unconventional in this sector of the job market.

CONCLUSION

This is probably the first time in the debate on the development of the urban working class during the twilight of slavery that it has been possible to unveil the characteristics of a sector of that class in such detail. We can go beyond the paradigm of "creolization" – from African to Brazilian – and transition – from slavery to freedom – to study the role of racial and, to a certain extent, ethnic characteristics in the formation of the free working class on the eve of abolition, with evident projections for the post-emancipation period.[62]

The *ganhadores*' registry book analysed above provides a map of the racial distribution of Salvador's street workers at the time of abolition. As noted earlier, race is understood here as meaning ethnic and skin-color differences that were often subtle. Presumably, ethnicity and certainly skin color were important but not always decisive factors in the *ganhadores*' internal organization. Africans and Brazilians, blacks, *pardos*, *cabras* and other "racial groups" were highly integrated in the world of Salvador's *cantos*. Apart from the still numerous work groups that were exclusively African, a legacy of the past, only a few *ganhadores* described as white or "nearly white" converged in the same group, and even so their group was mainly comprised of non-whites, including its leader.

Unlike some colonial institutions (some of which were also post-colonial) that were racially or ethnically segregated, such as the militia corps and Catholic confraternities – and even the *cantos,* two or three decades earlier – the *cantos* seen here appear to be moving towards an organization that was guided primarily by class-based principles. It is my suggestion that, just before abolition, race and ethnicity were still a basic hierarchical principle for Bahian society as a whole, but in the world of urban street labor (if not the entire working class) they tended to bear less weight. This trend may have been stimulated by the death throes and final demise of slavery, as freedom helped reduce the class differences between the street workers who had once been divided into free and freedmen on one hand, and slaves on the other. It may also have been stimulated by the fact that *ganhadores* were not just unskilled workers whose job was carrying loads on their shoulders. Because many of them had specialized trades, particularly in the construction sector, they earned wages from time to time, and therefore had worked under conventional employers. In other words, they had undergone the more "classic" experience of the working class.

However, I do not intend to exaggerate that classic side of this process. Any kind of class, racial or ethnic experience must be understood in context, and the context under consideration here is street labor in Salvador, which was mainly a job for "people of color". Just as the reification of class has long ceased to be intelligent, so we should not think that it is now intelligent to reify race or ethnicity. It is very tempting to do so in contexts that are as racially or ethnically charged as nineteenth-century Bahia. At the time of abolition, however, that temptation is easier to resist. We can see that, as they always had been, class, race and ethnicity were intertwined in a complex web, but at least in the pages of the 1887 registry book – and supposing that these things can be separated – the class factor seems to have taken the lead.

Still, when all of this is seen from the perspective of the *ganhadores*' place in Bahian society – and taking the complex relationship between class, race and ethnicity seriously – we can also conclude that in the *cantos,* a form of Afro-Brazilian identity was being formed that superceded differences in skin color and origins. In other words, pressured by the experience of class, the *ganhadores* were moving towards an identity in which Afro-Brazilians, and Africans recognized each other as fellow passengers on Bahia's social slave ship. I am fully aware that the racial ideology that predominated in Bahia at the time gave lighter-skin Afro-Brazilians enormous precedence over blacks. And I also believe that racial tensions must have existed between the two groups. Nevertheless, I suggest that, rather than embarking on divergent paths of identity, Afro-Brazilian workers were converging around the recognition that they were all – or nearly all – black or treated as such in a white-dominated society. This was the trend among street workers when slavery was abolished. Future studies may confirm or refute the extent to which this was true in the *cantos* and other sectors of the Bahian working class, and whether it continued after abolition.

APPENDIX

Police regulations concerning the services of workers in the commercial district

Clause 1 – Workers in the commercial district shall be divided into groups, each of which shall have a leader with the title of ***Canto* Captain,**[63] and an assistant who will substitute him [when he suffers] impediments.

Clause 2 – Each group may contain an unlimited number of workers.

Clause 3 – All workers must be registered with the Police by the *canto* captains, who for such purpose shall order them to present themselves before the Chief of Police, being forbidden to admit any who are not legally registered.

Clause 4 – The *cantos* shall be named **A., B., C.,** and so forth, according to the need for their location to transport objects.

Clause 5 – These workers must wear short-sleeved shirts, bearing on the right side in clearly visible letters, made from red nankeen, their registration number and above this, the letter of their respective *canto*.

Clause 6 – The appointment of "*canto* captains" and their assistants shall be effected by the workers in each *canto*, but will only be valid subject to the approval of the Chief of Police, who may dismiss them at his convenience.

Clause 7 – The Chief of Police shall present each *canto* captain free of charge a title of appointment and a true copy of these present instructions so that he may easily know all of his duties.

Clause 8 – Workers must obey their captains, who, each in his own *canto,* shall regularize their work in the best possible manner so that there is equality of work and interests among his subordinates.

Clause 9 – The captains shall be responsible to the Chief of Police for their subordinates who, during working hours, cause mayhem, gamble, become inebriated, use forbidden weapons, in sum, infringe upon any law or police regulation or commit a crime.

Paragraph 1 – They are also obliged to communicate any infractions or crimes, immediately sending the subordinates who commit them before the said authority for legal punishment, as the case requires, on pain of dismissal for incapacity.

Paragraph 2 – They shall also report deaths, sudden disappearances or any other event that may alter the number of workers [in their *cantos*].

Paragraph 3 – Such communications may be effected in person or in writing.

Clause 10 – Any and all public bearers, no matter what their condition, are expressly prohibited from working in the commercial district without having joined one of the *cantos* and without the clothing and badge described in these regulations.

Sole paragraph – This clause does not apply to internal workers at the Customs House, Companhia Bahiana, warehouses, storehouses or any other repository or place of business.

Clause 11 – These instructions may be altered, modified or reformed at the discretion of the Chief of Police of the Province of Bahia, 5 October 1880.

The Chief of Police
Virgilio Silvestre de Faria

ENDNOTES

1. This chapter is part of a more extensive study funded by the Brazilian Research Council-CNPq in which I discuss other "variables" about the *ganhadores* that were recorded by the police. I would like to thank Walter Fraga Filho and Wlamyra Albuquerque for suggesting important sources. I would also like to thank Flávio dos Santos Gomes, Mariângela Nogueira, Silvia Hunold Lara, Antônio Sérgio Guimarães and the members of the research seminar "Escravidão e invenção da liberdade" (Slavery and the invention of freedom) of the History Graduate Program of the Universidade Federal da Bahia (UFBa).
2. On the 1835 rebellion, see João José Reis, *Slave Rebellion in Brazil: The Muslim Uprising of 1835 in Bahia* (Baltimore: Johns Hopkins University Press, 1993). On African resistance to *canto* control after 1835, see João José Reis, "The Revolution of the Ganhadores: Urban Labour, Ethnicity and the African Strike of 1857 in Bahia, Brazil," *Journal of Latin American Studies* 29 (1997): 372-379.
3. For more information, see Reis, "The Revolution of the Ganhadores."
4. Arquivo Público do Estado da Bahia (hereafter APEBa), Polícia, Livro de Matrícula dos Cantos, maço (bundle) 7116.
5. B. J. Barickman, "Até a véspera: o trabalho escravo e a produção de açúcar nos engenhos do Recôncavo baiano," *Afro-Ásia* 21-22 (1998-99): 235; Kátia M. de Queirós Mattoso, *Bahia século XIX: uma província no Império* (Rio de Janeiro: Nova Fronterira, 1992), p. 111.
6. Robert Edgar Conrad, *The Destruction of Brazilian Slavery, 1850-1888* (Los Angeles: University of California Press, 1972), p. 285.
7. Luís Anselmo da Fonseca, *A escravidão, o clero e o abolicionismo* (Recife: Massangana, 1988 [1887]), p. 239.
8. Controlling free and freed workers was viewed as an important political issue throughout Brazil. A partial list of works on the subject include Lúcio Kovarik, *Trabalho e vadiagem* (São Paulo: Brasiliense, 1987), esp. pp. 36-69; Peter Eisenberg, *Homens esquecidos* (Campinas: Editora da UNICAMP, 1989), Part iii; Ademir Gebara, *O mercado de trabalho livre no Brasil* (São Paulo: Brasiliense, 1986), esp. chap. 2; Maria Lúcia Lamounier, *Da escravidão ao trabalho livre* (Campinas: Papirus, 1988); Hebe Maria Mattos de Castro, *Das cores do silêncio: os significados da liberdade no sudeste escravista, Brasil século XIX* 2nd ed. (Rio de Janeiro: Nova Fronteira, 1998, esp. chaps. 10 to 14; Joseli Maria Nunes Mendonça, *Entre a mão e os anéis* (Campinas: Ed. da UNICAMP/CECULT, 1999), esp. chap. 2; Regina Célia Xavier,

A conquista da liberdade (Campinas: Centro de memória da UNICAMP, 1996); Walter Fraga Filho, *Mendigos, moleques e vadios* (São Paulo: HUCITEC; Salvador: EDUFBA, 1996).

9. APEBa, Polícia, Livro de Matrícula dos cantos, maço 7116. This document is generally well preserved. However, during its recent restoration, some pages were put in the wrong order, which is often confusing for researchers. I will henceforth refer to it as the *Livro de Matrícula* or Registry Book.
10. *Livro de Matrícula,* fl. 29. Regarding the term *pardo* and other color designations, see the section "The colors of the *cantos*" below.
11. Ibid., fl. 80.
12. A similar phenomenon has been observed by historians of the city of Rio de Janeiro during the same period, including Carlos Eugênio Líbano Soares, when he discusses the increasingly frequent arrests of free and freed men and women in the *zungús,* lodgings and food service establishments controlled by black people. See, for example, his *Zungú: rumor de muitas vozes* (Rio de Janeiro: Arquivo Público do Estado, 1998), p. 79.
13. Alain Corbin, "Bastidores," in Michelle Perrot (ed.), *História da vida privada* (São Paulo: Companhia das Letras, 1995), IV, p. 430.
14. Although every effort has been made to ensure its accuracy, my count may have included some *ganhadores* twice if they changed *cantos.* It also includes workers who died after being registered and others who left the *cantos* to engage in another profession, or were banned from them because they broke the law or for some other reason.
15. This impression is confirmed by the festivals held on the docks, observed in the early twentieth century by Antonio Viana, *Quintal de nagô e outras crônicas, Cadernos do Centro de Estudos Baianos* No. 84 (Salvador: UFBa, n/d), p. 8.
16. See also Ana de Lourdes Ribeiro da Costa, "Espaços negros: '*cantos*' e 'lojas' em Salvador no século XIX," *Caderno CRH* Supplement (1991): 23-27, in which she emphasizes the importance of the docklands in the geography of the *cantos*, and maps some registered in the 1887 Registry Book, and others that are not listed, primarily through secondary sources. However, she identifies no more than twenty *cantos.*
17. See the photographic record of construction of the Bahia and São Francisco Railway, the railroad station and the urban settlement of the surrounding area in Gilberto Ferrez, *Bahia: velhas fotografias, 1858-1900* (Rio de Janeiro: Kosmos Editora; Salvador: Banco da Bahia Investimentos SA, 1988), pp. 71ff. The city had two *Gasômetros* that supplied the gas used to light its streets, one in Calçada and the other in Farol da Barra. See Eduardo Carigé, *Geographia Physica e Política da Província da Bahia* (Salvador: Imprensa Econômica, 1882), p. 75.
18. Ferrez, *Bahia,* pp. 44-45, 112, 187. This book of nineteenth-century photographs does not contain any images of sedan chairs. Regarding streetcars and the elevator built by Antônio Lacerda, see Carigé, *Geographia Physica e Política*, pp. 54 and 78.
19. Raymundo Nina Rodrigues, *Os africanos no Brasil* 4th ed. (São Paulo: Companhia Editora Nacional, 1976), p. 101.
20. Ibid, pp. 101-102.
21. See *Legislação da Província da Bahia sobre o negro: 1835-1888* (Salvador: Fundação Cultural do Estado da Bahia, 1996), pp. 172-175, 201-204. *Réis* was a Portuguese monetary unit, money of account, adopted in Brazil following independence in 1822.

22. Kátia M. de Queirós Mattoso, *Bahia: a cidade do Salvador e seu mercado no século XIX* (São Paulo: HUCITEC, 1978), p. 240, 343; Mattoso, *Bahia, século XIX*, p. 567.
23. See Maria Conceição da Costa e Silva, *Sociedade Montepio dos Artistas na Bahia* (Salvador: Fundação Cultural do Estado da Bahia, 1998).
24. Mattoso, *Bahia, século XIX*, p. 548. In 1887 one *real* was on average equal to 22.4 English pence. See Kátia M. de Queirós Mattoso, *Être esclave au Brésil, XVIe-XIXe siècles* (Paris: Hachette, 1979), p. 290.
25. According to Clause 4 of the regulations, the *cantos* were to be identified with letters of the alphabet.
26. *Livro de Matrícula*, fl. 79.
27. Ibid, fls. 24, 42, and 81.
28. Reis, "The Revolution of the Ganhadores," pp. 366-367.
29. See Manoel Querino, *A raça africana e seus costumes* (Salvador: Progresso, 1955), pp. 88-89.
30. Rodrigues, *Os africanos*, p. 100.
31. Reis, "The Revolution of the Ganhadores," pp. 390-391.
32. Again, the *Livro de Matrícula* recorded physical descriptions of *canto* members, which is why we know the color of their hair, as well as their ages. According to Conrad, *Destruction of Brazilian Slavery,* p. 288, only 1,001 sexagenarian slaves were registered in Bahia in 1886 and 1887. The best study on the so-called Sexagenarian Law is by Mendonça, *Entre a mão e os anéis*.
33. *Livro de Matrícula*, fls. 22 and 137.
34. On the national background of stevedores in Rio de Janeiro, see Maria Cecília Velasco e Cruz, "Tradições negras na formação de um sindicato: Sociedade de Resistência dos Trabalhadores em Trapiche e Café, Rio de Janeiro, 1905-1930," *Afro-Ásia* 24 (2000): 271-273.
35. *Livro de Matrícula*, fls. 29, 35, and 135.
36. See Fraga Filho, *Mendigos, moleques e vadios*, esp. chapter 8, and Barickman, "Até a véspera," pp. 228-234. The textile industrialist Luiz Tarquínio, writing under the pseudonym of "Cicinnatus", developed in 1885 an emancipation plan that, if put into practice, would last 10 years. He did not share the concerns of other members of the propertied class, particularly its rural branch, believing that freed men and women "rarely or unusually would leave the place [plantations] where everything is shown to them in a new light", in this case, the light of freedom. If the data presented in this chapter indicate a trend, he was mistaken. See Cicinnatus [Luiz Tarquínio], *O elemento escravo e as questões economicas do Brazil* (Bahia: Typographia dos Dois Mundos, 1885), pp. 86-87. However, many ex-slaves did stay in the plantation region, sometimes on the same plantations where they had served as slaves. On the experience of ex-slaves after emancipation, see Walter Fraga Filho, "Encruzilhadas da liberdade: histórias e trajetórias de escravos e libertos na Bahia, 1870-1910" (Ph. D. dissertation, Universidade Estadual de Campinas, 2003).
37. *Livro de Matrícula*, fls. 35 and 73.
38. Rodrigues, *Os africanos*, p. 98.
39. Ibid., p. 101.
40. I am working with the reasonable speculation that Brazilian *ganhadores* were still grouping in *cantos* at the time when Nina Rodrigues made his observations.

41. Rodrigues, *Os africanos*, p. 102.
42. On Candomblé in this period, see Raymundo Nina Rodrigues, *O animismo fetichista dos negros baianos* (Rio de Janeiro: Civilização Brasileira, 1935).
43. On this point, see Reis, "The Revolution of the Ganhadores," p. 383.
44. *Livro de Matrícula,* fls. 35 and 73. Age does not seem to have been a decisive factor in the choice of leadership among Africans or Brazilians. In Brazilian *cantos,* only 15 of the 37 captains were over 40; in African *cantos,* 55 percent were over 60 when 74 percent of their members were in that age group. In fact, younger men had an advantage when vying for leadership, which refutes the notion that Africans always maintained African traditions of the authority of elders in Brazil. Maturity, at least in the *cantos,* did not mean leadership.
45. Ibid., fl. 145.
46. Ibid., fl.133.
47. Ibid., fl. 94.
48. The captains' birthplace did not seem to have been a decisive factor in the workers' choice of *cantos.* In other words, there is no evidence that, for example, a captain from Santo Amaro would systematically bring workers from his hometown into his group.
49. *Livro de Matrícula*, fls. 144-5.
50. Ibid, fls. 5, 116, 119-20, and 124.
51. Ibid, fl. 51.
52. APEBa, *Livro de Registro de Testamentos*, vol. 61, fls. 156v-158v. My thanks to Walter Fraga Filho for having shared this document with me.
53. *Livro de Matrícula*, fl. 123.
54. Just as the term class, the term race is frequently used here as an analytical category. Regarding the reason for speaking of *race* in this context, see Antonio Sérgio A. Guimarães, *Racismo e Anti-Racismo no Brasil* (São Paulo: FUSP/Editora 34, 1999), esp. chaps. 1 and 2.
55. See Lilia Moritz Schwarcz, *O espetáculo das raças* (São Paulo: Companhia das Letras, 1993), and by the same author *Retrato em branco e negro: jornais, escravos e cidadãos em São Paulo no final do século XIX* (São Paulo: Companhia das Letras, 1987).
56. The association between being African and barbarism at that time was not restricted to "scientific racism". On the use of scientific racism in late nineteenth- and early twentieth-century Brazil, see Schwarcz, *O espetáculo das raças*. A Bahian example of the use of this theory is precisely the work by Nina Rodrigues referred above. On the persistance of the depreciation of African culture in early twentieth-century Bahia, see Wlamyra Albuquerque, *Algazarra nas ruas: comemorações da Independência na Bahia* (Campinas: Editora da UNICAMP/CECULT, 1999); and Meire Lúcia dos Reis, "A cor da notícia: discursos sobre o negro na imprensa baiana," M. A. thesis, Universidade Federal da Bahia, 2000, esp. chaps. 4 and 5.
57. For the persistense of the phenomenon nowadays, see Yvonne Maggie, "Introdução: cor, hierarquia e sistema de classificação," in *Catálogo: Centenário da Abolição* (Rio de Janeiro: CIEC/Núcleo da Cor/UFRJ, 1989), pp. 1-29.
58. The exceptional case of composition in *Canto* AL is discussed further below.
59. The 1872 census data are found in Manuel Jesuino Ferreira, *A Província da Bahia: apontamentos* (Rio de Janeiro: Typographia Nacional, 1875), pp. 32-33. The parishes of Sé, São Pedro Velho, Santana, Conceição da Praia, Vitória, Rua do Paço, Pilar,

Santo Antônio, Brotas, Mares, Penha, Itapoan, and Pirajá were included in this census. The last five were located on the outskirts of the city.

60. This is the predominant tone in Gilberto Freyre, *Sobrados e mucambos: decadência do patriarcado rural e desenvolvimento do urbano* 7th ed. (Rio de Janeiro: José Olympio Editora; Instituto Nacional do Livro, 1985), esp. chaps. 11 and 12. There is one passage (pp. 607-608) regarding poor "street" mulattoes (not workers) who are described as "socially pathological" (p. 607).
61. *Livro de Matrícula*, fl. 63.
62. For studies on the "transition" from slavery to freedom in Brazil, see ft. 8 above.
63. Emphasis given in the original document.

7

Leadership and Authority in Maroon Settlements in Spanish America and Brazil

Jane Landers

Several recent textbooks of colonial Latin American history have featured the famous sixteenth-century oil portrait of the maroons of Esmeraldas, Ecuador. This painting, depicts the *zambo* chieftains (persons of African and Indian heritage), Don Francisco de Arobe and his sons, Don Pedro and Don Domingo, dressed in Spanish finery of silk and lace, carrying lances of African design, and ornamented in golden and shell jewelry typical of the indigenous art of the coast.[1] This fascinating work illustrates nicely the cultural complexity of the maroon settlements. But perhaps the most striking aspect of the portrait for modern viewers, accustomed to think of the African experience in the Americas as totally degraded by slavery, is the confidence and authority with which Don Francisco stares out of the frame. While early modern viewers would have also been captured by the exoticism of the subjects, they would have immediately read in this painting many cues about the status of these men. Not only the honorific titles floating above their heads but their rich clothing and adornments, their weapons, their posture and Don Francisco's direct gaze all identified these men as "natural lords".[2]

This chapter examines questions about the leadership and social and political organization of maroon settlements in Spanish America and Brazil which have long been debated by scholars such as Roger Bastide, Raymond K. Kent, Richard Price, and Stuart Schwartz, to name only a few. Looking at the maroon experience across empires and centuries, Price theorized a sort of "progressive" continuum of political organization in which the earliest maroon communities drew on familiar African models of kingship while eighteenth-century groups adopted more modern organizational forms and elected creole leaders. Bastide, Kent, and Schwartz examined the maroon's attempts to recreate "kingdoms" and "states" in the Brazilian hinterlands. Using linguistic evidence primarily, Kent called the runaway slave community of Palmares a centralized kingdom and argued that "the model for Palmares could have come from nowhere else but central Africa" while Bastide and Schwartz acknowledged the multi-ethnic nature of the societies and made less dramatic claims about African retentions. Schwartz characterized Palmares as a "neo-African kingdom". This idea is supported by Igor Kopytoff's work on state formation on African frontiers. Kopytoff argued that Africa was a "frontier continent" with a long history of vast and often crisis-induced population movements which forced Africans repeatedly to create "new social order in the midst of institutional vacuum." The new states formed on the fringes of more complex societies reproduced something similar to what they knew, although in simpler form. The ethnogenesis Kopytoff described has parallels in the seventeenth century maroon communities herein examined–although the frontiers have been displaced across the Atlantic. And if hierarchy was, indeed, one of the organizing principles of African society as Kopytoff claims, then maroon settlements would have also established some form of it.[3] Located on the peripheries of European cities, and also on the fringes of indigenous worlds, maroon communities borrowed elements they found useful from both the dominant and native cultures. They drew as well on a variety of African cultural models–especially in the areas which reinforced the authority so necessary for the communities' survival. This chapter adopts Kopytoff's frontier thesis in examining the multiple sources of political and social authority which sustained maroon societies in the Americas.

Despite the often unflattering notions Europeans held of African religions and cultural practices the priests and military opponents sent to try to pacify or "reduce" maroons inevitably commented on the civil, military, and religious authority maroon leaders exercised in their culturally-mixed settlements.[4] The famous maroon chieftains of Gallque's painting were descendants of a shipload of "Guinea" slaves en route from Panama to Peru who shipwrecked on the coast of Ecuador at some point in the mid sixteenth-century, "sowed terror" among the local Pidi Indians and established a dynastic rule within the region.[5] The source of this foundational myth is the Spanish priest who first contacted the descendants of the escaped slaves in 1577 on a beach near the Esmeraldas River. His informants were Alonso Yllescas (a Cape Verdean who had taken the surname of his slave-trader/owner upon being baptized in Seville), his Indian wife, their children and spouses, and a sizeable entourage of gold-bedecked Indians and mulattos. Yllescas's years in Spain may have accounted for the peaceful reception granted the churchmen, but the first-hand knowledge he had of Spaniards also forearmed him. Although the *zambo* chief promised to produce more of his people for baptism, the priests waited in vain. A later search up the Esmeraldas River proved the maroons had destroyed their planted fruit trees and a fleet of canoes before withdrawing deeper into the jungle.[6] Subsequent Spanish efforts to drive a road from the interior capital of Quito to the coast, led to periodic, and often hostile, contacts with the maroons. Finally, in 1599, after almost a half-century of intermittent contact the maroon leaders of the portrait marched into Quito to swear vassalage to the Spanish King and receive their gifts of fine clothing from the governor, who served as godfather at their baptisms. Although never claiming to have descended from African kings, Yllescas could claim to have founded his community and successfully defended it for many years, thus earning the allegiance of his followers and the recognition of his dominion over them. The Esmeraldas maroons had drawn on African, Spanish, and indigenous backgrounds to create a creole dynasty which the ceremonies in

Quito helped validate. The territorial control and leadership of Don Francisco Arobe and his kin was confirmed by treaty and memorialized in oils.[7]

Nearby, the most famous Spanish American maroon community of San Basilio, in modern-day Colombia, was organized by one Domingo Bioho, who claimed to have been a ruler in Africa and who recreated a royal dynasty in Colombia, taking the name King Benkos. Benkos's wife was the queen of the community and his son was the heir designate. After many failed expeditions against him the governor of Cartagena struck a deal with Benkos, only to betray and hang him in 1619. Benkos's dynasty carried on without him and his settlement was not "reduced" into a legitimate and law-abiding town until 1686, by which time it had been in existence for almost seventy years and numbered more than 3000 inhabitants, including six hundred warriors, ruled by four war captains, each of his own "nation".[8]

Meanwhile, on another frontier, outlying the port of Vera Cruz in New Spain, another maroon community organized itself around a king. Like Benkos, Yanga (or Ñanga), an African of the Bran nation claimed royal lineage and ruled a mountaintop village which withstood retaliatory attacks for over thirty years before the Viceroy sent a major expedition against it in 1609. The accounts of a Jesuit priest who accompanied the Spanish expedition and Yanga's missives to his enemies highlight the multiple authorities which permitted Yanga, and later his successors, to rule so long.[9]

Yanga's initial source of authority rested on his having founded the settlement– as Yllescas and Benkos also had. His claim to royal lineage may have also been accepted by his followers. Moreover, Yanga had assumed the role of religious leader of his community–the sort of "sacred chieftainship" or "divine kingship" noted in other African societies. As military leader, he successfully defended his well-ordered community for many years, thereby maintaining another claim on the loyalty of his adherents/subjects and the bravery and haughtiness with which he faced the final attack are illustrative.

Yanga sent a letter to his pursuers via a released captive, recounting his many victories against previous expeditions, condemning the Spaniards as cruel, treacherous, and cowardly, and challenging them to follow the bearer back to his stronghold. Yanga assured the man he would not die because he had seen Yanga's face. [10] Safely down the mountain the Spaniard recounted how the maroons had split his comrade's head with a broadsword and after drinking cupped handfuls of his blood, had ridden back to their settlement with the man's scalp as their banner. Yanga and his captains had greeted the returning warriors as musicians played drums and cowbells for the procession.[11] In this account we see glimpses of ritual acts, warfare, courtly displays, diplomacy, and Yanga's claims to magical, as well as political, power.

The difficulty of the subsequent Spanish siege and the intricate defenses which protected Yanga's well-ordered town point to his strong central command. Yanga's flourishing community of over sixty households had devoted considerable resources to agriculture, fortification, and animal husbandry as well as to the banditry for which Spaniards condemned them.[12] Yanga's large house sat in the middle of town at the foot of a large tree topped by a sentinel's tower and it was filled with benches for seating. The Spaniards assumed it also served as a town meeting place although it might more accurately have been considered a royal compound or council house.[13]

In earlier years Yanga had led his own war parties, but by this time, he was aged, and his Angolan war captain, Francisco de la Matiza, now commanded the warriors.[14] The pattern of ethnic division of military responsibilities at San Basilio and Matudere (discussed below) where war captains commanded squadrons of their own nation would suggest that Yanga's camp included a number of Angolan men in addition to the Bran component. [15]

As Francisco and the younger men fought the Spanish forces, Yanga gathered the women in the community's small church and prayed before an altar covered with lighted candles and in front of which they had planted arrows in the ground. The meaning of this display is unknown but it appears that Yanga's community, like others discussed in this essay, observed forms of Catholic and African religious practices simultaneously. At nightfall, the maroons received word that the Spaniards were almost upon them, and Yanga led the women to the safety of another nearby palisaded fort.[16]

During one of the many battles which followed, Yanga's Angolan war captain was killed, and finally, after nine years of battling on the run, and in a starving state, Yanga sent the Spaniards a list of eleven conditions for peace. His demands included freedom for all those living in his town prior to 1608, legal recognition of the town from which Spaniards were to be excluded except on market days, and establishment of a recognized church. Yanga also demanded that his heirs would become governors after him.[17] In 1618 Spanish authorities accepted Yanga's terms and formally created the free black town of San Lorenzo de los Negros de Cerralvo.[18]

After long years of resistance Yanga had gained peace and recognition of a sort of dynastic right to succession for his sons. The Spaniards had agreed to similar terms at San Basilio in Ecuador and Colombia and although Spanish forces destroyed Matudere, another Colombian maroon community, that settlement also seemed to have attempted some form of dynastic rule. The claims of an aged African woman named Juana to have founded the settlement in 1681 were supported by her creole husband, Domingo, who styled himself Captain while his wife had adopted the title of *Virreina* (Vice-queen). It should be noted that although Spaniards described Domingo as a *criollo* (person of African descent born in the Americas) and *ladino* (or acculturated individual), his father, who also lived at Matudere, was born in Angola. Other maroons described as *muy viejos* or very old might also have been sources of direct knowledge about African social and political models.[19] The second largest ethnic group at Matudere were those identified as the Ararás, with 19 members and second only to the Minas who numbered 28: it is possible Juana's authority at Matudere may have resembled the role of reign-mates or queen mothers in Africa and the couple's two young sons may have been expected to later rule the settlement.[20]

Religious authority at Matudere was apparently divided between animist and Christian religious figures. An African shaman named Antonio provided the warriors with "poisoned arrowheads and cords and other demonic ideas," and assurances that they were invincible. He enjoyed great regard and was treated as a holy man. His adherents kissed his hand to show their respect and obeyed his every command, including his order to kidnap consorts from nearby haciendas. Antonio claimed to have a sack of powders he could set afire which would make Spanish attackers disappear. Antonio's implements and magic suggest he might have been from Central Africa.[21] The Christians at Matudere, who also enjoyed a loyal following, were led by Diego Biáfara and Francisco Arará whose services included reciting prayers and the rosary and officiating at sacraments of baptism and marriage in the church the maroons had constructed for their community.[22]

As was the case at San Basilio and also in the Mexican example, Matudere's war captains were African-born and seem to have led squadrons of their own countrymen. Pedro Mina led the most numerous African nation in the settlement and Francisco Arará led the second largest group. Pacho Congo and Miguel Pantoja (nation unstated) held subordinate military positions such as standard bearer (*alférez*).[23] In addition to maintaining jungle patrols and sentry systems, the maroons at Matudere had worked out a system of mutual defense and alliance with other nearby maroon settlements. Domingo Criollo also claimed to have established at least some infrequent contacts with larger maroon communities as far away as Santa Marta and Panama.[24] If this were true, Cartagena would have been encircled by a maroon alliance and the threat was too great not to address. Although Domingo Criollo attempted to treat for peace on several occasions, Spanish forces eventually destroyed Matudere, with some survivors escaping to allied settlements.[25]

Within the present-day limits of the United States, runaway slaves established the town of Gracia Real de Santa Teresa de Mose in Spanish Florida in 1738. Like the other maroon communities discussed above Mose was a multiethnic community in which cultural and material traditions of various African *naciones* (or nations)--Mandinga, Carabalí, Congo and Arará–blended with those of various Native American groups such as Yamasee, Apalache, and Timucua – and with Spanish and English traditions. A man of the Mandinga nation, baptized and renamed Francisco Menéndez, ruled Mose. Menéndez had fought in the Yamasee war against English settlers in Carolina and assumed military command of the free blacks to whom the Spaniards had granted sanctuary at Mose. He held his military position and the title of Captain for at least forty years and represented the villagers in all dealings with the Spaniards, thus combining military and civil leadership. He could claim authority as the founder of Mose. Spanish officials referred to the other residents of Mose as Menéndez's "subjects" and often commented on his character and the good example he set for his people. Menéndez was multi-lingual (speaking Spanish and Yamassee at least, but also probably English as well as his own language), was literate in Spanish and may have also been able to write in Arabic and English. In the context of eighteenth-century Spanish Florida, his literacy certainly distinguished him, including from many Spaniards in the colony, and this knowledge and "civility" would have been a source of additional authority and status for Menéndez. As a practicing Catholic he could not tap African religious power, at least openly, but Menéndez did assume another significant religious role as godfather to some of his villagers.[26] In this way Menéndez made kin of dependents and increased his authority over them, a strategy Kopytoff found African frontiersmen also practiced in new communities.[27] Because Mose is one of the few maroon settlements to be studied both through the documentary and material records, it has attracted the attention of archaeologists working on perhaps the most famous of all maroon settlements, Palmares.[28]

Located in the modern states of Alagôas and Pernambuco in Brazil, Palmares probably came into existence when slaves were first introduced in the sixteenth century. Over the course of the 17th century, it grew to encompass multiple village sites holding populations estimated at up to 20,000 persons. The maroons allegedly called their settlement *Angola janga* (little Angola), reflecting the Portuguese and later, even greater Dutch, importation of slaves from that region of Africa.[29] For approximately a century (1580-1680) Luanda was the primary port of embarkation for slaves entering Brazil and although they may have had distinct geographic origins they would have been Kimbundu or Umbundu-speakers. [30] The Angolan word *quilombo* by which Palmares was described at the end of that period refers to a male initiation society housed within a fortified war camp.[31] And Palmares was just that.

Beginning in 1612, the residents of Palmares endured and survived at least twenty-five military expeditions against them, many of which generated documentary evidence about the site. The leader of a Dutch expedition in 1645 reported that Macaco, the main village of Palmares, contained a large council house like Yanga's, 220 houses, a church, and four forges arrayed along a broad street, six feet wide and a half mile long. The village was fortified by a double palisade and its intervening trench filled with pointed stakes, a defensive technique Stuart Schwartz found the maroons still used in the 1760s at the Buraco de Tatú (Armadillo's Hole) *quilombo* in Bahia.[32] A contemporary drawing of Palmares shows nine African men pulling fishing nets from a river in which canoes float. In the background is a wooden watchtower and in the foreground a pot and a basket, all evidence of the economy and artisanry practiced by the maroons.[33] Portuguese accounts noted that like their counterparts in New Spain (Mexico) and New Granada (Colombia and Ecuador), the Brazilian maroons were industrious and skilled at exploiting the natural resources of their remote jungle terrain. They planted corn and a wide variety of vegetables that sustained them during the frequent sieges and also exploited the many nearby palm trees which provided them with fruit, wine, oil, butter, salt, clothing, thatching, cording and building materials. Fishing and hunting added to their food stores. In 1992 archaeologists mapped and conducted surface collections of materials at Macaco, locating remnants of a possible palisade, a variety of pottery shards, and some buried stone tools.[34] Little more could be determined by their brief investigation and, as is the case with other maroon sites, more is known through the documentary record.

Those inform us that between 1670 and 1694 the famed Ganga Zumba or Great Lord, ruled Palmares and its ten associated villages from the main village of Macaco.[35] Ganga Zumba's palace complex was staffed by courtiers and guards who prostrated themselves before him and the well-ordered city had grown to hold 1500-2000 houses. The order and scale of the main settlement, much grander than others discussed herein, the deference shown its ruler, and the existence of law (not to mention executions) all were cause for the Portuguese to marvel and to pay the ultimate compliment--observing that Macaco had all the attributes of a Republic. Not only were they amazed that "barbarians" could govern themselves "totally free of subjugation," they found that the maroons had also recreated the Catholic church in Macaco, just as the Colombian maroons of Matudere and Yanga's subjects did. Whereas at Matudere the "Catholics" decorated their chapel with paper images, the church at Macaco boasted images of the Christ child, Our Lady of the Conception (*Nossa Senhora da Conceição*) and Saint Bras (*São Brás*). As at Matudere, an acculturated maroon (*ladino*) performed baptisms and marriages in the church while congregants recited remembered Christian prayers.[36]

Such Christian observances did not apparently impede the practice of polygamy at Palmares for Ganga Zumba had three wives. His primary wife was a *mulatta* (female offspring of African women and white men), said to be the mother of his many children and two other wives were *criolas* or Brazilian-born women of African descent. His extended royal family helped Ganga Zumba govern the multiple villages associated with Palmares, most of which bore Central African names or the names of the village rulers. [37] Thus, although Ganga Zumba was said to have been "elected," he had, over time, created a ruling dynasty at Palmares. His brother, Gana Zona, ruled Subupira, the second largest city of Palmares which served as a military training camp and which boasted stone and wooden fortifications and 800 houses. Ganga Zumba's mother, Aqualtune/Acaine, ruled another fortified village nearby which carried her name, and his nephews, Zumbi and Andalaquituche ruled two others.[38]

An impressive array of military figures, many of them members of his own family, defended Ganga Zumba's kingdom. Those whose names survive include Ganga Muíça, identified as the war leader of the Angolans. This reference suggests that although Angolans were numerous in Brazil and in this settlement, Ganga Zumba and his family might not have been Angolans. Although he does not cite a source, Décio Freitas identifies Ganga Zumba as belonging to the "Arda" (Arará) nation. Others whose names have come down to us are Gaspar, the king's captain of the guard, and other "famous captains" such as João Tapuia (either an Indian or possibly a *zambo*), and Ambrósio. One of Ganga's own sons, Toculo, was said to be a "grand corsair". Contemporary documents also describe Zumbi, the son of Gana Zona and Ganga Zumba's nephew as a great warrior "of singular valor, great spirit, and rare constancy...the most spectacular of them all... his industry, judgement and fortitude served as an embarrassment to ours and to his an example."[39]

When the famed Brazilian slave catcher Pedro Fernão Carrilho and his forces attacked Subupira in 1676, they executed Ganga Muíça and other leaders whom they captured alive, but Zumbi and his uncle the king escaped with minor wounds. Ganga Zumba found shelter with many of his remaining family members at the large and well-fortified village of an allied maroon leader named Amaro but Carrilho's forces doggedly tracked the fugitives to that refuge. Again the Brazilians launched a devastating attack that almost wiped out Ganga Zumba's dynasty. They captured Ganga Zumba's children, Zambi and Acaiene (named for her grandmother?) along with some twenty of his grandchildren and cousins. They also killed Ganga Zumba's warrior son Toculo, and two other noted war leaders, Pacassa and Baubi, but once again Ganga Zumba escaped.[40]

The Portuguese accounts betray a certain admiration for the sophisticated settlements they destroyed and for the noted warriors they captured or killed. They also demonstrate that this long-lived maroon community had reached a complex level of political organization that the previous examples discussed aspired to and might have achieved given the same remote location and political and material conditions.

Carrilho's repeated attacks took such a severe toll that Ganga Zumba finally sued for peace. He sent three of his surviving sons (one of whom was badly wounded) and a delegation of other important maroon leaders into Pernambuco where they met with the governor and offered to end the war and to become loyal vassals of the King of Portugal in return for confirmation of Ganga Zumba's leadership and the freedom of the Palmaristas. The governor ordered the almost naked maroons be dressed and adorned with yellow ribbons, which generosity was said to have pleased them greatly. In another traditional act, the maroons were baptized while solemn masses were sung and the priest offered prayers to Saint Anthony. Unfortunately no portrait captured this event or the subsequent peace ceremonies in Macoco, but the high-level official rituals are reminiscent of those recorded for the maroon delegation to Quito in 1599 and for Yanga's peace accords in New Spain in 1619.[41]

The peace did not hold and the settlement was further undermined by internal divisions among Ganga Zumba's followers and others led by his Brazilian-born nephew, Zumbi. Distrustful of Portuguese promises Zumbi killed his uncle in 1687 and became the new ruler of Palmares. There may have been no other way for the younger man to acquire leadership despite his kinship and noted military skills, due to the hierarchic nature of African social relations and the tendency for political authority, once vested in an individual, to last a lifetime.[42]

Zumbi renewed the resistance of Palmares but ruled for less than a decade. The constraints of this paper do not permit a longer discussion of the subsequent attacks on Palmares but after two years of unabated war and a 45 day siege against Macaco a Brazilian force numbering about 6000 men claimed to have completed its destruction in 1695 and Zumbi was captured and beheaded.[43] Brazilian elation was premature because, of course, they had not eliminated the maroons. We now know that, rather, the survivors did what other maroons before and after had done when required to–they melted into the hinterlands to coalesce into new and more remote settlements and begin their free lives anew.

These case studies of Spanish and Brazilian maroon societies illustrate some of the mechanisms maroon leaders employed to establish and then legitimate authority in ethnically mixed settlements. Their sources of authority were varied and were based on such concepts as political seniority, religious power, military prowess, and corporate or familial connections. In some communities the maroons accommodated ethnic and religious difference by sharing leadership roles on the basis of proportional representation. Their attempts to create perpetual chieftainships or dynasties with acknowledged legitimacy were buttressed by origin myths, assumed titles, rituals, and in the case of Ganga Zumba, elaborate royal courts and large kinship networks that linked multiple village sites. When necessary and possible, maroons further stabilized their leadership and documented dynastic right through treaty with European powers.

ENDNOTES

1. Kenneth Mills and William B. Taylor, *Spanish America, A Documentary History* (Wilmington, DE: Scholarly Resources Press, 1998), cover and pp. 147-149. The painting is by the *mestizo* (male offspring of Amerindian females and white men) Andrés Sánchez Gallque, who like the subjects of his portrait, occupied an interstitial position between the worlds of his Spanish father and that of his Indian mother.
2. Ibid., p. 149, where it is stressed that the maroons have been "captured" by the portraitist–as "trophies, stuffed and mounted on a wall of blue." While it is true the men were offering allegiance to the Spanish king, the hierarchy I observe in the painting is that the two younger men stand behind Don Francisco, with Don Pedro standing closer to his father and Don Domingo standing slightly behind his father and older brother. Both young men gaze directly at their father as if accustomed to following his lead or deferring to him. On natural lordship see Amy Turner Bushnell, "Ruling the 'Republic of Indians' in Seventeenth-Century Florida," in Peter H. Wood, Gregory A. Waselkov, and M. Thomas Hatley (eds.), *Powahatan's Mantle: Indians in the Colonial Southeast* (Lincoln, NE: University of Nebraska Press, 1989), pp. 134-150.
3. Richard Price, *Maroon Societies: Rebel Slave Communities in the Americas* (Baltimore: Johns Hopkins University Press, 1996), p. 20; Roger Bastide, *African Civilisations in the New World* trans. Peter Green (New York: Harper and Row, 1971), p. 69; Stuart Schwartz, *Slaves Peasants and Rebels: Reconsidering Brazilian Slavery* (Urbana: University of Illinois Press, 1992), pp. 103-136; Igor Kopytoff, *The African*

Frontier: The Reproduction of Traditional African Societies (Bloomington: Indiana University Press, 1987), pp. 3-88.

4. European accounts also include valuable demographic information on the communities, as well as descriptions of their physical layout, subsistence patterns, and trade networks. For more on this subject see Jane Landers, "Cimarrón Ethnicity and Cultural Adaptation in the Spanish Domains of the Circum-Caribbean, 1503-1763," in Paul E. Lovejoy (ed.), *Identity in the Shadow of Slavery* (London: Continuum, 2000), pp. 30-54.
5. Audiencia de Quito (hereafter cited as AQ) 22/4, Arquivo General de Indias on microfilm at the Banco Central de Quito, Relación de Miguel Cabello Balboa, 1578; P. Rafael Savoia, "El negro Alonso de Illescas y sus descendientes (entre 1553-1867)," in P. Rafael Savoia (ed.), *Actas del primer congreso de historia del negro en el Ecuador y el sur de Colombia* (Quito: Centro Cultural Afro-ecuatoriano, 1988), pp. 29-61.
6. Relación de Miguel Cabello Balboa; Padre Joel Monroy, *Los religiosos de la Merced en el Antiguo Reino de Quito* (Quito: Editorial Labor, 1943), II, pp. 98-123, cited in Savoia, "El negro Aalonso de Illescas," pp. 28-29.
7. For an excellent discussion of the Esmeraldas maroons see Kris E. Lane, *Quito 1599: City and Colony in Transition* (Albuquerque: University of New Mexico Press, 2002).
8. Anthony McFarlane, "Cimarrones and Palenques: Runaways and Resistance in Colonial Colombia," *Slavery and Abolition* 6/3 (1985): 134-135; Arquivo General de Indias (hereafter AGI), Santa Fe 531, libro 11, folio 217, Real Cédula, July 13, 1686.
9. David Davidson, "Negro Slave Control and Resistance in Colonial Mexico, 1519-1650," *Hispanic American Historical Review* 46 (1966): 235-253; Colin A. Palmer, *Slaves of the White Gods: Blacks in Mexico, 1570-1650* (Harvard University Press, Cambridge: 1976), pp. 126-130; "Relación de la misión á que fué enviado el P. Juan Laurencio, acompañando a una escuadra de soldados que salía á la reducción de negros foragidos y salteadores," in Andrés Pérez de Ribes, *Crónica y historia religiosa de la Provincia de la Compañía de Jesús de México en Nueva España* 2 vols. (Mexico: Impr. Del Sagrado corazon de Jesús,1896), I, 282-294.
10. Davidson, "Negro Slave Control"; Palmer, *Slaves of the White God*, pp. 128-130.
11. Pérez de Ribes, *Crónica.*
12. Ibid.
13. Ibid.
14. Ibid. John K. Thornton describes dances as a central element of military training and war preparations in the Kongo. See his: "African Dimensions of the Stono Rebellion," *American Historical Review* 96/4(1991): 1112-1113; "African Soldiers in the Haitian Revolution," *Journal of Caribbean History* 25/1-2 (1991): 58-80.
15. Anthony McFarlane, "Cimarrones and Palenques,"; Landers, "Cimarrón Ethnicity."
16. Pérez Ribes, *Crónica.*
17. Archivo General de la Nación, Mexico, Commissary of Veracruz to the Inquisition in Mexico City, Inquisición, Vol. 283, fls. 186-187.
18. William B. Taylor, "The Foundation of Nuestra Señora de Guadalupe de los Morenos de Amapa," *The Americas* 26 (1970): 439-446.
19. AGI, Santa Fe 213, Report of Governor Martin de Cevallos, May 29, 1693.

20. Ibid. Matudere was home to 28 Minas, 19 Ararás, 3 Wolofs, 2 Caravlies, 1 Bran, 1 Goyo, 3 Popos, 10 Congos, 9 Luangos, and 5 Angolas. See also Edna G. Bay, *Wives of the Leopard: Gender, Politics, and Culture in the Kingdom of Dahomey* (Charlottesville: University of Virginia Press, 1998), pp. 13-21, 51-56.
21. AGI, Santa Fe 213, Report of Governor Martin de Cevallos, May 29, 1693. Kongo warriors were noted for their uses of poisons on arrows. John K. Thornton, *Warfare in Atlantic Africa, 1500-1800* (London: University College London Press, 1999), p.106. On Antonio's magic see Wyatt MacGaffey, *Religion and Society in Central Africa: The Bakongo of Lower Zaire* (Chicago: Chicago University Press, 1986), pp. 135-168.
22. AGI, Santa Fe 213, Father Fernando Zapata to Governor Martin de Cevallos, April 21, 1693.
23. Ibid. Within weeks after a priest visited the settlement, warriors from Matudere ambushed and defeated a Spanish force of some sixty men sent out against them, appropriated their weapons, and sent the commander's testicles wrapped in a cloth (like a charm?), back to the governor in Cartagena. Robin Law, "'My Head Belongs to the King': On the Political and Ritual Significance of Decapitation in Pre-Colonial Dahomey," *Journal of African History* 30 (1989): 399-415, shows that ritual decapitation and castration of enemies were important features of warfare in contemporary Dahomey until leaders forbade the practices late in the eighteenth century.
24. AGI, Santa Fe 213, Memorial of Baltasar de la Fuente, November 26, 1690.
25. For a discussion of this battle see Landers, "Cimarrón Ethnicity."
26. Jane Landers, "Gracia Real de Santa Teresa de Mose: A Free Black Town In Spanish Florida," *American Historical Review* 95 (1990): 9-30; idem, *Black Society in Spanish Florida* (Urbana: University of Illinois Press, 1999), Chapter 2.
27. Kopytoff, *The African Frontier*, p. 17.
28. Pedro Paulo de Abreu Funari, "A arqueologia de Palmares, Sua contribução para o conhecimento da história da cultura afro-americana," in João José Reis and Flávio dos Santos Gomes (eds.), *Liberdade por um fio: história dos quilombos no Brasil* (São Paulo: Companhia de Letras, 1996), pp. 26-51. Also see Charles E. Orser, Jr., *In Search of Zumbi: Preliminary Archaeological Research in the Serra da Barriga, State of Alagoas, Brazil* (Normal, IL: Midwestern Archaeological Research Center, 1992).
29. The earliest Portuguese references to Palmares date from 1605. Décio Freitas, *Palmares: A Guerra dos Escravos* 5th ed. (Porto Alegre: Mercado Alberto, 1984), p. 44. See also Stuart A. Schwartz, *Slaves, Peasants, and Rebels*, p. 125.
30. Joseph C. Miller, *Way of Death: Merchant Capitalism and the Angolan Slave Trade, 1730-1830* (Madison: University of Wisconsin Press, 1988), p. 452; David Eltis, *The Rise of African Slavery in the Americas* (Cambridge: Cambridge University Press, 2000), p. 189. John K. Thornton, "The African Experience of '20. and Odd Negroes' Arriving in Virginia in 1619," *William and Mary Quarterly* 3rd Series 55/3 (1988): 421-434, informs that between 1617-1621 the Portuguese exported about 50,000 slaves from Angola, most of whom were bound for Brazil.
31. Raymond K. Kent, "Palmares: An African State in Brazil," *Journal of African History* 6/2 (1965): 161-175, contends that Palmares was identified as a *mocambo* (from mukambo, the Ambundu/Mbundu/Kimbundu word for hideout) until the 18th century when the word *quilombo* first appears in Portuguese documents. Schwartz, *Slaves, Peasants and Rebels*, p. 125, found the earliest usage of *quilombo* dates to 1691 and refers specifically to Palmares.

32. Schwartz, *Slaves, Peasants and Rebels*, pp. 112-118. On recent archaeology of African city wall fortifications see Graham Connah, "African City Walls: A Neglected Source?," in David M. Anderson and Richard Rathbone (eds.), *Africa's Urban Past* (Oxford: Heinemann, 2000), pp. 36-51.
33. Orser, *In Search of Zumbi*, p. 6.
34. Charles E. Orser, Jr., "Toward a Global Historical Archaeology: An Example from Brazil," *Historical Archaeology* 28 (1994): 5-22.
35. The Portuguese considered the most populated and well-fortified villages to be Zambi, Acotirene, the dual villages of Tabocas, Dambrabanga, Subupira, Macaco, Osenga, Amaro, and Andalaquituche. In addition to these, they noted there were a number of other smaller settlements they did not name: "Relação das guerras feitas aos Palmares de Pernambuco no tempo do governador D. Pedro de Almeida, de 1675 a 1678," in Edison Carneiro, *O Quilombo dos Palmares* 4th ed. (São Paulo: Cia. Editora Nacional, 1988), pp. 201-222. See also "Memorias dos feitos que se deram durante os primeiros annos da guerra com os negros quilombolas dos Palmares, seu destroço e paz aceita em Junho de 1678," *Revista do Instituto Histórico e Geográfico Brasileiro* 39/1 (1876): 293-321, reproduced in Robert Conrad (ed.), *Children of God's Fire: A Documentary History of Black Slavery in Brazil* (Princeton: Princeton University Press,1983), pp. 369-377.
36. Carneiro, *O Quilombo*, pp. 203-204.
37. Kent, "Palmares," p. 169, identifies the origins of village names as follows: Macoco/Makoko (Loango); Tabocas/Taboka (Ambundu); Andalaquituche/Ndala Kafuche (Kisama); Osenga/Osanga/Hosanga (Kwango); Subupira (Zande); Dombabanga/Ndombe (a Benguela-Yombe composite).
38. Ibid. Also see: Conrad, "Memorias dos feitos," pp. 369-377; Carneiro, *O Quilombo*, pp. 57-58.
39. "Relação das guerras feitas," p. 214; Freitas, *Palmares*, p.102.
40. Ganga Zumba escaped in such haste that he allegedly discarded his gilded pistol and a sword. Carneiro, "Relação das guerras feitas aos Palmares," pp. 214-215; Conrad, "Memorias dos feitos," p. 374.
41. Apparently the men entered the town almost naked "with their natural parts alone covered. Some wore their beards in braids, others wore false beards and mustaches, and others were shaved and nothing more." One of Ganga Zumba's sons rode a horse because he was wounded. Conrad, "Memorias dos feitos," pp. 375-376; and Carneiro, "Relação das guerras feitas aos Palmares," pp. 219-220.
42. Kopytoff, *The African Frontier*, pp. 36-37.
43. On Zumbi's rule and fall see Carneiro, *O Quilombo*, pp.135-167; Mary C. Karasch, "Zumbi of Palmares: Challenging the Portuguese Colonial Order," in Kenneth J. Andrien (ed.), *The Human Tradition in Colonial Latin America* (Wilmington, DE: Scholarly Resources, Inc., 2002), pp. 104-120.

8

Enslavement, the Slave Voyage, and Astral and Aquatic Journeys in African Diaspora Discourse[1]

Monica Schuler

This chapter explores African diaspora accounts of astral and aquatic journeys, particularly successful and unsuccessful attempts to return to Africa. Often those accounts are set in a ritual context near trees and water, places where this world and the other world are believed to intersect. These narratives and commemorative ritual acts depict enslavement as witchcraft and cannibalism resulting from the victims' collective sin and the malice of slave dealers and slave owners.

Embodied memories may be detected in ritual processions, initiation ordeals and taboos. Processions seem to reenact Africans' journey as slaves to the Atlantic coast, traversing topography and landmarks characteristic of that journey. Ordeals generate trance- or dream-induced spirit travel, followed by hymns about boundary crossing, public narration of spiritual journeys, and baptism by immersion or other aquatic rites symbolizing death, rebirth and acquisition of new identities and kin. Allegorical captivity and release narratives relate stock tales about migration, repatriation, ritual and occult powers that interweave cosmology and history. They describe experiences in code or parable, preserving collective memory through a process of "mnemonic streamlining" whereby "whole groups of traditions . . . abraded to anecdotes, are situated and contrasted so that in every account details are sharpened, altered or left out to imprint the mark of their association on other accounts."[2] The discourse generated by the narratives probes the deeper meaning of enslavement, exile, and exploitation and the possibility of reunification in a blissful African homeland.[3]

Although slaves undoubtedly produced such narratives and rites in the first instance, descendants of a particular group of mid-nineteenth-century slaves captured and liberated by the British Navy also contributed their own versions. Transported from Sierra Leone, St. Helena, Rio de Janeiro and Havana to Guyana, Jamaica, Trinidad, and five smaller islands, liberated Africans, as they were known, made significant contributions to this anthology of memory and practice.[4] They help us to see the slave and liberated African traffic as formative, indeed, initiatory experiences in the development of the African diaspora.

Illness and death – the journey to the other world – pervaded the slave and liberated African immigrant experience to an extent significant for the elaboration of African worldviews in the Caribbean and Americas. The six-month-long march to the Angolan coast illustrates this vividly. It wound through highlands and valleys, across rivers and through marketplaces, past dead captives' sun-bleached "bones and wooden shackles" until coffles of 20-100 survivors reached overcrowded pens within sight and smell of unburied or half-buried corpses in a Luanda graveyard or Benguela beach. Across the Atlantic, slave warehouses in Rio de Janeiro adjoined a cemetery where partially interred, decomposing cadavers were burned periodically.[5] For liberated West Central Africans, St. Helena was no less grim. In 1859, the island's Anglican bishop described 500 disconsolate, skeletal slave ship survivors, many permanently blinded by eye diseases, "crawling on the beach" of the liberated African depot like "Charon and his crew of shades."[6] Medical personnel in St. Helena and Guyana attributed the high death rate among such Africans to "the depressing moral influence of fear and anxiety." "The victims of 'obeah' [sorcery] are thus destroyed," explained a Guyana doctor.[7]

West Central African cosmology situates both death and witchcraft in a comparable location along the slave ships' route from Africa – the red-tinted place of the setting sun where the rivers *Nzadi* (Congo) or Kwango and the Atlantic Ocean converge. West Africans have a similar concept. The crossing of this water – the boundary between this world and the next – represented a premature and unnatural death.[8] Overseas commerce with Europeans made Africans vulnerable. Increasing consumption of imported goods led to enormous expansion of rulers', merchants' and slave owners' personal prosperity, but also to mounting debt and increasing slave trafficking which people construed as the misappropriation of life. This judgment applied equally to slave traders, slave owners and employers of indentured labor, whom flight narratives describe as using "science" (i.e. sorcery) to prevent escape. African witchfinding trials, "the ritual production of slaves for the Atlantic trade," condemned many people to sale and disseminated "particular kinds of knowledge and subjectivity about witchcraft."[9]

SLAVE TRADE AND SLAVERY AS WITCHCRAFT

Twentieth century West and West Central African beliefs concerning the interrelated and finite nature of wealth, health and social harmony and assumptions that great wealth may be achieved only at the expense of others have a long history. Immoderate prosperity was equated with a loss of social equilibrium, blamed for social, medical and financial misfortune and even death, and represented as witchcraft, vampirism or cannibalism. The Diola of West Africa envisioned witches as flying away with their victims dangling from ropes to a place where their souls were used for gain. In West Central Africa, witches were believed to steal souls, force them to work, imprison them in containers and "eat" them. Congolese contrasted excessive wealth and furtive eating with African ideals that food should be shared generously, and they described vanished people toiling for the wealthy as "invisible slaves" long after their alleged burial. In this way, they "easily folded into familiar frames for remembering slave raiding."[10] The

Haitian populace pictured their counterparts as slaves of Chanpwèl – *Sans Poël* or Skinless Ones – witches who fly and who eat people, but who in actuality are secret societies that enforce social codes by turning transgressors into robot-like zombies lacking memory.[11]

Slave trafficking narratives described the processing of African body parts and blood to produce a variety of European or American imports into Africa – cheeses, red wines, red clothing, gunpowder, and black shoe leather.[12] The ubiquity of imported cloth and cowry shell currency in the Bight of Benin slave trade was attributed to Europeans who supposedly submerged West Central Africans in the ocean to weave trade cloth, or bred cowry shells on African cadavers and blood.[13] A seventeenth century Portuguese Jesuit commented, "[i]n Angola some of our slaves said . . . we were going to make use of them up to the point of devouring their bones."[14]

Two centuries later, liberated African Department personnel in Sierra Leone persuaded recaptives to refuse emigration to Guyana on the grounds that they would be decapitated, their heads boiled to make medicine to boost white men's intelligence, and their blood used to dye British soldiers' coats to make them brave.[15] The possibility of inadvertent pollution by such practices is suggested by a sailor's report in 1847 that he saw slavers butchering African children and old people to feed the rest.[16] The point is not whether some Africans or Europeans actually ate human flesh, but rather the way that standards of "good" (public) vs. "bad" (secret and excessive) eating permeated discourse and articulated with witch-finding divinations and slave trading.[17] Responding to African suspicions of European cannibalism, the eighteenth century English naval surgeon John Atkins argued that they were better grounded than European fears of being eaten by Africans, "for the next Cruelty to buying human Flesh, one would naturally think, should be to eat it; especially with Negroes, *who cannot conceive how their Labour can be used, that want so little for their own support*."[18] No wonder Africans described red slave ships flying blood red flags, the color of danger implying, in Rosalind Shaw's words, that "global [commercial] flows" were like "the flow of blood."[19]

References to red color in paint or trade goods are based on actual European commercial practices involving the exchange of red merchandise for slaves and the symbolism of the color red which denotes magical power, vulnerability and passage from one state to another.[20] European exports to Africa included red-colored textiles, apparel, and flags as early as the sixteenth century. New slaves received red kerchiefs or caps in Brazil and Cuba, and recruiters distributed red caps to Kru indentured workers bound for Guyana in the mid-nineteenth century.[21] The desire for European consumer goods made Africans vulnerable, the red narratives imply. As we shall see, the significance of red changed from dread to anticipation as West Indians used it to denote return to Africa.

Arrival in the Caribbean or Americas did not dispel fears of cannibalism. An early nineteenth century English traveler in Guyana, Henry Bolingbroke, witnessed the trepidation of a young African who assumed that Europeans attending a slave auction intended to eat him. In 1843, convinced that they were to be eaten, liberated Africans screamed and sobbed as their ship arrived in Port of Spain, Trinidad.[22] A mid-nineteenth century French visitor to Brazil described the shrieks of an African restaurant worker who believed that white diners planned the same fate for him. This notion of European depletion of African lives persisted in another set of traditions that recall Dutch, French or Spanish planters fleeing slave uprisings, but not before forcing slaves to bury their wealth and then murdering them so that their spirits might guard the treasure. In dreams or through divination, the spirits of these homicidal Europeans or murdered slaves offer to release the treasure hoard in return for the sacrifice of a child, thus projecting the consumption of humans into succeeding generations.[23] White discourse on slavery also revealed an understanding of slave trafficking as butchery and consumption. Two eighteenth century North American Quakers, John Woolman and Thomas Middleton, reported dreaming of whites eating African flesh; John Atkins alluded to slave dealing as "buying human Flesh", while Charles Brand referred to a Rio de Janeiro slave warehouse he visited in 1828 as a "flesh-shop".[24]

In 1805, insurrectionary Africans in Trinidad inverted the consumption metaphor, envisaging *themselves* grinding the bodies of white slave owners like sugar cane in a plantation mill and consuming their flesh and blood in Communion bread and wine. The slaves' fate was no metaphor, however, for as in the slave trade narratives, many were dismembered: three by beheading and others by having their ears severed.[25] In 1837, Daaga, a Porto Novo slave trader who was ambushed and enslaved while delivering slaves to a Portuguese slaver and subsequently liberated by the British Navy and enlisted in the 1st West India Regiment, vowed to repay his Portuguese captors by "attacking them in the night" (like a witch). Captured later for leading a mutiny in Trinidad, Daaga repeatedly threatened to eat "the first white man I catch after this."[26]

In the 1930s, remembrance of enslavement as European consumption of Africans was rejuvenated in Jamaica by access to North American publications. One of these books, *The Destiny of the Jews*, reiterated slave era assertions that African bodies "were going in machines and their bones, blood, flesh, [and] brain[s] were mixed with the manure and thrown into the roots of trees" as fertilizer. The secretary of Rastafarian leader Robert Hinds recalled seeing a cartoon in the *Pittsburgh Courier* illustrating how "the English . . . used to boil people in a big pot and eat them before the pot even boil."[27] The association of cannibalism and vampirism with exploitation persisted in post-colonial Caribbean discourse. A Haitian described as werewolves Protestant preachers who converted his six siblings, thereby severing their relationship with the ancestors.[28] In the 1970s, an associate of Haitian dictator François Duvalier became known as the Caribbean Vampire when he supplied cadavers and blood to foreign medical schools or hospitals.[29]

Like slaves, liberated Africans in Jamaica blamed malicious "scientists" or sorcerers for thwarting their efforts to return to Africa. The Africans mistakenly believed that they were *entitled* to free repatriation as a contractual right when in fact only a limited number of Sierra Leonians arriving in the 1840s had been guaranteed repatriation.[30] A liberated Central African descendant dreamed of a book with a red cover, a "present [received] in the old past" by people "who would come to Jamaica to work slave" (i.e. under indenture). In the dream, when a man asked the dreamer to hand him the "red-cover book", the dreamer urged him: "'[t]ake the ship!' . . . since them [the labor recruiters?] a give a present, take the ship that would carry him go a Africa, and come back and go back anytime we want [to] go."[31]

The dream suggests the intense feelings of betrayal transmitted by nineteenth century immigrants to their descendants. It explains the later insistence by Jamaican Rastafarians (discussed below), some of whom were liberated West Central African descendants, that far from requesting discretionary *emigration* to Africa, they were stipulating *repatriation* as a contractual right.[32] Red, associated with the boundary between the two worlds and with transitions, thus suggests the possibility of return journeys. Spiritual Baptists in St. Vincent tie a red band marked with a ship and the word "Africa" over other eye bands worn for spiritual journeys *back* to Africa, and they imagine a red, red-and-black, or red, yellow and green flag flying above their African destination.[33]

Jamaican flight narratives published[34] in Schuler, *"Alas, Alas, Kongo*", and the Guyanese narratives "Kramanti Mass Flight", recorded by Kempadoo in the 1970s, and "Carrion Crow" recorded by the author in 1984 and discussed below, exhibit stock elements found in descriptions of both collective and individual flight attempts in the Caribbean. These include refusal to perform hard labor, nostalgia for home, fidelity to African customs, singing, ring dancing, and drumming, proximity to trees and water, and transformation into a bird – a dove, vulture or carrion crow (associated with occult powers). Other important themes are the counter "science" of slave ship captains, slave owners or employers who plied Africans with salted food to destroy their occult powers, and the ability of some slaves to maintain a salt taboo.[35]

A characteristic escape narrative describes collective flight by several hundred Kramanti (the Guyanese pronunciation of "Coromantee", Akan-speakers exported from Ghana) slaves from Philippi plantation in Berbice, Guyana.[36]

KRAMANTI MASS FLIGHT

Objecting to the demand of the Philippi "slave master" that they perform a hated task, slaves gathered at the waterside near some "Kramanti trees". There they beat their drums and "about over 500 or 300 of them fly away."

> *1st Person*: [T]hese African people really had their culture, and they had their art and everything, and . . . [they knew] what tune to sing, and what sound of the drum, particular sound of the drum, and people would dance, stay just like

that and start to dance on their head and all those kind of thing. . . . They call it Komfa[37]. . . .

3rd Person: You see, ahm, it's a thing, they learn to fly, they know to fly. This flying business is to go 'way, but people use it to suck. *1st Person*: As he said, the evil part of it is to suck. . . . They doesn't eat salt. [When] they come, they don't eat salt. No salt at all. . . . You see when they want to fly, they mark a circle, and they [stand] back to back. And soon as they back-to-back, they use the leg, and they use the [hands?], and they gone! And if you only turn back, you left [behind]! *3rd Person*: The drum, the drum, the drum does lift them! The drum does lift them! And when they reach, *they know*. *1st Person*: And their leader – they always had a leader, indeed in Africa the tribes had their great leader, it's not everybody can do it, you see – and their leader would meet and start to sing this tune and thing, and beat this drum, and they would move. And then they [slave owners] start to apply science – salt – there's where the application of salt come in. . . . and the minute they give them salt, all gone, they can't fly no more. See, they becomes heavy.

CARRION CROW'S FLIGHT TO AFRICA

From her liberated West Central African father, Jungu, Mavis Morrison of Annandale, East Coast, Demerara heard the tale of "Carrion Crow", a taciturn, imperious and anti-social *Obeah* (private divination, healing and charm-making which frightened many) man. Carrion Crow faithfully observed his country's customs, even though his neighbors found them repellent. "He don't eat salt, he don't eat too much of flesh, but he want play boss of them." People considered him uncouth. At wedding feasts, he did not use a knife and fork but put his head on the table and cut meat with his teeth, served food with his hands, and anyone who refused the food died by the following morning. Children encountering him also died. Carrion Crow inspired the fear Haitians feel for Chanpwèl secret society members. He was considered a bad worker and even the estate manager feared him.[38]

One day, Carrion Crow said, "'Bro Jungu, me wan' go home. . . . This country too hard for me.'" So he invited all the Kongo from Georgetown to Berbice County to attend a farewell dance. They were happy to see him go. On the preceding day, he demarcated ritual spaces by digging a long ditch ("hole") and roping off a dance enclosure or *ganda* from which he barred others.[39] He tied two yards of cloth around his waist and early in the morning announced: "'Well, today is my last day.'" He ordered drumming until 6 p.m., "'[un]til me meet where me a' go.'" At noon he retired and emerged painted red, white, blue and black.[40] He commanded: "'throw rum right round, *throw rum*, *throw rum*! I going away now, now, *now*!'" As the men and women sang and danced back-to-back, he left the ring and jumped in the ditch three times.[41] "'At six o'clock, [Jungu] say, he [Carrion Crow] hand [arm] swell so [sprouting wings].'" A minute later, he took off. "'That's how dey get rid out of Carrion Crow. . . . *He is the onliest African [who] come at Guyana – the only one [to] go back*. He fly. Carrion Crow. *Wing*, I tell you, *wing*! He get de two foot [like a vulture], he get wing."

RITUAL

Since ritual believed to activate flight forms the context of the two previous narratives of return, it seems appropriate to investigate the relationship of ritual with journeying, including the slaves' march from point of capture to the coast and particularly their ocean voyage *from* Africa, which Jungu's ritual dance was designed to reverse.

Contemporary descriptions of the Atlantic slave voyage exhibit features typical of African initiations, a resemblance that could not have escaped the attention of adult Africans. These characteristics included separation from family and familiar surroundings, a journey, terror, corporal punishment, sensory and physical deprivation such as starvation, thirst, blinding by dark ship holds and eye diseases, shackling and long periods of immobility in which slaves were forced to lie on their sides or with heads on each others' laps, often in closely-packed spaces, dehydrated, dependent, depressed and probably hallucinatory.[42] Both the objective situation and the Africans' worldview would have made them understand this ordeal as a process of dying – a passage from the world of the living in Africa to the world of the dead across the "river of salt", the ocean.

The slave ship experience also forged new identities among shipmates and made them members of a new family similar to the spiritual family constituted by membership in a religious sect, while survival and recovery from the voyage resembled rebirth. At the end of the voyage, survivors underwent baptism or some rite of rebirth into a new identity and family, just as in an African initiation.[43] Novices could experience what slaves at sea could not – confession of sins, a Mass or prayer and hymn service, an affectionate and mournful leave-taking of friends and family prior to entering seclusion, and visits from friends during the later stages of initiatory isolation.[44]

Ordeals were a feature of pre-Atlantic slave trade African initiations, but captivity and the slave voyage added further layers of meaning to initiation ritual. Kongo slaves no sooner arrived in the Danish Virgin Islands, for instance, than they demanded baptism. Despite having felt the whip many times during their initial captivity, a flogging for sins committed in Africa preceded the ritual washing.[45]

"Every group", Paul Connerton states, "will entrust to bodily automatisms the values and categories which they are most anxious to conserve. They will know how well the past can be kept in mind by a habitual memory sedimented in the body."[46] A survey of Yoruba, West Central African, Fon and Ewe-inspired African and African diaspora initiations known as *kanzo*, *kouche*, *asiento*, *kari-ocha*, "flooring", or "mourning" among West Indians and African-North Americans reveals episodes resembling the quintessential African slave ship voyage. These include a number of melancholic and listless victims enduring head-shaving, fasting and other physical and sensory privations, incarceration in a hot, crowded room while lying on the floor, on their sides, ankles and wrists tied with raffia, rope or cloth bands, blinded by eye-bands, helpless, unwashed, undergoing physical and spiritual lashing and becoming increasingly somnolent and dissociated.[47] Although "[t]hese things may seem hard", a Vodun houngan informed McAlister, "this is what they [the enslaved ancestors] went through."[48] Other rationales for these ordeals are suggested by their resemblance to Yoruba *Itefa* ("Establishment of the Self") ritual and Ezekiel 4:4-8 where God condemns the prophet to expiate the sins of Israel and Judah by lying bound on his left side for 390 days and on his right side for 40 days, consuming only water and bread fouled by human waste.[49] Designed to break down the human personality as enslavement might have done, diasporan initiation ordeals end with neophytes' regeneration through baptism or ritual washing and their acquisition of godparents and new names.[50]

Both the ordeal of initiation and the findings of sensory deprivation experiments suggest that hallucinations produced by slaves' shipboard experiences centered on feelings of abandonment, remembered past life, and out of body experiences.[51] Captives' shipboard recollections of life in their homelands, I hypothesize, inspired subsequent efforts to re-experience the ordeal as a means of propelling the ship back across the Atlantic. The model of a ship's wheel or drawing of a turning wheel or compass which kept Revivalist and Spiritual Baptist travelers "spinning to different directions"; the office of Captain; the metaphor of the church, the hymn for the spiritual journey and the journey itself as ships (of Zion) steered by Captains to spiritual lands; a memorial stained glass window in New Mount Pilgrim Missionary Baptist Church, Chicago representing the torso of a black Christ as a crowded slave ship's hold; and the conceptualization of Brazilian *Candomblé* (religious institution, sacred place, religious community and its rituals) novices sequestered in a retreat cell (*ronco*) as passengers in a boat (*barco*), all strengthen this hypothesis.

These do not exhaust all the associations of "ship" with the slave trade. The word *malungu* in Kikongo and related languages originally meant "large canoe" but became transmuted to: "boat", "my ship"/"my companion in the same ship", "brother/relative", and significantly, "my companion in suffering" and "companion in the crossing of kalunga". Ruth Nicholls, a Trinidadian relating the experience of her grandfather, an Angolan Liberated African, condensed these images into a moving portrait of shipmates confined "in the belly of one woman . . . and . . . dying [together] in their mother's belly if the ship sink."[52] Haitians use the sailing ship as a symbol of the Vodun sea god Agwe; Cubans in *Regla de Ocha* (rule or path of the *orishas* or deities of the Yoruba pantheon, also known as *Santéria)* use a ship's helm or ship to represent the sea goddess Yemaya; and Brazilians invoke both Yemoja (Yemaya) and Oshun, the goddess of fresh water, every December 31 when they launch prayer-filled miniature ships in the ocean.[53]

Haitian Vodun novices visit calvaries, markets and churches, and Converted and Spiritual Baptist novices in St. Vincent and Trinidad, and *Regla de Ocha* novices in Cuba and the United States visit crossroads, markets, hills and, notably, rivers and the seashore and in dreams the Converted revisit these places as well as quarries, caves, a volcano, towns, the fish market, and a cemetery, which they represent as the Valley of Jehosaphat (Joel 3:12) or Ezekiel Cemetery or Ground, "the valley of dry bones" (Ezekiel 37:1-2). Typical of the vicinities through which captive ancestors journeyed on their way to the African coast and following arrival in the Americas, such sites become "stations of the cross" and points of contact with the dead to whom they address their rituals.[54]

While entranced, St. Vincentian Pilgrims desiring to visit "the valley of dry bones" in particular, wear a blindfold bearing the text, "The Valley of Ezekiel", along with stereotypical death symbols – skulls and crossbones, rib and bone fragments sealed and signed in chalk overlaid with drops of wax.[55] Although Wallace W. Zane considers bone fragments and tracings of the ubiquitous ship's wheel to be derivatives of eye spots, "stars" or "phosphenic patterns on the retina", the "cosmic graveyard" with its dry bones also evokes the bones of dead captives encountered on the slaves' march to the sea. Indigent Haitians may well recall such images whenever they communicate with ancestors whose bones rest in a "great anonymous heap" in the cemetery charnel house.[56]

In their visions, spiritual travelers in St. Vincent also visit other Caribbean islands and a variety of mystical "cities" or lands from Zion to Israel, Canaan, Jericho, Jerusalem, the Beulah Land of *Pilgrim's Progress*, and Africa. Some discover themselves sailing *on a sea of glass* (Revelation 4:6) through which the other world is visible.[57] When transported "in the spirit", travelers have the sensation of flying through clouds. Indeed, Claude Planson referred to Haitian Vodun initiatory seclusion as "*le vol des néophytes*". Margaret Thompson Drewal observed, "wherever Yoruba [and she might have written "African"] religion thrives – Brazil, Cuba, the United States – this practice of journeying through possession trance has been maintained." The concept of movement between the two worlds is so routine, that even when Rastafarians "play", they move markers across a game board, tracing a path from "Hell-Jamaica" to "Heaven-Ethiopia".[58]

WORLDVIEW

The narratives' and rituals' symbolism locates the slave and immigrant experience in the context of West and West Central African beliefs in parallel worlds of the living (blacks) and the dead (whites), separated by a mirror-like surface or a permeable body of water (West Central African *Kalunga*) which empowered people could cross. Versions of the spirit world share essential characteristics, but the names and details associated with them vary from people to people.[59] The two worlds may be conceptualized in a variety of ways, as two halves of a calabash, opposite mountains, above and under water, two banks of a river or two shores of the sea, village and forest, village and cemetery, two distant towns, a crossroad, night and day, Africa and Europe, or Africa and the Americas.

Any new or significant happening – the creation of the world, death, state building, the founding or expansion of a religion, international commerce, a migration, indeed, any fresh, meaningful experience – is registered in terms of magical passage between the two worlds.[60] Voyages in slave ships and dreams of miraculous returns to Africa were thus already modeled in people's understanding of the cosmos when they became enmeshed in the slave trade.

WATER

The water between the two worlds can be the Tano River for the Asante, the *Nzadi* (Congo) River or Atlantic Ocean for the Kongo, the Volta River for the eastern Ewe, the Niger and its Delta for Igbo and Kalabari, and the Jordan River or Red Sea for Afro-Christians.[61] Descriptions of heroes' or leaders' mysterious origins and final interment in water can be cited from many of the African regions whose inhabitants were enslaved in the Americas.[62] For their part, Africans in the Americas and Caribbean believed that at death they would make the "long journey across the blue water to the fatherland." For most of the living, however, the salty ocean "blocked the pass".[63]

Occult powers, correct ritual and moral rectitude make some of the living light enough to fly like angels or birds, as Jamaican Myalists (Native Baptists) claimed in 1842.[64] Others, like Vodun and Benin Kingdom (Nigeria) priests and priestesses and West Central African magicians and prophets, claim to have undertaken submarine initiatory sojourns among the dead, crossing rivers miraculously or disappearing alive underwater or into caves from which they return with occult knowledge or substances from water spirits who are connected with innovative but antisocial and deviant behavior.[65] The Mbundu (Angola) believe that should such visitors eat any food underwater they would be trapped there forever, a belief that may have translated into the African diaspora notion that eating the salted food of the Caribbean prevents their return to Africa. Vodun devotees who die supposedly spend at least a year and a day at the bottom of a lake or river.[66]

The magical nature of migration from one side of an ocean or a river to another is thus a widespread belief that can be found in the flight narratives and also in diaspora peoples' idealization of Africa and expectations of return. An African-North American memory of enslavement states,

> [T]he colored people one time was all on one side of the river. And the white people was all on this [the American] side. And they [the slave traders] had a red flag. . . . waving . . . and that caused them to get those slaves. . . . That's how they managed to come over here. . . . And when they got over here . . . they kep' 'em.[67]

To refer to the water between Africa and the United States of America as a river was to express the cosmological significance of the slave traffic – a voyage across water to the land of the dead from which return was uncertain. The Cuban maroon Esteban Montejo stated that a magical wall originally separated Africa and Cuba. Once the wall was breached (by implication through a combination of European trickery, African gullibility, and a ruler's dereliction of duty), the Africans were sent as slaves to Cuba. "After that they couldn't go back to their own country."[68] Being walled out is the reality that the people who flew tried to overcome.

West Central African descendants told Guyanese scholar Kean Gibson that the old Kongo used to perform riverside rites (Komfa) in the hope of returning to Africa.[69] The observation by J. Graham Cruickshank in 1917 that "[c]hief among the African dances kept up in the Canal [No. 1, in Guyana] are those in memory of – or to – the dead," suggests that the riverside rites described to Gibson were funeral rites to send the spirit of the deceased "home" to Africa.[70]

DREAM JOURNEYS

African ritual scripts had printed counterparts in Biblical texts or works such as *The Norwood Gypsey's Manual of Dreams* that the Guyana Garrison Chaplain found an African soldier reading around 1850.[71] The Bible provided texts guaranteeing a return home and a special African destiny that would justify the anguish and obloquy of the slave trade, exile, and slavery.[72] In 1892, fifty-eight years before Jamaican Rastafarians contemplated cutting a passage across the Atlantic with their beards and walking to Africa, Simon Buckaloo, an African-American preacher declared:

> We is de Lord's chillen of Israel of de nineteenth centery. . . . If we can't get to Liberia any oder way, de Lord He'll just have to open up a parf through the 'Lantic Ocean jes' as he did for dem oder chillen through the Red Sea . . . De days ob miracles ain't done yet.[73]

West and West Central Africans and West Indians set great store by messages and complex information communicated through guided dreaming exercises. These often involve travel through water or sky.[74] Religious guides or diviners provide the subject matter in the form of a personal Biblical chapter, a psalm or a hymn and help induce, interpret and edit dreams and visions into conventional narratives ("tracts" or "tracks"), often based on a particular teacher's master vision. Initially preserved by memory alone, in Jamaica such dream tracts were also disseminated in pamphlets or reported in local newspapers. Dreams are "incubated" by Spiritual or Native Baptists and Vodunists during fasting and seclusion. Cosmic diagrams inscribed on the floor or on white and multi-colored blindfolds and other body bands serve as maps for the dream journey. In the process, the body becomes a receiver and "transmitter of restorative forces, crossing varied landscapes, meeting shining beings, angels or other white-complexioned, white-garbed individuals believed to be spirit messengers from the other world where all is white. Rehearsed with a religious teacher, the dream is narrated and accompanied by simulated walking before a congregation in the Evangelical Protestant tradition that "made individual experiences an aspect of community." Repeated narration, analysis and feedback project new meanings onto the vision, producing an "ensemble of dreaming". Since visits from or to the other world are considered physically real, their association with actual events or places (e.g. Africa, India, China, Rome) connected with the Caribbean's diverse ethnic groups or religions make them the stuff of "geography", "history", and vocation.[75] A Trinidadian healer concluded that her dream of candles and calabashes of fresh water in the four corners of a house meant that she had traveled to Africa and was commissioned to heal in the Yoruba manner.[76] Detached from ritual, some dreams assume a life of their own as accounts of physical rather than conceptual journeys.

In the discourse of liberated African descendants, Jamaican Rastafarians and religious sects such as Guyana's Jordanites, a preoccupation with Africa as point of origin, role model and future destination remains evident. It is largely through such groups that perception of enslavement and exile as the definitive experience of Africans in the diaspora permeated public consciousness in the twentieth century.[77] Like Africans in 1768 Martinique who expected to be ransomed by an anonymous African monarch, Africans and Creoles in Guyana and the Caribbean trusted local or external leaders (ranging from Marcus Garvey, founder of the Universal Negro Improvement Association, to British monarchs and Emperor Haile Selassie) to liberate them.[78] Garvey's Black Star shipping line (1919-1926) was the culmination of a three hundred year old obsession, a flight narrative enacted on the Atlantic and the Caribbean. Euphoric West Indians greeted the arrival of each of the half dozen ships that plied the line's New York, Panama, Cuba, Jamaica circuit. Tony Martin compared Universal Negro Improvement Association members' obsession with the shipping line to "the desire to relocate in Liberia." The line had offices in Liberia and Sierra Leone, but never sent any ships there. With the line's failure,[79] the ocean-crossing saga became associated with Haile Selassie, a sovereign African king crowned emperor of Ethiopia in 1930. Part of Selassie's appeal was his legitimacy as a supposed descendant of David and Solomon, predicted by Psalm 68:31, "Ethiopia shall soon stretch out her hands to God." The West Central African nucleus of the Rastafarian movement that emerged around 1930 propagated the idea of Selassie as King Zambi (KiKongo: *kinzambi* God), an apocalyptic world emperor who would restore them to Africa and restore Africa to greatness. During 1936-1938, the *Pittsburgh Courier* serialized the futuristic tale written by conservative black journalist George Schuyler (alias Samuel I. Brooks), *Black Empire: An Imaginative Story of a Great New Civilization in Modern Africa*, as "Dr. Belsidus and the Liberation of Africa." Robert Hinds, an early Rastafarian, subscribed to multiple copies of the *Courier*, and had all 62 episodes transcribed and read aloud at meetings as if they were news bulletins.[80] Rastafarians, who allegedly associated the ruthless black liberator and scientist Belsidus with Haile Selassie, expected the emperor to fetch his scattered subjects in a huge ship or a whole flotilla, either in 1934, the anniversary of slave emancipation, or in 2000. When the ships failed to appear in 1934, Rastafarians reportedly planned to clear a path with their beards and walk across the sea to Africa. A Revivalist hymn has Selassie piloting a plane and in the United States, Nation of Islam leaders substituted space ships for wings and sailing vessels.[81]

TREES

Long associated metaphorically with the living and dead, deities, ritual space, political leaders, and witches in Africa, trees provide launching pads for heavenly flight and flight back to Africa. In the narratives this can be either implicit as in the flight ritual near some "Kramanti trees" at Philippi, or explicit as in Minott's and Manoka's efforts cited below. The tree is the cosmic tree by which shamans and spirits were believed to ascend and descend the different levels of the cosmos. The central pole in Haitian Vodun, Jamaican Kumina, Convince, and Revival, Trinidadian and St. Vincentian Spiritual Baptist temples symbolizes the tree whose base is anchored in the watery abyss beyond which Africa lies.[82] Trinidadian Spiritual Baptist "travelers" often express a wish to climb buildings, hills, mountains, poles or trees. When possessed by African spirits, Jamaican Maroon and West Central African Convince cult spirit mediums became "uncommonly interested in climbing" trees and rooftops, as did their Myal predecessors in 1842 Jamaica who would sit in hollow tree trunks or tall branches, singing. Devotees of Convince shot up swiftly and dived from heights "headfirst without using . . . arms or legs", rather like a Belgian Congo prophetic sect, aspiring Yaka diviners and members of Haitian secret societies.[83] Two Bobangi friends in Jamaica, the rainmaker Manoka Mvula and his friend George Minott, reportedly experimented with flying back to Africa using coconut trees for their launching. Minott climbed a tree, shouted "goodbye, everybody!" and jumped off. Manoka recited lengthy prayers in "language" and climbed on a tree stump. Neither man could sprout wings, however, and both fell.[84]

SECRET LANGUAGE

Flight narratives refer to fliers' knowledge of a language that they consider essential for achieving return to Africa. This is not surprising, since West Indians associate proficiency in a secret language with entrancement. Whether these languages were or are specific African languages, secret languages of initiates, or a type of vision speech or glossolalia remains controversial, but West Central African queens of Jamaican Kumina bands claim to have learned "the African language" (KiKongo) while in a state of trance. It is significant that both West Central African and Yoruba immigrant descendants in Jamaica and Guyana continue to use African languages in ritual contexts.[85]

SALT

Salt is a multi-layered, ambiguous and sometimes contradictory sign, open-ended and therefore subject to reinterpretation – a characteristic of symbols that express values about life.[86] People believed they could protect themselves from witch attacks by ingesting or applying salt, for witches believed that salt would make them lose their occult powers. The Kongo appreciated the Roman Catholic baptismal rite, considering the application of salt on the tongue as protection from evil and more significant than the rite of immersion or sprinkling with water. Yet the preferred Kongo term for baptism until the early twentieth century, "eat salt", is a loaded expression which can mean to become like Europeans or to lose one's power by associating with "ordinary", or uninitiated, people.[87] The Jamaican expression "you salt", means "you're unlucky".

Salt avoidance is associated with strengthening rituals and the acquisition of occult powers (such as witches possess) by West Central Africans embarking on difficult occult tasks. Salt, as in the Guyanese Kramanti flight tale, was also said to "sweeten" people, making them docile and submissive.[88] Haitian zombies, on the other hand, are supposed to remain *docile* as long as they get *no* salt. One encounter with salt, however, revives memory and recognition of their bondage. Enraged, they attack their master and his property. According to McAlister, "the metaphoric taste of salt" to the Haitian zombi-cum-slave is thus a "spark of political consciousness" capable of starting a revolution.[89]

In Africa and the Caribbean, salt was used to preserve fish or meat. So closely connected are they in the West Central African-Guyanese mind, that a locally compiled KiKongo-English word list confuses salt with the meat and fish preserved by it. Only when the desire is to say "salted fish" (*mbizi a mungwa*) does the lexicon get it right.[90] As mentioned above, many suspected that salted meat fed to them during the crossing from Africa was actually African flesh.[91] Moreover, salt had negative health associations for slaves. Dependence on salted and dried foods on slave ships contributed to Vitamin C deficiency or scurvy, a disorder that causes joint pain, bleeding gums, tooth loss, paralysis, and scaly gray or white skin; it killed nearly 15 percent of slaves in Johannes Postma's sample of Dutch slave cargoes.[92] Excessive salt intake is also associated with hypertension and swollen joints.[93] Salt was "probably the first [African] commodity involved in long-distance commerce", and the exchange of rock- or sea-salt for slaves was common.[94] "Gone to fetch salt in . . . Boma", the West Central African slave trade port, was a Kongo euphemism for death. Salt thus joined red cloth and cowry shells as currency and as symbols of labor extraction from Africa. The taboo against eating salted food is a constant reminder of enslavement.[95]

CONCLUSION

In analyzing Sierra Leonian perceptions of the transatlantic slave trade, witchcraft and witch-finding, Rosalind Shaw suggested that scholars investigate similar depictions in other parts of Africa.[96] As we have seen, such representations can be generalized to the African diaspora as well. The people left in the Americas by African repatriates blame their inability to return ("fly") on the treachery of practitioners of "science" (Obeah or witchcraft), who had them removed from Africa in the first place and then deliberately fed them salt so that they could not leave. As mediums of communal ethical judgment, the flight narratives criticize labor conditions and the treachery of slave owners and employers. They also prescribe correct behavior and envisage diaspora voluntary associations (e.g. religious initiation bands and churches) as ships, transforming the container for captives into an incubator of diaspora communities and at the same time into a magical naval, air or space ship for repatriation/escape.

ENDNOTES

1. Research for this paper was funded by grants from a National Endowment for the Humanities Fellowship in 1980-81, a Ford Foundation Postdoctoral Fellowship in 1984-85, a Wayne State University Humanities Center Fellowship in 1996, and Wayne State University Summer fellowships. I wish to thank Jamaican and Guyanese liberated African descendants, especially Mrs. Mavis Morrison of Annandale and Mr. Carmichael, Mr. Scott and Mr. Pere of Seafield who allowed me to interview them in the 1980s. My thanks also to the staff of the British Public Record Office, Guyana National Archives, the Georgetown Public Library, Libraries of the Universities of Guyana, University of the West Indies, Mona, Jamaica and Wayne State University, and Eusi Kwayana, Sister Noel Menezes and Sister Celine Kirsch of Guyana. Elizabeth McAlister of Wesleyan University shared insights on Vodun and Spiritual Baptist practices. Many participants in the Enslaving Connections: Africa and Brazil during the Era of the Slave Trade conference, October 2000, York University, Toronto, Canada, made helpful suggestions which I have tried to implement. Osumaka Likaka of the Wayne State History Department and Kay Johnson made perceptive comments and criticism and they and Marc Kruman, Chair of the Wayne State University History Department encouraged me to publish this paper. Any errors are my responsibility, of course.
2. Jan Vansina, *Oral Tradition as History* (Madison: University of Wisconsin Press, 1989), pp. 21-22, 89-90, 126, 139-146; Joseph C. Miller, "Introduction," in Joseph C. Miller (ed.), *The African Past Speaks* (Hamden, Conn.: Archon Books, 1980), pp. 7-8, 32, 33-52.
3. Vansina, *Oral Tradition*, pp. 20-21. See, for instance: Ethiopianism, Pan-Africanism, and back to Africa movements in Wilson Jeremiah Moses, *Classical Black Nationalism* (New York: New York University Press, 1996); idem, *Afrotopia: The Roots of African American Popular History* (New York: Cambridge University Press, 1998); and the Brazilian idealization of Luanda, the Angolan slave port, as *Aruanda*, the home of Amerindian and backwoods spirits in Jim Wafer, *The Taste Of Blood: Spirit Possession In Brazilian Candomblé* (Philadelphia: University of Pennsylvania Press, 1991), pp. 63, 70, 83.
4. The five islands were Tobago, St. Lucia, St. Vincent, St. Kitts and Grenada. Some 2,421 Kru men from the Liberian and Ivory Coasts also migrated as voluntary laborers: Howard Johnson, "The Liberated Africans in the Bahamas, 1811-1860," in Howard Johnson (ed.), *After the Crossing* (London: Frank Cass and Company, Ltd., 1988), pp. 16-40; Rosanne Marion Adderly, "'New Negroes from Africa': Culture and Community Among Liberated Africans in the Bahamas and Trinidad 1810 to 1900," Ph. D. dissertation, University of Pennsylvania, 1996; Maureen Warner-Lewis, *Guinea's Other Suns* (Dover, MA: The Majority Press, 1991); Lorna McDaniel, *The Big Drum Ritual of Carriacou* (Gainesville: University of Florida Press, 1998), pp. 2, 4, 57-59; Monica Schuler, *"Alas, Alas, Kongo": A Social History of Indentured African Immigration into Jamaica, 1841-1865* (Baltimore: The Johns Hopkins University Press, 1980), pp. 10-29; idem, "Liberated Africans in Nineteenth-Century

Guyana," in Brian L. Moore, et al (eds.), *Slavery, Freedom and Gender: The Dynamics of Caribbean Society* (Kingston, Jamaica: University of the West Indies Press, 2001), pp. 133-157; idem, "Kru Emigration to British and French Guiana, 1838-1870," in Paul E. Lovejoy (ed.), *Africans in Bondage: Studies in Slavery and the Slave Trade* (Madison: African Studies Program, University of Wisconsin, 1986), pp.154-156, 164; idem, "The Recruitment of African Indentured Labourers for European Colonies in the Nineteenth Century," in P. C. Emmer (ed.), *Colonialism and Migration: Indentured Labour before and after Slavery* (Dordrecht: Martinus Nijhoff Publishers, 1986), pp. 125-161; Kenneth M. Bilby and Fu-Kiau kia Bunseki, "Kumina: A Kongo--Based Tradition in the New World," *Les Cahiers du CEDAF* 8 (1983): 21-23, 43-45.

5. Joseph C. Miller, *Way of Death: Merchant Capitalism and the Angolan Slave Trade, 1730-1830* (Madison: University of Wisconsin Press, 1988), pp. 5, 381-392; Mary C. Karasch, *Slave Life in Rio de Janeiro, 1808-1850* (Princeton: Princeton University Press, 1987), pp. 36-39. See also note 54.

6. Schuler, *Alas*, pp. 27-28. Out of 4,908 people admitted to Rupert's Valley liberated African depot in St. Helena between September, 1848 and March 1849, 3,394 were hospitalized and 1,283 died. See Colonial Office, Public Record Office, Kew Gardens [hereafter CO] 247/74, "Report of the Liberated African Establishment, St. Helena: Dr. Vowell's Report," and "Extract of a Report of Dr. Rawlins, 25 May, 1849," enclosures in Ross to Grey, No. 7, 21 May, 1850 and 12 June, 1849; also "Return of Africans Brought to St. Helena and Their Disposal from 9 June, 1840 to 31 December, 1849," in Ross to Grey, No. 16, 6 June, 1850; Edward Griffith, R.N. to Lt. Colonel Clarke, 9 September, 1850, in No. 15, Slave Trade, Lt. Colonel R. Clarke to Grey, 25 September, 1850; United Society for the Propagation of the Gospel, London [hereafter USPG], D8, Letters from Natal, St. Helena, Sierra Leone, Mauritius, 1850-1859, Bishop Piers Claughton to Rev. W.T. Bullock, 29 December, 1859 and 17 January, 1860. Over 500 recaptives sailed on the *Broughton Hall* in January, 1860; see CO 111/326, James Crosby to Governor's Secretary, 4 February, 1860, in Henry Wodehouse to Newcastle, No. 17, 6 February, 1860.

7. CO 111/250, George R. Bonyun, M.D., "Remarks to Accompany Table A," in Light to Grey, No. 10, 11 January, 1848. Medical men described as *cachexy* extreme debility usually caused "by bad and insufficient food", but most often caused by prolonged fear. A discussion of *cachexia* is found in Karasch, *Slave Life in Rio*, p. 181.

8. Wyatt MacGaffey, *Religion and Society in Central Africa: The BaKongo of Lower Zaire* (Chicago: University of Chicago Press, 1986), pp. 5, 52, 57-62; René Devisch, *Weaving The Threads Of Life* (Chicago: University of Chicago Press, 1993), pp. 11, 54-58, 60-61, 119; C. G. A. Oldendorp, *History of the Mission of the Evangelical Brethren on the Caribbean Islands of St. Thomas, St. Croix, and St. John* Johann Jakob Bossar (ed.) (Ann Arbor: Karoma Publishers, 1987 [1877]), p. 215. See also William D. Piersen, "White Cannibals, Black Martyrs: Fear, Depression, and Religious Faith as Causes of Suicide Among New Slaves," *Journal of Negro History* 62/2 (1977): 147-159; C. K. Meek, *The Northern Tribes of Nigeria* 2 vols. (London: Frank Cass, 1971 [1921]), I, p. 36; A. B. Ellis, *The Ewe-Speaking Peoples of The Slave Coast Of West Africa* (Osterhout, Netherlands: Anthropological Publications, 1970 [1890]), pp. 107-109; J. D. Y. Peel, "For Who Hath Despised The Day of Small Things? Missionary Narratives And Historical Anthropology," *Comparative Studies in Society and History* 37/3 (1995): 594.

9. Ralph A. Austen, "The Moral Economy of Witchcraft: An Essay in Comparative History," in Jean and John Comaroff (eds.), *Modernity and its Malcontents* (Chicago: University of Chicago Press, 1993), p. 92; idem, "The Slave Trade as History and Memory: Confrontations of Slaving Voyage Documents and Communal Traditions," *William and Mary Quarterly* 58/1 (2001): 229-244; Rosalind Shaw, "The Production of Witchcraft/Witchcraft as Production: Memory, Modernity and the Slave Trade in Sierra Leone," *American Ethnologist* 24/ 4 (1997): 858, 862-869; idem, Memories *of the Slave Trade: Ritual and the Historical Imagination in Sierra Leone* (Chicago: University of Chicago Press, 2002), pp. 212-223.
10. See Robert Baum, *Shrines of the Slave Trade: Diola Religion and Society in Precolonial Senegambia* (New York: Oxford University Press, 1999), pp. 138-140, 161-162, 221; John K. Thornton, *The Kongolese Saint Anthony: Dona Beatriz Kimpa Vita and the Antonian Movement, 1684-1706* (New York: Cambridge University Press, 1998), pp. 83, 160-161; Wyatt MacGaffey, "Oral Tradition in Central Africa," *International Journal of African Historical Studies* 7/3 (1975): 425-426; idem, "Kongo and the King of the Americans," *Journal of Modern African Studies* 6/2 (1968): 181; Nancy Rose Hunt, *A Colonial Lexicon of Birth Ritual, Medicalization, and Mobility in the Congo* (Durham, NC: Duke University Press, 1999), pp. 179-195.
11. John K. Thornton provides West Central African sources for such beliefs about witches in "Cannibals: Witches, and Slave Traders in the Atlantic World," *William and Mary Quarterly* 60/2 (2003): 273-297. See also Hunt, *Colonial Lexicon*, p. 189; Wade Davis, *Passage of Darkness: the Ethnology of the Haitian Zombie* (Chapel Hill: University of North Carolina Press, 1988), pp. 75, 237-238, 249-284, 294, 299; Claude Planson, *Un initié parle* (Paris: Dulles, 1978), pp. 225, 231-233, 303; Alfred Métraux, *Voodoo in Haiti* (New York: Schocken, 1972), p. 282; Elizabeth McAlister, "A Sorcerer's Bottle: The Visual Art of Magic in Haiti," in Donald J. Cosentino (ed.), *Sacred Arts of Haitian Vodou* (Los Angeles: UCLA Fowler Museum of Cultural History, 1995), p. 314. I am grateful to Elizabeth McAlister for sharing prepublication excerpts from her book, *Rara! Vodou, Power and Performance in Haiti and Its Diaspora* (Berkeley: University of California Press, 2002), pp. 102-109.
12. Captain William Snelgrave, *A New Account Of Some Parts of Guinea and the Slave Trade* (London: Frank Cass, 1971 [1734]), pp. 162-163, 172; John K. Thornton, *Africa and Africans In The Making Of The Atlantic World, 1400-1800* (New York: Cambridge University Press, 1998 [1992]), pp. 153-162; idem, *Kongolese St. Anthony*, p. 206; Miller, *Way of Death*, pp. 4-5, 389, 409-410, 413-414, 425-426; Harms, *River of Wealth*, pp. 31, 240 note 15; Johannes Postma *The Dutch in the Atlantic Slave Trade: 1600-1815* (New York: Cambridge University Press, 1990), p. 165; William D. Piersen, *Black Legacy: America's Hidden Heritage* (Amherst, MA: University of Massachusetts Press, 1993), pp. 5-12; "Letter of Mr. Samuel Crowther to the Rev. William Jowett, in 1837 . . . Detailing the Circumstances Connected with his Being Sold as a Slave," in *Journals of the Rev. James Frederick Schön and Mr. Samuel Crowther Who Accompanied the Expedition up the Niger in 1841* (London: Frank Cass, 1970), p. 382; Quobna Ottobah Cugoano, *Thoughts and Sentiments on the Evil of Slavery* Vincent Carretta (ed.) (New York: Penguin Books, 1999 [1787]), pp. 13-14; Selena Axelrod Winsnes (ed.), *Letters on West Africa and the Slave Trade: Paul Erdmann Isert's Journey to Guinea and the Caribbean Islands in Columbia (1788)* (New York: Oxford University Press, 1992), pp. 175-177; Edward Long, *The History of Jamaica* 3 vols. (Frank Cass and Co., Ltd., 1970 [1774]), II, p. 397.

13. In Kongo, a standard-size piece of cloth, *libongo*, was used as money. John H. Weeks, *Among the Primitive Bakongo* (New York: Negro Universities Press, 1969 [1914]), pp. 294-295; Abiola Félix Iroko, "Cauris et esclaves en Afrique Occidentale entre le XVIe et le XIXe siècles," in Serge Daget (ed.), *De la traite à l'esclavage* 2 vols. (Nantes: Centre de Recherche sur l'Histoire du Monde Atlantique, 1988), I, pp. 199-200); Austen, "Moral Economy," pp. 89, 92; MacGaffey, *Religion and Society*, pp. 135-139, 162-168, 174.
14. Paul E. H. Hair, "Heretics, Slaves, and Witches – As Seen by Guinea Jesuits, c. 1610," *Journal of Religion in Africa* 28/2 (1998): 137.
15. See Shaw, "Production of Witchcraft," p. 867; and idem, *Memories of the Slave Trade*, pp. 222-223, 254, for beliefs that "big men" obtain power from medicines made from ritually murdered people. R. G. Butts, the Guyanese labor recruiter who related the incident, secured labor recruits only when the governor of Sierra Leone held recaptives from a Spanish slaver incommunicado to all except labor recruiters. See No. 200, Henry Light to Lord Stanley, enclosing R. G. Butts to Young, 23 July-7 August, 1844, CO 111/213; No. 57, Light to Stanley enclosing Butts to Young, 13 March, 1845, CO 111/221; Schuler, *Alas*, pp. 25-26, 28, 134 note 74. See also, for red associations: Michael A. Gomez, *Exchanging Our Country Marks: : The Transformation of African Identities in the Colonial and Antebellum South* (Chapel Hill: University of North Carolina Press, 1998), pp. 199-209; Piersen, *Black Legacy*, pp. 9-11, 35-42. Compare with Luise White, "Vampire Priests of Central Africa: African Debates About Labor and Religion in Colonial Northern Zambia," *Comparative Studies in Society and History* 35/4 (1993): 760-764, 767, 770-771.
16. Mechal Sobel, *Teach Me Dreams: The Search for Self in the Revolutionary Era* (New York: Oxford University Press, 2000), p. 270. Miller, *Way of Death,* p. 5, notes Africans' fears that salted meat served on slave ships was African flesh. See also: Gwendolyn Midlo Hall, *Africans in Colonial Louisiana: The Development of Afro-Creole Culture in the Eighteenth Century* (Baton Rouge: Louisiana State University Press, 1992), pp. 90-91; MacGaffey, "Kongo and King," pp. 174-177.
17. Thornton, "Cannibals," pp. 287-289, avers that the West Central African Imbangala, slave traders and unabashed practitioners of witchcraft and cannibalism, were an African "exception that proved the rule". See also, Bogumil Jewsiewicki and Bawele Mumbanza, "The Social Context of Slavery in Equatorial Africa during the Nineteenth and Twentieth Centuries," in Paul E. Lovejoy (ed.), *The Ideology of Slavery in Africa* (Beverly Hills: Sage, 1981), pp. 75-76; Miller, *Way of Death*, pp. 32, 147-149, 157; Shaw, "Production of Witchcraft," pp. 862-865; idem, *Memories of the Slave Trade*, pp. 231-232, 254. The failure of slaves to return was probably an additional factor.
18. John Atkins, *A Voyage to Guinea, Brasil, and the West Indies; in His Majesty's Ships, the Swallow and Weymouth* (London: Frank Cass, 1970 [1735]), p. 129, my emphasis.
19. Gomez, *Exchanging*, pp. 202, 204; Thornton, "Cannibals," p. 273; Shaw, "Production of Witchcraft," p. 869; idem, *Memories of the Slave Trade*, p. 224.
20. Gomez, *Exchanging*, pp. 200-202. For red color symbolism, see Thornton, *Kongolese St. Anthony*, pp. 82, 161; Baum, *Diola Religion*, pp. 161-162, Robert Farris Thompson, *Flash Of The Spirit* (New York: Vintage Books, 1984), pp. 6, 131; McAlister, "Sorcerer's Bottle," p. 310.

21. See George E. Brooks, *Landlords and Strangers: Ecology, Society, and Trade in Western Africa, 1000-1630* (Boulder, CO: Westview Press, 1993), p. 303. Terry Alford, *Prince Among Slaves* (New York: Oxford University Press, 1977), p. 21, mentions a red silk flag sold to Fulbe. For red caps see: Karasch, *Slave Life in Rio*, pp. 21, 35; Malcolm Cowley (ed.), *Adventures of An African Slaver . . . A True Account of The Life of Captain Theodore Canot* (New York: Albert and Charles Boni, 1928), p. 113; Schuler, "Kru Emigration," p. 171.
22. Schuler, *Alas*, pp. 28, 74 note.
23. See Winsnes, *Letters*, p. 182; Henry Bolingbroke, *Voyage to the Demerary* (Georgetown: The Daily Chronicle, 1942 [1807, 1809]), p. 142; Karasch, *Slave Life*, p. 39; Piersen, *Black Legacy*, pp. 9, 11; Richard Price, *Alabi's World* (Baltimore: Johns Hopkins University Press, 1990), p. 4. See also Métraux, *Voodoo*, pp. 313-317; Brackette Williams, "Dutchman Ghosts and the History Mystery: Ritual, Colonizer, and Colonized: Interpretations of the 1763 Berbice Slave Rebellion," *Journal of Historical Sociology* 3/3 (1990): 133-165, especially 144-145; Judith Roback, "The White-Robed Army: Cultural Nationalism and a Religious Movement in Guyana," Ph. D. dissertation, McGill University, 1973, p. 103; Elliott P. Skinner, "Ethnic Interaction in a British Guiana Rural Community: A Study in Secondary Acculturation and Group Dynamics," Ph. D. dissertation, Columbia University, 1955, p. 257; Arthur and Juanita Niehoff, *East Indians in the West Indies* (Milwaukee: Olsen Publishing Company, 1960), pp. 160-161; Georgia Writers' Project, *Drums and Shadows: Survival Studies Among the Georgia Coastal Negroes* (Athens: University of Georgia Press, 1986 [1940]), pp. 15, 41, 97, 124. For Kongo traditions of magical buried European goods, see Thornton, *Kongolese St. Anthony*, p. 159.
24. Sobel, *Teach Me Dreams*, pp. 65-74, 236-237; Atkins, *Voyage*, pp. 129, 131; Karasch, *Slave Life*, p. 38.
25. Lionel Mordaunt Fraser, *History of Trinidad* 2 vols. (London: Frank Cass, 1971 [1891]), I, pp. 269-272.
26. E. L. Joseph, *History of Trinidad* (London: Frank Cass, 1970 [1838], pp. 262, 268-269.
27. See Barry Chevannes, *Rastafari: Roots And Ideology* (Syracuse, N.Y.: Syracuse University Press, 1994), pp. 88, 129, 142. I could not locate such a book, but this title may have referred to Africans, not Jews, since many diaspora Africans consider the Biblical narratives of the enslavement of the Israelites as their own story. See p. 195 above and Simon Buckaloo sermon, and n. 73.
28. Planson, *Un initié*, p. 260; McAlister, "Sorcerer's Bottle," p. 317.
29. For Africa see White, "Vampire Priests". See also Paul Farmer, *The Uses of Haiti* (Monroe, Maine: Common Courage Press, 1994), pp. 49-51 and 378, notes 4 and 6. I wish to thank Elizabeth McAlister for providing this reference.
30. CO 111/221, Henry Light to Earl Grey, No. 57, 2 April, 1844, and enclosures including R. G. Butts to Light, 13 March, 1845. From Guyana 990 returnees have been documented, and 253 from Jamaica. See: Schuler, "Liberated Africans," pp. 12, 21 note 83; idem, *Alas*, pp. 88-93.
31. See Bilby and Bunseki, "Kumina," pp. 33-34 for the dream of a red book. Bilby's informant was West Central African, but see J. D. Y. Peel, *Religious Encounter and the Making of the Yoruba* (Bloomington: Indiana University Press, 2000), pp. 223-225, for Yoruba understanding of the Bible and school primer as "the Christian's personal

repository of power" comparable to the Ifa divination system. The "expression 'take book' exactly mirrors the Yoruba phrase used for receiving the Ifa palm nuts."

32. See the poem, "Repatriation: An Unfinished Business," in Barrett, *Rastafarians*, pp. 223, 154, 195; M. G. Smith, Roy Augier, and Rex Nettleford, *Report on the Rastafari Movement in Kingston, Jamaica* (Kingston: Institute of Social and Economic Research, U. W. I., 1968 [1960]), pp. 14-16, 19-20.
33. Wallace W. Zane, *Journeys to the Spiritual Lands: The Natural History of a West Indian Religion* (New York: Oxford University Press, 1999), pp. 84, 99.
34. Schuler, *Alas*, pp. 93-95.
35. Ibid., p. 93; Warner-Lewis, *Guinea's Other* Suns, pp. 28-29; Adderley, "'New Negroes from Africa,'" pp. 328, 341-345.
36. Peter Kempadoo, "Recordings of Folklore, Drama and Music Made in Guyana, 1971-3," University Library, University of Guyana, 1974, K104. This narrative may well preserve a memory of Maroon escape. See, for instance: Price, *Alabi's World*, pp. 17-18, 20-21; idem, *First Time: The Historical Vision of an Afro-American People* (Baltimore: Johns Hopkins University Press, 1983), pp. 54-59; John K. Thornton, "The Coromantees: An African Cultural Group in Colonial North America and the Caribbean," *Journal of Caribbean History*, 32/1-2 (1998): 161-178.
37. See Brian L. Moore, *Cultural Power, Resistance and Pluralism: Colonial Guyana 1838-1900* (Jamaica: University of the West Indies Press, 1995), pp. 139-142, and note 72.
38. Adeola James' interview with Mrs. Morrison in 1982 is available in mimeographed form in *Guyanese Oral Traditions: Interviews Conducted on the East Coast Demerara, West Coast Berbice, West Bank Demerara and the Essequibo Coast* (Turkeyen: University of Guyana, 1989), pp. 10-80. Maureen Warner-Lewis interviewed Mrs. Morrison in 1994 and in 2002 published an account of her father's enslavement: Maureen Warner-Lewis, *Central Africa in the Caribbean: Transcending Time, Transforming Cultures* (Jamaica: University of the West Indies Press, 2003), pp. 31-32. Neither was used for this chapter. Elizabeth McAlister, personal communication; and for other Haitian practices, see Planson, *Un initié*, pp. 225, 231-233, 303, and Davis, *Passage*, pp. 237-238, 249-284, 294, 299.
39. Some Kongo rituals require a trench to define the boundary between the two worlds, to indicate "the possibility of passage": MacGaffey, *Religion and Society*, pp. 107, 116; John Janzen, *Lemba, 1650-1930: A Drum of Affliction in Africa and the New World* (New York: Garland, 1982), pp. 193-194. *Ganda*: a proto-Bantu word meaning "social group", "quarter inhabited by a House", "clan", "enclosure of a leader", "quarter of a village", and "camp" was a microcosm like the trench: Jan Vansina, *Paths in the Rainforests: Toward a History of Political Tradition in Equatorial Africa* (Madison: University of Wisconsin Press, 1990), pp. 268-269.
40. Compare with the body paint of a Lemba priest in Janzen, *Lemba*, pp. 238, 192. The colors used in Lemba ritual are red (transition), white (*mpemba*-brilliance, the underworld) and black (*mundane*). According to MacGaffey, *Religion and Society*, pp. 45-46, 52, 110-111, there is no KiKongo word for blue and one wonders if Mrs. Morrison added blue because in Guyanese discourse the trio of red, white and blue is more customary. In Caribbean Spiritual Baptist iconography, red seems to represent Africa, particularly spirit travel to Africa. See Zane, *Journeys*, pp. 84, 99.

41. Compare with the dancing in "Kramanti Mass Flight," Kempadoo, "Recordings," K104.
42. For descriptions of slave ship conditions, see: Postma, *Dutch in Atlantic Slave Trade*, pp. 232-256; Snelgrave, *New Account*, pp. 163-191; Robert Edgar Conrad (ed.), *Children of God's Fire: A Documentary History of Black Slavery in Brazil* (Princeton: Princeton University Press, 1983), pp. 14, 22, 27, 32-39, 44-48; Cowley, ed., *Adventures of An African Slaver*, p. 110; Thornton, *Kongolese St. Anthony*, pp. 205-206; Warner-Lewis, *Central Africa in the Caribbean*, pp. 31-38. For diseases and depression en route to Brazil, see Karasch, *Slave Life*, esp. pp. 35-36, 40-41, 162, 182.
43. Oldendorp, *Mission of the Evangelical Brethren*, p. 263; Métraux, *Voodoo*, p. 33; Schuler, *Alas*, p. 84; Igor Kopytoff, "Revitalization and the Genesis of Cults in Pragmatic Religion: The Kita Rite of Passage among the Suku," in Ivan Karp and Charles S. Bird (eds.), *Explorations in African Systems of Thought* (Washington, D. C.: Smithsonian Institution Press, 1987), pp. 191-197; Thornton, *Kongolese St Anthony*, pp. 57, 133-134. MacGaffey, *Religion and Society*, p. 204, mentions confessions heard by Capuchin missionaries in 1600s Kongo. See also: Janzen, *Lemba*, pp. 190-192; Drewal, *Yoruba Ritual*, pp. 63-72. For shipmates, see: Orlando Patterson, *Sociology of Slavery* (Rutherford, NJ: Fairleigh Dickinson University, 1969), p. 150; Karasch, *Slave Life*, pp. 39, 44, 146, 298.
44. See Isabel Castellanos, "From Ulkumí to Lucumí: A Historical Overview of Religious Acculturation in Cuba," in Arturo Lindsay (ed.), *Santeria Aesthetics in Contemporary Latin American Art* (Washington: Smithsonian Institution Press, 1996), pp. 42-43, 48, 55; Métraux, *Voodoo*, pp. 199, 202; Planson, *Un initié*, p. 163; Brown, *Mama Lola*, p. 325; Walter F. Pitts, *The Old Ship of Zion: The Afro-Baptist Ritual in the African Diaspora* (New York: Oxford University Press, 1993), pp. 31-32, 117-122, 127; Zane, *Journey*, pp. 111-113; Jeannette Hillman Henney, "Spirit Possession Belief and Trance Behavior in a Religious Group in St. Vincent, British West Indies," Ph. D. dissertation, Ohio State University, 1968, pp. 114-115; George Eaton Simpson, 'The Shango Cult in Trinidad," in George Eaton Simpson (ed.), *Religious Cults of the Caribbean: Trinidad. Jamaica and Haiti* 3rd ed. (Rio Pedras, Puerto Rico: Institute of Caribbean Studies, University of Puerto Rico, 1980), pp. 33, 44; W. F. Elkins, *Street Preachers, Faith Healers and Herb Doctors in Jamaica, 1890-1925* (New York: Revisionist Press, 1977), pp. 21, 22; "Bedward," *Star* (14 May, 1976); Beryl DeLeon, "The Prophet of August Town," *Jamaica Times* (Saturday 29 November, 1930): 20-21. For baptism before departure from Angola, see Miller, *Way of Death*, pp. 402-404.
45. Oldendorp, *Mission of the Evangelical Brethren*, p. 263. Rastafarians in Jamaica believe that African sins, not witchcraft caused their enslavement, but God pardoned them long ago and only the trickery of white men prevented their return to Africa. See Leonard Barrett, *The Rastafarians: A Study in Messianic Cultism in Jamaica* (Rio Pedras, Puerto Rico: Institute of Caribbean Studies, 1969), p. 131.
46. Paul Connerton, *How Societies Remember* (New York: Cambridge University Press, 1989), p. 102. See also Elizabeth McAlister, "Love, Sex, and Gender Embodied: The Spirits of Haitian Vodou," in Joseph Runzo and Nancy M. Martin (eds.), *Love, Sex and Gender in the World Religions* (Oxford: One World, 2000), p. 131.
47. See Pitts, *Old Ship*, pp. 116-122, 127-128; Wafer, *Taste*, pp. 121-136, 150-154; Stephen D. Glazier, "Contested Rituals of the African Diaspora," in Peter B. Clarke (ed.),

New Trends and Developments in African Religions (Westport, CT: Greenwood Press, 1998), pp. 114-116; Zane, *Journeys,* pp. 25, 27, 35-37, 49, 76, 93-94, 99, 107, 109, 181; Métraux, *Voodoo*, pp. 192-211; Wafer, *Taste*, p. 121-131, 135, 150-154; Thos. Wynter, Buff Bay to Editor, *Jamaica Times* (Saturday 1 June, 1907): 6; "Bedward," *Star* (14 May, 1976); A. A. Brooks, *History of Bedwardism* 1st ed. (Kingston: F. A. Benjamin Manufacturing Co., 1909), p. 18. Katherine Dunham's description of her Vodun initiation ordeal so resembles slave ship conditions that it convinced me that Haitian, other Caribbean, and American initiation rituals must be commemorations of the slave voyage. See Katherine Dunham, *Island Possessed* (Chicago: University of Chicago Press, 1994 [1969]), pp. 60-65, 68-70, 75-79, 86-94. In Kongo, binding induced ritual death and signified salvation and faith: Thornton, *Kongolese St. Anthony*, pp. 57, 133-134; Schuler, *Alas*, p. 4. But see also: Suzanne Preston Blier, *African Vodun: Art, Psychology, and Power* (Chicago: University of Chicago Press, 1995), pp. 26-27; Kopytoff, "Kita Rite," pp. 191-197; Michael Barkun, *Disaster and the Millennium* (New Haven: Yale University Press, 1974), pp. 147-149, 165.

48. I wish to thank Elizabeth McAlister for confirming my hypothesis from her interview with Oungan François, New York, 1988.

49. Drewal, *Yoruba Ritual*, pp. 63-88, esp. 64-65 and plate 5.7. Zane, *Journeys*, p. 37 cites Ezekiel 3:24-25, albeit inaccurately, as the authority for the Spiritual Baptist practice.

50. See, for instance: Castellanos, "Ulkumí to Lucumí," pp. 42-43, 55; Métraux, *Voodoo*, pp. 33, 210-211; Brown, *Mama Lola*, p. 325; Deren, *Divine Horsemen*, p. 222; Planson, *Un initié*, p. 163, 173, 217-223; Desmangles, *Faces*, pp. 86-87; Wafer, *Taste*, pp. 122-129; Melville J. Herskovits and Frances S. Herskovits, *Trinidad Village* (New York: Alfred A. Knopf, 1947), pp. 201-204.

51. Henney, "Spirit Possession," pp. 111-121. Initiation is not the only occasion for ritual travel. Traveling can be repeated during church services, when it is called "doption". Zane, *Journeys*, pp. 100-102, 140-147 disagrees with Henney's interpretation.

52. Desmangles, *Faces*, p. 106, 151-153, 172; Métraux, *Voodoo*, pp. 103-104, 164; Deren, *Divine Horsemen*, p. 121, Castellanos, "Ulkumí to Lucumí," p. 47; Wafer, *Taste*, p. 112; Henney, "Spirit Possession," pp. 55-56; Zane, *Journeys*, p. 101-102, 140; Murphy, *Working The Spirit*, pp. 44, 51, 174, 240, 243-244; Pitts, *Old Ship*. My thanks to the Lusophone/phile participants in the Enslaving Connections conference, October 2000, for pointing out the usage of the term *barco* (boat), and especially to José C. Curto for referring me to Robert W. Slenes, "Malungu, Ngoma's Coming!" Africa Hidden and Discovered in Brazil," in Nelson Aguilar (ed.), *Mostra de redescobrimento: Negro de Corpo e Alma, Black in Body and Soul* (São Paulo: Associação Brasil 500 Anos Artes Visuais, 2000), pp. 222-223. The New Mount Pilgrim Missionary Baptist Church window is described and illustrated with a photograph in *The New York Times* (9 February 2001). Ruth Nicholls is quoted in Warner-Lewis, *Central Africa in the Caribbean*, p. 38.

53. See Robert Farris Thompson, *Face of the Gods: Art and Altars of Africa and the African Americas* (Prestel, Munich and New York: The Museum for African Art, 1993), pp. 210-211, 212, 270-280. Virgílio Coelho contrasts ancient images of beneficent nature spirits of the ocean and fresh water around Luanda, Angola with the bogus image of a western-type mermaid as a promotional "brand" for post-independence Luanda: "Imagens, Símbolos e Representações. 'Quiandas, Quitutas, Sereias': Imaginários

locaias, identidades regionais e alteridades. Reflexões sobre o quotidiano urbano luandense na publicidade e no universo do *marketing*," *Ngola. Revista de Estudos Sociais* (Luanda), 1 (1997): 127-191. My thanks to José C. Curto for this reference.

54. See note 5 above. See also: Miguel "Willie" Ramos, "Afro-Cuban Orisha Worship," in Lindsay, *Santeria Aesthetics in Contemporary Latin American Art,* p. 59; Henry John Drewal and John Mason, "Ogun and Body/Mind Potentiality: Yoruba Scarification and Painting Traditions in Africa and the Americas," in Sandra T. Barnes (ed.), *Africa's Ogun: Old World and New* 2nd ed. (Bloomington: Indiana University Press, 1997), p. 350, note 4; Zane, Journeys, pp. 20, 67, 80, 83-84; Karasch, *Slave Life*, pp. 38-39. There is also considerable evidence that springs were visited regularly: Hesketh J. Bell, *Obeah; Witchcraft in the West Indies* (Westport, CT: Negro Universities Press, 1970 [1889]), pp. 38-42; DeLeon, "Prophet of August Town," pp. 20-21; Métraux, *Voodoo,* pp. 211, 329-330; Wyatt MacGaffey, *Modern Kongo Prophets: Religion in a Plural Society* (Bloomington: Indiana University Press, 1983), pp. 124, 126; idem, *Religion and Society,* pp. 46, 84, 116.
55. Zane, *Journeys,* pp. 37, 98, 140; and Ezekiel 3:24-25.
56. Desmangles, *Faces*, pp. 115-117; Brown, *Mama Lola*, pp. 369-371; Miller, *Way of Death*, pp. 391, 392; Zane, *Journey*, pp. 140-141. I wish to thank David Richardson, University of Hull for suggesting that I explore how Africans might have commemorated the slaves' march to African ports. This exploration is by no means complete and deserves more consideration than I can give it here.
57. See Murphy, *Working the Spirit*, pp. 139-144 on spiritual travel in Jamaican Revival Zion, and pp. 170-175 on African American associations of the Biblical Promised land, Canaan and River Jordan with "the [African] homeland of the past". See "Hold the wind . . . Don't let it blow! I'm going to stand on a sea of glass!" in John Work (ed.), *American Negro Songs and Spirituals* (New York: Bonanza Books, 1940), pp. 159, 161; Zane, *Journeys*, p. 87. Deren, *Divine Horsemen*, p. 34, considers the mirror "the metaphor for the cosmography of Haitian myth." A West Central African source of Brazilian, North American and Caribbean adoption of reflective or transparent surfaces as the crossing to the Promised Land is confirmed by Slenes, "Malungu," p. 223. Muslim-influenced divining with mirrors in West Africa as described by Shaw, *Memories of the Slave Trade*, pp. 91-92, 94-95, may be relevant also.
58. Zane, *Journeys*, pp. 4, and 50, 73, 83, 86, 94, 95-96, 100, 141, describes *Pilgrim's Progress* as a "guidebook to the spiritual realm in which the Converted [i.e. Spiritual Baptists] travel." See also: Planson, *Un initié*, pp. 160-175, 186-187; Drewal, *Yoruba Ritual*, p. 33; Murphy, *Working the Spirit*, pp. 21-24; Wafer, *Taste*, pp. 112, 196. "[T]he journey as metaphor" has other possible African cultural sources: Judy Rosenthal, *Possession, Ecstasy, & Law in Ewe Voodoo* (Charlottesville: University of Virginia Press, 1998), pp. 27, 68, 252-253, note 1, 5; Janzen, *Lemba*, pp. 190-197; MacGaffey, *Religion and Society*, pp. 43-56; Thompson, *Face of the Gods*, pp. 49-55; George Eaton Simpson, "The Ras Tafari Movement: Political Cultism in West Kingston, Jamaica," in Simpson (ed.), *Religious Cults of the Caribbean*, p. 222.
59. For example, *Mpemba* or *Mputu* (Kongo), *Asaman* (Asante), Kutome (Ewe), *Orun* (Yoruba), *Housandioume* (Diola, Senegal), a Temne tripartite realm known as *ro-soki, ro-kerfi, and ro-seron*, and *Teme* (Kalabari, Niger Delta). For *Kalunga* in West Central Africa and Brazil, see MacGaffey, *Religion and Society*, pp. 80-81; Slenes, "Malungu," p. 223; T. J. Desch-Obi, "Combat and the Crossing of the Kalunga, in

Linda M. Heywood (ed.), *Central Africans and Cultural Transformations in the American Diaspora* (New York: Cambridge University Press, 2002), pp. 353-370. See also Ivor Wilks, *Forests of Gold* (Athens: Ohio University Press, 1993), pp. 232-234; Ellis, *Ewe-Speaking Peoples*, p. 107; Henry John Drewal, John Pemberton III, Roland Abiodun, and Henry Wardwell (eds.), *Yoruba: Nine Centuries of African Art and Thought* (New York: Harry N. Abrams, Inc., 1989), pp. 14-15; Baum, *Diola Religion*, pp. 50-51; Shaw, "Production of Witchcraft," pp. 856-857; 29-47; Desmangles, *Faces*, pp. 100-102; Robin Horton, "The Kalabari World View: An Outline and Interpretation," *Africa* 32:3 (1962): 199.

60. Wyatt MacGaffey, *Custom and Government in the Lower Congo* (Berkeley: University of California Press, 1970), pp. 17-35; idem, "Oral Tradition," pp. 418-419, 421-422; Anne Hilton, *Kingdom of Kongo* (Oxford: Clarendon Press, 1985), pp. 179, 198, 199-210, 218-223; Thornton, *Kongolese St. Anthony*, pp. 138, 177-184; 204-211; Adrian Hastings, "The Christianity of Pedro IV of the Kongo, 'The Pacific' (1695-1718)," *Journal of Religion in Africa* 28/2 (1998), pp. 149-150, 152-155; Susan Herlin Broadhead, "Beyond Decline: The Kingdom of the Kongo in the Eighteenth and Nineteenth Centuries," *International Journal of African Historical Studies* 12/4 (1979): 650; Harms, *River of Wealth*, pp. 30-32, 120-122; Vansina, *Paths*, pp. 220-222; idem, *Tio Kingdom*, p. 277.
61. James Fernandez, *Bwiti: An Ethnography of the Religious Imagination in Africa* (Princeton: Princeton University Press, 1982), pp. 491-493; Ellis, *Ewe-Speaking Peoples*, pp. 107-108; Captain R. S. Rattray, *Ashanti* (New York: Negro Universities Press, 1969 [1923]), pp. 199-200; McAlister, "Sorcerer's Bottle," p. 426, note 12; Richard N. Henderson, *The King in Every Man: Evolutionary Trends in Onitsha Ibo Society and Culture* (New Haven: Yale, 1972), pp. 109-125; Horton, "Kalabari World-View," pp. 201-203; Zane, *Journeys*, p. 87.
62. See Babatunde Lawal, "The Living Dead: Art and Immortality among the Yoruba of Nigeria," *Africa* 47/1 (1977): 16; Dominique Zahan, *The Religion, Spirituality, And Thought Of Traditional Africa* (Chicago: University of Chicago Press, 1983), pp. 20-25, 94; Pierre de Maret, "Archeological and Other Prehistoric Evidence of Traditional African Religious Expression," in Thomas D. Blakeley, Walter E. A. van Beek, and Dennis Thomson (eds.), *Religion in Africa* (Portsmouth, NH: Heinemann, 1994), p. 190; Harms, *River of Wealth* pp. 120-122, 134; Georgia Writers' Project, *Drums and Shadows*, pp. 184-185.
63. W. J. Gardner, *A History of Jamaica from its Discovery by Christopher Columbus to the Year 1872* (London: Frank Cass, 1971 [1873]), pp. 386-387; Atkins, *Voyage*, p. 175; Schuler, *Alas*, pp. 95-96; McDaniel, *Big Drum Ritual*, p. 57.
64. Gardner, *History of Jamaica*, p. 460, reported that in 1842, Myalists "ran about with arms outstretched, and declared that they were flying." Rev. Hope Masterton Wadell, *Twenty-Nine Years in the West Indies and Central Africa: A Review of Missionary Work and Adventure 1829-1858* (London: Frank Cass, 1970 [1863]), p. 189, attributed the resurgence of witchfinding in 1841 to the influence of liberated Africans who began to arrive that year. Compare his description of wheeling Myal dancers with McDaniel, *Big Drum Ritual*, pp. 29, 80-83, 110, 111, 113, 169. See also Monica Schuler, "Myalism and the African Religious Tradition in Jamaica," in Margaret E. Crahan and Franklin W. Knight (eds.), *Africa and the Caribbean: The Legacies of A Link* (Baltimore: The Johns Hopkins University Press, 1979), pp. 65-79.

65. See Vansina, *Paths*, pp. 72, 258-260; MacGaffey, "Oral Tradition," pp. 418-421; idem, *Religion and Society*, pp. 14, 234,: idem, "Kongo," pp. 176, 178; Wilks, *Forests Of Gold*, pp. 232-234; Baum, *Diola Religion*, p. 72; Shaw, "Production of Witchcraft," pp. 856-857; idem, "Splitting Truths from Darkness: Epistemological Aspects of Temne Divination," in Philip M. Peek (ed.), *African Divination Systems: Ways of Knowing* (Bloomington: Indiana University Press, 1991), p. 143; Henderson, *King in Every Man*, p. 123; Drewal, et al, *Yoruba*, pp. 14-15; Desmangles, *Faces*, pp. 100-108; Robin Horton, *Patterns of Thought in Africa and the West* (New York: Cambridge University Press, 1997), pp. 25, 38, 217-219; Métraux, *Voodoo*, pp. 63, 258-259; Planson, *Un initié*, pp. 186-187; Paula Girshick Ben Amos, "The Promise of Greatness: Women and Power in an Edo Spirit Possession Cult," in Blakeley, van Beek and Thomson, *Religion in Africa*, p. 125; and Brown, "Systematic Remembering," p. 67.
66. Harold Courlander, *A Treasury of American Folklore* (New York: Smithmark Publishers, 1996 [1976]), pp. 32-35; 62-63, 577-579.
67. Piersen, *Black Legacy*, pp. 36-37.
68. Esteban Montejo, *The Autobiography of a Runaway Slave* (New York: Vintage Books, 1973 [1968]), p. 16. Shaw's discussion of Temne reliance on concealed fortified towns during the era of the Mane invasions and Atlantic trade in *Memories of the Slave Trade*, p. 58, may be applicable here.
69. Kean Gibson, personal communication; idem, "A Celebration of Life," Cinema Guild video, undated.
70. J. Graham Cruickshank, "Among the Aku (Yoruba) in Canal No. 1, West Bank, Demerara River," *Timehri* 3rd Series 4 (1917): 78; idem "An African Dance in the Colony," *Supplement to the West India Committee Circular*, 29/666 (14 February, 1924): 8-9. Cruickshank identified as *s'iku*, a Yoruba funeral rite for an old man (*isinku* in Yorubaland): also see Drewal, *Yoruba Ritual*, pp. 19, 38-39.
71. USPG, Letters Received British Guiana 1850-59, Extracts, Garrison Chaplain's Letter, undated.
72. See Psalm 68:31, "'Ethiopia shall stretch out her hands to God" and Revelations 7:8, "'The sealing of the last tribe'" and Joel 1-10. See also Brooks, *History Of Bedwardism*, pp. 11, 20-21; Morton Marks, "Uncovering Ritual Structures in Afro-American Music," in Irving I. Zaretsky and Mark P. Leone (eds.), *Religious Movements in Contemporary America* (Princeton: Princeton University Press, 1974), pp. 92-93, 100-101, 105-109. Marks concludes that rhythmic percussion induces "going home" during trance. See Work, *American Negro Songs*, for many African-American spirituals referring to home as the goal. See also, George Eaton Simpson and Joseph G. Moore, "A Comparative Study of Acculturation in Morant Bay and West Kingston, Jamaica," *Zaïre* 11 (1957): 992-996, 1002-1004. Compare with Peel, *Religious Encounter*, pp. 223-225.
73. Albert Raboteau, *Slave Religion* (New York: Oxford University Press, 1978), pp. 262-265, 239. The 1892 sermon of Simon Buckaloo quoted in *The New York Sun*, is in Elias Farajaje-Jones, *In Search of Zion: The Spiritual Significance of Africa in Black Religious Movements* (Bern: Peter Lang, 1990), p. 33; W. R. F. Browning, *Oxford Dictionary of the Bible* (New York: Oxford University Press, 1996), pp. 125-129; *Book of Exodus*; Murphy, *Working the Spirit*, pp. 142-144, 188-189. Compare with

the Jordan and river-crossing in prayers and songs in the American South in Pitts, *Old Ship*, pp. 66, 69, 71, 72, 78, 89, 159.

74. See Vansina, *Oral Tradition*, pp. 156-157, 158-161, 165-173, 194-199 for legitimating devices.
75. Thompson, *Flash*, pp. 108-116, 227-267; Métraux, *Voodoo*, pp. 66, 68, 69, 163-166; Planson, *Un initié*, pp. 163-172; Henney, "Spirit Possession," pp. 54, 71-87, 119, 124-130, 141-143, 200-204; Zane, *Journeys,* pp. 18-28, 76, 95-99, 107-118, 132-135; Herskovits and Herskovits, *Trinidad Village*, pp. 199-202, 205; Stephen D. Glazier, *Marchin' The Pilgrims Home* (Salem, WI: Sheffield, 1991), pp. 29-30, 49-58, 145-146; George Eaton Simpson, *Black Religions in the New World* (New York: Columbia University Press, 1978), pp. 118-121; idem, "Ras Tafari," pp. 209-210, 222; Shirley C. Gordon, *God Almighty Make We Free* (Bloomington: Indiana University Press, 1996), pp. 44, 126; Schuler, *Alas*, pp. 41, 73-75; Chevannes, "Jamaican Lower Class Religion," pp. 95-96; idem, *Rastafari*, pp. 30, 59-60, 84-86, 111-114; Martha Beckwith, "Some Religious Cults in Jamaica," *American Journal of Psychology* 34 (1923): 33, 34, 39-40; "Bedward," *Star* (14 May, 1976); Roback, "White-Robed Army," pp. 40-43, 46-47, 68-69; Mechal Sobel, *Trabelin' On* (Princeton, N. J.: Princeton University Press, 1988 [1979]), pp. 93, 96-97, 101, 107-12; Thornton, *Africa and Africans*, pp. 244, 257-262; Leigh E. Schmidt, "Time, Celebration and the Christian Year," in Mark A. Noll, et al (eds.), *Evangelicalism* (New York: Oxford Unversity Press, 1994), p. 103; M. C. Jedrej and Rosalind Shaw (eds.), *Dreaming, Religion and Society in Africa* (Leiden and New York: E. J. Brill, 1992), pp. 9-11, 18 n. 3, 46; Brooks, *History Of Bedwardism*, pp. 5-6, 22-23.
76. See Simpson, ed., *Religious Cults of the Caribbean*, p. 78; and Zane, *Journeys*, pp. 94-95.
77. Chevannes, *Rastafari*, pp. 151-152, 157-158, 215, 244-245, 248-249; Roback, "White-Robed Army," pp. 1, 24, 81-82, 175-240; Glazier, *Marchin' the Pilgrims*, pp. 56-57; McDaniel, *Big Drum Ritual*, p. 106; Schuler, *Alas*, pp. 92-96.
78. See L. Peytraud, *L'esclavage aux Antilles françaises avant 1789, d'après des documents inédits des archives coloniales* (Paris: Hachette et cie, 1897), p. 372; David Patrick Geggus, "Slavery, War, and Revolution in the Greater Caribbean, 1789-1815," in David Barry Gaspar and David Patrick Geggus (eds.), *A Turbulent Time: The French Revolution and the Greater Caribbean* (Bloomington: Indiana University Press, 1997), pp. 7-11, p. 35 note 33; Simpson, "Ras Tafari," p. 218.
79. Tony Martin, *Race First* (Dover, MA: Majority Press, 1986 [1976]), pp. 12-13, 16-17, 49-50, 151-167.
80. See also George Samuel Schuyler, *Black Empire* Robert A. Hill and R. Kent Rasmussen (eds.) (Boston: Northeastern University Press, 1991). Schuyler himself considered the book "hokum and hack work". See African American Literature Reviews, *Black Empire* (1936-38), George S. Schuyler [writing as Samuel L. Brooks], http://www.brothersjudd.com/webpage/africanamlit.htm; Chevannes, *Rastafari*, pp. 33-34, 42-43, 133-136. "The spirit of David jump into Solomon, the spirit jump out of Solomon into Ras Tafari," in Simpson, "Ras Tafari," pp. 209, 216.
81. Chevannes, *Rastafari*, pp. 110-117, 157-158, 161, 220-221, 241-244, 248; Robert Hill, "Leonard P. Howell and Millenarian Visions in Early Rastafari," *Jamaica Journal* 16/1 (1981): 34, 35; Kenneth M. Bilby, "Jamaica," in Peter Manuel (ed.), *Caribbean Currents: Caribbean Music from Rumba to Reggae* (Philadelphia: Temple

University Press, 1995), pp. 61, 146-150, 159-164; Kenneth M. Bilby and Elliott Leib, "Kumina, the Howellite Church and the Emergence of Rastafarian Traditional Music in Jamaica," *Jamaica Journal* 19/3 (1986): 22-28. See Mattias Gardell, *In the Name of Elijah Muhammad: Louis Farrakhan* (Durham: Duke University Press, 1996), pp. 37-63, 99-135, 158-165 for the Nation of Islam.

82. Mircea Eliade, *Shamanism* (Princeton: Princeton University Press, 1974), pp. 269-274 for the cosmic tree. See also: McDaniel, *Big Drum Ritual*, p. 58; Métraux, *Voodoo*, pp. 107-108; Wafer, *Taste*, pp. 172-174; Donald M. Hogg, "The Convince Cult in Jamaica," in Sidney W. Mintz (ed.), *Papers in Caribbean Anthropology* (New Haven: Department of Anthropology, Yale University, 1960), pp. 3-7, 9, 13-16; Schuler, *Alas*, pp. 74, 78; Thompson, *Flash*, pp. 135-136; idem, "Kongo Influences on African-American Culture," in Joseph E. Holloway (ed.), *Africanisms in American Culture* (Bloomington: Indiana University Press, 1990), pp. 172-173; Montejo, *Autobiography*, pp. 139-140; Marks, "Uncovering Ritual Structures," p.102; Charles L. Perdue and Robert K. Phillips (eds.), *Weevils in the Wheat* (Charlottesville: University of Virginia Press, 1997 [1976]), p. 222; Murphy, *Working the Spirit*, pp. 28-29; Desmangles, *Faces*, pp. 104-108; Parks, "Conceptualization," pp. 48-49.

83. Gardner, *History of Jamaica*, p. 460; Schuler, "Myalism and the African Religious Tradition in Jamaica," pp. 65-79; Bilby and Bunseki, "Kumina," pp. 22, 23; MacGaffey, *Religion and Society*, pp. 55, 56, 129-133, 135; Planson *Un initié*, pp. 165-167, 225-233, 303; Davis, *Passage of Darkness*, pp. 294, 299; Hogg, "Convince Cult," pp. 10, 15, 16. Compare Convince trance behavior with Kongo ecstatic behavior described by Ephraim Andersson, *Messianic Popular Movements in the Lower Congo* (Uppsala: Studia Ethnographica Upsaliensa, 1958), pp. 73, 171-172, with Eliade, *Shamanism*, p. 126, 480-481. See also Thornton, *Kongolese St. Anthony*, pp. 161, 188. The silk cotton tree (*ceiba pentendra*) is associated with spirits and magic in the Caribbean and Africa: Beckwith, *Black Roadways*, pp. 171-172; Moore, *Colonial Guyana*, pp. 148-149, Desmangles, *Faces*, pp. 111, 197n; Ellis, *Ewe-Speaking Peoples*, pp. 49-52, 210, 311; Herskovits and Herskovits, *Trinidad Village*, pp. 66-67; Parks, "Conceptualization," pp. 81-82; René Devisch, "Mediumistic Divination among the Northern Yaka of Zaire," in Peek (ed.), *African Divination Systems*, p. 115.

84. Bilby and Bunseki, "Kumina," pp. 22-23, 44-45. Such tales are probably the sources of rumors that elders in the Jamaican prophet Alexander Bedward's church tried to fly. See for example, W. Adolph Roberts, "Bedward the Revivalist," and A.E.T. Henry, "Dip Dem Missa Bedward, dip dem," *Sunday Gleaner* (January 31, 1960), p. 14, and (November 10, 1968), p. 8, respectively.

85. Schuler, *Alas*, pp. 73-75; Herskovits and Herskovits, *Trinidad Village*, p. 205. See also Kenneth M. Bilby, "How the 'Older Heads' Talk: A Jamaican Maroon Spirit Possession Language and Its Relationship to the Creoles of Suriname and Sierra Leone," *Nieuwe West-Indische Gids/New West Indian Guide* 57/1-2 (1983): 38-41, 58-62; Hogg, *Convince Cult*, pp. 11, 13-14; Murphy, *Working the Spirit*, pp. 139, 172; John P. Homiak, "Dub History: Soundings on Rastafari Livity and Language," in Barry Chevannes (ed.), *Rastafari and Other African-Caribbean World Views* (Basingstoke: MacMillan and the Institute of Social Studies, the Hague, 1995), pp.163, n.180; Bilby and Bunseki, "Kumina," pp. 23, 44. Roback, "White-Robed Army," pp. 178-179, stated that the Jordanite sect held Igbo classes. See Warner-Lewis, *Guinea's Other Suns*, pp. 79-114; Pitts, *Old Ship Of Zion*, p. 116; Deren, *Divine Horsemen*, pp. 69, 196.

86. Vansina, *Tio Kingdom*, pp. 234-237; Moore, *Colonial Guyana*, p. 147; Judith Roback, "The White-Robed Army: An Afro-Guyanese Religious Movement," *Anthropologica* New Series 16/2 (1974): 245. It is difficult to distinguish European from African beliefs about salt. Newbell Niles Puckett, *Folk Beliefs of the Southern Negro* (New York: Dover Publications, 1969), pp. 154-156, 160-161; Thornton, *Africa and Africans*, p. 8.
87. Oldendorp, *Mission of the Evangelical Brethren*, p. 263; Thornton, *Kongolese St. Anthony*, pp. 17, 149-150, 175, 206; Hilton, *Kingdom Of Kongo*, p. 98. Thanks to Duane Harris of Jamaica for pointing out the expression. See also Chevannes, *Rastafari*, p. 35.
88. Fernandez, *Bwiti*, p. 303; Kempadoo, "Recordings," K104.
89. Skinner, "Ethnic Interaction," p. 235; Métraux, *Voodoo*, pp. 282-283; McAlister, "Sorcerer's Bottle," pp. 314, 318; Moore, *Colonial Guyana*, p. 147; Roback, "White-Robed Army," p. 245. In the West Central African Lemba cult, the "unsalted" novices' meal was actually *meatless*. Salt denotes deliberate and constructive anger in Lemba. See Janzen, *Lemba*, pp. 190, 196.
90. The lexicon is reproduced in Monica Schuler, "Liberated Central Africans in 19th Century Guyana," in Linda Heywood (ed.), *Central Africans and Cultural Transformations in the American Diaspora* (New York: Cambridge University Press, 2001), pp. 319-352.
91. Schuler, *Alas*, p. 96; Bilby and Bunseki, "Kumina," pp. 21-22; Miller, *Way of Death*, p. 5; MacGaffey, *Religion and Society*, p. 133; idem, *Modern Kongo Prophets*, p. 134.
92. See Postma, *Dutch in the Atlantic Slave Trade*, p. 246.
93. Africans in Rio de Janeiro's slave market attributed their crusty whitish skin (called *sarna* or *mal de loanda* in Brazil) to salted food fed them on the slave ship: Conrad, *Children of God's Fire*, p. 51; Karasch *Slave Life*, pp. 35, 40, 166, 179, 182-18; Schuler/Carmichael, Schuler/Scott interviews, Seafield, Berbice, 1984; Kempadoo, "Recordings," K104. While Thomas W. Wilson and Clarence E. Grim, "The Possible Relationship between the Transatlantic Slave Trade and Hypertension in Blacks Today," in Joseph E. Inikori and Stanley Engerman (eds.), *The Atlantic Slave Trade* (Durham, NC: Duke University Press, 1992), pp. 350-353, suggest that attempts to replace salt lost through sweating, vomiting and diarrhea on slave ships and during "seasoning" by feeding extra salt to slaves might have contributed to hypertension in African Americans, Philip D. Curtin disputes the connection in "The Slavery Hypothesis for Hypertension among African Americans: The Historical Evidence," *American Journal of Public Health* 82/12 (1992): 1681-1686. See Brown, *Mama Lola*, p. 40 for swollen ankles and salt and pp. 42-44 for meanings of food to Haitians.
94. Miller, *Way of Death*, pp. 37, 56-7, 64, 143-144, 214-215, 236, 274-276, 395, 396, 402-404, 685; Ralph A. Austen and Jonathan Derrick, *Middlemen of the Cameroons Rivers: The Duala and their Hinterland c. 1600-c. 1960* (New York: Cambridge University Press, 1999), pp. 28, Table 2.5, 49, 54, 71-72, 199 note 6, 205 note 96; E. Ann McDougall, "Salts of the Western Sahara: Myths, Mysteries and Historical Significance," *International Journal of African Historical Studies* 23/2 (1990): 235-236, 239-241, 250, 255, 256; idem, "Salt, Saharans and the trans-Saharan slave trade: Nineteenth-century developments," *Slavery and Abolition* 13/1 (1992): 61-80; Robin Law, *The Slave Coast of West Africa: The impact of the Atlantic Slave Trade on an*

African society (Oxford: Clarendon Press, 1991), pp. 42-43; 45-46, 57, 206, 220; Shaw, "Production of Witchcraft," pp. 864-865.

95. Wyatt MacGaffey, "The West In Congolese Experience," in Philip D. Curtin (ed.), *Africa and the West: Intellectual Responses to Western Culture* (Madison: University of Wisconsin Press, 1972), p. 55; Gomez, *Exchanging*, pp. 199-209; Iroko, "Cauris et esclaves". Taboos are reminders of something important in the past. See Jennifer Cole, "The Work of Memory in Madagascar," *American Ethnologist* 25/4 (1998): 614.

96. Shaw, "Production of Witchcraft," p. 869 and *Memories of the Slave Trade*. For West Central Africa, see pp. 186-188 above, and notes 10-14, 16-19.

Plate 12: Mrs. Mavis Morrison, Jungu's daughter

Source: Photograph by Monica Schuler (with permission from Mrs. Mavis Morrison)

9

Ancestors, Saints, and Prophets in Kongo-dominguois Root Experience: A Revisionist Reading of Transatlantic African Resistance

Terry Rey

CHARISMA AND ROOT EXPERIENCE IN KONGO-DOMINGUOIS RELIGION

Revisionist historical analyses of African traditions in the New World[1] have provided new and exciting insights into the root sources of African American cultures from Virginia to Bahia. This paper follows suit by exploring the particular question of Kongolese influence on religious prophecy in the Haitian Revolution, with focus on the identities, charisma, and impact of Makandal, Macaya, and Romaine-la-Prophétesse, three *dominguois*[2] rebel prophets. In doing so we show that the most influential source of Haitian Catholic saint cults is Kongolese rather than Iberian or *Breton* (people, culture, and of language of Bretagne, France), and that understanding saint cults generally in popular Haitian religion demands consideration of Kongolese religious "root experiences", since, as we will see below, Catholic saints featured centrally in such experiences for the baKongo. Tens of thousands of Kongolese Catholics were an essential collective agent in the creation of Haitian culture and all of its main features, the cult of the saints paramount among them. Hence Kongolese root experiences held impressive sway over the baKongo and their progeny in Saint-Domingue, just as Jewish root experiences like Moses on Mt. Sinai and the Holocaust still hold sway for Jews in such diasporic cities as New York and Bogotá today.[3]

The late fifteenth century introduction by the Portuguese of Catholic saints in the kingdom of Kongo, and the baKongo's subsequent appropriation of the saints over the next quarter millennium, is a taproot of what John K. Thornton has called "a new Afro-Atlantic religion", or "Afro-Atlantic Christianity".[4] Given the strength and nature of the indigenous Kongolese ancestor and *bisimbi* (spirits of the soil and terrestrial waters) cults and the cosmology in which they were framed, Catholic saints, who like ancestors were white and would have to traverse waters (*nzadi*) were they ever to visit the world of the living (*nza yayi*), resonated quite harmoniously with traditional Kongolese religious notions. Wyatt MacGaffey argues that the critical factor in the impressive and voluntary acceptance of Catholicism among the baKongo was their belief that European Catholic visitors, like the Kongolese dead, lived either under the ocean or the earth and belonged "specifically to the category of spirits of the soil and terrestrial waters, which were responsible for fertility and communal well being" – arguably the most cherished of traditional African values. Consequently, baptism into the new religion brought by the Portuguese "was understood as an initiation into the powers of a new and improved version of the cult of local spirits."[5]

In Kongolese religious consciousness, Catholic saint cults soon transcended the geographic limitations of the *bisimbi* cults, which centered on topographic features like springs and hills. As such, Catholic saints functioned in a universal way that is more akin to West African spirits like the *orishas* (spirits/deities) than anything typical of traditional Kongolese religion. Because of this, saints would come to play leading roles in what we can call the root experiences of Kongo religion in the sixteenth through eighteenth centuries, as will be shown below. "Root experience" is a term coined by the great Jewish philosopher and historian Emil Fackenheim to identify any essential, "*more* than epoch-making" event that has indelibly shaped Judaism:

> These events each made a new claim upon the Jewish faith and, indeed, could not be epoch-making if it were otherwise. They did not, however, produce a new faith. What occurred instead was a confrontation in which the old faith was tested in the light of contemporary experience. . . . The strain of confrontation may often have come near a breaking point, yet present experience, however new, unanticipated, and epoch-making, never destroyed the past faith. Its claim upon the present survived.[6]

Three conditions must be met in order for an event to be considered a root experience, for Fackenheim: 1) that "a past experience legislate to the present" (which in Kongolese experience resulted in saints being grouped with *bisimbi* and ancestors); 2) that the event have a "public historical character", and 3) that the past be accessible to the present, not as "events dead and gone" but "*as a present reality*".[7]

The theoretical focus of Fackenheim's root experience model can be sharpened by Max Weber's similar notion of "breakthrough". For Weber, religions change not gradually over time but in sudden, explosive bursts, or breakthroughs, which are inspired by charismatic prophets, the most obvious examples being those of Jesus, who inspired Christianity out of Judaism, and Buddha, who inspired Buddhism out of Hinduism. Weber defines the prophet as "the purely individual bearer of charisma, who by virtue of his mission proclaims a religious doctrine or divine commandment."[8] That is to say, "the prophet's claim is based on personal revelation and charisma." There are, for Weber, two kinds of charisma, one that is "wholly merited, based purely on personal calling", and another that lies dormant in the prophet and is "produced artificially... through some extraordinary means."[9] Often the two types merge. In any case, charisma "cannot be acquired by [just] any means.... Charisma is a gift that inheres in an object or person simply by virtue of natural endowments."[10]

Concerned primarily with "religion as a source of the dynamics of social change",[11] Weber uses the notion of charisma to explain the prophet's impact, and develops the notion of breakthrough (a sudden and major prophet-provoked shift in a religion's development) to understand "the effect of religious views upon the conduct of life."[12] It is the prophet, thus naturally endowed with charisma, who is the root cause of such an effect. "The essential criterion of prophecy for Weber is whether or not the message is a call to break with an established order."[13] Doubtless, such a (theological and/or political) break was the central factor in the agenda of each of the prophets here under consideration. Furthermore, the prophet, in order to activate and legitimate the break or stir his/her following to loyalty, must appeal to some accepted moral authority and exhibit "signs" or "proofs" of his/her calling. As the case below of the early eighteenth century Kongolese prophet Beatriz Kimpa Vita demonstrates, such authority was embodied by Saint Anthony, just as for the *dominguois* prophets Macaya and Romaine-la-Prophétesse it was embodied by the Magi and the Virgin Mary respectively. Over and above the degree of legitimation of the prophet that is thus wrought, it is by virtue of the messenger's charisma, for Weber, that a "breakthrough" is inspired. Such breakthroughs, in any event, are usually fundamental to root experiences.

Whereas the function of charismatic leadership in millenarian and protest movements has received considerable attention among sociologists and historians of religion, it has never featured prominently in studies of Kongo prophecy or the Haitian Revolution. Our understanding of such individuals as Beatriz, Makandal, Macaya, and Romaine-la-Prophétesse thus stands to gain much from such historical sociological analysis. Weber's classic argument about the role of prophets, their charisma, and the breakthroughs they effect can help us here by identifying the legitimating authority of Kongolese and *dominguois* prophecy, and thereby further elucidate the origins and impacts of historical figures like these. In effect, Weber's theory reveals some of the content of root experience in *dominguois* slave religion that is continuous with Kongolese root experience: Catholic saints served as legitimating authority to prophecy, and a promise of freedom and the unification of a kingdom resounded with the religious needs of the faithful. In other words, Weber's discussion of charisma and breakthrough helps reveal the depth structure of Kongo-*dominguois* root experience by directing attention to the legitimating authority upon which charisma and prophecy depend for their success. In eighteenth century Kongo, Catholic saints provided such authority, which legitimated the prophets' charisma. And this, in turn, inspired breakthroughs, or root experiences, several of which are discussed below.

MERGING ANCESTORS AND SAINTS IN KONGO

According to Kongolese beliefs, some *bisimbi* were once ancestors and share the same world of the dead *(nsi a bafwa),* along with other "forces who inhabit the other or invisible world and mediate between Nzambi (God) and living beings."[14] It follows logically that once they learned about the lives of Catholic saints, the baKongo identified them with "this larger class of the dead" to which the *bisimbi* belonged, especially in light of their role as mediums between God and humans. Resulting from such assimilation between saints and ancestors in Kongo, for example, "[Saint] Anthony, patron saint of marriage, was eventually incorporated in charms called Toni Malau, bringers of good fortune";[15] and "(o)ne of Kongo's earliest and most important churches was built directly over a graveyard, and for that reason was called *mbila*, which means grave in Kikongo."[16] Ancestor/Saint assimilation, furthermore, readily explains why in Kongo "All Souls' Day and All Souls' Eve (Halloween) were popular holidays that were celebrated by all-night vigils at the graves of family members, followed by days of fasting, prayer, and hearing mass."[17] Such syncretic African/Catholic devotions, which in extended forms continue to thrive in the Americas today, derived from the credence that the baKongo lent to both ancestors and Catholic saints and their intercessory powers. This was perhaps the most essential "co-revelation" in slave-era Kongolese and Afro-*dominguois* religion (or more specifically Kongo-*dominguois* religion).[18]

An impressive variety of beliefs about the dead aside, Kongolese ancestor cult activity usually took place around the graves of the recently departed. This kind of ritual life, which depended in large part on local geographic features – in this case graves – were the most difficult to perpetuate in the New World. Consequently there resulted a gap in Kongolese New World religion that was soon filled by an inflation of Catholic saint cults. This dynamic went far in shaping Afro-Atlantic Christianity and was a major factor in the establishment and development of Catholic saint cults in places with high concentrations of Kongolese slaves, such as Saint-Domingue, Cuba, and Brazil.

This process of course took many and varied forms. Whereas some of them are probably historically irretrievable, our revisionist reading of African diaspora history does yield insight into the ways that Catholic saints were and continue to be perceived in the African diaspora. For instance, in the eighteenth and nineteenth centuries, both in Haiti and Kongo, saints were popularly perceived as governing the rains and political struggle, which were once the exclusive powers of *bisimbi* and the dead.[19] It is thus evident that Kongolese popular hagiography has had a far-reaching influence on saint cults in Haitian Catholicism. I am referring, in particular, to a kind of appropriation of Catholic saints – something which might be labeled an Afro-Atlantic Christian tradition – in which saints possess powers of influencing the results of political, military, and even class struggles. Such powers enabled saints to play pivotal roles in Afro-Atlantic religion's root experiences, as in Saint James's 1506 battlefield appearance to the future Kongolese King Afonso, and, two centuries later across the Atlantic, in the Virgin Mary's inspiration of Romaine-la-Prophétesse in the Haitian Revolution.

CATHOLIC SAINTS IN KONGOLESE ROOT EXPERIENCES

A few years after the Portuguese first visited the Kongo in 1483, King Nzinga a Nkuwu sent an ambassador to Lisbon to request that Catholic priests come to the kingdom of Kongo to baptize him. Lisbon consented and in May 1491 Nzinga Nkuwu was baptized João I. Any misgivings that members of his court may have held in following suit were likely allayed when "two members of his nobility had

had the same dream about being encouraged to have hope by a beautiful woman", who later would be identified as the Virgin Mary,[20] thereby centering a Catholic saint in this quintessential root experience of Kongolese religion.

Whereas later in his life King João would waver somewhat in his commitment to the new faith (in part due to his commitment to polygamy), his son and heir, Afonso I, possessed remarkable and enduring Catholic zeal, vigorously studying Catholic theology with especial interest in the lives of the saints. Once having become himself king in 1509, the devout Catholic Afonso I "attempted to create a synthesis between the religious beliefs of the Kongolese people and Christianity" and, with the help of a significant tradition of Kongolese Catholic intellectuals that he created, became the driving force behind the initial spread of Christianity in the kingdom.[21] Afonso's own son Henrique was ordained Kongo's first bishop in 1518.

Kongolese devotion to Catholic saints gained steam following the Virgin's simultaneous apparitions to two of João's nobles. This devotion would next be encouraged with strong and lasting effect by Afonso's battlefield vision of Saint James the Greater in 1506. During a dynastic military struggle over the throne early in his rule, Afonso found his troops numerically overwhelmed and, facing imminent defeat, cried out in despair: "Santiago! Santiago!" In dutiful response, Saint James appeared in the sky leading a division of divine cavalry to drive Afonso's adversaries to surrender and flee.

As reflected in the following explanation by Thornton, these dreams and visions of saints in the kingdom of Kongo are root experiences of Kongolese (and Afro-Atlantic) Christianity, and as such would forever guide its course:

> The Kongolese idea of the Other World as being inhabited by the souls of the once living was reinforced by their interpretation of the principal figures of Catholic Christianity as it was presented to Afonso in the early sixteenth century. For Afonso and other Kongolese, the revelations of the late fifteenth and early sixteenth centuries had established the existence of a number of these figures in the Other World. The dream of the two nobles was clearly a revelation of the Virgin Mary....Afonso's opponents had seen Saint James Major and others of the Heavenly host in that fateful battle in 1506. Christian history as Afonso understood it, and indeed as it had been presented in the texts he read, made all of these beings formerly living humans, whose lives were recorded in the gospels or the Lives of the Saints. It was not difficult to reconcile this concept with that of the long dead souls who became territorial deities (*simbi*), since historical record revealed they had indeed lived many centuries before.[22]

Given the pivotal roles played by saints in earlier Kongolese Christian root experiences, there is nothing anomalous to their appearance at the heart of the most significant "heretical" movement in early Kongolese Christianity, the Antonians. Whereas the permanent possession of a young women named Beatriz Kimpa Vita by Saint Anthony was indeed the cynosure of the Antonian movement, earlier communications from the Virgin Mary to two peasant women created the ripe climate that nurtured Antonianism's impressive and rapid spread in 1704-

06. In one of these visions, the Virgin announced that "Jesus was angry with the Kongolese and that they must ask his mercy. To do this, it was necessary to say the Hail Mary three times, following it with three calls for mercy."[23] It was not long before thousands of Kongolese were caught up in this ritual and possessed by the kind of expectancy that usually precedes messianic and millenarian movements. Out of this widespread anticipation, which also drew force from the despair and ruin of a series of civil wars that racked the region beginning in 1641,[24] "a Kongolese woman [Beatriz] possessed by Saint Anthony led a mass movement to restore the Kingdom of Kongo. The movement was violently suppressed by the religious and political authorities of the country, and she was burned at the stake as a witch and heretic in 1706 – but not before she had drawn thousands of people to her in the ruins of the country's ancient capital."[25]

Beatriz set something of a new standard in Kongolese prophecy, not simply as the generator of yet another Kongolese Catholic root experience wherein saints played a central role, but in the degree of license she took in contorting Catholic doctrines, myths, and symbols. And while syncretism had always characterized Kongolese Catholicism, burning crosses, claiming her own pregnancy to be an immaculate conception, declaring Christ to have been born in the kingdom of Kongo, and the like, were simply beyond what the Portuguese clergy and their elite Kongolese patrons were willing to tolerate. Beatriz's creative symbolism and performance also implied a transgendered self-identification in that she claimed to be the reincarnation of a male saint. Such gender inversion, as demonstrated by James Sweet, was a common feature of West Central African spiritual mediumship, though mainly this took the form of men self-inverting as women rather than the opposite as in the case of Beatriz.[26] It is interesting that similar transgendered claims would be made later in the eighteenth century by Macaya and Romaine in Saint-Domingue, which is further evidence of their Kongolese origins, a point to revisit below. In any case, the root experience that Beatriz augured, along with the radical degree of her appropriation of Christianity came at a critical juncture in the history of Afro-Atlantic Christianity and would thus have far reaching influence in such distant places as Bahia, South Carolina, and Saint-Domingue.[27]

SAINTS AND POLITICAL STRUGGLE IN SAINT-DOMINGUE

Haitianists who have considered the impact of West Central Africa on Haitian religious culture have, for the most part, limited their scope to traditional Kongolese religious influences on Vodou, all but totally ignoring the forceful historical reality of popular Catholicism among the tens of thousands of Kongolese who comprised roughly half of Saint-Domingue's slave population on the eve of Haitian Revolution.[28] Studies of religion in Haiti have become redundant in their imbalanced portrayal of the assimilation of "West African" religious traditions with first Spanish and then French Catholicism, which – in the context of the social domination and resistance that characterized colonial plantation society in Saint-

Domingue/Haiti – underwent an explosive transformation and became Haitian Vodou. A case in point is the portrait painted, not that long ago, by Maya Deren:

> ... all these West Africans had certain basic beliefs in common: ancestor worship, the use of song, drums and dancing in the religious rituals, the possession of the worshipper by the god...they integrated, around this core of what they had in common, the great diversity of their tribal systems. Obviously, since each people had a complete religious system with its own set of major deities, there was much overlapping to be resolved.... And yet, because Vaudoun was a collective creation, it did not exact the abandonment of one tribal deity in favor of another. On the contrary, it seemed rather to delight in as generous an inclusion as possible.[29]

While acknowledging that "certainly Congo and Angola were forced to contribute by the French slavers of Saint-Domingue", Alfred Métraux mistakenly claims that "the annual intake from the African coast consisted mainly of blacks from Dahomey and Nigeria",[30] since at least half of slave imports to the colony derived from West Central Africa. Métraux lists some Kongolese contributions to Vodou's spirit pantheon, yet concludes that "Voodoo...in structure and in spirit has remained essentially Dahomean."[31] Karen McCarthy Brown's 404 page *Mama Lola* relegates the discussion of Kongo influences on Vodou to one sentence and a single footnote referencing Robert Farris Thompson, someone far less familiar with Haiti than she.[32] It is curious that affirming one of Vodou's most important rites, *petwo*, as Kongo-derived – as most scholars in fact do – has not inspired greater consideration of the implications.[33] Scholarly discourse of Vodou, furthermore, is mostly based on ethnography done in southern Haiti, which leads to conclusions like Métraux's and focuses like Deren's and Brown's, wherein Vodou indeed appears largely West African. In the north, however, Vodou demonstrates a greater focus on ancestors than on spirits, which is only curious until one considers that higher concentrations of Kongolese slaves settled in the north, and traditional Kongolese religion, while possessing local nature spirit cults, was chiefly characterized by its ancestor cult.

Although Thornton has demonstrated, for more than two decades, the influence of Kongolese Catholicism on *dominguois*/Haitian religious culture, Haitian studies remain plagued by the assumption that anything Catholic in Vodou is merely residue from the colonial era when enslaved Africans had to employ saints as masks for their forbidden homeland spirits.[34] More recently, a couple of scholars have been fruitfully following Thornton's lead and employing a revisionist approach toward understanding the influence of Kongolese Catholics on both Vodou and popular Haitian Catholicism. I have argued elsewhere, for instance, that Haitian saint cults and pilgrimage traditions are traceable to the kingdom of Kongo.[35] Hein Vanhee advances an interesting argument that one class of Vodou's ritual specialist, the *pret savann*, probably descends from the Kongolese cathechist who had been so essential to the spread of Catholicism in the Kongo.[36] This line of inquiry raises other important questions. Were there other baKongo among the celebrated rebel prophets of the Haitian Revolution?

And what were the influences of Kongolese Catholic root experiences on their leadership and message?

Armed slave uprisings first occurred in Hispaniola in 1522, and several others erupted during the twenty-five year period between 1679 and 1704. But such violent insurrections were actually rather infrequent in Saint-Domingue prior to 1791, making the case of Makandal all the more significant. "The Makandal conspiracy" of the 1750's spread from plantation to plantation, involving unknown numbers of slaves and maroons (escaped slaves) in a "network of resistance" aiming "to overthrow the white regime, whereby the blacks would become the new masters of Saint-Domingue", as Carolyn Fick explains. "It was the first real attempt in the long history of slave resistance at disciplined, organized revolt aiming not only at the destruction of the white masters and of slavery, but at the political notion of independence, albeit historically premature and expressed in messianic overtones."[37] The impressive longevity (18 years) of Makandal's movement drew from the elusive nature of maroon raiders in Saint-Domingue, and Makandal would serve as a model for later rebel prophets in this regard.[38] This "was a case of a maroon band with a formidable leader operating in a permanent state of marronage, but one that extended itself, at the same time, to set afoot a vast movement of resistance."[39] Although captured and, like Beatriz half a century earlier, burned at the stake in 1758, Makandal set an important precedent both as a charismatic leader of rebellion against the slave regime and an example of the potency of maroon-based resistance: thus "his memory was sufficient to nourish the long and bitter struggle that would one day lead to emancipation."[40] We shall turn to the question of Makandal's origins later.

By August of 1791, scattered armed slave uprisings nourished a nascent national revolution following the legendary Vodou ceremony at Bois Caïman led by Boukman Dutty, in which a pig sacrifice and a stirring sermon amounted to, "in essence, a call to arms."[41] While charismatic leadership of the kind displayed by Makandal and Boukman would remain instrumental over the course of the Haitian independence struggle, it was especially during the early years of the revolution that popular religion made its resounding impact on the insurrection, serving as an organizational vehicle, an inspiration for legendary feats of courage, providing talismans for defense and the promise of immortality in Africa for martyrs and, perhaps most importantly, creating a worldview in which charismatic prophets could rise in stature and lead the slaves to victory and freedom.

Claims of Boukman's Jamaican origins have, as far as I know, never been questioned. And though the origins of most maroon leaders in Saint-Domingue remain debatable, the nature of Romaine's person and performance suggest that he was Kongolese. The Kongolese identity of Macaya is only somewhat more certain. As for the first prophet to inspire the only successful national slave revolt in world history, Fick finds the notion of Makandal's Kongolese origins to be tenuous. Vanhee nonetheless argues that Makandal was Kongolese, despite good reasons to doubt this, such as the fluent Arabic that contemporary sources report

Makandal to have spoken. Both Fick and Vanhee suggest possible ways to link Makandal to Kongo, such as his name and the names of his closest conspirators, Mayombe and Teyselo. Fick posits that Makandal may have originally been from MaKanda in the West Central African kingdom of Loango, and hence named after his hometown. Vanhee, meanwhile, speculates that his name may have "derived from "Makonda", meaning Kongo *nkisi* [charm], or from "*makanda*", meaning a medicinal plant".[42] While finding it thus "tempting to try and link the origins of the Saint-Domingue maroon leaders with this place [the kingdom of Kongo], or at any rate with the surrounding region," Fick rightly concludes, however, that "such a linkage would still be little more than conjecture."[43] It is noteworthy that David Geggus finds evidence that Makandal, like Boukman, may have come from the British West Indies.[44] The paradigm that I am employing here, in any case, may just as well be used to refute claims of specific origins as to demonstrate them: for example, since no features of Kongolese root experience are evident in the Makandal conspiracy, it is further unlikely that he was Kongolese.

That the names of Makandal and his associates sound Kongolese is in itself not enough to demonstrate that they themselves were. Instead, could Makandal's prolific production and distribution of poison and ensorcelling packets, which were comparable to certain forms of *nkisi* used in the Kongo, convince us of this? No, for it is just as likely that Makandal learned such practices, along with *petwo* rites, from other maroons who were in fact Kongolese. Furthermore, the baKongo, although by some New World accounts renowned in the colonial era for their proclivity for sorcery, by no means held a monopoly on the destructive supernatural arts. One contemporary source from Saint-Domingue, in fact, notes that among slaves it was "especially those of the nations from the Gold Coast" who "have knowledge of various plants containing poisons or the necessary elements with which to compose them."[45]

The most forceful counter-evidence to the claim that Makandal was Kongolese was his fluent Arabic and Islamic devotion.[46] It is possible that prior to his enslavement in Africa he had been a Koranic scholar. And despite Moreau de Saint-Mery's observation that some West Central African slaves in Saint-Domingue professed beliefs in "Mohametism", it is unlikely that any of them would have possessed the command of Arabic that was reported of Makandal.[47] Prematurely denying Makandal's Islamic background runs the risk of missing what could have been his central religious motivation: the Islamic notion of *jihad* [holy war]. It is quite plausible that any Muslim slave in revolutionary era Saint-Domingue, however few there may have been, perceived of the entire resistance struggle against the slave regime as a veritable *jihad*, much as this notion helped fuel such resistance among Islamic slaves in Bahia during the following century.[48] I do not mean to argue that Islam played any major role in *dominguois* insurgence – for surely it did not; I am only suggesting that it may have been central to Makandal's perception of his struggle and of himself. This suggestion is admittedly speculative, but it is more plausible than the argument that Makandal was Kongolese. The revisionist interpretation of this history, in any case, demands careful consideration of the entire spectrum of religious and ideological forces behind African agency in New World slave resistance.

Macaya, a maroon leader who operated largely independently in the north from 1793-1796, is a safer bet to have been Kongolese than either Makandal or Romaine. Yet even here the argument basically hinges upon linguistic connections alone, albeit more tenable ones than those suggested for Makandal. "That Macaya was a Kongolese," writes Thornton, "might be inferred from his name, which can be attested as a personal name in Kongo from the late seventeenth century."[49] Geggus calls Macaya a "pro-Royalist black chief" who in 1793 was "stirring up his fellow 'Congos' at Acul."[50] Jacques De Cauna simply calls Macaya a Kongo without revealing a source for this important piece of information, though probably deducing as much from Macaya's famous declaration, "I am the Subject of three kings: the king of the Kongo, the master of all blacks; the king of France, who represents my father, and of the king of Spain, who represents my mother. These three Kings are the descendants of those who, led by a star, came to adore God made man."[51] Macaya's contortion of Christian myth and symbolism in this statement is typical of Kongolese prophetic tradition and root experience. The lack thereof in reports on Makandal further weakens claims that he was Kongolese. Its relative abundance in the case of Romaine-la-Prophétesse, on the other hand, is the most compelling hint that this intriguing rebel prophet may very well himself have been Kongolese.[52]

Claiming to be both the godson of the Virgin Mary and a king, Romaine led a band of several thousand maroons on violent raids of plantations between Leogane and Jacmel from December 1791 to March 1792. The style and content of his prophecy indicates that Romaine may have been Kongolese. For example, in preaching Mass before an inverted cross and placing his head inside the tabernacle of his church to retrieve the Virgin's handwritten message, Romaine appropriated Catholic symbolism and myth in radical ways that were consistent with Kongolese prophetic tradition, since indeed "Kongolese ideologues had reworked Christian concepts in similar ways for years."[53]

From the time of the Kongo kingdom's initial contact with Europeans in the late fifteenth century, Kongolese traditions of religious leadership came to be largely defined in terms of prophetism, and prophets from Beatriz to the twentieth century's Simon Kimbangu have had unparalleled and enduring influence on Kongolese religious life.[54] It is the prophet (*ngunza*) who has eclipsed all other forms of religious specialists for the Kongo "laity". Romaine's very title of "la Prophétesse" raises the question as to whether he and his followers (many, if not most, of whom were in fact Kongolese) viewed him as a prophet in the traditional Kongolese sense of the term. MacGaffey identifies basically two conditions that define the prophet "in popular Kongo consciousness": "his exercise of healing powers in the public interest…[and he] represents a hierarchical dispensation of healing power mediated through him personally."[55] Note here that Romaine was widely renowned as a healer. Besides healing, Kongo ideologues are also marked as prophets by their capacity for transcendental mediumship with "the invisible world", as Kongo religion assumes "a cosmology describing relationships between the visible and invisible worlds and a limited set of contrasted mediating roles. These assumptions compose the structure of Kongo religion."[56] Romaine's mediating role, to wit, involved his communication with the Virgin Mary, much as Beatriz's involved her being Saint Anthony. These each represent examples of the kind of appeal to an accepted and transcendent moral authority that, according to Weber, legitimates prophecy. As a healer and a medium whose ultimate objective, the liberation of an enslaved people, was obviously "in the public interest", Romaine quite unambiguously fits the description of a *ngunza*, suggesting either that he was himself a Kongo prophet, or at least that he was perceived as a *ngunza* by his Kongolese followers. For Romaine, moreover, as is the case for Kongo prophets in general, prophetic leadership entailed both religious and political responsibilities. All of this illustrates that in both the kingdom of Kongo and Saint-Domingue "the appearance of the prophets represented an utterly new divine dispensation of power intended to redress the balance between Africans and Europeans."[57]

Besides the royalist overtones of his message, Romaine's subversive appeal to the Virgin Mary and his claims to be both her relative and medium also are evidence that either he was Kongolese or, at least, that he was deeply influenced by Kongolese religious thought and that he sculpted his message and performance accordingly. While appeal to Catholic saints or biblical personages was a common feature of *dominguois* popular religion, claims by religious leaders to be related to and in direct communication with them were not. Such claims were, however, typical of Kongo prophets, further demonstrating Kongolese influence on both Romaine's self-understanding and the religious needs of his followers. The campaign of terror that Romaine and his following of renegade slaves orchestrated against the whites of Leogane, Jacmel, and environs was believed by the insurgents to have been commanded of them by the Virgin Mary. This, anyway, is what Romaine preached that his "godmother" had ordered.

What makes the case of Romaine still more compelling than that of either Macaya or Makandal is its reflection of each of the three Kongolese root experiences of Afro-Atlantic Christianity outlined above: Romaine received revelations from the Virgin Mary, as in the simultaneous dreams of two of King João I's nobles; he was guided to victory in battle by a Catholic saint, just as Afonso had been by Saint James the Greater in 1506; and he set about to defeat the forces of enslavement and restore some kind of kingdom in Saint-Domingue, as Beatriz had done earlier that century in the kingdom of Kongo.

Finally, like Beatriz, who claimed to be Saint Anthony, Romaine's self-identification as "prophetess" rather than "prophet" inverted his gender. This transgendered self-identification is further suggestive of Romaine's Kongolese origins. By the sixteenth century in West Central Africa, the spiritual power of transgendered male prophets was, as Sweet demonstrates, well established and "universally known": "the feminization of these men, as measured by their social and sexual roles as females, rendered them vulnerable to the spirit world...."[58] Hence Romaine may very well have taken the feminine title "*la prophétesse*" as a reflection of a feminized passivity that made him penetrable by the spirit world, and hence an effective medium. In such a transgendered state, his mediumship was made both possible and understandable to his Kongo-*dominguois* followers. One might, moreover, consider in similar terms Macaya's inversion of the King of Spain in his famous declaration, quoted above, in which he refers to this king as "my mother". Such transgendered references thus served to further legitimize the charisma of Macaya and Romaine in the stunning root experience of the Haitian Revolution.

CONCLUSION

Attention to root experiences in African history sharpens revisionist focus on the most forceful religious and ideological forces behind African and African-based resistance in the Americas, as our exploration of Kongolese influences in revolutionary Saint-Domingue demonstrates. This theoretical approach, furthermore, especially once sharpened by application of Weber's theory of prophecy and charisma, breeds new insights into the origins and identities of leading rebel prophets of the Haitian Revolution, such as Makandal, Macaya, and Romaine-la-Prophétesse. Peter Worsley's suggestion about the social grounding of charisma reflects well this chapter's central point about these *dominguois* prophets and their Kongolese forbearers, all of them leaders of social movements in which:

> followers with possibly utopian or at least diffuse and unrealized aspirations cleave to an appropriate leader because he articulates and consolidates their aspirations. He then specifies and narrows these aspirations, converting them both into more concrete and visible goals towards whose achievement collective action can be oriented and organized, and into *beliefs* which can be validated *by reference to experience.*[59]

This contribution argues that Kongolese notions of prophecy and conceptions of Catholic saints were the keys to "specifying and narrowing" such "diffuse and unrealized aspirations". In Saint-Domingue, Macaya and Romaine transformed and validated these aspirations "by reference to [root] experience" in the kingdom of Kongo.

Yet these conclusions are but the tip of the iceberg, for revisionist readings of slave resistance in Saint-Domingue hold potential to do more than shed light on the origins and impacts of the colony's leading rebel prophets. In his discussion of Kongolese ideological contributions to the Haitian Revolution, for instance, Thornton notes that "attention to the ideological orientation of the mass of the slaves might be important even if many of their leaders were creoles with no immediate African background, since they would still have to appeal to their followers in terms that resonated with their ideology."[60] This suggestion can help us understand, for example, the conflicting accounts of revolutionary creole military leader Jean-Jacques Dessalines's ripping the white out of the French flag to create the red and blue flag of the new Haitian republic at *le Congrès d'Archahaie* in 1806: by some accounts he was possessed by Ogun (the originally West African spirit of iron) when so capping the overthrow of the French; by others, Dessalines's possession was by the Virgin Mary, who, moreover, commanded him to desecrate *les tricouleurs* while cursing "in Congo language".[61]

ENDNOTES

1. "A revisionist interpretation of the dispersal of enslaved Africans in the era of the trans-Atlantic slave trade . . . concentrates on the role of Africa in the genesis and ongoing history of the diaspora. This revisionist approach emphasizes the continuities in African history and the extension of that history into the diaspora." Paul E. Lovejoy, "Revisionist Interpretations of Ethnicity, Culture and Religion under Slavery," *Studies in the World history of Slavery, Abolition and Emancipation* 2/1 (1997): 1, http://www2.h-net.msu.edu/~slavery/essays/esy9701love.html, 1/18/01.
2. I use the French term "*dominguois*" as the adjectival form of Saint-Domingue throughout this essay. I also use the term Kongo-*dominguois* as an identifier of a specific contiguous transatlantic African Diasporic culture, or a particular strain of Afro-Atlantic culture that is born in the kingdom of Kongo and lives in Saint-Domingue/Haiti.
3. At the time of the outbreak of the Haitian Revolution in 1791, there were over half a million slaves in Saint-Domingue. More than half of them had been born and raised in Africa. During the second half of the eighteenth century, a majority of these, furthermore, were derived from the Kongo. See the chapter in this volume by David Eltis, Stephen Behrendt, and David Richardson.
4 See John K. Thornton, *Africa and Africans in the Making of the Atlantic World, 1400-1800* (Cambridge: Cambridge University Press, 1998, [1992]), chapter nine.
5. Wyatt MacGaffey, "Dialogues with the Deaf: Europeans on the Atlantic Coast of Africa," in Stuart Schwartz (ed.), *Implicit Understandings* (New York: Cambridge University Press, 1994), pp. 249-267, 257.
6. Emil Fackenheim, *God's Presence in History: Jewish Affirmations and Philosophical Reflections* (New York: New York University Press, 1970), p. 9.
7. Ibid., pp. 9-11. Fackenheim's thesis is especially relevant for revisionist studies of African diasporic religious history because it is, obviously, concerned with the quintessential diasporic experience, that of the Jews, and since it insists that the Holocaust itself is a root experience in Judaism, in much the same way the transatlantic slave trade should itself be considered a root experience in Afro-Atlantic religion, since in both cases no sense can be made of subsequent history and collective religious experience without careful consideration of the legislative powers of radical oppression over a people's destiny and identity. In other words, Jews, diasporan Africans (and certainly even many continental Africans), and their religions would never be the same after the Holocaust and the transatlantic slave trade respectively.
8. Max Weber, *The Sociology of Religion* (Boston: Beacon, 1963), p. 46.
9. Ibid., p. 2.
10. Ibid.
11. Talcott Parson, "Introduction," in Weber, *The Sociology of Religion*, p. xxx.
12. Weber, *The Sociology of Religion*, p. 9.

13. Parson, p. xxxiii.
14. Wyatt MacGaffey, "Cultural Roots of Kongo Prophetism," *History of Religions* 17 (1977): 185.
15. Ibid., p. 187.
16. John K. Thornton, "Perspectives on African Christianity," in Vera Lawrence Hyatt and Rex Nettleford (eds.), *Race, Discourse, and the Origins of the Americas* (Washington: Smithsonian Institution, 1995), p. 177.
17. Ibid. It is noteworthy that such All Saints' Day devotions remain popular in Haitian Vodou today.
18. "Africans became Christians not because the priests or the converts sought to match or replace their cosmologies. Instead, they converted because they received "co-revelations;" that is, revelations in the African tradition that dovetailed with the Christian tradition. The conversion was accepted because Christians also accepted this particular set of revelations as valid." Thornton, *Africa and Africans in the Making of the New World*, p. 255.
19. See Terry Rey, "A Consideration of Kongolese Catholic Influences on dominguois/ Haitian Popular Catholicism: A Sociohistorical Exploration," in Linda M. Heywood (ed.), *Central Africans and Cultural Transformations in the American Diaspora* (New York: Cambridge University Press, 2001), pp. 265-285.
20. Thornton, "Perspectives on African Christianity," p. 172.
21. Ibid., p. 173.
22. Ibid., p. 177.
23. John K. Thornton, *The Kongolese Saint Anthony: Dona Beatriz Kimpa Vita and the Antonian Movement, 1684-1706* (New York: Cambridge University Press, 1998), p. 105.
24. On the Kongo civil wars, see John K. Thornton, *The Kingdom of the Kongo: Civil War and Transition, 1641-1718* (Madison: The University of Wisconsin Press, 1983).
25. Ibid., p. 1.
26. James H. Sweet, "Male Homosexuality and Spiritism in the African Diaspora: The Legacies of a Link," *Journal of the History of Sexuality* 7 (1996): 184-202.
27. I follow here Thornton's provocative suggestions about such transatlantic continuities in chapter nine of *The Kongolese Saint Anthony*.
28. See Jean Price-Mars, "Lemba-Pétro: un culte secret, son histoire, sa localisation géographique, son symbolisme," *Revue de la Societé d'Histoire et de Géographie d'Haïti* 9/28 (1938): 12-31; Robert Farris Thompson and Joseph Cornet, *The Four Moments of the Sun: Kongo Art in Two Worlds* (Washington, DC: National Gallery of Art, 1981); John Janzen, *Lemba; 1650-1930: A Drum of Affliction in Africa and the New World* (New York: Garland, 1982); Robert Farris Thompson, *Flash of the Spirit: African and Afro-American Art and Philosophy* (New York: Random House, 1983); Luc de Heusch, "Kongo in Haiti: A New Approach to Religious Syncretism," *Man (Journal of the Royal Anthropological Institute)* 24 (1989): 290-303; Lilas Desquiron, *Les racines du vaudou* (Port-au-Prince: Deschamps, 1990); John K. Thornton, "On the Trail of Voodoo: African Christianity in Africa and the Americas," *Americas* 44 (1988): 261-278; idem, "'I Am the Subject of the King of Congo': African Political Ideology and the Haitian Revolution," *Journal of World History* 4 (1993): 181-214; Elizabeth McAlister, "A Sorcerer's Bottle: The Visual Art of Magic in Haiti," in

Donald J. Cosentino (ed.), *Sacred Arts of Haitian Vodou* (Los Angeles: University of California 1995), pp. 304-321.

29. Maya Deren, *The Divine Horsemen: The Living Gods of Haiti* (New Paltz, NY: Documentex, McPherson, 1983 [1970]), pp. 58-59.
30. Alfred Métraux, *Voodoo in Haiti* (New York: Schocken Books, 1972 [1959]), p. 26.
31. Ibid., p. 29.
32. Karen McCarthy Brown, *Mama Lola: A Vodou Priestess in Brooklyn* (Los Angeles: University of California Press, 1991), p. 100.
33. Vodou spirits, or *lwas*, generally have various manifestations, which are classified into different branches of the pantheon. The main branches are *rada*, which derive mostly from West Africa, and *petwo*, which are more likely of West Central African origins. See Leslie G. Desmangles, *The Faces of the Gods: Vodou and Roman Catholicism in Haiti* (Chapel Hill: The University of North Carolina Press, 1992).
34. Métraux is an important exception to this.
35. Rey, "Kongolese Catholic Influences on Haitian Popular Catholicism," pp. 272-276.
36. Hein Vanhee, "Central African Popular Christianity and the Making of Haitian Vodou Religion," in Linda M. Heywood (ed.), *Central Africans and Cultural Transformations in the American Diaspora* (New York: Cambridge University Press, 2001), pp. 262-263.
37. Carolyn E. Fick, *The Making of Haiti: The Saint Domingue Revolution from Below* (Knoxville: The University of Tennessee Press, 1990), p. 62.
38. Métraux, *Voodoo in Haiti*, p. 47, in fact refers to Romaine-la-Prophétesse and Hyacinthe, another revolutionary era rebel prophet, as "imitators of Makandal".
39. Fick, *The Making of Haiti*, p. 62.
40. Ibid., p. 63. So much legend surrounds the ceremony at Bois Caiman that one scholar questions whether it ever actually took place. See Léon François Hoffmann, "Un mythe nationale: la cérémonie du Bois Caïman," in Gerald Barthélemy and C. Girault (eds.), *La république haïtienne* (Paris: Karthala, 1993), pp. 434-448. From a vast literature on Bois Caiman, see especially Robin Law, "La cérémonie du Bois Caiman et le 'pacte du sang' dahoméen," in Laënnec Hurbon (ed.), *l'Insurrection des esclaves de Saint-Domingue* (Paris : Karthala, 2000), pp. 131-147; and David Patrick Geggus, "La cérémonie du Bois Caiman," in ibid, pp. 149-167.
41. Ibid., p. 93.
42. Vanhee, "Central African Popular Christianity."
43. Fick, *The Making of Haiti*, p. 291, n.70.
44. David Patrick Geggus, *Slavery, War, and Revolution: The British Occupation of Saint-Domingue 1793-1798* (New York: Oxford University Press, 1982), p. 40.
45. "Mémoire fait par un habitant d'Ouanaminthe sur les evénements arrivés a cette paroisse jusqu'au 15 janvier 1792, certifié par Alexandre la Fosse, le Cap, 22 sept. 1792," as cited in Fick, *The Making of Haiti*, p. 291, ft. 70.
46. Thomas Madiou, *Histoire d'Haïti, tome 1*(Port-au-Prince: Deschamps, 1989 [1847]), p. 35. Madiou may have relied for this information on M. de C., "Makandal, histoire veritable: extrait du *Mercure de France* 15 septembre 1787," which is cited in Fick, *The Making of Haiti*, p. 291 ft. 69. Sidney Mintz and Michel-Rolph Trouillot question the claim that Makandal was a Muslim: "A great deal of imaginative reconstruction surrounds François Makandal's personal history. He is thought to have been of

"Guinea" origin – some claim of the Muslim faith. It is said that he was enslaved at the age of twelve. (There is to our knowledge no conclusive evidence for any of this.)" See Sidney W. Mintz and Michel-Rolph Trouillot, "The Social Character of Haitian Vodou," in Donald J. Cosentino, (ed.), *Sacred Arts of Haitian Vodou* (Hong Kong: South Sea Press, 1995), p. 136.

47. M.E.L. Saint-Mery, *Déscription topographique, physique, civil, et historique de la partie française de l'isle de Saint-Domingue* 3 vols. (Paris: Societé de l'histoire des colonies française, 1959 [1797]), I, p. 53.
48. Paul E. Lovejoy, "Background to Rebellion: The Origins of Muslim Slaves in Bahia," in Paul E. Lovejoy and Nicholas Rogers (eds.), *Unfree Labour in the Development of the Atlantic World* (London: Frank Cass, 1994), pp. 151-180.
49. Thornton, "'I Am the Subject of the King of the Kongo,'" p. 185.
50. Geggus, *Slavery, War, and Revolution*, p. 182.
51. Jacques De Cauna, *Haïti: l'eternelle révolution* (Port-au-Prince: Deschamps, 1997), p. 207. De Cauna does not provide his source for Macaya's declaration, which is cited by Thornton, "'I Am the Subject of the King of the Kongo,'" p. 181, as François-Joseph-Pamphile de Lacroix, *Mémoires pour servir a l'histoire de la revolution de Saint-Domingue* (Paris: Chez Billet Ainé, 1819), I, p. 25.
52. For a fuller discussion of Romaine-la-Prophétesse, see Terry Rey, "The Virgin Mary and Revolution in Saint-Domingue: The Charisma of Romaine-la-Prophétesse," *Journal of Historical Sociology* 11 (1998): 341-369.
53. Thornton, "'I am the Subject of the King of the Kongo,'" p. 189.
54. On Kimbanguism, see Wyatt MacGaffey, "Kimbanguism and the Question of Syncretism in Zaire," in Thomas D. Blakeley, Walter E. A. van Beek, and Dennis L. Thompson (eds.), *Religion in Africa* (Portsmouth, NH: Heinemann, 1994), pp. 241-256; idem, *Modern Kongo Prophets: Religion in a Plural Society* (Bloomington, IN: Indiana University Press, 1983; Susan Asch, *"l'Eglise du Prophète Simon Kimbangu: de ses origins à son role actuel au Zaïre* (Paris: Karthala, 1983).
55. Wyatt MacGaffey, "Cultural Roots of Kongo Prophetism," pp. 177-193, 179.
56. Ibid., p. 192.
57. Ibid., p. 190.
58. Sweet, "Male Homosexuality and Spiritism in the African Diaspora," p. 193.
59. Peter Worsley, *The Trumpet Shall Sound: A Study of "Cargo" Cults in Melanesia* (New York: Schocken Books, 1968), p. xiv. Second italics mine.
60. Ibid., p. 183.
61. "In Léogane in the 1970s I heard people recount that Dessalines cut out the white strip of the French flag while possessed by the warrior spirit Ogou. [Haitian novelist Timoléon] Brutus in l'Homme d'airain (1946) presents an even more compelling version. He tells a story of "undying memory," heard and passed on to Justin Lhérison in his history class at the Lycée Pétion in Port-au-Prince in the 1930s. It was not a spirit of African origins that possessed Dessalines, but "the Holy Virgin, protectress of the Blacks." Then, Dessalines cursed in "Congo language...." Joan Dayan, *Haiti, History, and the Gods* (Berkeley: University of California Press, 1995), p. 52.

10

The Afro-Brazilian Communities of Ouidah and Lagos in the Nineteenth Century: A Comparative Analysis

Elisée Soumonni

The section of the West African Coast extending from the present-day Republic of Ghana to modern Nigeria got its infamous appellation of the Slave Coast because of its deep involvement in the transatlantic slave trade between the seventeenth and nineteenth centuries. Many localities of this coast served as ports of embarkation of enslaved Africans, the largest proportion of whom went to Brazil. The same ports of embarkation were also to serve as disembarkation for those Africans and their descendents who were lucky to return home. This return movement started as early as the eighteenth century, but it did not become significant until the 1830s, largely in the aftermath of the Muslim rebellion of 1835 in Bahia. The constitution of what can be termed an Afro-Brazilian community, with a specific identity, was therefore basically a nineteenth century phenomenon. Similarly, the existence in the Bight of Benin of cities with communities referred to as Brazilians, Afro-Brazilians or Aguda, is the living illustration of the long and active Portuguese and Brazilian participation in the slave trade of this part of the West African coast. Ouidah and Lagos, the two major slave-trading ports in the region, are two significant examples of such cities. Despite the common features of their Afro-Brazilian communities, a comparative approach is needed in their study. As a matter of fact, prevailing local conditions of their establishment and further development were responsible for striking differences between them. It is this comparative analysis that is the focus of this chapter.[1]

The history of the constitution of the Afro-Brazilian communities in Ouidah and Lagos is a reflection of the participation of both cities in the transatlantic slave trade. Unlike Lagos, Ouidah was an early major slave-trading port, even before 1727 when it was incorporated into the fast expanding Kingdom of Dahomey. The roots of its Brazilian community can be traced to the establishment, in 1721, of the Portuguese Fort São João Baptista de Ajuda whose links "were to Brazil rather than directly to Portugal, or the local West African headquarters of Portuguese administration on the island of São Tomé." The directors of the fort "were appointed by and reported to the viceroy of Bahia."[2] The location of the fort was to become the center of the original community of Ouidah, the early establishment of which resulted from the fact that, at the beginning of the eighteenth century, Ouidah was already a notorious center of the slave trade, a position that its conquest by Dahomey in 1727 was to confirm till the mid-nineteenth century. During this long period, "Portuguese, based mainly in Brazil, and native-born Brazilians" were undoubtedly the leading merchants.[3] Operating along the coast, these merchants established a community with the offspring of their unions with local women that would continue to grow with the return movement of liberated Africans from Brazil in the nineteenth century.

Unlike Ouidah, Lagos's direct involvement in export trade in slaves was a nineteenth century development. Before the first decade of this century, it had limited contact with the hinterland. The participation of its inhabitants in trade with the interior, if any, might have been marginal or informal, through middlemen. The situation was however to change from the early decades of the nineteenth century as a result of inter-related factors. The collapse of Oyo and the resulting struggle among Yoruba states competing for its succession created a permanent state of warfare aggravated by pressure from the Fulani-led *jihad* (Muslim holy war). War captives fell prey to slave traders who continued to operate despite the abolition of the traffic. Profiting from the situation thus created, but also from the fact that the activities of the British Preventive Squadron were then concentrated on other parts of the coast, Lagos and Badagry emerged as important centers of the Atlantic slave trade.[4] The subsequent British reaction to such a development was of great significance for the Afro-Brazilian communities of both Lagos and Ouidah. It was also illustrative of the political situation prevailing in the two slave-trading ports in the mid-nineteenth century. Realizing that diplomatic pressures to convince the rulers of Lagos and Dahomey to give up slave-trading were not producing the desired effect, the British resorted to more severe and dissuasive measures to force them to sign an anti-slave trade treaty. This result was achieved in Lagos, subjected, after a long blockade, to a bombardment on December 24, 1851, by the British West African Squadron. King Kosoko was forced out of power and replaced by his rival Akitoye. The latter quickly agreed to sign, on 1 January 1852 the long sought treaty for the suppression of the slave trade, the banning of human sacrifices, and the protection to Christian missionaries and their converts.[5]

Though subjected, like Lagos, to the British blockade in 1851, Ouidah did not suffer the same bombardment. It would have been risky for the British. King Ghezo of Dahomey was not Kosoko. He had no Akitoye or a puppet rival who could be helped to replace him if forced out of power. He could also count on the compromising attitude of the French envoys to his kingdom, less committed than their British counterparts to forcing him to sign an anti-slave trade treaty.[6] The imposition of such a treaty on Akitoye, followed by the establishment of the British consulate, was to make the clandestine export of slaves from Lagos more difficult because of stricter surveillance. From then on, Ouidah and Porto-Novo were to provide the needed outlets for enslaved victims of the various conflicts in Yorubaland.

From the above considerations, it appears clear that Lagos and Ouidah, in the context of the campaign for the abolition of the transatlantic slave trade and the tense rivalry it generated between the French and the British, were two strategic positions. This context must be taken into account in any attempt to properly grasp the flow, establishment and development of their Afro-Brazilian communities.

Returnees from Brazil found a more familiar environment in Ouidah than in Lagos. A small but influential community of Brazilians made up of traders from Portugal and Brazil, their close associates, and their offspring from unions with local women was already well established. Their common protector was Felix Francisco de Souza, a famous slave trader who played a significant role in the plot that brought Ghezo to the throne in 1818 and who, as a result, was a prominent figure in Dahomean political life till his death in 1849.[7] Throughout this period, he remained committed, like his royal friend Ghezo, to a trade abolished by the British since 1807. Most of the members of his Afro-Brazilian community, especially traders from Brazil and Portugal, were directly or indirectly involved in the same activity. In fact, their counterparts, expelled from territories under British influence took refuge in Porto-Novo, Agoué, and Ouidah where returnees from Sierra Leone, thought to be English spies, were not well received as a reaction against the British policy.[8] Living in such a milieu, some liberated Africans who returned from Brazil could not resist the temptation of engaging themselves in the slave trade.[9]

The political situation of Lagos to which Afro-Brazilians were returning from the 1830s, though significantly different from that of Ouidah in many respects, presents a striking similarity by the mid-nineteenth century. Like Ghezo in Dahomey, Oba Kosoko in Lagos was committed to the slave trade, entertaining good relationships with slave traders established in his kingdom. When dynastic disputes created an opportunity for the British intervention discussed earlier, he sought and received the assistance of the Brazilian and Portuguese traders, while Akitoye could count on British support, since, unlike his rival, he expressed his readiness to sign a treaty abolishing the slave trade and protecting legitimate commerce. As a result of the situation thus created, slave traders, mainly Portuguese and Brazilians, as well as returning liberated Africans from Brazil would find themselves in strikingly different situations, depending on where they ended up. This notwithstanding, liberated Africans from Sierra Leone were expected to be of vital assistance in bringing about a new order in West Africa.

The Sierra Leonian factor was probably a significant element of difference between the Afro-Brazilian communities of Lagos and Ouidah. It was also, as this chapter will show, the most striking reflection of the impact of the rivalry between the French and the British in the sub-region. The Sierra-Leonians or Saros, it must be recalled, were slaves shipped for the Americas but on the way rescued by the British West African squadron and taken to Freetown in Sierra Leone. Victims of various conflicts in the aftermath of the breakup of the Oyo Empire, the majority of them were of Yoruba origin. Settled outside Freetown itself, they came to create relatively homogenous Yoruba villages referred to as Aku town or Egba town.[10] This enabled them to retain their customs and traditions, an important factor in the process of their reintegration to their homeland from the 1830s. The education most of them received while in Sierra Leone was consonant with the mission the British expected them to play, once back home. The focus was on religion since the British "civilizing mission" itself was entrusted to religious organizations. The opening, in February 1827 of Fourah Bay College, with Samuel Ajayi Crowther as its first Aku student, is to be seen in this perspective. The college was to play an important role in the translation of the Bible into African languages such as Yoruba.

Though the Afro-Brazilians' movement to Lagos was contemporaneous with that of the Sierra Leonians, their different experience abroad was to be a significant factor in the fortunes of their respective communities. Despite the presence among them of Muslims, the Afro-Brazilians found a rallying point in the Roman Catholic Church, "so much so that the word Aguda came to refer indiscriminately to Brazilians and Catholic alike."[11] Faithful to Luso-Brazilian traditions, they could not be relied upon in the implementation of the British philosophy of salvation, enlightenment and modernization. The Saros, on the other hand, were prepared to play such a role. They were grateful to the British who saved them from American slavery, brought them to Sierra Leone and set them free.[12]

Apart from the differences of experience and position with respect to the British influence, and despite the simultaneous character of their movement to Lagos, it is worth noting that before the Afro-Brazilians started arriving in any significant numbers, the Saros of Sierra Leone were buying condemned slave-vessels to trade down the coast as far as Badagry and Lagos, where some of them found people they knew and renewed old family ties.[13] They were therefore more familiar with Yorubaland and apparently likely to be more easily integrated to local populations, since they had not been gone for too long.

Despite their differences and rivalries, however, both Brazilians and Saros occupied the same structural position in the fast changing situation of Lagos after the 1851 bombardment of the city. They constituted an emerging elite and "a rising bourgeoisie which saw itself as the natural heir of the colonial regime."[14] Such expectations must have been stronger among Sierra Leonians than among Afro-Brazilians who, faithful to Luso-Brazilian traditions, showed little inclination to be part of the British venture and were reluctant to adopt English as their lingua franca.[15] Both were to be frustrated in their expectations in this respect because the British preferred to control and use traditional rulers as agents of their colonial administrative system. Probably because of this frustration and this reality, they found it necessary and useful to enhance their African and ethnic identity. As a matter of fact, from the 1880s onwards, there was a noticeable tendency to change Brazilian and English names to African names. Yet, they continued to harbor a Western lifestyle, living in separate and distinct areas of the city. The Brazilian quarter, located on the eastern part of the island of Lagos, was a transposition of Brazil to the African continent, or more specifically, a reproduction of Bahia with its festivals and typical dishes. More significantly, the Brazilian quarter was also a business center with a great impact on the development of the city. Afro-Brazilians invested substantial parts of their savings to build houses, not only to live in, but also for rental,[16] thereby introducing speculation on housing and urban land.

The situation in Ouidah was quite different. Unlike Lagos, Ouidah received an insignificant number of returnees from Sierra Leone for reasons discussed earlier. However the migration of the latter to Badagry and Lagos and their movement to and establishment in Abeokuta did affect indirectly the Afro-Brazilian community of Ouidah. British protection of the missionaries in Abeokuta, where many Sierra Leonians of Egba origin had moved to, became a source of increased tension with Dahomey. Ouidah, in such a context, crystallized this tension, making it inhospitable to the Sierra Leonians.

Its Afro-Brazilian community, unlike that of Lagos, was not predominantly Yoruba, but more ethnically heterogeneous. Liberated and/or expelled enslaved Africans from Brazil arriving in the city in increasingly significant numbers from the 1830s faced less serious initial problems of settlement than their counterparts in Lagos. They could count on the "ancestor and godfather" in the person of Francisco Felix de Souza who, from 1818 until 1849, was the chief intermediary between the King of Dahomey and the European traders operating in his kingdom. He was also, as a result, the actual governor of Ouidah. Apart from the privileged political position he enjoyed in Dahomey, Francisco Felix de Souza could be seen as a convenient transition from the first generation of Afro-Brazilians to the post-1835 return movement of liberated Africans from Brazil. By the 1830s, the "Brazilian" community of Ouidah was already quite substantial, including not only white Brazilians who married local women and fathered "Afro-Brazilian" families, such as Francisco Felix de Souza himself, but also free returnees to Africa and even Africans who had never been to Brazil but who had assimilated Brazilian culture as a result of their close association with Brazilian settlers.[17] Before the more substantial post-1835 return of emancipated enslaved Africans, the Brazilian community of Ouidah already had a heterogeneous character that would be compounded by the new arrivals. The integration of the latter to the established community, as well as their interaction with local populations, was facilitated by the life and experience of Francisco Felix de Souza. The famous Brazilian slave trader adopted the basic characteristics of African culture and of Dahomean traditions. His alliance with Ghezo, whom he helped to ascend to the throne in 1818, was concluded with a blood pact, in a purely local tradition. His family life was that of a chief, or even of an African "king", with an impressive number of wives and children.[18] He died in Dahomey and was buried there, not in Brazil. It could not have been otherwise. The *Chacha*[19] was so integrated to the local culture that he became, despite his Catholic faith, a Vodun worshipper with his own family Vodun cult.[20]

The prestigious position which the title of *Chacha* conferred on Francisco Felix de Souza and the political influence it implied constituted a consolidation of the Afro-Brazilian interests in Ouidah, starting naturally from his own interests and those of his family's members, associates and dependents. The quarter he founded on the south-west of the city, known as Brazil was populated by this kind of extended family. Another quarter of Ouidah, the Maro quarter, founded in 1812 by returnees from Brazil, was to benefit from Francisco Felix de Souza's patronage and political influence. Its further and continuous development during the nineteenth century was a reflection of the increasing rate of the return movement in the aftermath of the 1835 Bahia Muslim rebellion. By and large, the development of the Afro-Brazilian community of Ouidah in the nineteenth century was Francisco Felix de Souza's handiwork or his legacy. As far as we can tell from the historical record, there was no such leading figure in Lagos, nor, indeed, in any other coastal city of the sub-region where returning Afro-Brazilians settled in relatively significant numbers.[21]

During the nineteenth century, the impact of the Afro-Brazilians of Ouidah and Lagos upon their respective cities was similar but, in many respects, occurred at a variable scale owing to differences in the prevailing local conditions of their establishment. Both communities were confronted with two basic problems: the assertion of an Afro-Brazilian identity and the necessary interaction with and integration to the local populations. Interaction with other groups and progressive integration in the new social milieu is always a key factor in the success or failure of new immigrants. In this respect, Afro-Brazilians' relationship with indigenous African communities was of paramount importance. How the new-comers would be received in the first instance depended on prevailing local conditions as previously argued, but also on the nature of initial relationships established. There were, as to be expected, cases of disappointment among the returnees. Difficulties encountered on the return to the fatherland were responsible for these early disillusionments.[22] All the same, the new settlers were generally welcome. Some factors contributed to that. As argued by Lorenzo D. Turner,[23] the enslaved Africans in Brazil had been keeping in touch with Africa in a number of ways long before the abolition of slavery. By purchasing their freedom, many families found it possible to go back to Africa and then return to Brazil after slavery was abolished, sometimes with their African-born children. Trade between Lagos and Brazil was a golden opportunity for such contacts. Those engaged in this trade would carry to Africa such Brazilian products as tobacco, sugar, alcohol, etc., and on their return they would bring such African products as kola nuts, palm oil, black soap, pepper, beans, etc., to be sold in Brazil. As a result of these uninterrupted contacts, not all the returnees were lost while getting back to the homeland. Moreover, this movement was not that massive and sudden enough to provoke a shock or rejection by the indigenous populations. This does not, of course, exclude isolated cases of some forms of antipathy between the two communities.[24] The procurement of land for settlement upon arrival was also a potential source of tension. Lagos, unlike Ouidah, was an illustration of this potential danger, not only because of the prevailing local conditions, but also because of the location and physical features of the city as noted earlier. Moreover, Afro-Brazilians' speculation over land conflicted with the traditional concept of its communal use.

Not only did Afro-Brazilians of Ouidah and Lagos overcome the initial problems of settlement, their absorption into African society was rather rapid on the whole. This is worth noting in view of their experience and background, different in many respects from the overwhelming majority of the indigenous population.[25] Differences in local conditions notwithstanding, it is this shared common experience and background that constitute the basic similarity between the Afro-Brazilian communities of Ouidah and Lagos and explains the features of their influence on the two coastal cities.

Members of the Afro-Brazilian communities of Ouidah and Lagos shared the same attachment to the Portuguese language and the need for schools for their children. They built churches and welcomed missionaries not only because they found a rallying point in the Roman Catholic Church but also because they associated such developments with the increased establishment of schools and the promotion of the Portuguese language. This fact was clearly attested to by the activities of the *Société des missions africaines de Lyon* (SMA) from the 1860s onwards.

Founded in 1860 by Reverend Father Borghero, an Italian priest, the SMA was present in Ouidah the following year. The Afro-Brazilian community of the city, because of its experience of Catholicism, became the focus of activity of the newly implanted religious order. It did not take long before the arrival of the SMA missionaries produced the expected result. By May 1862, the mission school of Ouidah had over 60 students.[26] Moreover, instruction was given in Portuguese, a gesture highly appreciated by the Afro-Brazilian community, but not by the French officials and agents living in Ouidah.

During a visit to Lagos in September 1862, Borghero was welcomed by Afro-Brazilians of the city anxious to follow the example of Ouidah, and obtain their own mission and school so that they would not have to send their children to the Methodist schools of the Sierra Leonians. There too, Portuguese was to be the language of instruction, not English.

The use of Portuguese in the schools of both Ouidah and Lagos was illustrative of the status of this language on the West African coast during the nineteenth century, a status to be challenged by both the French "assimilation" and the British "indirect rule" policies. In the process, Afro-Brazilians of the sub-region lost an original feature of their identity; but many other aspects of the impact of their culture in the costal cities where they settled in any significant numbers during the nineteenth century remain visible today. This is particularly the case with architecture.

The Brazilian-style architecture introduced by returning former slaves and their descendents was reflected in churches, mosques, and more importantly, in private houses. The first Catholic Church in Lagos, first named *Igreja do Bonfim*, and then Holy Cross, was built in 1880 by Afro-Brazilian artisans led by Marcos Cardoso who, before returning home with his father a decade earlier, had been trained in Brazil as a carpenter and a joiner. Cardoso built other churches outside Lagos. He is also credited with having built the first spiral stairway in Lagos.[27] In Ouidah, the central mosque was more or less a replica of the cathedral of the same city, inspired by the Brazilian model of a Catholic Church.[28] This is not peculiar to Ouidah or Lagos. Major mosques on the coast of the Bight of Benin in the second half of the nineteenth century and early twentieth century followed the same pattern. Projects for their construction were often a source of conflicts between Afro-Brazilian and indigenous members of the Muslim communities of the cities concerned. Such conflicts or controversies underline the significance of the Islamic factor in the experience of the Afro-Brazilians. Because of the emphasis on Christianity and Catholicism, this Islamic factor, which played such a critical unifying role in the Bahia uprising of 1835, is not generally given the attention it deserves in the study of Afro-Brazilian communities.[29] As I have argued elsewhere,[30] without tolerance, understanding, and coexistence between different ethnic groups on the one hand, and between Muslims and non-Muslims on the other, the planning of that uprising would have been difficult, indeed impossible. To achieve the sacred objective of freedom, Islam in Brazil had to be tolerant and accommodating. It is true that Afro-Brazilian Muslims' knowledge of the Koran was rather poor, especially among those who were converted in the Americas. It is also true that back home they found themselves "much closer to the ways and style of living of the Brazilian Catholics than to their own fellow-believers who had remained in Africa."[31] It is not surprising therefore that the latter did not always consider them as serious Muslims, failing to realize or understand that "the spirit of tolerance and mutual understanding that existed in Bahia was carried over to Africa."[32] This spirit is probably one of the most significant aspects of the Brazilian legacy on the West African coast. Many Afro-Brazilian families of Lagos and Ouidah, indeed of most cities where returnees established relatively important communities, had and continue to have a Christian branch and a Muslim branch. Muslims continue to bear two or even three names: Muslim, Christian, and African, symbolic of their African religion. This capacity of conciliating Christianity, especially its Catholic brand, Islam, and African religions is probably one of the major contributions of emancipated Africans from Brazil.[33] Religious syncretism was certainly one of the most successful survival strategies of the enslaved Africans in the Americas. Back home, it remained the yardstick of the capacity of their readjustment, re-adaptation, and re-integration to the new abode. The Aguda of Ouidah, more than their counterparts of Lagos, seem to have taken the lead in this respect, following to some extent the path set by Francisco Felix de Souza, a devout Catholic and a Vodun worshipper as well. However, both communities, by the time of the colonial conquest of the end of the nineteenth century were largely absorbed into the local society without losing their Afro-Brazilian identity.

In Lagos, though the returning Sierra Leonians were predisposed and prepared to play the role of reliable agents, the British realized early the advantage they could derive from Afro-Brazilian repatriates. The experience and skills they brought home as artisans and craftsmen were highly appreciated. In Ouidah, where the Sierra Leonian factor was negligible, the French relied heavily on the Afro-Brazilians for the establishment of their administration and the implementation of their education program. Their continuous return was officially encouraged as early as 1895. A list of those already in the colony and whose level of education and expertise could be helpful to the new administration was established.[34] Though both European administrations appreciated and used the Afro-Brazilians' expertise, they did not however allow them to play the political role they could legitimately expect from their relatively privileged position. In this respect, it has been argued[35] that the French, unlike the British in Lagos, were successful in transforming the Aguda of Ouidah into loyal agents of their colonial administration. This assumed achievement is accounted for by "the initial advantage of the Roman Catholic background common to both the French and the Portuguese-speaking Brazilians", or "the common linguistic aspect of their Latin background coupled with the history of close contacts between France, Portugal, and consequently Brazil", thus making "things less arduous for the French to welcome them and actually place them in some sort of middle-class situation." If such a view is questionable, it remains true that there is a difference in the respective fortunes of the Afro-Brazilians of Ouidah and Lagos before, during and after the colonial administration. The former, more than the latter, seem to have enjoyed a privileged status. The roots of this difference have been highlighted throughout this essay. They attest to an interaction of several factors as well as the intrinsic significance of similarities between the two communities.

ENDNOTES

1. Pierre Verger, *Flux et Reflux de la traite des Nègres entre le Golfe de Bénin et Bahia de Todos os Santos, du XVIIe au XIXe siècle* (Paris: Mouton, 1968), remains a valuable source of material for such a study. In this chapter, quotations from this monumental work are taken from the English translation: *Trade Relations Between the Bight of Benin and Bahia,17th to 19th Century* trans. Evelyn Crawford (Ibadan: University of Ibadan Press, 1976). Among the most recent publications, see: Robin Law and Kristin Mann, "West Africa in the Atlantic Community," *William and Mary Quarterly* 3rd Series 56/2 (1999): 307-334; Elisée Soumonni, "Afro-Brazilian Communities of the Bight of Benin in the Nineteenth Century," in Paul E. Lovejoy and David V. Trotman (eds.), *Trans-Atlantic Dimensions of Ethnicity in the African Diaspora* (London: Continuum, 2003), pp. 181-194.
2. Robin Law, "The Evolution of the Brazilian Community in Ouidah," *Slavery and Abolition* [Special Issue, Kristin Mann and Edna G. Bay (eds.), *Rethinking the African*

Diaspora: The Making of a Black Atlantic World in the Bight of Benin and Brazil] 22 (2001): 22-41.

3. Robin Law and Kristin Mann, "West Africa in the Atlantic Community," p. 312.
4. Jean Herskovits Kopytoff, *A Preface to Modern Nigeria: The 'Sierra Leonians' in Yoruba, 1830-1890* (Madison: University of Wisconsin Press, 1965), p. 11.
5. Robert S. Smith, *The Lagos Consulate: 1851-1861* (London: The Macmillan Press, 1978) pp. 30-31; Kopytoff, *Preface to Modern Nigeria*, p. 79.
6. See Elisée Soumonni, "The compatibility of the slave and palm oil trades in Dahomey, 1818-1859," in Robin Law (ed.), *From Slave Trade to 'Legitimate' Commerce: The Commercial Transition in Nineteenth Century West Africa* (Cambridge: Cambridge University Press, 1995), p. 79.
7. Francisco Felix de Souza appears in many studies of pre-colonial Dahomey. See, among others: David Ross, "The first Chacha of Whydah: Francisco Felix de Souza," *Odu* New Series 2 (1969): 19-28; Law, "Evolution of the Afro-Brazilian community in Ouidah," pp. 22-41; Elisée Soumonni, "Some Reflections on the Brazilian Legacy in Dahomey," *Slavery and Abolition* 22 (2001): 61-71; Robin Law, "Francisco Felix de Souza in West Africa, 1800-1849," in José C. Curto and Paul E. Lovejoy (eds.), *Enslaving Connections: Changing Cultures of Africa and Brazil During the Era of Slavery* (Amherst, NY: Humanity Books, 2004), pp. 189-213.
8. Verger, *Trade Relations*, p. 536.
9. Ibid, p. 538.
10. Kopytoff, *Preface to Modern Nigeria*, p. 21: "Aku" is the term applied to Yoruba-speaking peoples in Freetown, and according to various sources, its derivation is the greeting they used: "Oku". The Aku belonged, in their majority, to the Egba subgroup of the Yoruba-speaking peoples.
11. Marianno Carneiro da Cunha, *From Slave Quarters to Town Houses: Brazilian architecture in Nigeria and the People's Republic of Benin* (São Paulo: Nobel, 1985).
12. J. F. Ade Ajayi, *Christian Missions in Nigeria. The Making of a New Elite* (Evanston: Northwestern University Press, 1965) pp. 27-28.
13. Ibid., p. 27.
14. Cunha, *From Slave Quarters to Town Houses*, p. 32.
15. Tundonu A. Amosu, "The Jaded Heritage: Nigeria's Brazilian Connection," *África* (Revista do Centro de Estudos Africanos, Universidade de São Paulo) 10 (1987): 43-51.
16. Cunha, *From Slave Quarters to Town Houses*, p. 50. Land for settlement, especially in urban areas, was one of the immediate problems of returning Afro-Brazilians. The central section of Lagos, which came to be known as the Brazilian quarter, was the only place where many new families could be accommodated. For further details, see Richard D. Ralston, "The Return of Brazilian Freedmen to West Africa in the 18th and 19th Centuries," *Canadian Journal of African Studies* 3/3 (1969): 589.
17. Law and Mann, "West Africa in the Atlantic Community," pp. 324-325.
18. The tradition has it that he left, at his death, "25 boys and 25 girls, chosen and recognized by him among the 312 children of his 302 wives"! See Reynier, "Eléments sur la reorganisation du commandement indigène à Ouidah (1917)," *Mémoire du Bénin* (matériaux d'histoire) 2 (1993): 41. According to Prince de Joinville, quoted by Pierre Verger, *Trade Relations*, p. 407, "he is the father of eighty male children; the girls have not been counted. All of his sons are well brought up. I see them walking

about dressed in white and wearing Panama hats. They are generally speaking handsome mulattoes."

19. *Chacha* was the official title of Francisco Felix de Souza in Dahomey. It became hereditary within the family. The coronation of the current holder, Honore Feliciano Julião de Souza, took place on 7 October, 1995. See Soumonni, "Some Reflections on the Brazilian Legacy in Dahomey," pp. 61-71. Though the actual meaning of *chacha* is unclear, it is likely to derive from an onomatopoeia suggesting nimble movements.
20. Dana Rush, "Afro-Brazilian and Afro-Portuguese Arts and Cultures along Coastal Benin," Unpublished paper presented at the symposium on Rethinking the African Diaspora: The Making of a Black Atlantic World in the Bight of Benin and Brazil, Emory University, Atlanta, April 1998.
21. As evidenced in Silke Strickrodt, "Afro-Brazilians of the Western Slave Coast in the Nineteenth Century," in Curto and Lovejoy (eds.), *Enslaving Connections*, pp. 215-247.
22. Difficulties sometimes started on board the ships that brought repatriated Africans home, before disembarkation. Most of them were forced to travel from Brazil on Portuguese vessels whose crew sometimes confiscated their belongings for alleged non-payment of the costs of crossing. See Pierre Verger, *Trade Relations*, pp. 545-546. Returnees could also be welcomed by some disagreeable surprises, such as the imposition of heavy duty on every family landing at the coast, as was the case in Lagos under Akitoye and his successor and son Dosunmu: Ibid., p. 546. Finally, nostalgia for Brazil, and more particularly for Bahia, could also be partly responsible for this early disappointment.
23. Lorenzo D. Turner, "Some Contacts of Brazilian ex-slaves with Nigeria, West Africa," *Journal of Negro History* 27 (1942): 55-67.
24. This was the case in some cities of the Niger delta, especially Bonny. Brazilian repatriates are also reported to have returned disappointed to Brazil "because of the aloofness of the reception they received or the suspicion and antagonism which they encountered." See Ralston, "Return of Brazilian Freedmen to West Africa," pp. 586-587.
25. Ibid., pp. 590-591.
26. Jerry Michael Turner, "Les Brésiliens: The Impact of Former Brazilian Slaves upon Dahomey," Ph. D. dissertation, Boston University, 1975, p. 162.
27. Turner, "Some Contacts of Brazilian ex-slaves with Nigeria," p. 61.
28. Alain Sinou (ed.), *Ouidah et son patrimoine* (Paris: ORSTOM/PUB, 1991), p. 249.
29. João José Reis, *Slave Rebellion in Brazil: The Muslim Uprising of 1835 in Bahia* (Baltimore: Johns Hopkins University Press, 1993); Paul E. Lovejoy, "Background to Rebellion: The Origins of Muslim Slaves in Bahia," in Paul E. Lovejoy and Nicholas Rogers (eds.), *Unfree Labour in the Development of the Atlantic World* (London: Frank Cass, 1994), pp. 151-180; José A. T. Cairus, "Jihad, Cativeiro e Redenção: escravidão, resistência e irmandade, Sudão Central e Bahia (1835)," M. A. thesis, Universidade Federal do Rio de Janeiro, 2002; Alberto da Costa e Silva, *Um Rio Chamado Atlântico: A África no Brasil e o Brasil na África* (Rio de Janeiro: Editora Nova Fronteira, 2003), esp. Chapter 8 - "Sobre a Rebelião de 1835 na Bahia," pp. 189-214.
30. Soumonni, "Some Reflections on the Brazilian Legacy in Dahomey," pp. 61-71.
31. Verger, *Trade Relations*, p. 535.

32. Ibid., p. 536: "In Bahia, some of them were at the same time altogether Catholic through the authority of their masters, Muslims in opposing this servitude, and kept ties with the worship of the ancestral orisha and vodun."
33. Olabiyi B. Yai, "The Identity, Contributions, and Ideology of the Aguda (Afro-Brazilians) of the Gulf of Benin: A Reinterpretation," *Slavery and Abolition* 22 (2001): 72-82.
34. Anne-Marie C. Sanvi (born da Matha), "Les Métis et les Brésiliens dans la Colonie du Dahomey," M. A. thesis, Université Nationale du Bénin, 1977, pp. 69-70.
35. Amosu, "The Jaded Heritage: Nigeria's Brazilian Connection," pp. 43-51.

11

Mozambique-Brazil: Cultural and Political Influences Caused by the Slave Trade

José Capela

Translated by Renée Soulodre-La France

Aside from its inherent economic and social effects, the slave trade conferred very particular characteristics upon the cultural and political relations that developed between Mozambique and Brazil.[1] Relations between these Portuguese colonial landscapes, especially Maranhão in Brazil and Sofala and Rios de Sena in Mozambique, were markedly different prior to and following the establishment of systematic slave trading. Once the Portuguese began their maritime voyages to the Indian Ocean, relations between Brazil and Mozambique developed naturally. During the 1500s and the first half of the 1600s, contact between both Portuguese colonies did not transcend what was made possible by the sporadic voyages from Lisbon to India and the various ports of call along that route. Links were limited, quite incapable of creating strong mutual influences. To be sure, a number of cultural practices and techniques, such as sugar cultivation, did arrive in Mozambique from Brazil.[2] Nevertheless, relations between the two colonies did not attain notable levels until after the middle of the seventeenth century.

Brazilian interest in Mozambique did not truly develop until the second quarter of the seventeenth century, when the Dutch occupied the Portuguese colonies of Brazil and Angola. Although of relatively short duration, this occupation significantly reduced the flow of new slave labor into Brazil from its major supplying region, West Central Africa. With Brazilians prevented from meeting their servile labor needs in Angola, Mozambique thereafter emerged as a reasonable alternative. Ships with slave cargoes from Mozambique began to sporadically arrive in Brazilian ports. The early slave traders who went to southeastern Africa from Portugal and Brazil to engage in this commerce often ended up staying in Mozambique. But they dedicated themselves, instead, to other commercial activities between local ports and Asia, especially Macao and the coast of western India. Attempts to supply Brazil with slaves from Mozambique were to remain, at best, intermittent until the end of the eighteenth century. When Dom Pedro Miguel de Almeida Portugal, who had been Governor and Captain-General of São Paulo and of Minas Gerais in Brazil, passed through Mozambique in 1744 on his way to India, he was nothing less than astounded at the number of slaves available there and their low price compared to those sold at Mina,[3] West

Africa, where Brazil by then also secured a great deal of captive labor. Given his Brazilian experience, this was quite a revelation for Dom Almeida Portugal.

Until the middle of the eighteenth century, most of Mozambique's external trade was limited to India. The second half of the 1700s, however, saw a major transformation take place. During the 1720s and 1730s, the French in the Mascarene Islands began to purchase slaves in Mozambique. Soon thereafter, they established regular commercial relations that subsequently flourished. By the 1770s, the French also began to supply their market in Saint Domingue with captive labor from this southeastern African source. Their interest in slave labor from Mozambique coincided with a strategy that Portuguese colonial policy-makers had long contemplated: that is, to solve Brazilian labor shortages by importing slaves from southeastern Africa. This shift in the epicenter of Portuguese colonial interests, from the East (India) to Brazil, and Mozambique's role in that shift, was part and parcel of the Colonial Pact outlined by the Marquis of Pombal, the de facto ruler of Portugal between 1750 and 1777. It was then that Mozambique began to be seriously considered to supply part of the continuously expanding labor needs of Brazil, particularly Maranhão in the northeast. To bring this project to fruition, a number of measures were put into place: first, Mozambique was given its administrative independence from India; second, customs duties were implemented at Mozambican ports; third, subjects of the Portuguese Crown were allowed to engage in free trade throughout its overseas territories; fourth, a group of slave traders based in Mozambique was allowed to emerge; and, finally, payment for merchandise imported from Portugal was made possible through slaves exported to Brazil.[4]

Beyond the instructions and orders emanating from the central government in Lisbon, the determining factor in the transformation of Mozambique's external commerce was the entrance of French slavers on the scene. It was thanks to them that the colony's public funds attained new heights: Captains-general, Governors, officers and civil servants were seduced by this trade and, in the process, secured huge fortunes. Moreover, groups of local slave traders, first in Mozambique and later in Quelimane, began to engage in regular and systematic trade to Brazil at the turn of the eighteenth century. Once these two different, but intertwined, processes coalesced, they led to a series of intense cultural and political impacts upon this part of southeastern Africa.

It was with French, Brazilian, Portuguese and Spanish slave traders, for example, that news of the French Revolution arrived in Mozambique. However, they carried more than news of this event. Slave traders also brought with them literature that proclaimed the ideology of the French Revolution and of the Freemasons. It was they, moreover, who played the initial role in the local manifestations of the Portuguese liberal revolution of 1820. And among those individuals who financed this revolution, there were Mozambican slave traders acting from Rio de Janeiro.

Indeed, Mozambique even came to experience some "seditious" movements of its own. First of all, locals not only adhered to the liberal movement of 1820 in Portugal but, in the process, also rejected the Captain-general who had been sent out there by the Portuguese Court still based in Rio de Janeiro. And following the 1822 Proclamation of Brazilian Independence, a network of individuals in Rio de Janeiro, Rios de Sena, Mozambique, Luanda, and Benguela attempted to draw Portugal's colonies in Africa to adhere to Brazil. In this project too the revolutionaries were slave traders. By the early 1800s, a more or less permanent flow of seditious ideas had been established between Rio de Janeiro and Mozambique.

When the Portuguese Court was transferred to Rio de Janeiro in November 1807, Brazil suddenly assumed the role of metropolis. As such, Mozambique became one of its colonies. This occurred not only because the center of imperial political power had moved from Lisbon to Rio de Janeiro, but also due to the fact that the axis of Mozambique's external commerce had shifted from the Indian Ocean to the South Atlantic. The relationship between Brazil and Mozambique was by then a symbiotic one. Mozambique's prosperity depended on the Brazilian market and Brazil depended, if only partially, on slaves from Mozambique. We can better capture and evaluate the significance of this economic relationship through the following symbolic act. When the Island of Mozambique was elevated to the status of city on 17 September, 1818, the decision was not taken in Lisbon. Rather, it originated in Rio de Janeiro.

Mozambique was radically transformed as this relationship unfolded. At the end of the eighteenth century, slave traders from Havana, Bahia, Rio de Janeiro and Montevideo joined the French operating in the ports of this part of southeastern Africa. Alongside these newcomers came a wave of political deportees; conspirators from the 1789 *Inconfidência Mineira* in Brazil,[5] including the famous poet Tomas António Gonzaga, as well as liberals from mainland Portugal. Moreover, Portuguese officers who had fought in France under Napoleon and had been influenced by new ideologies brought these with them when stationed in Mozambique. The children of the wealthiest slave traders were, in turn, sent to study in Goa, Lisbon, Rio de Janeiro, Buenos Aires and Mauritius. While those who went to Mauritius returned "very French", some who returned from Europe and America were suspected of bringing subversive ideas with them. In each and every case, they brought with them everything that was new.

Fears of ideological contagion arose very early in Mozambique. As early as 1792, for example, the Captain-general of Mozambique received instructions to ensure that the "abominable and destructive principles of Liberty and Equality are not spread."[6] The Governor of Lourenço Marques, Luis Correia Monteiro de Matos, was advised to be on his guard against the French, especially the "clubs" on their Indian Ocean islands that preached to the enslaved that they should rise in insurrection against their masters and, thereby, subverted the political and social order that supported the traditional monarchy. He was cautioned to "redouble his precautions" regarding French ships, from which nobody should be allowed to disembark. Those French citizens already on land were not to be allowed to communicate with those on board. Every French arrival was to be apprehended and delivered to Mozambique with precise and top-secret details of their arrest handwritten by the Governor himself.[7] Although the Captain-general took responsibility for the captaincy's subjects,[8] these orders were reissued in 1800: "the external defense of the country must be a special preoccupation of the Governors, especially in a period when the French, common enemies warring, less with arms and more with their pernicious ideas, against all nations, never let an opportunity pass to invade and infest other States by one means or another." It was especially necessary to watch the government of Mauritius.[9] The Captain-general in Mozambique continued to reassure Lisbon: there was nothing to worry about; relations between the French and Mozambique were fine; and it was the Governor of the Island of Reunion who was the first to inform him about the Proclamation of Peace.[10] If the Captain-general meant that Mozambique was protected from ideological contagion, the truth of the matter was that there were already plenty of people in the area who were carriers of what was feared the most: liberal ideology.

In 1799 Vicente Guedes da Silva e Sousa returned to Mozambique. The eldest son of João da Silva Guedes, the important Mozambique slave trader, he had been studying in Lisbon for eight years. There he had boarded with traders and had certainly maintained contacts with José Nunes da Silveira, himself a significant slave trader, not to mention notorious liberal and suspected mason, who was represented in Mozambique by Vicente Guedes's father. The return from Lisbon was made aboard the *Nossa Senhora da Conceição e Santo António*, a large ship carrying 243 prisoners to India. Separate from the prisoners on board were two cadets and Francisco Álvaro da Silva Freire, who had studied in England, Paris and Holland. When the *Nossa Senhora da Conceição e Santo António* stopped over in Rio de Janeiro, Silva Freira and Vicente Guedes were both searched. Several of the books carried by Silva Guedes' son were confiscated. These included works by Helvetius and Rousseau, five manuscript notebooks detailing Masonic rites, and correspondence signed with three small points.[11] This notwithstanding, once back in Mozambique, Vicente Guedes was named secretary of government in 1802.[12] Lisbon demanded that the Captain-general have his behavior constantly monitored. But the latter responded with the guarantee that Vincente Guedes "held none of those principles that are labeled erroneous jacobite maxims."[13]

There were other people in Mozambique with compromising pasts. Added to the poet Gonzaga and some of his companions from the *Inconfidência Mineira*, there were the deported Portuguese liberals who would manifest themselves later. Eleutério José Delfim, the son of a wealthy merchant from Rio de Janeiro was there from at least 1797. He was linked both to Masonry and to the revolutionaries in Minas Gerais. He had studied at Montpellier, established himself in Goa in 1792 and from there moved on to Mozambique, where he became a major slave trader. Also masons or linked to Masonry were the Captain-general (1793-1797) Dom Diogo de Sousa Coutinho, who would later become the Count of Rio Pardo, and the *Ouvidor* (chief justice of the Portuguese Crown) Tavares de Sequeira.[14] During the early nineteenth century, the subversive attitudes and liberal principles of individuals such as these did not go beyond suspicion. Amongst them, Masonic solidarity was most probably a reality, although this is not clearly evidenced by the documentation at hand. Commerce was thriving for the dominant class and there was no reason to suspect the convulsions that would later occur.

In 1820, important individuals like the Captain-general João da Costa de Brito Sanches, the municipal *Ouvidor* Amaro Guedes da Silva (brother of Vincente Guedes), the *Juiz de Fora* (external, independent Magistrate) Joaquim António de Gouveia, the Brigadier Francisco Carlos da Costa Lacé, the commanders of the African batallion (*sipais*) Joaquim António Ribeiro and João Vicente de Cardinas, the secretary of government Carlos Maia Rosa, the junior military aids (*ajudantes de ordems*), and others carried out the parody of a funeral for religion.[15] Joaquim António Ribeiro was none other than the man who would later become the leader of Mozambique's reply to the liberal uprising in Portugal. The event took place after the Captain-general absolved those who, on a Holy Saturday, had hung in effigy the previous prelate, Father Superior José Nicolau de Jesus Maria Pegado, O.P. We should highlight that the spoof took place before the liberal revolution in Porto. Given the individuals involved, its blasphemous character was considered of the gravest concern regarding the rule of law and the dominant mentality.

On 25 June of the following year, Captain-general João da Costa de Brito Sanches was forced out of office and arrested. A provisional liberal government assumed power. The Court, still in Rio de Janeiro, subsequently appointed João Manuel da Silva as the new governor of Mozambique. The provisional government, arguing that it followed orders only from the *Côrtes* or representative assembly in Lisbon, found the appointment unacceptable. The conspirators in this revolt included several of the people who had attended the anti-religious demonstration of 1820: Joaquim Ribeiro, Joaquim Gouveia and even the *escrivão* or clerk of the *Junta da Fazenda* (Treasury Board) Joaquim António de Menezes.[16] Cardinas, who had attended the funeral for religion, was himself part of the provisional government.

Eight years after the liberal revolt of 1821, the then governor, Paulo José Miguel de Brito envisioned the expulsion of certain "revolutionaries" from Mozambique.

> There are employed in this captaincy, certain military officers who should be expelled in order to maintain public order, obedience and loyalty to the King. They were the regenerators of Mozambique, carried out the 1821 revolution here, came to the King's palace and arrested his representative, the Captain-general João da Costa de Brito Sanches, took over the government, gave each other military posts, raised the troops' salaries etc. And after all of this, some fled, others went to Portugal, where his Highness D. João VI pardoned them,

> confirmed the posts that they had given themselves, and even appointed a few as governors of the very captaincy where they had revolted (...).[17]

At the time, of the four individuals who had been most active in the 1821 revolt, one had died, Joaquim António Ribeiro had been expelled and sent to Rio de Janeiro,[18] Lieutenant Colonel Domingos Correia Arouca was governor of Inhambane, and Captain José Amante de Lemos was governor of the Islands of Cabo Delgado.[19]

Throughout this revolutionary period, relations with Brazil were far from interrupted. The provisional government of Bahia not only assisted in advancing the revolutionary cause in southeastern Africa: it also formally recognized the provisional government of the Province of Mozambique.[20]

The mutual dependence that had developed between Brazil and Portugal's most important colonies in Africa becomes even more apparent when we recognize that Angola experienced exactly the same type of agitation as did Mozambique. In November 1822, the president of the provisional government (*Junta Governativa)* in Luanda, D. Frei João Damasceno, was obliged to resign because he opposed the union of Angola with Brazil. He was insulted verbally and through a series of seditious postures both in Luanda and in Rio de Janeiro, where he was burned in effigy. In Luanda, the party favoring Angola's unification with Brazil was numerous and quite diligent. The newspaper "*Gazeta do Rio de Janeiro"* published correspondence from Luanda's provisional government to the Prince of Brazil, informing of its intention to unite with the newly independent state. According to a subsequent governor of Angola, power actually rested with "a club of slave traders, who governed for their own profit." Their interests were such that they viewed Brazil "as their natural homeland." In Benguela, the situation was even more serious.[21] In 1821 Elias Vieira de Andrade was arrested there: possessing a freemasonry manual was his principal crime. The provisional government in Benguela, always claiming to obey Luanda, was almost exclusively made up of members who were by and large partisans of Brazil. They too wanted nothing less than to fly the Brazilian flag in Benguela. In 1823, their provisional government even received legislation from Brazil to be applied locally.[22] This port town and its hinterland, whose slaving ties with Rio de Janeiro were particularly intense, came close to seeing unification with Brazil a reality.[23]

Mozambique was thus not an isolated incident. But the situation here was further complicated by other factors. One of these was the influence of deputies from Goa on their way to the *Côrtes* in Lisbon. They included Lima Leitão, who enjoyed great popularity in Mozambique since he had been its Physician-general, and Bernardo Peres da Silva, a *canarin* (Indians from the area of Goa, including Christians and Hindus, of whatever caste; a term which came increasingly to have a pejorative connotation in the 1800s) and notorious revolutionary with relatives in Mozambique: "their main objective is to depose the actual government to replace it with another formed only with members of [their] faction."[24] Other individuals from Goa agitated and provoked Mozambicans to force the local election of deputies to the *Côrtes*, which had been cancelled under the pretext that there was not a large enough population. Moreover, the deputies from Goa wanted to sail directly to Lisbon: the Prince Regent, still in Brazil, was in conflict with the Lisbon *Côrtes* and they did not want to pass through Rio de Janeiro. The captain of the ship on which they were sailing was of a different opinion: he refused to continue directly to Lisbon and then declined to reimburse the sums that the deputies had paid at Goa for their sustenance, money which had to be handed over to the Treasury in Rio de Janeiro. The deputies from Goa, unlike the two from Angola who adhered to the link with Brazil, preferred to maintain their ties to Portugal, a fact that would perturb relations between Mozambique and Brazil.[25] João Manuel de Silva, who meanwhile had managed to take over the direction of the provisional government, "ended up by seeing himself free of the deputies from Goa." But that was not the case with the local revolutionaries. As he dishearteningly stated, "having fled from revolutions over the course of fourteen years, it is in Mozambique that I finally encountered one."[26]

The worst was that there was an upsurge in Mozambique of those who wanted to "declare this Province linked to Brazil." The group was made up of individuals who had been forced out of their jobs, the majority soldiers, but officers as well, almost all of whom were "natives of the land, Brazilians, and relatives and friends of the revolutionary band."[27] Then, in 1826, after Brazilian independence had been formally recognized by Portugal, the subjects of the Emperor of Brazil who resided in the Island of Mozambique were allowed to celebrate his holiday (*o dia do seu nome).*[28] Masons were then able to appear in public for this grand occasion. This explains the important role that Masons played in relations between Mozambique, Brazil and Portugal during the troubled period that followed, both in political as well in commercial issues related to the slave trade.

There had been Masons in Mozambique since the last decade of the eighteenth century, at the very least. Still, the first known reference to an organized Masonic lodge in Mozambique concerns the *União Fidelidade*, of Scottish rite, which was functioning in 1828. This lodge sustained the liberals deported to Mozambique through Dom Miguel's policy of ridding Portugal of revolutionary ideals and restore royal absolutism. Governor Paulo José Miguel de Brito, a "straightforward realist," "well-intentioned, who could pass for a Mason", helped the deportees financially and did not imprison them. Was this a metaphoric manifestation of the links between the governor and Masonry?[29] Governor Miguel de Brito had received very clear instructions to "turn a blind eye to certain political unorthodoxies in the colonies, and this principally in Mozambique, where relations are presently so varied that it is separated from all dependence and interest with the metropolis; even if the end of the slave trade will subsequently tie this colony more to Portugal, it is necessary to overcome the crisis and promote what is conducive to that effect."[30] The discourse was seemingly more about tolerance towards the slave trade than political behavior. But it is clear that leaders in Lisbon recognized the distance that had grown between Mozambique and the metropolis, as the colony had become more dependent on Brazil. Masonry was manifesting and exercising its power, something that would continue to grow in Mozambique over the following decades.

The references on the tolerance of Governor Miguel de Brito were written long after his tenure. They appear trustworthy. But it is also true that he never stopped acting in a drastic manner against local liberal agents. He took possession of his post on 21 August, 1829. On 7 July his predecessor had celebrated the acclamation of the reactionary Dom Miguel: there were "no signs of dissidence in the city."[31] However, immediately afterwards, in referring to the general political climate, Miguel de Brito informed the central government in Lisbon that "over the last nine years, the liberal party (more or less moderate)" was dominant and, as a result, the public spirit was not good. The party dominated because a majority of the military officers belonged to it. He promised to act in order to lessen its influence.[32] Governor Miguel de Brito considered that in Mozambique there was not "the least enthusiasm in favor of the political order existing in Portugal"; and, with respect to the military situation, he further noted that, beyond the fact that the armed forces were insufficient, almost all of the officers were constitutionalists, the Commander of the *corpo de caçadores* (body of troops for rapid deployment) was Brazilian, and the Commander of the Infantry battalion was a "native son and closely related to some of the wealthiest local families."[33]

After the return to power of the absolutist Dom Miguel in 1828, all of the inhabitants of Mozambique had to swear on the Holy Scriptures, in a church, to never having, throughout their lives, belonged to a secret society.[34] On 21 January, 1830, an arrest warrant was issued for Captain João Rufino Ramos, Captain Policarpo José da Costa, *alferes* (ensign) Urbano da Costa Matoso, and the adjutant of the *corpo de caçadores*, José da Costa Assis, for "public rejection of the external forms of religion." These officers neither accompanied their troops to mass, nor to church. They were "as opposed to the Alter as they were to the Throne."[35] Once again, subsequent instructions noted that colonial officials needed to guard against the introduction of seditious literature. It was asked, in particular, that "inquiries and investigations be carried out in that city to determine the existence of societies made suspicious by their members, as well as the places or houses where they meet and the hours at which these persons get together."[36]

On 6 September, 1830, a brig arrived from Rio de Janeiro with news of the establishment of the Regency on the Island of Terceira, in the Azores. It also carried the periodical "*O Brasil Imparcial*", which the governor deemed "scandalous".[37] Brazil had by then recognized the Regency in Terceira and accepted the credentials presented by the Count of Sabugal as its Ambassador to the new country: Portugal's Consul in Rio de Janeiro, loyal to the Regency, continued to take care of all Portuguese affairs. It was this Consul who sent the governor of Mozambique some publications that dealt with the "state of the French Revolution and news from other parts of Europe."[38] It was through the hands of this same diplomat that the Mozambique slave traders João Bonifácio Alves da Silva, Manuel Sumatra

Campeão, and António José Pedrosa offered the Regency a ship, rice, *aguardente* (distilled grape spirit), sugar and tobacco.[39]

Revolutionary fervor nevertheless persisted in Mozambique. At the beginning of 1831, an armed rebellion was organized by political deportees, soldiers and military officers. The rebellion was aborted and the perpetrators were brought before a military tribunal.[40] But this type of seditious act soon spread to Quelimane and Rios de Sena. On the King's birthday in 1831, the Judge of Quelimane, João Mariano Coutinho, refused to proclaim the traditional good wishes and was arrested by the governor. António Mariano da Cunha, in turn, was circulating copies of "*O Brasil Imparcial*" which had been sent to him by *canarins* resident in Brazil. Themselves *canarins*, they were accused of all failings by the absolutist and racist governor of Quelimane, Vasconcelos Cirne. According to Cirne, the *canarins* were organized into clubs, the "*grancarias",* in which they celebrated the "misfortunes of Europe". Dom Pedro's abdication of the throne of Brazil and subsequent return to Portugal in 1831 as its constitutional monarch, as well as the "system of a Republic manifested in Brazil", encouraged them. They decided to unite the captaincy of Rios de Sena to Brazil, a goal towards which *canarins* resident in Brazil were also working.[41] The governor of Rios de Sena, José Francisco Alves Barbosa, was himself considered a "partisan of Brazil".[42]

Joaquim Dinis da Costa, who had succeeded Miguel de Brito in early 1832 as president of the provisional government, informed Lisbon "that there was an incessant agitation of the revolutionary spirit."[43] In his opinion, its sustaining winds were blown from Rio de Janeiro. The principal revolutionaries were Captain João de Sousa Machado, surgeon José Pinto de Lemos, Rafael António de Carvalho, the deputy-clerk of the *Junta da Fazenda*, Francisco Justiniano da Cunha, as well as the Brazilian José Alves Machado de Carvalho. All were "anti-monarchists, highly exalted and much revered in the revolutionary sect."[44] Propaganda aboard the ship *S. Gualter*, recently arrived from Rio de Janeiro, served as encouragement to the revolutionaries who distributed pamphlets and sang the constitutional anthem. A military detachment at Fernão Veloso Bay revolted: the rebels declared themselves constitutionalists and deserted. Captain Machado and surgeon Lemos were both arrested and deported on a ship, the *feitor* or factor Rafael António de Carvalho was sent to Lisbon for accountability purposes, and the Brazilian was expelled.[45]

The political transformations occurring in both Portugal and Brazil inevitably had repercussions in Mozambique. With the interruption of the slave trade to Brazil in 1830 and the final and definitive liberal victory in Portugal in 1834, seditious displays became more commonplace in Mozambique. This notwithstanding, local Masons supported the acclamation of the Queen, Dona Maria II, on 13 March, 1834, in Portugal: on that same day, political deportees and those who had been banished were granted full liberty.[46] Once the differences between liberals and absolutist Portuguese were resolved, trade with Brazil again was slowly reestablished, operating normally; until, that is, the liberals enacted the first abolitionist measures against the slave trade. It was then that the Masonic lodges threw in their full weight into the Mozambique-Brazil-Lisbon axis.

On 10 December 1836, Sá da Bandeira, the liberal Minister of the Colonies, published a decree abolishing the slave trade from all Portuguese possessions. Opposition to this decree was both immediate and general throughout the colonies. Slave traders in Brazil and in Africa, linked as they were through commercial relations and membership in secret societies, worked towards preserving the continuity of their business. When Governor Domingos Saldanha de Oliveira Daum arrived in Luanda in 1836, he found 40 ships loaded with slaves in the port. In Mozambique, as was the case in Angola, Governors not only failed to apply the decree of December 10, 1836, but they even went so far as to regulate and stimulate the now illegal trade.

In 1839, the Ambassador of Portugal in Brazil denounced a group of slave traders in Rio de Janeiro who were planning to annex the Portuguese colonies in Africa to Brazil. He knew them and was watching them. The group, in his view, had spread its tentacles to Angola and Mozambique.[47] This was the very same organization that the governor of Quelimane, Vasconcelos Cirne, had referred to seven years earlier as underpinned by *canarins*. The Portuguese Consul in Rio de Janeiro not only confirmed the Ambassador's findings, but also revealed that the slave traders intended to assassinate the governor of Angola. In his view, their opinions on the advantages of the union of the African colonies with Brazil, based on their near exclusive commercial relations with and closer proximity to Brazil, as well as the fact that they identified far more strongly with Brazil than with Portugal, were as notorious as they were public knowledge. The Consul further added that there was absolutely no doubt that all of Brazil and all of Portuguese Africa remained interested in the slave trade: the moment that definitive measures were taken to end the slave trade, those interested persons would scheme to prevent their implementation.[48] In Rio de Janeiro, slave traders were already harassing Portugal's Ambassador in Brazil, Joaquim César de Figuanière e Morão, because of his anti-slave trade activities.[49]

The slave traders were well organized, particularly around secret societies, where their presence had a long history. These secret societies, although not necessarily affiliated by the same rites, nonetheless converged in the defense of common interests. At the end of the 1830s, an individual named Menezes, former clerk of the *Junta da Fazenda* in Mozambique and in Angola who shared the slavers' views on the annexation of Portugal's African colonies to Brazil, had risen to Grand Master of a Masonic lodge in Lisbon.[50] In Mozambique, at the time, the Masonic lodge was Carlist. Almost all of the personalities residing in the colonial capital belonged to it: it had a correspondent in Lisbon and maintained close links to Rio de Janeiro, Pernambuco, and Havana. This lodge had been established in 1835. It was within it that had developed all opposition against abolishing the slave trade. Its members not only acted in concert; they also sought to occupy the most important administrative positions so as to take part in the Governing

Council and the *Junta da Fazenda*, through which they could oppose or replace the Governor.[51] This was the *União* lodge which, in 1840, registered with the *Grande Oriente Lusitano* in the metropolis, headed by Grand Master José da Silva Carvalho.[52] The first Senator from Mozambique, Domingos Correia Arouca, and the first Deputy, Theodorico José de Abranches, who were then in Lisbon, were both masons and interested in the slave trade. Indeed, all, or nearly all, of the most important residents of Mozambique seem to have been linked to this lodge. According to Governor Joaquim Pereira Marinho, one could not even count on the *Juiz de Direito* (Justice of the Peace) to take measures against the directors of the Company of Industry, Commerce and Agriculture, because he was "hand in hand with the directors and linked to them through a Masonic lodge."[53] The lodge *União* from Mozambique Island changed its name to *União e Fidelidade* in 1842, and there are records of its activities at least until 1849.[54]

Yet another fact highlights well the links that had emerged between the Masons and the slave trade lobby. That is, the apparent ease through which the Senator and the Deputy from Mozambique, once in Lisbon, were able to secure the resignation of Brigadier Pereira Marinho, the first Governor to have seriously sought to put an end to the slave trade in this part of southeastern Africa.[55] He was removed from his post in a most humiliating manner.

The Mozambique slave trade to Brazil continued, albeit clandestinely, until the 1850s, when the commerce came to an end. The intense relationships that had developed between these two landscapes through this economic activity were also maintained until then. With the decline of the commerce, imposed first by the English and later by the international community, slave traders began to lose both interest and the capacity to pursue the transfer of Portugal's colonies in Africa to Brazil's tutelage. Nonetheless, Brazil remained the country of preference to which the wealthy of Mozambique retired. Those traders who left in the wake of the 1830 ban on slaving in the South Atlantic, like João Bonifácio Alves da Silva and Pedrosa, were also landowners. Headed for Brazil, they took with them money, as well slaves to sell. And they also took artisans from their former landed properties: that is to say, local slaves skilled in a variety of occupations – carpenters, stonemasons, smiths, and the like – and who effectively constituted the greatest wealth in Mozambique. Other individuals behaved in much the same way. A case in point are the lords of the Crown estates (*prazos*) on the Zambezi who, without having been slave traders themselves, periodically sought official authorization to leave Mozambique. The most flagrant example of this behavior was the Count de Montaury, a wealthy inhabitant of the city of Tete, who left with his local-born wife, their children and other relatives. They retired to Rio de Janeiro with all of their goods, which were considerable.[56] Of all the effects resulting from the Mozambique slave trade to Brazil, the best thus ended up in the southwestern part of the Atlantic. Over and beyond a few hundred thousand unskilled slaves, this included the artisans, a good part of the capital accumulated through the trade, as well as the culture of all.

CONCLUSION

In Mozambique, the development of systematic, long-distance slave trading to Brazil in the latter 1700s created conditions that favored the arrival of liberal practices and ideologies from Europe. The first reports of the French Revolution, as well as the ideology that fueled it, arrived in Portugal's southeast African colony through slave traders, especially those operating from Rio de Janeiro. The crews manning the Brazilian vessels that frequented Mozambique ports were also carriers of the seeds of this ideology. Masonry arrived in this part of the Indian Ocean along the same routes. The slave traders who operated within the Mozambique-Angola-Brazil axis used this organization to promote the annexation by Brazil of Portugal's most important colonies in Africa and to fuel their strong opposition to the abolition of the slave trade. Mozambique slave traders who, following 1829, left the colony, preferred to resettle in Brazil. It was from Rio de Janeiro that some of them helped to finance the liberal revolution in Portugal. The multifaceted effects of systematic slave trading were not confined to the landscapes where heavy demand for servile labor existed, as in Brazil. As we have shown in the case of Mozambique, they also reverberated throughout the regions of supply in Africa. They even spilled beyond these immediate confines; yet another story that remains to be told in full.

ENDNOTES

1. Aside from the contribution by Edward A. Alpers in this collection, see also: Herbert S. Klein, "The Trade in African Slaves to Rio de Janeiro, 1795-1811: Estimates of Mortality and Patterns of Voyages," *Journal of African History* 10 (1969): 533-549; idem, "O Tráfico de Escravos Africanos para o Porto do Rio de Janeiro, 1825-1830," *Anais de História* 5 (1973): 85-101; Edward A. Alpers, *Ivory and Slaves in East Central Africa* (Berkeley: University of California Press, 1975); Mary C. Karasch, *Slave Life in Rio de Janeiro 1808-1850* (Princeton: Princeton University Press, 1987); José Capela, "O Tráfico da Escravatura nas Relações Moçambique-Brasil," *História: Questões e Debates* (Curitiba) 9/16 (1988): 187-192; José Capela and Eduardo Medeiros - *O tráfico de escravos para as Ilhas do Índico, 1720-1902* (Maputo: INLD / UEM, 1988); Aurélio Rocha, "Contribuição para o estudo das relações entre Moçambique e Brasil no séc. XIX (Tráfico de escravos e relações políticas e culturais)," *Estudos Afro-Asiáticos* 21 (1991): 200-204; Manolo G. Florentino, *Em Costas Negras: Uma História do Tráfico Atlântico de Escravos entre a África e o Rio de Janeiro (Séculos XVIII e XIX)* (São Paulo: Companhia das Letras, 1997); José Capela, *O Tráfico de Escravos Nos Portos de Moçambique, 1733-1904* (Porto: Edições Afrontamento, 2002); Edward A. Alpers, "Mozambique and 'Mozambiques': a global perspective," Unpublished paper presented at the UNESCO Slave Route Conference, Maputo, Mozambique, 17-19 March, 2004; Eduardo Medeiros, "The Mozambiqueanisation of Slaves Embarking at Mozambiquean Ports," *Portuguese Studies Review* 12/2 (2004, forthcoming).
2. At Sena, "(...) there is much cane from which to make excellent sugar: some mulattoes from Bahia made excellent sugar and instructed Africans to do so." Quote from João

Baptista de Montaury, "Moçambique, Ilhas Querimba, Rios de Sena, Vila de Tete, Vila de Zumbo, Manica, Vila de Luabo, Inhambane, c. 1778," in António Alberto Banha de Andrade (ed.), *Relações de Moçambique Setecentista* (Lisbon: Agência-Geral do Ultramar, 1955), p. 362.

3. Arquivo Histórico Ultramarino, Lisbon [hereafter AHU], Códice [Codex, hereafter Cód.] 448, folio 3v, cited in Manuel Artur Norton, *D. Pedro Miguel Almeida Portugal* (Lisbon: Agência-Geral do Ultramar, 1967), p. 93.
4. Fritz Hoppe, *A África Oriental Portuguese no Tempo do Marquês de Pombal (1750-1777)* (Lisbon: Agência-Geral do Ultramar, 1970), pp. 132, 205 and 434. See also Alexandre Lobato, *Evolução Administrativa e Economica de Moçambique, 1752-1763* (Lisbon: Agência-Geral do Ultramar, 1957) for chronological developments and institutional acts. Neither of these authors mentions the decision to establish Mozambique's administrative independence from India in the Colonial Pact of the Marquis de Pombal.
5. This conspiracy, organized by a small group of enlightened intellectuals, ecclesiastics, prominent land and slave owners, and miners in Minas Gerais, sought to overthrow the Portuguese colonial regime in Brazil in the wake of the reassertion of imperial control and the levying of new taxes. See João Pinto Furtado, *O manto de Penélope: história, mito e memória da Inconfidência Mineira de 1788-9* (São Paulo: Companhia das Letras, 2002); Herculano Gomes Mathias, *Autos da Devassa da Inconfidência Mineira: Complementação Documental (Belo Horizonte: Editora UFMG, 2002);* Kenneth Maxwell, *A Devassa da Devassa:* A *Inconfidência Mineira, 1750-1808* (Rio de Janeiro: Paz e Terra, 1985); Câmara dos Deputados e Governo do Estado de Minas Gerais, *Autos da Devassa da Inconfidência Mineira* 2nd ed. 10 Vols. (Belo Horizonte: Imprensa Oficial de Minas Gerais, 1976-1983); A. Tenório d'Albuquerque, *A maçonaria e a Inconfidência Mineira: movimento de carater maçônico, a bandeira maçônica dos inconfidentes* 2nd ed. (Rio de Janeiro: Editora Aurora, 1970). See also notes 11 and 14 below.
6. AHU, Moçambique, Caixa [box, hereafter Cx.] 63, Documento[document, hereafter Doc.] 32 , Minister to Governor-general, 21 February, 1792.
7. Alexandre Lobato, *História do Presídio de Lourenço Marques, II (1737-1799)* (Lisbon: Junta de Investigações do Ultramar, 1960), pp. 114 and 196.
8. AHU, Moçambique, Cx. 63, Doc. 32, Governor-general to the Secretary of State, 30 August, 1792.
9. Biblioteca Nacional de Lisboa [hereafter BNL], Reservados, Colecção Tarouca, No. 53, Instructions from the Prince Regent to Governor Isidro de Sousa e Sá, 16 October, 1800.
10. Ibid, Captain-general to Viscount Anadia, 10 November, 1802.
11. Paulo Gomes Leite, "A Maçonaria, o Iluminismo e a Inconfidência Mineira," *Revista Minas Gerais* 33 (1991): 18-23. See also *Suplemento Literário do Jornal Minas Gerais*, 21/4/1992.
12. AHU, Moçambique, Cx. 88, Doc. 63, Governor-general to D. Rodrigo de Sousa Coutinho, 22 August, 1801.
13. Ibid, Cx. 95, Doc. 40, Isidro de Sousa e Sá to João Rodrigues de Sá e Mello, 16 November, 1802.
14. Adelto Gonçalves, *Gonzaga, o Poeta do Iluminismo* (Rio de Janeiro, Nova Fronteira, 1999), p. 408, *passim*. My thanks to Ambassador Alberto da Costa e Silva for this

reference. See also AHU, Cód. 1365, fls. 106v, 149v, and 199v; ibid, Moçambique, Cx. 77, Doc. 76; Cx. 93, Doc. 18; Cx. 99, Doc. 19; Cx. 105, Doc. 24; Cx. 106, Doc. 22.

15. BNL, Reservados, Fundo Geral, Cód. 9452, Report from the Bishop of S. Tomé and prelate of Mozambique, 25 May, 1820.
16. AHU, Moçambique, Cx. 181, Doc. 41, João Manuel da Silva to the King's Central Government, 15 and 25 October, 1821.
17. BNL, Reservados, Fundo Geral, Cód. 9452, Report from the Bishop of S. Tomé and prelate of Mozambique, 25 May, 1820.
18. See Joaquim António Ribeiro, *Memoria* (Lisbon: Typographia Patriotica, 1822).
19. Francisco José Gingeira Santana, *Documentação Avulsa Moçambicana do Arquivo Histórico Ultramarino* (Lisbon: Centro de Estudos Históricos Ultramarinos, 1960), I, pp. 759-1829. 3 Vols.
20. AHU, Moçambique, Cx. 184, Doc. 80, 10 June, 1822.
21. Ralph Delgado, *A Famosa e Histórica Benguela: Catálogo dos Governadores (1779 a 1940)* (Lisbon: Edições Cosmos, 1940), pp. 73-104, 457-480.
22. Manuel dos Anjos da Silva Rebelo, *Relações entre Angola e Brasil, 1808-1830* (Lisbon: Agência-Geral do Ultramar, 1970), pp. 221 and ff.
23. Ibid; Delgado, *Famosa e Histórica Benguela*; José C. Curto "Movers of Slaves: The Brazilian Community in Benguela, c. 1722-1832," Unpublished paper presented at the Angola on the Move: Transport Routes, Communications, and History conference, Centre for Modern Oriental Studies, Berlin [Germany], 24-26 September, 2003.
24. AHU, Moçambique, Cx. 185, Doc. 37, 5 August, 1822; Cx. 186, Doc. 113, Governor João Manuel da Silva to Cândido José Xavier, 22 October, 1822.
25. José Honório Rodrigues, *Brasil e África: Outro Horizonte* (Rio de Janeiro: Civilização Brasileira, 1961), pp. 135 and ff.
26. AHU, Moçambique, Cx. 181, Doc. 41, Joâo Majuel da Silva to the King, 15 October, 1821.
27. Ibid, Cx. 188, Doc. 20, João Manuel da Silva to Cândido José Xavier, 22 February, 1823.
28. Ibid, Cx. 204, Doc. 54, 16 October, 1826.
29. Biblioteca Municipal do Porto, Cód. 1317, Delfim José de Oliveira, "Diário da Viagem de Lisboa a Tete (1859-1860)".
30. Count de Basto to Paulo José Miguel de Brito, 4 May 1829, in Santana, *Documentação Avulsa Moçambicana*, I, pp. 948 and ff.
31. Paulo José Miguel de Brito to Count de Basto, 28 August, 1829, in ibid, p.749.
32. Idem to idem, 28 September, 1829, in ibid, p. 750.
33. Idem to idem, 10 October, 1829, in ibid, p. 752.
34. AHU, Moçambique, Cx. 192, Doc. 128, Commander of Tete to the Governor of Rios de Sena, 29 October, 1829.
35. Santana, *Documentação Avulsa Moçambicana*, I, pp. 1066-1067.
36. AHU, Moçambique, Cx. 237, Doc. 31, Order of the Governor-general, 9 September, 1830.
37. Ibid, Cx. 237, Doc. 31, Governor-general to Count de Basto, 13 September, 1830.
38. Ibid, Cx. 248, Doc. 42, Consul João Baptista Moreira to the Governor-general of Mozambique, 30 November, 1830.

39. Ibid, Cx. 237, Doc. 31, Governor-general to Count de Basto, 13 September, 1830.
40. Ibid, Cx. 246, Doc. 10, idem to idem, 1 March, 1831
41. Ibid, Cx. 253, Doc. 4, Governor of Quelimane to the Governor-general, 3 January, 1832.
42. AHU, Avulsos de Moçambique, Maço [bundle] 9, Count de Subserra to Xavier Botelho, n/d.
43. Ibid, Avulsos de Moçambique, [Documents of] Governadores subalternos to Conde de Basto, 8 October, 1832.
44. AHU, Moçambique, Cx. 188, Doc. 20, João Manuel da Silva to Cãndido Josér Xavier, 22 February, 1823.
45. Santana, *Documentação Avulsa Moçambicana*, III, pp. 536 and *passim.*
46. Oliveira, "Diario de Viagem".
47. Arquivo Histórico de Moçambique [hereafter AHM], Cód. 11-2396, fl. 12v, Portuguese Minister [Ambassador] in Rio de Janeiro to the Secretary of State for Foreign Affairs, 12 September, 1839.
48. Ibid, fl. 13, Ex-Vice-Consul of Portugal in Rio de Janeiro, 14 October, 1839.
49. AHU, Sala 12, Pasta 4, Doc. 5, Joaquim Pereira Marinho to Baron Ribeira de Sabrosa, 24 November, 1839.
50. Ibid, Sala 12, Pasta 6, Doc. 1, Joaquim Pereira Marinho to Count of Bonfim, 19 October, 1840.
51. Ibid, Sala 12, Pasta 8, Doc. 1, António Júlio de Castro Pinto de Magalhães to the Minister, 5 January, 1842.
52. Personal communication from Ilídio Rocha and Fernando Carneiro.
53. Santana, *Documentação Avulsa Moçambicana,* I, p. 233.
54. Personal communication from Fernando Carneiro. In 1874 the *Loja União a Fidelidade,* number 84 of the Ancient Scottish Rite was resuscitated and accepted.
55. AHM, Cód. 11-2396, fls. 199 and ff., Representation by Arouca and Abranches to the Queen, 16 December, 1840; AHU, Sala 12, Pasta 5, Doc. 2, Pereira Marinho to the Minister, 26 September, 1840. For Pereira Marinho's version of these events see his *Memória de Combinações sobre as ordens de Sua Magestade a Senhora D. Maria II. Passados pelo Ministerio da Marinha e Ultramar, por diferentes Ministros da mesma repartição ao Brigadeiro Pereira Marinho como Governador Geral de Moçambique* (Lisbon: Typographia de Gouveia, 1842).
56. Santana, *Documentação Avulsa Moçambicana,* I, pp. 961 and ff.

12

The Conundrum of Culture in Atlantic History[1]

Colleen Kriger

> Few today are interested in Negro history because they feel the matter already settled: the Negro has no history. This dictum seems neither reasonable nor probable. I remember my own rather sudden awakening from the paralysis of this judgment taught me in high school and in two of the world's great universities. Franz Boas came to Atlanta University where I was teaching history in 1906 and said to a graduating class: You need not be ashamed of your African past; and then he recounted the history of the black kingdoms south of the Sahara for a thousand years. I was too astonished to speak.
> -W.E.B. Du Bois[2]

> The dominant theory of ethnology at the time Boas entered anthropology was that culture – or society, as it was variously phrased – had evolved, and was evolving from simple to complex forms, from lower to higher modes of life. It was, like all theories, a product of its times.
> -M. Herskovits[3]

Nine years after Franz Boas' visit to Atlanta University, W.E.B. Du Bois published his first scholarly book seeking to reunite the Americas with their African heritage.[4] Like Boas, he saw that the problem of the color line had become intricately entangled with judgements about people based on their cultural beliefs and practices. "Culture", defined generally as a set of behaviors, values, beliefs, arts, and other expressions or products of human thought, has been used in the past as a gauge to measure, compare, and rank human achievement. In the 19th century, for example, ethnologists employed it in their social evolutionary theory to classify much of the colonized world as "primitive" and then claim those peoples as their own scholarly domain.[5] Circular reasoning maintained this apparently clear division: only when "primitive" societies reached a certain specified level of social and cultural complexity (using standards based mainly on European examples) would they be considered participants in historical time and worthy of study by historians. Both the theory and the reasoning relied on *ad hoc* cultural criteria and comparisons. Similarly, some scholars today are placing increased emphasis on cultural factors in economic history, such as the recent works of David Landes and Thomas Sowell which seek to explain economic inequalities between societies as a result of differences in cultural values and attitudes.[6] But "culture" as an abstract concept presents a conundrum. While it may be convenient to use in characterizing and rank ordering groups of people, it is also recognized that broad generalizations and value judgements based on culture are both difficult to make and often inappropriate. In any case, it is both difficult and cumbersome to identify and trace historically the specific values and attitudes this catch-all concept supposedly represents. Furthermore, it is often difficult to distinguish between peoples' cultural beliefs and practices and their social identities. The two are closely related and each contributes to the other, but they are not exactly the same. The difference can be seen most clearly in specific cases, where a society is multicultural, for example, or when a cultural belief transcends ethnic and national affiliations.

Making these kinds of analytical distinctions is crucial in Atlantic history.[7] From the earliest scholarly studies of the Atlantic slave trade, slavery, and Africa's contributions to the creation of New World societies, cultural comparisons and judgements have been frequent, though not always explicitly stated, systematically examined, or well supported. Moreover, the multiple ways people formed collective identities and affiliations have not been as well spelled out for Africa as they have been for the Americas. This chapter discusses these and other methodological issues in cross-cultural history, especially as they pertain to research on precolonial Africa and the Atlantic basin. More specifically, I argue here for the writing of culture histories in Africa – the writing of them *by historians using historical methods*. I will be focusing in particular on West Central Africa, since that region predominated as the homeland of slaves in the trans-Atlantic trade[8] and future research depends so much, therefore, on knowledge of its cultural history.

This chapter is divided into five parts. First, I tackle some of the methodological difficulties of studying culture and cultural change, especially the African heritage of New World societies. Second, I argue that the study of Africa's cultural record must be grounded in the kind of source criticism and skepticism that historians are trained to provide. Third, I discuss the challenge of fitting Africa more fully into Atlantic history while also delineating and portraying Africa's cultural heritage in historical terms. And fourth, I sketch out some issues having to do with historical sources, emphasizing that Africanist historians researching precolonial culture will need to wrestle once again with *varieties* of sources, including unconventional ones. I will be illustrating some of my points with selected recent studies and then will conclude with several recommendations.

CULTURE AND ATLANTIC HISTORY

Scholarly research on African-American history began in earnest during the first decades of the 20th century, though groundbreaking works had been published earlier.[9] Then, as now, the forced migration of millions of Africans to the New World was acknowledged, either explicitly or implicitly, as a foundational historical event but one that presents special challenges to the researcher. As with much social and economic history over the long term, there is scant direct evidence for identifying and tracing the contributions made by peoples of African descent in creating new societies in the Americas. Added to this methodological handicap is the even more daunting problem of how to reconstitute and convey the lived experiences of slavery, especially when practiced on such an unprecedented scale. The very magnitude of racialized slavery in the New World, its political and moral dimensions, and its tragically unresolved legacies lend a particular urgency to the topic, an urgency that inevitably sparks intense debates.[10] One of the most prominent of these debates took place in the United States during the 1930s and 40s – between the anthropologist Melville Herskovits and the sociologist E. Franklin Frazier – and it has generated a rich and vibrant literature on "slave culture". This chapter is not a comprehensive review of that literature. The focus here is on several major milestones in the development of this literature because, taken together, they offer a well-articulated context for identifying and confronting several problematics in the researching and writing of cultural histories for West Central Africa.[11]

The Myth of the Negro Past is valuable and still relevant today as a useful (though for some scholars old-fashioned) introductory guide to Atlantic history. It is useful for several reasons: a) it brings together most of the important themes that have emerged as research topics in Atlantic history over the past four decades; b) it outlines very clearly an approach to the topic of African-American cultural history that has been followed (at least in part) by many researchers of the Atlantic slave trade (whether they actually read or cited Herskovits or not); and c) Herskovits' comprehensive overview allows us to identify and assess certain problems that remain in place as barriers to understanding the social and cultural history of the Atlantic basin. In other words, like all great works of synthesis, *The Myth of the Negro Past* offers numerous points of reference, intended to be continually revised, for assessing past results and suggesting future avenues of research.

Herskovits' main interest was in the transformative realm of acculturation, more specifically the new cultures created in the Americas during the slave trade era, and the various ways these new cultures drew from aspects of their African heritage. This complex topic is often referred to by such catchword terms as "Africanisms", "African traits", or "survivals" in the New World. What this terminology fails to capture are the multifarious historical *processes* of cultural continuity, rupture, revision, and adaptation that particularly drew Herskovits' attention.[12] He laid out his recommended approach to the study of American cultural history and its ties with Africa by highlighting three major interrelated areas that required basic research from the outset: 1) slavery and slave societies; 2) the specifics of the Atlantic slave trade; and 3) the specific origins of African slaves in the New World. Since the time of his writing, scholars have generated enormous literatures for the first two of these areas. The third one has so far received less attention, though it is now becoming a focus of current research.[13] Herskovits referred to it as the "tribal origins" of blacks in the New World. For him, identifying slaves' geographical or ethnic origins was an essential first step toward the larger goal of ascertaining their African cultural heritage. He envisioned that this goal could only be achieved through cross-disciplinary, comparative study – relying on sources and methods from both history and ethnology and carrying out rigorous comparative analyses of societies.[14] Most importantly, those comparisons would be made *between African societies* as well as between societies in Africa and the New World. In other words, he called for the writing of cultural histories over the entire African continent, including but not confined to the areas of slaves' origins, in order to provide a baseline for assessing whether or not there were identifiable "survivals of African traditions and beliefs" in the New World.[15]

To carry on with this unfinished project means confronting some major problems having to do with methodology and sources. The very unruliness of cultural change is so confounding, for example, that we are tempted to tidy it up, to describe it more simply in the abstract or to merge it with other historical units of analysis. In Atlantic history, cultural forms and elements have often been folded into the social groups that carry them, thereby collapsing cultural history in the Atlantic basin with demographic trends and patterns. Cultural change, however, is ruled by contingent factors and not necessarily by a logic based on numbers. It is therefore erroneous to trace it by simply following the slave trade census figures. Cultural change over time is not the product of numerical trends such as "majority rules" – that is, one should not expect that there will be a clear and consistent correlation between the numbers of people and the degree of their cultural impact in a new social environment. One charismatic or powerful individual can exert a tremendous and lasting influence on a particular community, while circumstances may conspire to minimize or even stifle the potentially strong influence of a large social group. In other words, the study of culture in historical terms cannot be simply a reiteration or reflection of what the demographic trends tell us about populations. Demography, an essential starting point for Atlantic history, cannot be expected by itself to portray the complex dynamics of cultural change.[16]

Demographic and other social trends, however important for social histories of the Atlantic basin, take us only part of the way toward writing Atlantic cultural histories. Culture operates both independently of and within social groups and institutions. We implicitly acknowledge this when we recognize that just as people have multiple facets to their social identities, their cultural values and practices can include combinations of many disparate elements. Nevertheless, culture is often described in terms that refer to single, specific aspects of the people who partake in or express it. For example, culture may be tied to class ("high" or "popular" or "folk" culture), social status ("slave" culture), geographical setting ("urban" or "rural" or "frontier" culture), national identity (Canadian culture), religious affiliation (Islamic culture), or ethnic identity, which tends to be equated with language (French or Japanese culture). That these are not mutually exclusive or timeless categories only complicates matters further. To portray the dynamics of cultural change means showing how specific cultural beliefs and practices cross into and out of social groups and categories such as these. And in order to do so, culture must be first taken out of the abstract and broken down into its constituent forms or "elements" (for want of a better word). Then, disentangled from their human producers and carriers, those cultural elements can be tracked as they play out, that is, as they move around in social space and change with time's passing. This is common practice in the study of European culture, where, for example, particular ideas, conventions, and attitudes can be traced across many individual works of art over time, and those same works of art can also be studied in relation to the artists who made them and their social milieux.

Much of what is outlined above was acknowledged by Sidney Mintz and Richard Price in 1973,[17] when they surveyed the literature on "Creole" societies in the Caribbean, in order to build on the earlier methodological and theoretical foundation laid by Herskovits. Like him, they stressed that the social and cultural histories of the New World could not be understood without appreciating continuities with the Old World, and that central to this long-term history was the forced migration of Africans. And they, too, placed special emphasis on the way that new African-American social and cultural forms were created that were not restricted to peoples of African descent, just as new Euro-American social and cultural forms were not restricted to peoples of European descent. But they also urged for some revision and refinement of Herskovits, and proposed to complicate American (Atlantic) history by maintaining a sharp analytical distinction between culture and the social institutions through which it operates. Doing so highlights the processes of acculturation in the New World rather than simply cataloguing the end results, for by separating "the cultural" from "the social" one is able to suggest or even gauge their interaction over time. Mintz and Price illustrated very effectively the usefulness of their revised approach by looking at the cultural and social dimensions of language. The former include the distinctive features and particular character of the language and how they came to be so, while the latter include other aspects of language such as if, how, and when it was standardized and how and by whom it was used.[18] The intricate way the two are tied together can best be shown by separating them for analytical purposes: changes in the features of language are produced in and through the changing social contexts of speaking and/or writing.

Just that kind of dialectical, interactive process of cultural change is an implicit theme in Gregory Guy's recent, elegant argument about African contributions to Brazilian Portuguese.[19] This work also provides a model example of how systematic comparative analyses can be used to leverage scant and indirect evidence into a convincing conclusion. Guy starts off by acknowledging the lack of documentation for languages spoken by Brazilians of African descent in the colonial and imperial periods, and describes the resulting mainstream view that the impact of African languages on Brazilian Portuguese was minimal. What allows him to question this mainstream view is his understanding of creole languages and how they are formed.

This body of knowledge was itself created out of comparative analyses, which allowed historical linguists to begin to see creole languages as special – that is, they constitute a special group by sharing a certain kind of history that also sets them apart from other languages. In short, they were shaped in their very particular ways by the historical context of European colonial expansion.[20] Guy hypothesizes that, based on this shared history, popular Brazilian Portuguese might be considered a creole language, which would explain some of the striking differences between it and standard Portuguese. He then goes on to identify and discuss certain formal features (i.e. cultural elements) of popular Brazilian Portuguese which are indeed what one would expect to find in creole language usage, and he is able to trace these to African languages and speech patterns. Certain of these elements are transfers from African languages (such as patterns of negation and plural marking) while others are social products – they are the "language learning effects" derived from the particular speech communities that make creoles distinctive (with features such as absence of agreement and reduction in the number of verb forms). Although this linguistic evidence comes from languages spoken today, it becomes more compelling historically when compared to other creole languages and what is known about them, especially if supplemented with other types of evidence from historical demographics and the social histories of slave communities. Guy demonstrates not only the importance of separating "the cultural" from "the social", as emphasized by Mintz and Price, but also the value of a cross-disciplinary, comparative approach as recommended by Herskovits.

This brings me to another major problem, that of primary sources, which is addressed by Herskovits but hardly at all by Mintz and Price. It has already been established that many of the captives exported from ports along the West Central African coast came from the hinterland, and that the slaving frontier reached further and further eastward over time. According to estimates by Joseph C. Miller and Jan Vansina, the supply area extended as far as the Kasai basin by the beginning of the peak period of the trade in the mid-17th century, and had expanded upriver to the upper Congo and into the western portion of the central Congo basin by about 1830.[21] This presents us with a major problem: for the inner Congo basin, the geographical area of origin for many of the captives exported from this major supply area, there are no written primary sources from before 1850, the period in question.[22] And as Anne Hilton has pointed out so effectively, even when there are excellent early written records, as is the case for the kingdom of Kongo, they pose difficult methodological problems, especially when the research centers on social and cultural topics.[23]

The paucity, unevenness, and Eurocentric biases of written primary sources need not present insurmountable barriers to the writing of early central African history. However, unlike the adventurous days of the 1960s and 70s, when Africanists relished the challenges of writing histories of societies for which few written sources existed, recent scholarship appears by comparison to be much more cautious and, in some cases, unnecessarily anxious to conform to the prevailing methods and assumptions of western historiography – either by focusing entirely on topics and periods for which there do exist written archival sources, or by uncritically selecting topics and theoretical positions that are current in European or U.S. history.[24] The historiography for 20th century Africa is therefore growing, while many aspects and periods of precolonial African history are being neglected and remain poorly understood.[25] Compounding this emphasis on the recent past is the general tendency of Africanist historians to cede the study of culture to scholars in other disciplines, such as anthropology, archaeology, and art history. The end result is that we still know very little about cultural values in Africa and how they changed during the era of the Atlantic slave trade.

METHODOLOGY, OR WHY HISTORY?

So far very little research on culture in Africa has been carried out by historians or social scientists with historical methods. What difference does this make and why is it important? Let me illustrate. A small but substantial corpus of studies on cultural values, practices, and institutions in the kingdom of Kongo, for example, can be misleading when brought into discussions of Atlantic history. These studies are often cited by scholars doing research on the cultural impact of Kongo in the Americas. The art historian Robert Farris Thompson, to take but one example, presents considerable evidence of "Kongoisms" – or continuities of "Kongo culture" – in the New World, but his sources often prove problematic in various ways from the standpoint of historical methodology. In other cases, what is discussed by Thompson as a "Kongo" phenomenon is a cultural form or element that has not been established as something that was particular to the kingdom of Kongo.[26]

Similarly, the impressive works by Wyatt MacGaffey[27] are also of limited use for research in Atlantic history. Based on mostly 20th century evidence – particularly the Karl Laman papers and collections of artifacts – they raise important methodological issues. Laman's notebooks do provide rich and vivid testimony about Kongo society by some of its own members in the KiKongo language: but these texts have not yet been subjected to the kind of source criticism that would qualify their weight and reliability as historical evidence. They are valuable sources, but are limited in several important ways. One is the special interest and unusual perspective of the authors as Protestant converts writing the notebooks at the request of their Swedish missionary superior, Laman. This problem is compounded by the particular time of their writing – the final years of the notorious Congo Independent State and the early years of Belgian colonial rule when the new regime was seeking to define "African traditions" as a basis for colonial policy. Hence the notebooks were written strategically and for posterity, during a time of profound conflict, and they should be evaluated and interpreted accordingly. Another limitation is their geographical specificity, that is, the individuals writing the notebooks were mainly from environs between eastern Mayombe and Malebo Pool, and so did not represent the central Kongo region as a whole. Although

MacGaffey points out this geographical specificity, he nevertheless relies heavily on these sources to construct a more comprehensive argument about "the principal forms of legitimate power as the BaKongo understood it in 1900."[28] There are also unresolved questions surrounding the time depth for some of the phenomena that were being described. For example, the collection of *minkisi* (divination paraphernalia) might well reflect late 19th - early 20th century inventions or revivals, rather than the "ancient rituals" that MacGaffey understands them to be.[29] In short, the Laman archive becomes problematic when used as a source for all of "the BaKongo of lower Zaire" or "Kongo religion" in general, and even more so for the era of the Atlantic slave trade.

Particularities of place and time are essential starting points for portraying culture and the dynamics of cultural change. Culture is neither "bounded" nor static, yet there is a tendency to describe it in just that way, in geographically fixed and timeless terms. To return to my earlier example, the linguistic evidence related to *minkisi* (sing. *nkisi*) provides an illustration. According to my preliminary analysis of the available linguistic data,[30] I would suggest more precisely that what is "ancient" here is the linguistic form – the Bantu root for the word *nkisi* – but it was not limited to the KiKongo-speaking area, and its semantic field was neither uniform nor unchanging. Words derived from this root form existed in western and eastern Bantu languages meaning either "spirit" or "fetish, charm" – two distinct and potentially related principles, one metaphysical, the other a material apparatus or substance. What is significant for our purposes is that both were distributed in both branches of the Bantu language family, demonstrating that *nkisi* is not a specifically "Kongo" phenomenon. If there are "Kongo" versions of *nkisi*, that is, versions particular to either the kingdom of Kongo or speakers of KiKongo, they have yet to be identified by systematic comparative analyses. The many examples of *minkisi* in the Laman archive and collection include modifiers in their terminology – e.g *nkisi Kubungu* – which specialize and localize the general principles, but to my knowledge no systematic analyses of these modifiers have been carried out. Moreover, there are other vocabulary items in KiKongo for the same and related phenomena, such as "charm", "spirit", and "medicine", not to mention objects similar to *minkisi* that were made and used in other central African locales,[31] all of which further complicate the matter. What we find here are layers and facets of semantic distinctions and relatedness that should not be forced into one neat descriptive category. The particularities matter a great deal and they must be spelled out and analyzed in order to show that far from being "bounded" or static, culture is contingently formed and changed. It is about unpredictable variabilities in time and place – that is, it *has history*.

LANGUAGE AND CULTURE

Cultures in Africa, however, still tend to be classified into seemingly self-contained, unchanging units. In the past, scholars used the term "tribe", while more up-to-date terminology uses categories of ethnicity or language, but even the latter are misleading.[32] Language, in Africa and in the rest of the world, is not a consistent or overriding cultural indicator. For central and southern Africa the terminology problem is especially acute, where the Bantu language family and language groups within it are often treated as uniform cultural units. In a recent synthesis of Atlantic history, one that does the valuable work of placing Africa more fully in the picture, John K. Thornton runs into difficulty trying to define cultural groups. He states, for example, that language can be a "first-line indicator", but also that it is "not the sole mediator" of culture.[33] This complexity gets lost, however, in the map he presents of "African Cultural Groups" – groups that he defines by language families (e.g. Mande, Eastern Kwa, Western Bantu). Contradictions emerge again when Thornton discusses the map, describing linguistic differences within the separate "culture zones" while admitting that those differences would be minimized by the unifying effects of economic exchange taking place within the zone.[34] In calling attention to the way Africa has been left out of Atlantic history and then trying to reinsert it, he gets caught up in the conundrum of culture.

Thornton is focusing not on cultural history in Africa but on the transformation of "African cultures into Afro-Atlantic cultures."[35] His difficulties can be traced to Mintz and Price's "encounter model" and the very general comparisons they made between European and African cultures. By constructing this model, Mintz and Price were attempting to theorize "creolization", a complex term for the creation of new cultures in the Americas by peoples from different continents.[36] Thornton engages with an issue that has been under debate, which is the degree to which these peoples' cultures were homogeneous or heterogeneous, and how those factors played out in the making of "creole" cultures. For example, Mintz and Price compared Europeans with Africans, pointing out that many Europeans migrated freely to the Americas and settled in certain locales by choice, while diverse groups of African slaves were purchased on the African coast, forced across the Atlantic, and then deliberately randomized in their New World slave settings. Added to this process is the way Mintz and Price characterized Europeans and Africans culturally: European culture was, to them, more homogeneous, while African culture was more heterogeneous. As a result, Mintz and Price concluded that continuity of African institutions and cultural forms was difficult if not impossible to achieve.[37] Thornton seems to be arguing against African heterogeneity, and tries to show that cultural groupings in Africa were large, and that, by extension, there was greater potential for African cultural continuity than Mintz and Price allow.

Although Thornton is not able to resolve this particular issue, he does open the way to further advancements in Atlantic history by directly challenging certain aspects of the "encounter model". Mintz and Price, after all, never intended it to serve as a scholarly blueprint or as a permanent replacement for the work of earlier scholars, and they were very careful to explain the precisely drawn parameters of their essay. Nevertheless, since the "encounter model" is sometimes made to serve as a general model of cultural change, Thornton's questions are timely and welcome. One of the most important limitations of both the model and the essay is its narrow analytical framework. Mintz and Price deliberately chose to focus almost entirely on plantation societies in the New World – a dramatic departure from the broad framework of Herskovits, which embraced both the Old and New Worlds. The contrast can be seen clearly in their respective bibliographies: of the 364 sources listed in Herskovits' *The Myth of the Negro Past*, 102 (28%) concern Africa; while the 1992 version of Mintz and Price's essay lists 72 sources, only 12 (7%) of which relate to Africa, and these are mostly secondary sources. Its development in relation to New World situations and conditions limits the "encounter model" to societies in the Americas, which should not be mistaken as a statement that Africa is only a distant backdrop to Atlantic history.

Another problem has to do with how Mintz and Price defined the cultural heritage of African slaves. Shifting away from the formal and overt "cultural elements" that are so closely associated with Herskovits, Mintz and Price proposed that cultural continuities were much more likely to have taken place at the deeper, sometimes unconscious levels of values and attitudes. They called these phenomena "cognitive orientations", noting also that Herskovits himself had suggested that scholars should study these deeper levels of culture. However, their examples are so general that they are not likely to be useful for comparative purposes. They admitted as much when they called for research that would spell out just what were the cultural differences between Africans and also what were the values that they held in common.[38] Although Mintz and Price were well aware of how provisional their proposed approach was at the time, it is sometimes misinterpreted by others to mean that researchers should steer away from pursuing the more overt forms of African cultural continuities.

Since Mintz and Price wrote their essay in 1973, research on African-American social and cultural history, on creole languages in the Atlantic basin, and on the demography of the slave trade has suggested that there be some revision of aspects of their "encounter model". While they were certainly right to emphasize the enormous difficulties faced by Africans attempting to maintain their cultural heritage under New World slave regimes, it is now well established that cultural continuities of many kinds and on many levels could be and were achieved. Monica Schuler's chapter in this volume brilliantly portrays a continuation of slaves' world views and therefore serves as an exemplar of the "cognitive orientation" approach. She meticulously and exhaustively combed archival sources in locales throughout the Atlantic basin to retrieve contemporary (19th century) accounts of West and West Central African rituals and ideologies, slaves' memories of their African homelands, and their attempts to return. By tracking recurrent images and tropes appearing in those accounts, Schuler is able to convey a powerful evocation of the remembered experience of the middle passage and slavery from the perspective of the slaves and presented in the symbolic language of their own value systems. More overt continuities are demonstrated in a recent study by Judith Carney, sure to be a landmark in Atlantic historiography, which traces the history of a multi-ethnic system of rice cultivation technology created by African women and men along the grain coast of West Africa. Like Schuler, Carney worked on both sides of the Atlantic. She broke the agricultural system down into its constituent elements, detailing its technical complexities while also showing how skilled slaves brought it to the New World and adapted it to various North and South American ecological settings.[39] In other recent scholarship, case studies of languages show many types of linguistic continuities, from the preservation of vocabulary items, phonological preferences, and naming practices, to the making of creole languages, pidgins, and *lingua francas*, where free and unfree Africans could and did overcome the formidable barrier of unintelligibility and generate new languages out of unrelated ones. Equally provocative is the demographic evidence revealed in the recently compiled Atlantic slave trade database which challenges Mintz and Price's characterization of slaves as a heterogeneous "crowd".[40] According to David Eltis' analyses of shipping data, enslaved Africans were not as randomized as was earlier believed, and instead, "like free and indentured servant trades, systematic geographic patterns existed."[41] As we attempt to identify, flesh out, and understand those geographic patterns and why they existed, Africa and Africanist research is sure to occupy a prominent place in Atlantic history.

These questions and revisions aside, a central point in Mintz and Price's essay still stands as a major contribution to research methodology. Their "encounter model" took us beyond language or cultural groups as units of analysis and focused more on the *institutional contexts* of change in African-American history. By making this shift, they were able to suggest an array of possible social situations in which confrontations and exchanges of cultural values could take place. Limiting their discussion to the particular structures of plantations and the plantation regime, the most important of these situations were: labor relations, such as negotiation and supervision of work assignments; the more private dimensions of plantation life, which centered on running the household and included family and sexual relations; and the more public types of settings where trade and commercial transactions took place. This emphasis on situations and transactions – the sites and dynamics of social conflict and interaction – invites more contingent and therefore more effective portrayals of cultural change. Their model also aims to complicate the process by highlighting the contradictory aspects of slavery as an institution, where strict social divisions were coupled with daily intimacies, and a violent domination was coupled with interdependence and negotiation.[42]

To sum up, scholars pursuing research on cultural history in West Central Africa will do well to draw from some of these important lessons in African-American cultural history. The "encounter model", though it was developed specifically for analyzing New World plantation societies, offers a way out of the trap of equating culture with language groupings and provides units of analysis that are more useful than population numbers, ethnic identities, and their movements. It suggests other situations, in addition to religious organizations, where cultural exchange could take place – such as labor institutions and practices, technological and knowledge systems, household and family structures, sex and gender relations, and commercial transactions. Applying the model to Africa will also allow us to test and revise it further. For example, how successfully can the "encounter model" be applied beyond plantation societies to other "creolizing" contexts such as slave trading depots and maroon communities? And how closely, if at all, does cultural change follow the patterns of language change? Is all cultural change under slave regimes qualitatively different from cultural change in other social environments? Comparative analyses between African societies and between Africa and the New World, as Herskovits suggested, will take us closer to answering these and other theoretical questions.

SOURCES

The cultural impacts of West Central Africans in the Atlantic basin still remain to be assessed (and should not be assumed), a situation which poses some prickly problems. The most important of these is, of course, what kinds of historical sources are available for establishing a cultural history baseline for West Central Africa, especially in the areas of supply networks for the Atlantic trade before the 19th century. As mentioned earlier, the lack of written documentation presents a severe and obvious problem. Less obvious are the problems with what written sources do exist. The "use and abuse" of the many explorers' accounts, travelogues, and ethnographies written about Africa has become a subject of historiographical debate in the last several decades.[43] Although such source material can be relied upon to make certain specific contributions to the historical literature, an example being the monumental work by Isabel de Castro Henriques,[44] these texts will be necessarily confined to those societies and topics that were considered important to the (mainly) European writers who created the documents. And the European perspective was very selective indeed. Its particularities and peculiarities are spelled out very thoroughly in publications by scholars such as Robert Thornton, Jan Vansina, and Johannes Fabian, whose systematic examinations of ethnographic and explorers' accounts have revealed the distinct patterns of intellectual conventions, obsessions, and avoidances that characterized many European observers living in or travelling through Africa.[45]

Given the problems with and paucity of written documentation, other kinds of sources must be consulted, all of which have their own limitations. Certain such "alternative" sources seem to be more readily acceptable to historians than others. Oral testimony, for example, whether gathered in interviews by the researcher herself or dislodged from previously written accounts and documents, is now considered invaluable historical evidence even when there are ample written sources available as well.[46] Much more problematic are the various forms of oral traditions, which have been subjected to severe criticism though not dismissed entirely.[47] Notwithstanding their drawbacks, oral traditions can provide significant evidence representing dominant ideologies and/or political elites, and are especially effective when considered alongside additional sources that represent different and competing interests and perspectives.

Still other kinds of sources tend to be considered "unconventional" for historical research, or deemed outside its domain and belonging to entirely separate scholarly disciplines. Linguistic data, for example, have hardly begun to be tapped and exploited by historians, though recent major studies have proven their value.[48] They are a particularly promising body of evidence for West Central Africa, especially its social and cultural history, since the essential groundwork has been laid by research over the past century in comparative Bantu languages.[49] The prospect of building on this solid groundwork, which sets out the historical relationships of the over six hundred Bantu languages of Central, Eastern and Southern Africa, therefore bodes very well for research in Atlantic history also.

Visual representations and material artifacts, above all, seem to be most difficult for historians to accept. Of these, photographs and drawings are more likely to be considered useful, perhaps because of their presumed literary and documentary functions, though recent critical studies underscore many of the problems they present as sources for African history.[50] Material objects and physical remains, which often carry determining weight as forensic evidence in courts of law, seem to pose the biggest hurdle. These kinds of sources are most often associated with the disciplines of art history, anthropology, and archaeology, though they are of great potential use to historians as well. And historians have much to offer in exchange. For example, the often understaffed public museums in Africa, Europe, and North America would benefit from the kinds of source criticism historians would have to apply to their holdings. Once thoroughly documented and evaluated as evidence, collections of African art and material culture can offer rich and eloquent insights into African cultural history that no other sources can provide.[51] In short, the separation of history from the disciplines of art history, anthropology, and archaeology, and the proprietary claims these disciplines have made over certain kinds of sources and evidence, do much to hinder the development of African cultural history, where the prominence of orality and visual communication demand that scholars be willing and equipped to handle sources beyond those of the written or spoken word. Moreover, a conventional periodization that distinguishes between prehistory and history based on the presence or absence of written records, is, for Africa as well as for much of the rest of the world, irrelevant and therefore unworkable.[52]

Elsewhere I have argued that Africanist historians must use a *variety* of conventional and unconventional data, bringing to bear on them the rigors of our research methods – especially documentation of sources, critical evaluation of them, and corroboration of evidence – and an emphasis on delineating changes over time.[53] Recent major contributions to cultural history in the Atlantic basin reiterate this position, though it seems that some of the most rigorously historical work focusing on culture is still being done by scholars in other disciplines. Carney, a historical geographer, overcame the lack of written sources about rice production by amassing a rich array of data from botany, the built environment and archaeology, material culture, and oral testimonies, which she then supplemented with historical descriptions gathered from European and Islamic accounts. These sources, together with her effective use of comparative analyses, allowed her to reconstitute much of the technological and knowledge base necessary for rice cultivation and to then trace its transfer to the Americas. Luis Nicolau Parés, an anthropologist trained in historical methods of research, also demonstrates the value of using a variety of sources. His chapter in this volume traces a multi-ethnic aggregation of religious deities and their worship over the long term – on the Slave Coast of Africa and from there to a new social environment in Bahia, Brazil. By combining various fragments of indirect evidence drawn from linguistics, oral traditions, and careful projection into the past of 20th century ethnography, Parés convincingly develops and fleshes out the sketchy and sometimes indecipherable picture presented in the sparse written documentation for religious history in the Atlantic basin. He shows the regional development of sea and thunder vodun worship in the Slave Coast region of West Africa, how and when these deities were taken across the Atlantic, and how they were there combined with Yoruba deities into a much larger pantheon. His study highlights not only the transfer of religious belief but especially the *process* of culture creation and change in Africa, and that *this same process* was replicated in Brazil. He therefore makes an important contribution not only to the history of religion but also to the cultural history of Africa, the African diaspora, and New World communities. We see a rendering of historical change that takes us beyond the false dichotomy of continuity vs. discontinuity and reaches a new level in Atlantic history – *both* "cultural elements" and "cognitive orientations" being reworked and reshaped through rupture, innovation, and transformation.

CONCLUSIONS

Historicizing African culture means not only thinking about it in new ways but also portraying more fully and convincingly the dynamics of cultural change. To do so requires that what remains of a lingering colonial/anthropological view of Africa as a continent made up of "primitive", "tribal", or small scale societies be supplanted by research projects that can decipher and highlight exchanges that took place within larger regional contexts and over the long term. Again, we can borrow from African-American history and look at the way scholars have reconceptualized the Atlantic trading system. Formerly described rather simply as a triangle trade, which calls to mind a mechanistic series of unidirectional crossings and migrations, it is now being recognized and appreciated as an intercommunication zone, that is, a dense network of multidirectional social movements and cultural reverberations between the continents of Europe, Africa, and the Americas. Including Africa in the Atlantic world means not only redefining African culture and reuniting the Americas with their African heritage, but also trying to assess the impact of the Atlantic trade on Africa's cultural history. Cultural change – including the most intense and coerced – surely happened all around the Atlantic basin, not just in the New World. And now that scholars are returning to a more comprehensive and intercontinental analytical framework,[54] we can take up the comparative study of culture in Africa with more refined strategies of analysis and interpretation.

To more fully integrate Africa into New World studies, three things will prove helpful: disaggregating culture in Africa; analyzing it in frameworks that are unlikely to create tautologies; and broadening the periodization along with the geographical scope of Atlantic history. Disaggregating culture means separating cultural forms and elements from social institutions and language groups in order to track those forms and elements across time and space. Borrowing from Atlantic history, preferable frames of reference and analysis would be the intercommunication zones of economic networks -- not only river basins, but also precolonial currency zones. And periodization is crucial. Bringing Africa into Atlantic history means beginning the stories of cultural change further back in time, in the Old World, showing long term transformations in Africa and how these contributed to further change in New World contexts.

ENDNOTES

1. I would like to thank George Dimock and Paul E. Lovejoy for suggestions on this and earlier drafts, and I am especially grateful to José C. Curto for his generous editorial help and comments.
2. W. E. B. Du Bois, *Black Folk, Then and Now* (New York: Henry Holt and Co., 1939), p. vii.
3. Melville J. Herskovits, *Franz Boas: The Science of Man in the Making* (New York: Charles Scribner's Sons, 1953), p. 51.
4. W. E. B. Du Bois, *The Negro* (New York: Henry Holt and Co., 1915). This became the basis for his later book, *Black Folk Then and Now*.
5. Adam Kuper, *The Invention of Primitive Society: Transformations of an Illusion* (London: Routledge, 1988). See also the volumes, beginning in 1983, of the History of Anthropology Series edited by George Stocking.
6. David Landes, *The Wealth and Poverty of Nations: Why Some are so Rich and Some so Poor* (New York: W. W. Norton, 1998); Thomas Sowell, *Conquests and Cultures: An International History* (New York: Basic Books, 1998). See also the review essays on "Explaining European Dominance," *American Historical Review* 104/4 (1999): 1240-1257.
7. I use the term '"Atlantic history" rather than "African-American history" or "history of slavery" in order to emphasize the point that the impact of Africa on the Atlantic world was not limited to African-Americans or the slave sectors of societies.

8. See David Eltis, "The Volume and Structure of the Transatlantic Slave Trade: A Reassessment," *William and Mary Quarterly* 3rd Series 58/1 (2001): 33 and Table II.
9. Among the earliest were: George Washington Williams, *A History of the Negro Race in America from 1619 to 1880: Negroes as Slaves, as Soldiers, and as Citizens* (New York: G. P. Putnam's, 1882); Raymundo Nina Rodrigues, *O animismo fetichista dos negros bahianos* (Rio de Janeiro: Civilização Brasileira, 1935 [but originally published in *Revista Brasileira*, 1896-1897). Both men died young, in their forties. Later scholars, such as W. E. B. Du Bois, Carter Woodson, Arthur Ramos, and Gilberto Freyre, are usually credited with being the pioneers of African-American history.
10. For a useful summary of recent issues in the literature on U. S. slavery, see George M. Fredrickson, "The Skeleton in the Closet," *New York Review of Books* 2 November, 2000.
11. Melville J. Herskovits, *The Myth of the Negro Past* (New York: Harper and Brothers, 1941); Sidney W. Mintz and Richard Price, "An Anthropological Approach to the Afro-American Past: A Caribbean Perspective," *ISHI Occasional Papers in Social Change* 2 (1976), reprinted with minor additions as *The Birth of African-American Culture: An Anthropological Perspective* (Boston: Beacon Press, 1992); John K. Thornton, *Africa and Africans in the Making of the Atlantic World, 1400-1800*, (Cambridge: Cambridge University Press, 1998 [1992]).
12. Herskovits made it quite clear that his use of the word "trait" had created misunderstandings of what he intended in acculturation studies. He saw the identification of cultural elements (or "traits") as an integral early step in his method, which was inductive and historical, and not as a mechanistic end in itself. See Melville J. Herskovits, *Acculturation: The Study of Culture Contact* (Gloucester, Mass.: Peter Smith, 1958 [1938]), pp. 28-29.
13. For example, the chapters in this volume and in José C. Curto and Paul E. Lovejoy (eds.), *Enslaving Connections: Western Africa and Brazil during the Era of Slavery* (Amherst, NY: Humanity Books, 2004). See also Paul E. Lovejoy (ed.), *Identity in the Shadow of Slavery* (London: Continuum, 2000); *Slavery and Abolition* [Special Issue, Kristin Mann and Edna G. Bay (eds.), *Rethinking the African Diaspora: The Making of a Black Atlantic World in the Bight of Benin and Brazil*] 22 (2001); Linda M. Heywood (ed.), *Central Africans and Cultural Transformations in the American Diaspora* (New York: Cambridge University Press; 2002); Paul E. Lovejoy and David V. Trotman (eds.), *Trans-Atlantic Dimensions of Ethnicity in the African Diaspora* (London: Continuum Press, 2003).
14. Herskovits' comparative method follows on that of Boas, and is not to be confused with diffusionist and other approaches. See Boas' critique (first published in 1896), "The Limitations of the Comparative Method of Anthropology" in *Race, Language, and Culture* (New York: Macmillan, 1940). Nevertheless, many scholars still associate comparative analysis with ahistorical approaches such as diffusionism, "psychic unity", "collective unconscious", etc.
15. Herskovits, *Myth*, p. 7.
16. Herskovits warned against such a mechanistic approach, as did Mintz and Price, who called it a "bipartite model of culture contact." See Herskovits, *Myth*, pp. 6-10; Mintz and Price, "Anthropological Approach," pp. 7-8.
17. I emphasize the date here because the timing *of the writing* is important to keep in mind. The essay was written in 1973, first published in 1976, and then republished

with few changes in 1992. Therefore, this most recent version is still very much a product of the 70s, and does not exhibit the reflexivity and critical rethinking of their discipline that anthropologists have been engaged in since the early 1980s.

18. Mintz and Price, "Anthropological Approach," p. 11.
19. See Gregory Guy, "Muitas Linguas: The Linguistic Impact of Africans in Colonial Brazil," in Curto and Lovejoy (eds.), *Enslaving Connections*, pp. 125-137.
20. For the sake of simplicity here, I use the term "creole" as a general category, though there are many different creoles and pidgins, as well as mixed languages and lingua francas. What distinguishes creoles as a group of languages is the way they have developed – they came into existence abruptly, through "linguistic violence", unlike the gradual historical process of slow change from generation to generation that is associated with other languages. See Jacques Arends, Pieter Muysken, and Norval Smith (eds.), *Pidgins and Creoles: An Introduction* (Amsterdam: Benjamins Publishing, 1994), especially pp. 3-39.
21. Joseph C. Miller, *Way of Death: Merchant Capitalism and the Angolan Slave Trade, 1730-1830* (Madison: University of Wisconsin Press, 1988), Chapter 5; Jan Vansina, *Paths in the Rainforest: Toward a History of Political Tradition in Equatorial Africa* (Madison: University of Wisconsin, 1990), pp. 198-207.
22. See the maps constructed and published by Adam Jones in "The Dark Continent: A Preliminary Study of the Geographical coverage in European Sources, 1400-1880," *Paideuma* 33 (1987): 19-26.
23. Anne Hilton, "European Sources for the Study of Religious change in Sixteenth and Seventeenth Century Kongo," *Paideuma* 33 (1987): 289-312.
24. Africanist historians working in the new field of Cultural Studies tend to focus on modernity, colonial discourse, and/or commodities in capitalist economies, which reinforces the stereotype of precolonial Africa as timeless and "traditional". A recent example is Timothy Burke, *Lifebuoy Men, Lux Women: Commodification, Consumption, and Cleanliness in Modern Zimbabwe* (Durham, NC: Duke University Press, 1996). Burke devotes a mere several pages to a description of what he calls "indigenous" hygiene practices – and as a result, there appears to have been no historical development of them and no precolonial manufacture of products for them. In other words, history begins with the influence of Europe and western capitalism.
25. See Jan Vansina, "The Doom of Early African History?," *History in Africa* 24 (1997): 337-343.
26. Robert Farris Thompson, *Flash of the Spirit: African and Afro-American Art and Philosophy* (New York: Random House, 1983); Robert Farris Thompson and Joseph Cornet, *The Four Moments of the Sun: Kongo Art in Two Worlds* (Washington, D.C.: National Gallery of Art, 1981).
27. Most prominent among them: Wyatt MacGaffey, *Custom and Government in the Lower Congo* (Berkeley: University of California Press, 1970), based on field work and colonial (20th century) records; idem, *Religion and Society in Central Africa: The BaKongo of Lower Zaire* (Chicago: University of Chicago Press, 1986); idem, *Art and Healing of the BaKongo commented by themselves* (Stockholm: Fokens Museum - Etnografiska, 1991); idem, *Kongo Political Culture: The Conceptual Challenge of the Particular* (Bloomington: Indiana University Press, 2000). The latter three are all based mainly on the Karl Laman collection of *minkisi* and notebooks written in KiKongo, along with field work.

28. MacGaffey, *Kongo Political Culture*, p. 43.
29. MacGaffey, *Art and Healing*, p. 7. MacGaffey himself refers to the proliferation of poison trials in the early 20th century, presumably brought on by the turmoils of colonial conquest and exploitation. It would not be surprizing if new forms of *minkisi* proliferated during this time as well.
30. Malcolm Guthrie, *Comparative Bantu* 4 vols. (Farnborough, England: Gregg, 1969-70), CS 1072 and CS 1073, and the semantically related forms CS 619 and CS 1534. MacGaffey, *Kongo Political Culture*, p. 243, ft. 1, mentions the root form, but does not list the distributions of it. Moreover, he misrepresents the evidence in Guthrie when he edits the full semantic set (fetish, charm, spirit), omitting the term "charm" and focusing mainly on the use of the term "fetish." Interestingly, given his deep interest and expertise in language issues, he does not mention or comment on the etymology proposed by Jan Vansina, *Paths in the Rainforest*, p. 297.
31. For an excellent study of objects from the Tio kingdom which are materially and/or morphologically related to "*nkisi*-objects", see Marie-Claude Dupré and Etienne Féau, *Batéké: Peintres et Sculpteurs d'Afrique Centrale* (Paris: Musée National des Arts d'Afrique et d'Océanie, 1998).
32. In the literature on African art, for example, language is presented as synonymous with culture, though political and religious ideologies are increasingly being appreciated as major factors affecting cultural production and change. Vansina recommended that the "artificial nomenclature" based on language be abandoned. Jan Vansina, *Art History in Africa* (London: Longman, 1984), pp. 29-33. Nevertheless, language continues to be the predominant descriptive term for culture. See Judith Perani and Fred Smith, *The Visual Arts of Africa* (Upper Saddle River, NJ: Prentice-Hall, 1998).
33. Thornton, *Africa and Africans*, pp. 185-186.
34. Ibid., Map 5, p. xiv. Thornton's discussion of African cultural groups serves mainly as the prologue to his more detailed discussion of cultural change in the New World: see pp. 183-192.
35. Ibid., 184.
36. Creole as a term for either people or their culture usually refers to either Euro-Americans, Afro-Americans, Euro-Africans, or Afro-Euro-Americans, though it often means intercontinental mixings in general. English usage in the 17th and 18th centuries has it referring to children born in the New World to parents who were originally from the Old World, either Europe or Africa.
37. Mintz and Price, "Anthropological Approach," p. 4.
38. Ibid., pp. 5-6.
39. Judith A. Carney, *Black Rice: The African Origins of Rice Cultivation in the Americas* (Cambridge, MA: Harvard University Press, 2001).
40. Mintz and Price, "Anthropological Approach," p. 9; David Eltis et al (eds.), *The Trans-Atlantic Slave Trade: A Database on CD-ROM* (New York: Cambridge University Press, 1999).
41. Eltis, "The Volume and Structure of the Transatlantic Slave Trade," p. 41. See also: Robin Law and Silke Strickrodt (eds.), *Ports of the Slave Trade (Bights of Benin and Biafra)* (Stirling: Centre of Commonwealth Studies, University of Stirling, 1999); David Eltis, *The Rise of African Slavery in the Americas* (Cambridge: Cambridge University Press, 2000).

42. Mintz and Price, "Anthropological Approach," pp. 12-19.
43. *Paideuma* 33 (1987) [Special Issue, Adam Jones and Beatrix Heintze (eds.), *European Sources for Sub-Saharan Africa before 1900: Use and Abuse*].
44. Isabel de Castro Henriques, *Commerce et Changement en Angola au XIXe siècle: Imbangala et Tshokwe face à la Modernité* 2 vols. (Paris: l'Harmattan, 1995).
45. Robert Thornton, "Narrative Ethnography in Africa, 1850-1920: The Creation and Capture of an Appropriate Domain for Anthropology," *Man* New Series 18/3 (1983): 502-520; Jan Vansina, "The Ethnographic Account as a Genre in Central Africa" *Paideuma* 33 (1987): 433-444; Johannes Fabian, *Out of our Minds: Reason and Madness in the Exploration of Central Africa* (Berkeley: University of California Press, 2000).
46. See, for example, Robert Harms, *River of Wealth, River of Sorrow: The Central Zaire Basin in the Era of the Slave and Ivory Trade* (New Haven: Yale University Press, 1981); idem, *Games Against Nature: An Eco-cultural History of the Nunu of Equatorial Africa* (Cambridge: Cambridge University Press, 1987); Ralph A. Austen and Jonathan Derrick, *Middlemen of the Cameroons Rivers: The Duala and their Hinterland c. 1600-c. 1960* (New York: Cambridge University Press, 1999).
47. See David Henige, *The Chronology of Oral Tradition: Quest for a Chimera* (Oxford: Oxford University Press, 1974); idem, *Oral Historiography* (London: Longman, 1982); Jan Vansina, *Oral Tradition as History* (Madison: University of Wisconsin Press, 1985). The value of oral tradition as evidence of political ideology is demonstrated in Joseph C. Miller, *Kings and Kinsmen: Early Mbundu States in Angola* (Oxford: Clarendon, 1976); Jan Vansina, *Children of Woot* (Madison: University of Wisconsin Press, 1978). See also Beatrix Heintze, "Written Sources, Oral Traditions, and Oral Traditions as Written Sources: The Steep and Thorny Way to Early Angolan History" *Paideuma* 33 (1987): 263-288.
48. Vansina, *Children of Woot*; idem, *Paths in the Rainforest*; David Lee Schoenbrun, *A Green Place, A Good Place: Agrarian Change, Gender, and Social Identity in the Great Lakes Region to the 15th century* (Portsmouth, NH: Heinemann, 1998).
49. Y. Bastin, "Bibliographie Bantoue Selective," *Archives d'Anthropologie* (Tervuren, Belgium) 24 (1975): 1-56; Jan Vansina, "New Linguistic Evidence and 'The Bantu Expansion'" *Journal of African History* 36 (1995): 173-195.
50. See, for example, the case studies in Elizabeth Edwards (ed.), *Anthropology and Photography 1860-1920* (New Haven, CT: Yale University Press, 1992). For an overview of major theoretical and interpretive issues, see Jessica Evans and Stuart Hall (eds.), *Visual Culture: The Reader,* (London: Sage Publications, 1999).
51. Colleen E. Kriger, "Museum Collections as Sources for African History," *History in Africa* 23 (1996): 129-154. See also Beatrix Heintze, "Zur materiellen Kultur der Mbundu im 16. und 17. Jahrhundert," in Beatrix Heintze, *Studien zur Geschichte Angolas im 16. und 17. Jahrhundert. Ein Lesebuch* (Köln: Köppe, 1996): 253-282; idem, "A cultura material dos Ambundu segundo as fontes dos séculos XVI e XVII," *Revista Internacional de Estudos Africanos* 10-11 (1989): 15-63.
52. See Daniel A. Segal, "'Western Civ' and the Staging of History in American Higher Education," *American Historical Review* 105/3 (2000): 770-805.
53. Colleen E. Kriger, *Pride of Men: Ironworking in 19th century West Central Africa* (Portsmouth, NH: Heinemann, 1999).

54. For example, see Ira Berlin, "From Creole to African: Atlantic Creoles and the Origins of African-American Society in Mainland North America," *William and Mary Quarterly* 3rd Series 53/2 (1996): 251-288.

Glossary

acaboclada. Person with Amerindian looks in Brazil.

acè. Spiritual power.

africanos livres. Liberated African slaves seized from slave ships in the mid-1800s who were landed in Brazil.

aguardente. Distilled grape spirit.

Aguda. Afro-Brazilians in the Bight of Benin.

ako (also *hennu*). Voduns whose worship was the exclusive responsibility of a particular lineage.

alforrias. Manumissions.

alferes. Ensign in Mozambique.

alférez. Standard bearer in a Colombian maroon community.

ajudantes de ordems. Junior military aids in Mozambique.

aliamba (also *diamba*, *liamba*, and *riamba*). Brazilian word(s) for marijuana.

almas. Souls.

andador. Alms collectors.

Angola janga. Little Angola; term by which the maroons of Palmares allegedly called their settlement.

aringa. Fortified retreat for African chiefs; stockade.

arraial. Hamlet.

Asiento. License by the Spanish Government to trade in slaves.

atimevodun. Tree vodun.

avermelhada. Reddish.

babalorixá. Individuals in Bahia who directed the worship of all deities installed in voduns temple.

barco. Boat.

batuques. African drumming, associated with dance celebrations in Brazil.

bisimbi (also *simbi*). Kongolese spirits of the soil and terrestrial waters.

Bozal. Slaves recently arrived in Brazil from Africa.

branco. White.

Breton. People, culture, and language of Bretagne, France.

cabelos pretos anelados. Curly black hair.

caboclo. Offspring of Amerindian and white or black parents in Brazil.

cabras. Individuals with skin color somewhere between black and brown.

cachaça. Distilled molasses; Brazilian cane brandy.

cachimbo. Smoking pipe.

cadeiras de arruar. Sedan chairs or litters.

cafuzos. Persons of Amerindian and African descent.

calava. "Reddish copper" slave from Mozambique with "blue-black" cicatrizations.

calundus. Healing and oracular activities for the service of individual clients, performed by a single religious expert.

canarin(*s*). Indians from the area of Goa, including Christians and Hindus, of whatever caste; a term which came increasingly to have a pejorative connotation in the 1800s.

Candomblé. Religious institution, sacred place, religious community and its rituals, created by Africans in Brazil, largely Yuroba in origin.

cantos. Groups of "incidental workers", divided into ethnic groups that hung about the commercial districts and docks of Bahia.

capataz. Foreman of the *cantos*.

capineiros. Weeders.

capitão de canto. Captain of the *canto*.

capoeira. Martial art of Angolan origin.

caracaxá. Small rattle used to entertain babies.

carapinha. Nappy (frizzy) hair.

Casa das Minas. House of the Mina in Brazil.

Chacha. Official title of Francisco Felix de Souza in the Kingdom of Dahomey.

cinta de vidro. See *maçambique*.

Compagnie du Sénégal. French slave trading company during the 17th century.

Companhia do Grão-Pará e Maranhão. Pombaline government-chartered company (1759-1778) that opened direct slave trading between Guinea-Bissau and distant Brazilian captaincies in Amazonia.

Companhia Geral de Pernambuco e Paraíba. Pombaline government-chartered company (1759-1782) that supplied northeastern Brazilian with slave labor, especially from the Slave Coast and West Central Africa.

compromisso. Incorporating statutes of black, lay religious brotherhoods in Brazil.

condição. Legal status as slave or free.

congada. Dances in Brazil that accompanied celebration of the coronation of the King and Queen of Congo.

côr. Color.

corpo de caçadores. Body of troops for rapid deployment.

coronel conselheiro. Counselor colonel of *canto* workers in Bahia.

corrido. Very straight hair.

Côrtes. Representative assembly established in Lisbon in 1821.

criollo. Spanish term for person of African descent born in the Americas.

crioulo. Generic Portuguese term for a black person born in Brazil; also male Brazilian-born black; *crioula* or *criola* for female.

definidor. High ranking official in the black, lay religious brotherhoods of Brazil.

dengue. Kimbundu and Tsonga word for acute infectious disease or fever.

Documentos Históricos. Series of documents, including tobacco licenses for ships leaving Bahia, published by the National Library, Rio de Janeiro, Brazil.

dominguois. Adjectival form of Saint-Domingue.

engagés. Individuals who were slaves when they left Africa, but technically free upon arrival on French islands during the mid-1800s.

engoma. Type of drum.

escrivão. Clerk.

escura. Dark.

fazer. To name a governor in the each (African) nation.

feitor. Factor.

fidalgos. Nobles.

fimbo. Wooden lance or spear used by *cafres* (southern Africans).

folias. Festive dances and coronations held on feast days.

forros. Freed slaves.

fulo. Lighter skinned black person in Brazil.

ganda. Dance enclosure in Guyana.

ganhadores. Slaves and freedmen who worked for hire on the streets of Brazilian cities.

governadora. Female governor of certain professions.

grancarias. Clubs organized by *canarins*.

gungunhana. Brazilian term for Africans from southern Mozambique.

*Gurunci (*or *Grunci).* Probably Gurensi from north of Ashanti in the Bight of Benin.

Hulahun. Sea voduns.

hunve. Red vodun.

Inconfidencia Mineira. The conspiracy of 1879 organized by a small group of enlightened intellectuals, ecclesiastics, prominent land and slave owners, and miners in Minas Gerais that sought to overthrow the Portuguese colonial regime in Brazil in the wake of the reassertion of imperial control and the levying of new taxes.

Ioba. Unidentified East African language.

Itefa. Yoruba "Establishment of the Self" ritual.

iteques. Tiny figurines for religious purposes.

iyalorixá. Same as *babalorixá.*

jihad. Muslim holy war.

Juiz de Direito. Justice of the Peace in the Portuguese colonial world.

Juiz de fora. High-ranking, independent judge in the Portuguese colonial world; appointed from outside the area of jurisdiction.

Junta da Fazenda. Treasury Board.

Junta Governativa. Provisional Government.

kachasu. East Central African drink similar to *cachaça.*

Kalunga. Designation in West Central Africa for a permeable body of water.

kanzo (also *kouche*, *asiento*, *kari-ocha*). African and African diaspora inspired initiations; flooring or mourning among West Indians and African-North Americans.

kinzambi (also *nzambi*). God in KiKongo.

Knobneusen. Derogatory name for the Tsonga among the Afrikaners of northern South Africa.

ladino. Acculturated individual.

la prophétesse. Female prophet.

le vol des neophytes. Haitian Vodun initiatory seclusion.

les tricouleurs. Tri-colour, flag of France.

libertos. Freed persons.

Livro de Matrícula. Registry Book.

livros cabalisticos. Secret books.

Lloyd's List. English Shipping Gazette with records beginning in 1741.

maçambique. Special kind of belt made of glass.

macumba. "Umbrella" term used for two principle forms of African spirit worship in Brazil, *Candomblé* and *Umbanda.*

makanda. KiKongo for medicinal plant.

Malês. Term by which the Muslims involved in the 1835 Bahia revolt were known.

malungu. KiKongo for large canoe.

malungos. Term by which enslaved shipboard comrades were known in Brazil.

marimba. African keyboard percussion instrument consisting of tuned wooden bars with a resonator below each bar with notes that usually span several octaves.

mbila. Grave in Kikongo.

mbizi a mungwa. Salted fish in KiKongo.

mestre do campo. Field sergeant.

mestiço(s). Portuguese term for persons of mixed ancestry in Brazil; *mestizo* in Spanish.

mineiro. From Minas Gerais.

minkisi (sing. *nkisi*). Kongolese divination paraphernalia.

minhoca. Worm in Brazilian Portuguese, related meaning from the Bantu root, *nyoka*. "snake."

moçambiqueiros. Dancers of the Moçambique dance.

mordomos. Stewards.

morena. Brownish.

mulatto(s). Offspring of African women and white men.

mulungu. Supreme being; has variant meanings from a drum used in *candomblé* (in Bahia) to "an African idol worshipped in *macumba* cults".

nação. Nation; also ethnicity.

Naciones. Spanish for nations.

negros. Blacks.

ngunza. KiKongo for prophet.

nkisi. Charm(s) in Kikongo.

Nossa Senhora da Conceição. Our Lady of the Conception.

nsi a bafwa. KiKongo for world of the dead.

Nyambana. People who inhabited the coast between Delagoa Bay and Sofala; *Inhambane* in Portuguese.

nza yayi. World of the living in KiKongo.

Nzadi. KiKongo for waters; also Congo River.

Obeah. Sorcery; private divination, healing and charm-making person which frightened many.

o dia do seu nome. Emperor of Brazil's name day.

oficiais. Officers.

ordre de grandeur. Order of magnitude.

orikis. Praise songs recounting the attributes or deeds of an *orisha*.

orisha(*s*). Generic designation for the deities of the Yoruba pantheon.

Ouvidor. Chief justice of the Portuguese Crown.

paiá. Leg bells.

Pândegos de África. (Revelers of Africa) A wealthy Bahian carnival club.

parda acaboclada. Amerindian brown in Brazil.

parda afogueada. Reddish brown in Brazil.

parda clara. Light brown in Brazil

parda macilenta. Pale brown in Brazil.

pardo. Light-skinned mulatto, brown, or person of mixed black and white ancestry.

patentes. Governors' commissions.

peças de India. Prime male adult slave; standard against which all slaves were valued.

petwo. Branch of the pantheon of vodou spirits.

pombeiras. Female pigeon peddlers.

por devoção. Out of devotion.

prazos. Lords of Crown estates along the Zambezi valley.

preta anêmica. Anemic black in Brazil.

preta escura. Dark black in Brazil.

preto. Generic term in Portuguese for black person; black male.

pretos minas. Mina [nation] blacks.

pretos. Same as *negros*.

pret savann. Class of Vodou's ritual specialist, probably descended from Kongolese cathechists.

procuradores. Procurators or persons in Brazil usually responsible for informing lay religious brotherhood members of important events, illness or death of a member.

provedor. Supervisor.

quilombos. Communities of escaped slaves in Brazil; male initiation society housed within a fortified war camp in Angola.

quimovia. Mavia or lowland Makonde.

quingoge. Language spoken by slaves from Angoche; a dialect of Makua or possibly even Koti.

réis. Portuguese monetary unit, money of account, adopted in Brazil following independence.

regenta. Female regent.

Regla de Ocha. Rule or path of the *orishas* in Cuba; also known as *Santéria*.

rodilha. Twisted cloth pad worn on head.

ronco. Retreat cell in *Candomblé*.

Sans Poël. Chanpwèl or skinless ones in Haiti; witches who fly and who eat people, but who in actuality are secret societies that enforce social codes by turning transgressors into robot-like zombies lacking memory.

São Brás. Saint Bras.

Saros. Slaves, largely of Yuroba origin, liberated from slave ships in the 1800s and landed in Freetown, Sierra Leone.

senzalas. Slave residential areas in Brazil.

Setohun. Hevioso thunder voduns, deities of the Seto.

sexo. Gender.

sipais. Commanders of African battalions.

terreiros. Portuguese term for vodun cult houses.

União Fidelidade. Scottish rite Masonic lodge in Mozambique.

vila. Large town.

vodunons. Priests, literally "owners" of the vodun.

yabas. Female *orishas*.

Yehwe. Thunder voduns according to Hevioso congregations from Heve.

zambo. Persons of African and Indian heritage.

Bibliography

Abreu, Martha. *O Império do Divino: Festas religiosas e cultura popular no Rio de Janeiro, 1830-1900* (Rio de Janeiro: Nova Fronteira, 1999).

Adderly, Rosanne Marion. "'New Negroes from Africa': Culture and Community Among Liberated Africans in the Bahamas and Trinidad 1810 to 1900," Ph. D. dissertation, University of Pennsylvania, 1996.

Agbonon II, Fio. *Histoire de Petit Popo et du royaume Guin* (Nicoué Lodjou Gayibor, ed.) (Lomé: Université du Benin, 1984 [1934]).

Aguiar, Marcos Magalhães de. "Vila Rica dos confrades: a sociabilidade confrarial entre negros e mulatos no século XVIII," M. A thesis, Universidade de São Paulo, 1993.

Ajayi, J. F. Ade. *Christian Missions in Nigeria. The Making of a New Elite* (Evanston: Northwestern University Press, 1965).

Albuquerque, Wlamyra. *Algazarra nas ruas: comemorações da Independência na Bahia* (Campinas: Editora da UNICAMP/CECULT, 1999).

Alencastro, Luiz-Felipe de. *O Trato dos Viventes: Formação do Brasil no Atlântico Sul* (São Paulo: Companhia das Letras, 2000).

Alford, Terry. *Prince Among Slaves* (New York: Oxford University Press, 1977).

Algranti, Leila Mezan. *O Feitor Ausente: Estudo sobre a escravidão urbana no Rio de Janeiro* (Petrópolis: Vozes, 1988).

Alpers, Edward A. "Mozambique and 'Mozambiques': a global perspective," Unpublished paper presented at the UNESCO Slave Route Conference, Maputo, Mozambique, 17-19 March 2004.

Alpers, Edward A. "Becoming 'Mozambique': Diaspora and Identity in Mauritius," in Vijaya Teelock and Edward A. Alpers (eds.), *History, Memory and Identity* (Port-Louis: Nelson Mandela Centre for African Culture and the University of Mauritius, 2001), pp. 117-155.

Alpers, Edward A. *Ivory and Slaves in East Central Africa* (Berkeley: University of California Press, 1975).

Alves-Silva, Juliana, et al. "The Ancestry of Brazilian mtDNA Lineages," *American Journal of Human Genetics* 76 (2000): 444-461.

Amenumey, D. E. K. "Geraldo da Lima: A Reappraisal," *Transactions of the Historical Society of Ghana* 9 (1968): 65-78.

Amos, Alcione M. "Afro-Brasileiros no Togo: a história da família Olympio, 1882-1945," *Afro-Ásia* 23 (1999): 175-197.

Amos, Paula Girshick Ben. "The Promise of Greatness: Women and Power in an Edo Spirit Possession Cult," in Thomas D. Blakeley, Walter E. A. van Beek and Dennis Thomson (eds.), *Religion in Africa* (Portsmouth, NH: Heinemann, 1994), pp.119-134.

Amosu, Tundonu A. "The Jaded Heritage: Nigeria's Brazilian Connection," *África* (Revista do Centro de Estudos Africanos, Universidade de São Paulo) 10 (1987): 43-51.

Andersson, Ephraim. *Messianic Popular Movements in the Lower Congo* (Uppsala: Studia Ethnographica Upsaliensa, 1958).

Andrade, Marcos Ferreira de. "Rebelião escrava na Comarca do Rio das Mortes, Minas Gerais: o caso Carracas," *Afro-Ásia* 21-22 (1998-1999): 45-82.

Andrade, Maria José de Souza. "A mão-de-obra escrava em Salvador, de 1811 a 1860: um estudo de História Quantitativa," M. A. thesis, Universidade Federal da Bahia, 1975.

Anonymous. "Relation du royaume de Judas en Guinee, de son gouvernement, des moeurs de ses habitants, de leur religion, et du négoce qui s'y fait," Archives d'Outre-Mer, Aix-en-Provence: Dépôt des Fortifications des Colonies, Côte d'Afrique ms 104, undated, (certainly post-1708, and pre-1727).

Apter, Andrew. "Notes on Orisha Cults in the Ekiti Yoruba Highlands," *Cahiers d'Études Africaines* 35/138-139 (1995): 369-401.

Araújo, Alceu Maynard. *Folclore Nacional, I: Festas, Bailados, Mitos e Lendas* (São Paulo: Melhoramentos, 1964).

Arends, Jacques, Muysken, Pieter, and Smith, Norval. (eds.) *Pidgins and Creoles: An Introduction* (Amsterdam: Benjamins Publishing, 1994).

Asch, Susan. *l'Eglise du Prophète Simon Kimbangu: de ses origins à son role actuel au Zaïre* (Paris: Karthala, 1983).

Atkins, John. *A Voyage to Guinea, Brasil, and the West Indies; in His Majesty's Ships, the Swallow and Weymouth* (London: Frank Cass, 1970 [1735]).

Austen, Ralph A. "The Slave Trade as History and Memory: Confrontations of Slaving Voyage Documents and Communal Traditions," *William and Mary Quarterly* 58/1 (2001): 229-244.

Austen, Ralph A. "The Moral Economy of Witchcraft: An Essay in Comparative History," in Jean and John Comaroff (eds.), *Modernity and its Malcontents* (Chicago: University of Chicago Press, 1993), pp. 89-110.

Austen, Ralph A., and Derrick, Jonathan. *Middlemen of the Cameroons Rivers: The Duala and their Hinterland c. 1600-c. 1960* (New York: Cambridge University Press, 1999).

Austin, Allen D. *African Muslims in antebellum America: transatlantic stories and spiritual struggles* (New York: Routledge, 1997).

Avé-Lallemant, Robert Christian Berthold. *Viagem pelo norte do Brasil, no ano de 1859* (Rio de Janeiro: Instituto Nacional do Livro, 1961).

Bailyn, Bernard. "The Idea of Atlantic History," *Itinerario* 20 (1996): 19-44.

Bandelt, H.-J., et al. "Phylogeography of the human mitochondrial haplogroup L3e: a snapshot of African prehistory and Atlantic slave trade," *Annals of Human Genetics* 65 (2001): 549-563.

Barickman, B. J. "Até a véspera: o trabalho escravo e a produção de açúcar nos engenhos do Recôncavo baiano," *Afro-Ásia* 21-22 (1998-99): 177-238.

Barkun, Michael. *Disaster and the Millennium* (New Haven: Yale University Press, 1974).

Barnes, Sandra T. "The Many Faces of Ogun: Introduction to the First Edition" in Sandra T. Barnes (ed.), *Africa's Ogun: Old World and New* (Bloomington: Indiana University Press, 1997), pp. 1-26.

Barlaeus, Gaspar. *Historia dos feitos recentementes Praticados durante Oito Anos no Brasil* trans. Cláudio Brandão (Rio de Janeiro: Ministério de Educação, 1940).

Barrett, Leonard. *The Rastafarians: A Study in Messianic Cultism in Jamaica* (Rio Pedras, Puerto Rico: Institute of Caribbean Studies, 1969).

Bastide, Roger. *Sociologia de la Religion* [*Les religions africaines au Brésil*] (Gijón: Ediciones Jucar, 1986 [1960]).

Bastide, Roger. *African Civilisations in the New World* trans. Peter Green (New York: Harper and Row, 1971).

Bastin, Y. "Bibliographie Bantoue Selective," *Archives d'Anthropologie* (Tervuren, Belgium) 24 (1975): 1-56.

Baudin, Paul. *Fetichism and Fetish Worshippers* (New York: Benziger Bros., 1885 [1884]).

Baum, Robert. *Shrines of the Slave Trade: Diola Religion and Society in Precolonial Senegambia* (New York: Oxford University Press, 1999).

Bay, Edna G. *Wives of the Leopard: Gender, Politics, and Culture in the Kingdom of Dahomey* (Charlottesville: University of Virginia Press, 1998).

Beckwith, Martha. "Some Religious Cults in Jamaica," *American Journal of Psychology* 34 (1923): 32-45.

Bell, Hesketh J. *Obeah; Witchcraft in the West Indies* (Westport, CT: Negro Universities Press, 1970 [1889]).

Bennett, Herman L. *Africans in Colonial Mexico: Absolutism, Christianity, and Afro-Creole Consciousness, 1570-1640* (Indiana University Press, 2003).

Bento, Cláudio Moreira. *O Negro e Descendentes na Sociedade do Rio Grande do Sul (1635-1975)* (Porto Alegre: Grafosul and Instituto Estadual do Livro, 1976).

Bergad, Laird W. *Slavery and the Demographic and Economic History of Minas Gerais, Brazil, 1720-1888* (Cambridge; Cambridge University Press, 1999).

Berlin, Ira. *Many Thousand Gone: The First Two Centuries of Slavery in North America* (New York: Oxford University Press, 1998).

Berlin, Ira. "From Creole to African: Atlantic Creoles and the Origins of African-American Society in Mainland North America," *William and Mary Quarterly* 3rd Series 53/2 (1996): 251-288.

Bethell, Leslie. *The Abolition of the Brazilian Slave Trade: Britain, Brazil and the Slave Trade Questions, 1807-1869* (Cambridge: Cambridge University Press, 1970).

Bethell, Leslie, and Carvalho, José Murilo de. "Empire, 1822-1850," in Leslie Bethell (ed.), *Brazil: Empire and Republic, 1822-1930* (Cambridge: Cambridge University Press, 1989), pp. 45-112.

Biblioteca Nacional do Rio de Janeiro, *Documentos Históricos da Biblioteca Nacional do Rio de Janeiro* 110 vols. (Rio de Janeiro: Government of Brazil, 1929-1955).

Bilby, Kenneth M. "Jamaica," in Peter Manuel (ed.), *Caribbean Currents: Caribbean Music from Rumba to Reggae* (Philadelphia: Temple University Press, 1995), pp. 143-182.

Bilby, Kenneth M. "How the 'Older Heads' Talk: A Jamaican Maroon Spirit Possession Language and Its Relationship to the Creoles of Suriname and Sierra Leone," *Nieuwe West-Indische Gids/New West Indian Guide* 57/1-2 (1983): 37-85.

Bilby, Kenneth M., and Bunseki, Fu-Kiau kia. "Kumina: A Kongo-Based Tradition in the New World," *Les Cahiers du CEDAF* 8 (1983): 1-114.

Bilby, Kenneth M., and Leib, Elliott. "Kumina, the Howellite Church and the Emergence of Rastafarian Traditional Music in Jamaica," *Jamaica Journal* 19/3 (1986): 22-29.

Birmingham, David. *Trade and Conflict in Angola: The Mbundu and Their Neighbours Under the Influence of the Portuguese, 1483-1790* (Oxford: Clarendon Press, 1966).

Blier, Suzanne Preston. *African Vodun: Art, Psychology, and Power* (Chicago: University of Chicago Press, 1995).

Boadi-Siaw, S. Y. "Brazilian Returnees of West Africa," in Joseph E. Harris (ed.), *Global Dimensions of the African Diaspora* (Wash. D.C.: Howard University Press, 1993, 2nd edition), pp. 421-439.

Boas, Franz. *Race, Language, and Culture* (New York: Macmillan, 1940 [1896]).

Bolingbroke, Henry. *Voyage to the Demerary* (Georgetown: The Daily Chronicle, 1942 [1807, 1809]).

Boogart, Ernst van den, and Emmer, Pieter. "The Dutch Participation in the Atlantic Slave Trade, 1596-1650," in Henry A. Gemery and Jan S. Hogendorn (eds.), *The Uncommon Market: Essays in the Economic History of the Atlantic Slave Trade* (New York: Academic Press, 1979), pp. 353-375.

Borghero, Francesco. *Journal de Francesco Borghero, premier missionnaire du Dahomey (1861-1865)* (Renzo Mandirola and Yves Morel, eds.) (Paris: Karthala, 1997 [1865]).

Boschi, Caio César. *Os leigos e o poder: Irmandades leigos e política colonizadora em Minas Gerais* (São Paulo: Editora Ática, 1986).

Bosman, William. *A New and Accurate Description of the Coast of Guinea* (London: Frank Cass & Co. Ltd., 1967 [1704]).

Bowen, T. J. *A Grammar and Dictionary of the Yoruba Language* (Washington: Smithsonian Institution, 1858).

Braga, Julio. *Na Gamela do Feitiço. Repressão e Resistência nos Candomblés da Bahia* (Salvador: EDUFBA,1995).

Braga, Júlio Santanna "Notas Sobre o 'Quartier Bresil' no Daomé," *Afro-Ásia* 6-7 (1968): 56-62.

Broadhead, Susan Herlin. "Beyond Decline: The Kingdom of the Kongo in the Eighteenth and Nineteenth Centuries," *International Journal of African Historical Studies* 12/4 (1979): 615-652.

Brooks, A. A. *History of Bedwardism* 1st ed. (Kingston: F. A. Benjamin Manufacturing Co., 1909).

Brooks, George E. *Landlords and Strangers: Ecology, Society, and Trade in Western Africa, 1000-1630* (Boulder, CO: Westview Press, 1993).

Brown, Karen McCarthy. *Mama Lola: A Vodou Priestess in Brooklyn* (Los Angeles: University of California Press, 1991).

Browning, W. R. F. *Oxford Dictionary of the Bible* (New York: Oxford University Press, 1996).

Burke, Timothy. *Lifebuoy Men, Lux Women: Commodification, Consumption, and Cleanliness in Modern Zimbabwe* (Durham, NC: Duke University Press, 1996).

Burton, Richard *A mission to Gelélé King of Dahomey* (London: Routledge & Kegan Paul, 1966 [1864]).

Bushnell, Amy Turner. "Ruling the 'Republic of Indians' in Seventeenth-Century Florida," in Peter H. Wood, Gregory A. Waselkov, and M. Thomas Hatley (eds.), *Powahatan's Mantle: Indians in the Colonial Southeast* (Lincoln, NE: University of Nebraska Press, 1989), pp. 134-150.

Butler, Kim D. *Freedoms Given, Freedoms Won: Afro-Brazilians in Post-Abolition São Paulo and Salvador* (New Brunswick, NJ: Rutgers University Press, 1998).

Cáceres, Rina. (ed.) *Rutas de la Esclavitud en África y América Latina* (San José, Costa Rica: Editorial de la Universidad de Costa Rica, 2001).

Cairus, José A. T. "Jihad, Cativeiro e Redenção: escravidão, resistência e irmandade, Sudão Central e Bahia (1835)," M. A. thesis, Universidade Federal do Rio de Janeiro, 2002.

Câmara dos Deputados e Governo do Estado de Minas Gerais, *Autos da Devassa da Inconfidência Mineira* 2nd ed. 10 vols. (Belo Horizonte: Imprensa Oficial de Minas Gerais, 1976-1983).

Capela, José. *O Tráfico de Escravos Nos Portos de Moçambique, 1733-1904* (Porto: Edições Afrontamento, 2002).

Capela, José. "Apontamento sobre os negreiros da Ilha de Moçambique, 1900-1920 [*sic*], *Arquivo – Boletim do Arquivo Histórico de Moçambique* 4 (1988): 83-90.

Capela, José. "O Tráfico da Escravatura nas Relações Moçambique-Brasil," *História: Questões e Debates* (Curitiba) 9/16 (1988): 187-192.

Capela, José, and Medeiros, Eduardo. *O tráfico de escravos para as Ilhas do Índico, 1720-1902* (Maputo: INLD / UEM, 1988).

Capo, H. B. C. *Comparative Phonology of Gbe* (Berlin and New York: Foris Publications, 1991).

Carigé, Eduardo. *Geographia Physica e Política da Província da Bahia* (Salvador: Imprensa Econômica, 1882).

Carney, Judith A. *Black Rice: The African Origins of Rice Cultivation in the Americas* (Cambridge, MA: Harvard University Press, 2001).

Cardozo, Manoel S. "The Lay Brotherhoods of Colonial Bahia," *Catholic Historical Review* 33/1 (1947): 12-30.

Carreira, António. *As Companhias Pombalinas* 2nd. ed. (Lisbon: Editorial Presença, 1983).

Carretta, Vincent. "Olaudah Equiano or Gustavus Vassa? New Light on an Eighteenth Century Question of Identity," *Slavery and Abolition* 20 (1999): 96-105.

Carvalho, Marcus J. M. de. *Liberdade, Rotinas e Rupturas do Escravismo no Recife, 1822-1850* (Recife: Editora Universitária da UFPE, 1998).

Cascudo, Luís da Câmara. *Dicionário do Folclore Brasileiro* 4th ed., revised and enlarged (São Paulo: Edições Melhoramentos e Instituto Nacional do Livro, 1979).

Castellanos, Isabel. "From Ulkumí to Lucumí: A Historical Overview of Religious Acculturation in Cuba," in Arturo Lindsay (ed.), *Santeria Aesthetics in Contemporary Latin American Art* (Washington: Smithsonian Institution Press, 1996), pp. 39-50.

Castillo, Nicolás del. *Esclavos negros en Cartagena y sus aportes léxicos* (Bogotá: Insituto Caro y Cuervo, 1982).

Castro, Hebe Maria Mattos de. *Das cores do silêncio: os significados da liberdade no sudeste escravista, Brasil século XIX* (Rio de Janeiro: Nova Fronteira, 1998 [1995]).

Castro, Yeda Pessoa de. "Língua e nação de candomblé," *África* (Revista do Centro de Estudos Africanos, Universidade de São Paulo) 4 (1981): 57-77.

Chambers, Douglas. "'My own nation': Igbo Exiles in the Diaspora," *Slavery and Abolition* 18/1 (1997): 72-97.

Cherinda, Marcos. "Praia de Moçambique no Brasil," *Tempo* (Maputo) 119 (29 March,1992): 38-43.

Chevannes, Barry. *Rastafari: Roots And Ideology* (Syracuse, N.Y.: Syracuse University Press, 1994).

Churchill, Awnsham, and Churchill, John. *A Collection of Voyages and Travels* 6 vols. (London: H. Lintot, 1744-1746).

Cicinnatus [Luiz Tarquínio]. *O elemento escravo e as questões economicas do Brazil* (Bahia: Typographia dos Dois Mundos, 1885).

Codo, Bellarmin C. "Les Afro-brésiliens de retour," in Doudou Diene (ed.), *La Chaine et le lien: une vision de la traite negrière* (Paris: Unesco, 1998), pp. 95-105.

Coelho, Virgílio. "Imagens, Símbolos e Representações. 'Quiandas, Quitutas, Sereias': Imaginários locaias, identidades regionais e alteridades. Reflexões sobre o quotidiano urbano luandense na publicidade e no universo do *marketing*," *Ngola: Revista de Estudos Sociais* (Luanda) 1 (1997): 127-191.

Cole, Jennifer. "The Work of Memory in Madagascar," *American Ethnologist* 25/4 (1998): 610-633.

Connah, Graham. "African City Walls: A Neglected Source?," in David M. Anderson and Richard Rathbone (eds.), *Africa's Urban Past* (Oxford: Heinemann, 2000), pp. 36-51.

Connerton, Paul. *How Societies Remember* (New York: Cambridge University Press, 1989).

Conrad, Robert Edgar. *World of Sorrow: The African Slave Trade to Brazil* (Baton Rouge: Louisiana State University Press, 1986).

Conrad, Robert Edgar. *Children of God's Fire; A Documentary History of Black Slavery in Brazil* (Princeton: Princeton University Press, 1983).

Conrad, Robert Edgar. *The Destruction of Brazilian Slavery 1850-1888* (Berkeley: University of California Press, 1972).

Corbin, Alain. "Bastidores," in Michelle Perrot (ed.), *História da vida privada* (São Paulo: Companhia das Letras, 1995), IV, pp. 413-611.

Costa, Ana de Lourdes Ribeiro da. "Espaços negros: '*cantos*' e 'lojas' em Salvador no século XIX," *Caderno CRH* Supplement (1991): 49-68.

Costa, Emília Viotti da. *Da Senzala à Colônia* (São Paulo: Difusão Européia do Livro, 1966).

Costa, Joaquim José. *Breve notícia da irmandade de Nossa Senhora do Rosário e São Benedito dos homens pretos do Rio* (Rio de Janeiro: Tipografia Politécnica, 1886).

Costa e Silva, Alberto da. *Um Rio Chamado Atlântico: A África no Brasil e o Brasil na África* (Rio de Janeiro: Editora Nova Fronteira, 2003.

Costa e Silva, Maria Conceição da. *Sociedade Montepio dos Artistas na Bahia* (Salvador: Fundação Cultural do Estado da Bahia, 1998).

Coughtry, Jay. *The Notorious Triangle: Rhode Island and the African Slave Trade, 1700-1807* (Philadelphia: Temple University Press, 1981).

Courlander, Harold. *A Treasury of American Folklore* (New York: Smithmark Publishers, 1996 [1976]).

Cowley, Malcolm. (ed.) *Adventures of An African Slaver . . . A True Account of The Life of Captain Theodore Canot* (New York: Albert and Charles Boni, 1928).

Cruickshank, J. Graham. "Among the Aku (Yoruba) in Canal No. 1, West Bank, Demerara River," *Timehri* 3rd Series 4 (1917): 70-82.

Cruickshank, J. Graham. "An African Dance in the Colony," *Supplement to the West India Committee Circular*, 29/666 (14 February, 1924): 8-9.

Cugoano, Quobna Ottobah. *Thoughts and Sentiments on the Evil of Slavery* Vincent Carretta (ed.) (New York: Penguin Books, 1999 [1787]).

Cunha, Marianno Carneiro da. *Da Senzala ao Sobrado: A Arquitectura Brasileira na África Ocidental / From Slave Quarters to Town Houses: Brazilian architecture in Nigeria and the People's Republic of Benin* (São Paulo: Nobel, 1985).

Cunha, Manuela Carneiro da. *Negros, Estrangeiros: Os Escravos Libertos e Sua Volta à África* (São Paulo: Brasilience, 1985).

Cunha, Manuela Carneiro da. "Religião, Comércio e Etnicidade: Uma Interpretação Preliminar do Catolicismo Brasileiro em Lagos, no Século XIX," *Religião e Sociedade* 1 (1977): 51-60.

Curtin, Philip D. *Atlantic Slave Trade: A Census* (Madison: University of Wisconsin Press, 1969).

Curtin, Philip D. "The Slavery Hypothesis for Hypertension among African Americans: The Historical Evidence," *American Journal of Public Health* 82/12 (1992): 1681-1686.

Curto, José C. *Alcoól e Escravos: O comércio luso-brasileiro do alcoól em Mpinda, Luanda e Benguela durante o tráfico atlântico de escravos (c. 1480-1830) e o seu impacto nas sociedades da África Central Ocidental* (Lisbon: Editora Vulgata, 2002).

Curto, José C. "The Story of Nbena, 1817-1820: Unlawful Enslavement and the Concept of 'Original Freedom' in Angola," in Paul E. Lovejoy and David V. Trotman (eds.), *Trans-Atlantic Dimensions of Ethnicity in the African Diaspora* (London: Continuum, 2003), pp. 43-64.

Curto José C. "Movers of Slaves: The Brazilian Community in Benguela, c. 1722-1832," Unpublished paper presented at the Angola on the Move: Transport Routes, Communications, and History conference, Centre for Modern Oriental Studies, Berlin [Germany], 24-26 September, 2003.

Curto, José C. "The Anatomy of a Demographic Explosion: Luanda, 1844-1850," *International Journal of African Historical Studies* 32 (1999): 381-405.

Curto, José C. "The Legal Portuguese Slave Trade from Benguela: A Quantitative Re-Appraisal," *África* (Revista do Centro de Estudos Africanos, Universidade de São Paulo) 16-17 (1993-1994): 101-116.

Curto, José C. "A Quantitative Reassessment of the Legal Portuguese Slave Trade from Luanda, Angola," *African Economic History* 20 (1992): 1-25.

Curto José C., and Lovejoy, Paul E. (eds.) *Enslaving Connections: Western Africa and Brazil during the Era of Slavery* (Amherst, NY: Humanity Books, 2004).

Curto, José C., and Gervais, Raymond R. "The Population History of Luanda During the Late Atlantic Slave Trade, 1781-1844," *African Economic History* 29 (2001): 83-121.

Curto, José C., and Paul E. Lovejoy, "Introduction: Enslaving Connections and the Changing Cultures of Africa and Brazil during the Era of Slavery," in José C. Curto and Paul E. Lovejoy (eds.), *Enslaving Connections: Changing Cultures of Africa and Brazil during the Era of Slavery* (Amherst, NY: Humanity Books, 2004), pp. 11-18.

d'Albuquerque, A. Tenório. *A maçonaria e a Inconfidência Mineira: movimento de carater maçônico, a bandeira maçônica dos inconfidentes* 2nd ed. (Rio de Janeiro: Editora Aurora, 1970).

Dantzig, Albert van. (ed.) *The Dutch and the Guinea Coast, 1674-1742: A Collection of Documents at the General State Archive at The Hague* (Accra: GAAS, 1978).

Dapper, Olfert. *Naukeurige Beschrijvinge der Afrikaensche Gewesten* (Amsterdam: J. van Meurs, 1668 [1676]).

Davidson, David. "Negro Slave Control and Resistance in Colonial Mexico, 1519-1650," *Hispanic American Historical Review* 46 (1966): 235-253.

Davis, Wade. *Passage of Darkness: the Ethnology of the Haitian Zombie* (Chapel Hill: University of North Carolina Press, 1988).

Dayan, Joan. *Haiti, History, and the Gods* (Berkeley: University of California Press, 1995).

Debret, Jean Baptiste. *Viagem Pitoresca e Histórica ao Brasil* 2 vols., trans. Sergio Milliet (São Paulo: Livraria Martins, 1940 [1834-1839]).

De Cauna, Jacques. *Haïti: l'eternelle révolution* (Port-au-Prince: Deschamps, 1997).

Delgado, Ralph. *A Famosa e Histórica Benguela: Catálogo dos Governadores (1779 a 1940)* (Lisbon: Edições Cosmos, 1940).

Deren, Maya. *The Divine Horsemen: The Living Gods of Haiti* (New Paltz, NY: Documentex, McPherson, 1983 [1970]).

Desch-Obi, T. J. "Combat and the Crossing of the Kalunga, in Linda M. Heywood (ed.), *Central Africans and Cultural Transformations in the American Diaspora* (New York: Cambridge University Press, 2002), pp. 353-370.

Desmangles, Leslie G. *The Faces of the Gods: Vodou and Roman Catholicism in Haiti* (Chapel Hill: The University of North Carolina Press, 1992).

Desquiron, Lilas. *Les racines du vaudou* (Port-au-Prince: Deschamps, 1990).

Devisch, René. *Weaving The Threads Of Life* (Chicago: University of Chicago Press, 1993).

Devisch, René. "Mediumistic Divination among the Northern Yaka of Zaire," Philip M. Peek (ed.), *African Divination Systems: Ways of Knowing* (Bloomington: Indiana University Press, 1991), pp. 112-132.

Dias, Maria Idila Leite da Silva. *Quotidiano e poder em São Paulo no século XIX* (São Paulo: Brasiliense, 1984).

Diouf, Sylviane. *Servants of Allah: African Muslims enslaved in the Americas* (New York: New York University Press, 1998).

Drewal, Henry John, and Mason, John. "Ogun and Body/Mind Potentiality: Yoruba Scarification and Painting Traditions in Africa and the Americas," in Barnes, *Africa's Ogun*, pp. 332-352.

Drewal, Henry John, et al (eds.), *Yoruba: Nine Centuries of African Art and Thought* (New York: Harry N. Abrams, Inc., 1989).

Drewal, Margaret Thompson. "Dancing for Ògún in Yorubaland and Brazil," in Barnes, *Africa's Ogun*, pp. 199-234.

Du Bois, W. E. B. *Black Folk, Then and Now* (New York: Henry Holt and Co., 1939).

Du Bois, W. E. B. *The Negro* (New York: Henry Holt and Co., 1915).

Dunham, Katherine. *Island Possessed* (Chicago: University of Chicago Press, 1994 [1969]).

Dunkerley, James. *Americana: The Americas in the World, Around 1850 (Or "Seeing the Elephant" as the Theme for an Imaginary Western)* (London: Verso, 2000).

Dupré, Marie-Claude, and Féau, Etienne. *Batéké: Peintres et Sculpteurs d'Afrique Centrale* (Paris: Musée National des Arts d'Afrique et d'Océanie, 1998).

Ebel, Ernst. *O Rio de Janeiro e seus arredores em 1824* (São Paulo: Editora Nacional, 1972).

Edwards, Elizabeth. (ed.) *Anthropology and Photography 1860-1920* (New Haven, CT: Yale University Press, 1992).

Eisenberg, Peter. *Homens esquecidos* (Campinas: Editora da UNICAMP, 1989).

Eliade, Mircea. *Shamanism* (Princeton: Princeton University Press, 1974).

Elkins, W. F. *Street Preachers, Faith Healers and Herb Doctors in Jamaica, 1890-1925* (New York: Revisionist Press, 1977).

Ellis, A. B. *The Ewe-Speaking Peoples of The Slave Coast Of West Africa* (Osterhout, Netherlands: Anthropological Publications, 1970 [1890]).

Eltis, David. *The Rise of African Slavery in the Americas* (Cambridge: Cambridge University Press, 2000).

Eltis, David. *Economic Growth and the Ending of the Transatlantic Slave Trade* (New York: Oxford University Press, 1989).

Eltis, David. "The Volume and Direction of the Transatlantic Slave Trade: A Reassessment," *William and Mary Quarterly* 58/1 (2001): 17-46.

Eltis, David. "The British Transatlantic Slave Trade Before 1714: Annual Estimates of Volume and Direction," in Robert L. Paquette and Stanley L. Engerman (eds.), *The Lesser Antilles in the Age of European Expansion* (Gainesville: Florida University Press, 1996), pp. 182-205.

Eltis, David. "Volume and African Origins of the Seventeenth Century English Transatlantic Slave Trade," *Cahiers d'Études Africaines* 138 (1996): 617-627.

Eltis, David. "The Volume, Age/Sex Ratios and African Impact of the Slave Trade: Some Refinements of Paul Lovejoy's Review of the Literature," *Journal of African History* 31 (1990): 550-567.

Eltis, David, Behrendt, Stephen, Richardson, David, and Klein, Herbert. *The Transatlantic Slave Trade: A Database on CD-ROM* (New York: Cambridge University Press, 1999).

Emmer, Pieter. "Jesus Christ was Good, but Trade was Better:' An Overview of the Transit Trade of the Dutch Antilles, 1634-1795," in Paquette and Engerman, *Lesser Antilles in the Age of European Expansion*, pp. 206-222.

Evans, Jessica, and Hall, Stuart. (eds.) *Visual Culture: The Reader,* (London: Sage Publications, 1999).

"Explaining European Dominance," *American Historical Review* 104/4 (1999): 1240-1257.

Fabian, Johannes. *Out of our Minds: Reason and Madness in the Exploration of Central Africa* (Berkeley: University of California Press, 2000).

Fackenheim, Emil. *God's Presence in History: Jewish Affirmations and Philosophical Reflections* (New York: New York University Press, 1970).

Farajaje-Jones, Elias. *In Search of Zion: The Spiritual Significance of Africa in Black Religious Movements* (Bern: Peter Lang, 1990).

Farmer, Paul. *The Uses of Haiti* (Monroe, Maine: Common Courage Press, 1994).

Fehderau, Harold W. *Dictionnaire Kituba (Kiongo ya Leta)-Anglais-Français et Vocabulaire Français-Kituba* (Kinshasa: Editions Cedi, 1992).

Fernandez, James. *Bwiti: An Ethnography of the Religious Imagination in Africa* (Princeton: Princeton University Press, 1982).

Ferreira, Manuel Jesuino. *A Província da Bahia: apontamentos (*Rio de Janeiro: Typographia Nacional, 1875).

Ferretti, Sérgio Figueiredo. *Querebentan de Zomadonu. Etnografia da Casa das Minas do Maranhão* (São Luis: EDUFMA, 1996 [1985]).

Ferrez, Gilberto. *Bahia: velhas fotografias, 1858-1900* (Rio de Janeiro: Kosmos Editora; Salvador: Banco da Bahia Investimentos SA, 1988).

Fick, Carolyn E. *The Making of Haiti: The Saint Domingue Revolution from Below* (Knoxville: The University of Tennessee Press, 1990).

Filho, Aires de Mata Machado. *O Negro e o Garimpo em Minas Gerais* (Rio de Janeiro: Livraria José Olympio Editora, 1943).

Filho, Alexandre José de Mello Moraes. *Festas e tradições populares do Brasil* (Luís da Câmara Cascudo, rev. and ed.) (Rio de Janeiro: Tecnoprint Gráfica S.A., 1967).

Filho, Melo Morais. *Festas e Tradições Populares do Brasil* 3rd ed. (Rio de Janeiro: F. Briguiet & Cia., 1946).

Filho, Walter Fraga. *Mendigos, moleques e vadios* (São Paulo: HUCITEC; Salvador: EDUFBA, 1996).

Filho, Walter Fraga. "Encruzilhadas da liberdade: histórias e trajetórias de escravos e libertos na Bahia, 1870-1910" (Ph. D. dissertation, Universidade Estadual de Campinas, 2003).

Florence, Alfonso Bandeira. "Nem escravos, nem libertos: os 'africanos livres' na Bahia," *Cadernos do CEAS* (Salvador) 121 (1989): 58-69.

Florentino, Manolo G. *Em Costas Negras: Uma História do Tráfico Atlântico de Escravos entre a África e o Rio de Janeiro (Séculos XVIII e XIX)* (São Paulo: Civilização Brasileira, 1997 / São Paulo: Companhia das Letras, 2002, 2nd edition).

Florentino, Manolo G., and Góes, José R. "Slavery, Marriage and Kinship in Rural Rio de Janeiro, 1790-1830," in Paul E. Lovejoy (ed.), *Identity in the Shadow of Slavery* (London and New York: Continuum, 2000), pp. 137-162.

Fonseca, Luís Anselmo da. *A escravidão, o clero e o abolicionismo* (Recife: Editora Massangana, 1988 [1887]).

Forbes, Frederick E. *Dahomey and the Dahomeans* 2 vols. (London: Longman, Brown, Green, and Longmans, 1851).

Fraser, Lionel Mordaunt. *History of Trinidad* 2 vols. (London: Frank Cass, 1971 [1891])

Fredrickson, George M. "The Skeleton in the Closet," *New York Review of Books* 2 (November 2000).

Freitas, Décio. *Palmares: A Guerra dos Escravos* 5th ed. (Porto Alegre: Mercado Alberto, 1984).

Freyre, Gilberto. *Sobrados e mucambos: decadência do patriarcado rural e desenvolvimento do urbano* 7th ed. (Rio de Janeiro: José Olympio Editora; Instituto Nacional do Livro, 1985).

Freyre, Gilberto. *Sobrados e mucambos: decadência do patriarcado rural e desenvolvimento do urbano* 5th ed. 2 vols. (Rio de Janeiro: Livraria José Olympio Editora, 1977).

Freyre, Gilberto. *O Escravo nos Anúncios de Jornais Brasileiros do Século XIX* (Recife: Imprensa Universitária, 1963).

Friedemann, Nina S. de. "Cabildos de Negros: Refugios de Africanía en Colombia," *Caribbean Studies* 23/1-2 (1990): 82-97.

Funari, Pedro Paulo de Abreu. "A arqueologia de Palmares, Sua contribução para o conhecimento da história da cultura afro-americana," in João José Reis and Flávio dos Santos Gomes (eds.), *Liberdade por um fio: história dos quilombos no Brasil* (São Paulo: Companhia de Letras, 1996), pp. 26-51.

Furtado, João Pinto. *O manto de Penélope: história, mito e memória da Inconfidência Mineira de 1788-9* (São Paulo:Companhia das Letras, 2002).

Gardell, Mattias. *In the Name of Elijah Muhammad: Louis Farrakhan* (Durham: Duke University Press, 1996).

Gardner, W. J. *A History of Jamaica from its Discovery by Christopher Columbus to the Year 1872* (London: Frank Cass, 1971 [1873]).

Gayibor, Nicoué Lodjou. *Les Peuples et Royaumes du Golfe du Bénin* (Lomé: Université du Benin, 1986).

Gebara, Ademir. *O mercado de trabalho livre no Brasil* (São Paulo: Brasiliense, 1986).

Geggus, David Patrick. *Slavery, War, and Revolution: The British Occupation of Saint-Domingue 1793-1798* (New York: Oxford University Press, 1982).

Geggus, David Patrick. "La cérémonie du Bois Caiman," in Laënnec Hurbon (ed.), *l'Insurrection des esclaves de Saint-Domingue* (Paris : Karthala, 2000), pp. 149-167.

Geggus, David Patrick. "Slavery, War, and Revolution in the Greater Caribbean, 1789-1815," in David Barry Gaspar and David Patrick Geggus (eds.), *A Turbulent Time: The French Revolution and the Greater Caribbean* (Bloomington: Indiana University Press, 1997), pp. 1-50.

Georgia Writers' Project. *Drums and Shadows: Survival Studies Among the Georgia Coastal Negroes* (Athens: University of Georgia Press, 1986 [1940]).

Gengenbach, Heidi. "Boundaries of Beauty: Tattooed Secrets of Women's History in Magude, Southern Mozambique," *Journal of Women's History* 14/4 (2003): 106-141.

Gibson, Kean. "A Celebration of Life," Cinema Guild video, undated.

Gilroy, Paul. *The Black Atlantic: Modernity and Double Consciousness* (Cambridge, MA.: Harvard University Press, 1993).

Glazier, Stephen D. "Contested Rituals of the African Diaspora," in Peter B. Clarke (ed.), *New Trends and Developments in African Religions* (Westport, CT: Greenwood Press, 1998), pp. 104-119.

Glazier, Stephen D. *Marchin' The Pilgrims Home* (Salem, WI: Sheffield, 1991).

Glélé, Maurice Ahanhanzo. *Le Daxomé: Du pouvoir Ajá à la nation Fon* (Cotonou: Nubia, 1974).

Gomez, Michael A. *Exchanging Our Country Marks: The Transformation of African Identities in the Colonial and Antebellum South* (Chapel Hill and London: University of North Calorina Press, 1998).

Gonçalves, Adelto. *Gonzaga, o Poeta do Iluminismo* (Rio de Janeiro, Nova Fronteira, 1999).

Gordon, Shirley C. *God Almighty Make We Free* (Bloomington: Indiana University Press, 1996).

Goulart, Mauricio. *Escravidão africana no Brasil (das orignes à extinção do tráfico)* (São Paulo: Editora Alfa-Ômega, 1975).

Graden, Dale T. *From Slavery to Freedom in Brazil: Bahia, 1835-1900* (Albuquerque: University of New Mexico Press, forthcoming).

Graden, Dale T. "'An Act Even of Public Security': Slave Resistance, Social Tensions and the End of the International Slave Trade to Brazil, 1835-1856," *Hispanic American Historical Review* 76/2 (1996): 249-282.

Guimarães, Antonio Sérgio A. *Racismo e Anti-Racismo no Brasil* (São Paulo: FUSP/ Editora 34, 1999).

Guran, Milton. *Agudás: os "brasileiros" do Benim* (Rio de Janeiro: Editora Nova Fronteira, 1999).

Guthrie, Malcolm. *Comparative Bantu* 4 vols. (Farnborough, England: Gregg, 1969-1970).

Guy, Gregory. "Muitas Linguas: The Linguistic Impact of Africans in Colonial Brazil, in Curto and Lovejoy, *Enslaving Connections*, pp. 125-137.

Guyanese Oral Traditions: Interviews Conducted on the East Coast Demerara, West Coast Berbice, West Bank Demerara and the Essequibo Coast (Turkeyen: University of Guyana, 1989).

Gyekeye, Kwame. *Tradition and Modernity: Philosophical Reflections on the African Experience* (Oxford: Oxford University Press, 1997).

Hair, Paul E. H. "Heretics, Slaves, and Witches – As Seen by Guinea Jesuits, c. 1610," *Journal of Religion in Africa* 28/2 (1998): 131-144.

Hair, Paul E. H., Jones, Adam, and Law, Robin. (eds.). *Barbot on Guinea: the writings of Jean Barbot on West Africa 1678-1712* 2 vols. (London: Hakluyt Society, 1992 [1688]).

Hale, Horatio. *Ethnography & Philology*, a separate volume in Charles Wilkes, *United States Exploring Expedition. During the Years 1838, 1839, 1840, 184, 1842. Under the Command of Charles Wilkes, U.S.N.* (Philadelphia: Lea and Blanchard, 1846).

Hall, Gwendolyn Midlo. (ed.), *Databases for the Study of Afro-Louisiana, 1699-1860* (Baton Rouge: Louisiana State University Press, 2000).

Hall, Gwendolyn Midlo. *Africans in Colonial Louisiana: The Development of Afro-Creole Culture in the Eighteenth Century* (Baton Rouge: Louisiana State University Press, 1992).

Handler, Jerome S. "Survivors of the Middle Passage: Life Stories of Enslaved Africans in British America," *Slavery and Abolition* 23/1 (2002): 25-56.

Handler, Jerome S. "Life Histories of Enslaved Africans in Barbados," *Slavery and Abolition* 19 (1998): 129-141.

Harding, Rachel Elizabeth. "Candomblé and the alternative spaces of black being in nineteenth century Bahia, Brazil: a study of historical context and religious meaning," Ph. D. dissertation, University of Colorado, 1997.

Harms, Robert. *Games Against Nature: An Eco-cultural History of the Nunu of Equatorial Africa* (Cambridge: Cambridge University Press, 1987).

Harms, Robert. *River of Wealth, River of Sorrow: The Central Zaire Basin in the Era of the Slave and Ivory Trade* (New Haven: Yale University Press, 1981).

Hastings, Adrian. "The Christianity of Pedro IV of the Kongo, 'The Pacific' (1695-1718)," *Journal of Religion in Africa* 28/2 (1998): 145-159.

Heintze, Beatrix. "Zur materiellen Kultur der Mbundu im 16. und 17. Jahrhundert," in Heintze, Beatrix. *Studien zur Geschichte Angolas im 16. und 17. Jahrhundert. Ein Lesebuch* (Köln: Köppe, 1996): 253-282.

Heintze, Beatrix. "A cultura material dos Ambundu segundo as fontes dos séculos XVI e XVII," *Revista Internacional de Estudos Africanos* 10-11 (1989): 15-63.

Heintze, Beatrix. "Written Sources, Oral Traditions, and Oral Traditions as Written Sources: The Steep and Thorny Way to Early Angolan History" *Paideuma* 33 (1987): 263-288. [Special Issue *European Sources for Sub-Saharan Africa before 1900: Use and Abuse*, Adam Jones and Beatrix Heintze (eds.).]

Henderson, Richard N. *The King in Every Man: Evolutionary Trends in Onitsha Ibo Society and Culture* (New Haven: Yale, 1972).

Henige, David. *Oral Historiography* (London: Longman, 1982)

Henige, David. *The Chronology of Oral Tradition: Quest for a Chimera* (Oxford: Oxford University Press, 1974).

Henney, Jeannette Hillman. "Spirit Possession Belief and Trance Behavior in a Religious Group in St. Vincent, British West Indies," Ph. D. dissertation, Ohio State University, 1968.

Henriques, Isabel de Castro. *Commerce et Changement en Angola au XIXe siècle: Imbangala et Tshokwe face à la Modernité* 2 vols. (Paris: l'Harmattan, 1995).

Henriques, Isabel Castro, and Sala-Molins, Louis. (eds.) *Déraison, esclavage ideologiques et juridiques de la traite négrière et de l'esclavage* (Paris: Éditions UNESCO, 2002).

Hernaes, Per O. *Slaves, Danes, and African Coast Society: The Danish Slave Trade from West Africa and Afro-Danish Relations on the Eighteenth Century Gold Coast* (Trondheim: Department of History, University of Trondheim, 1995).

Herskovits, Melville J. *Acculturation: The Study of Culture Contact* (Gloucester, Mass.: Peter Smith, 1958 [1938]).

Herskovits, Melville J. *Franz Boas: The Science of Man in the Making* (New York: Charles Scribner's Sons, 1953).

Herskovits, Melville J. *The Myth of the Negro Past* (New York: Harper and Brothers, 1941).

Herskovits, Melville J. *Dahomey, an ancient West African kingdom* 2 vols. (New York: J.J. Augustin Publisher, 1938).

Herskovits, Melville J., and Herskovits, Frances S. *Trinidad Village* (New York: Alfred A. Knopf, 1947).

Herskovits, Melville J., and Herskovits, Frances S. *An Outline of Dahomean Religious Belief* Memoirs of the American Anthropological Association 41 (Menasha WI: American Anthropological Association, 1933).

Heusch, Luc de. "Kongo in Haiti: A New Approach to Religious Syncretism," *Man* (Journal of the Royal Anthropological Institute) 24 (1989): 290-303.

Heywood Linda M. (ed.) *Central Africans and Cultural Transformations in the American Diaspora* (New York: Cambridge University Press; 2002).

Heywood, Linda M. "The Angolan-Afro-Brazilian Cultural Connections," *Slavery and Abolition* 20 (1999): 9-23.

Higgins, Kathleen J. *"Licentious Liberty" in a Brazilian Gold-Mining Region: Slavery, Gender, and Social Control in Eighteenth-Century Sabará, Minas Gerais* (University Park, PA: Pennsylvania State University Press, 1999).

Hill, Robert. "Leonard P. Howell and Millenarian Visions in Early Rastafari," *Jamaica Journal* 16/1 (1981): 24-39.

Hilton, Anne. *Kingdom of Kongo* (Oxford: Clarendon Press, 1985).

Hilton, Anne. "European Sources for the Study of Religious change in Sixteenth and Seventeenth Century Kongo," *Paideuma* 33 (1987): 289-312 [Special Issue *European Sources for Sub-Saharan Africa before 1900: Use and Abuse*, Adam Jones and Beatrix Heintze (eds.)].

Horton, Robin. *Patterns of Thought in Africa and the West* (New York: Cambridge University Press, 1997).

Hoffmann, Léon François. "Un mythe nationale: la cérémonie du Bois Caïman," in Gerald Barthélemy and C. Girault (eds.), *La république haïtienne* (Paris: Karthala, 1993), pp. 434-448.

Hogg, Donald M. "The Convince Cult in Jamaica," in Sidney W. Mintz (ed.), *Papers in Caribbean Anthropology* (New Haven: Department of Anthropology, Yale University, 1960), pp. 1-24 plus 6 plates.

Homiak, John P. "Dub History: Soundings on Rastafari Livity and Language," in Barry Chevannes (ed.), *Rastafari and Other African-Caribbean World Views* (Basingstoke: MacMillan and the Institute of Social Studies, the Hague, 1995), pp. 127-176.

Hoppe, Fritz. *A África Oriental Portuguese no Tempo do Marquês de Pombal (1750-1777)* (Lisbon: Agência-Geral do Ultramar, 1970).

Hunt, Nancy Rose. *A Colonial Lexicon of Birth Ritual, Medicalization, and Mobility in the Congo* (Durham, NC: Duke University Press, 1999).

Inikori, Joseph E. "The Volume of the British Slave Trade, 1655-1807," *Cahiers d'Études Africaines* 32 (1992): 669-676.

Iroko, Abiola Félix. "Cauris et esclaves en Afrique Occidentale entre le XVIe et le XIXe siècles," in Serge Daget (ed.), *De la traite à l'esclavage* 2 vols. (Nantes: Centre de Recherche sur l'Histoire du Monde Atlantique, 1988), I, pp. 193-204.

Isert, Paul Erdman. *Voyage en Guinée et dans les îles Caraïbes en Amérique* (Nicoué Lodjou Gayibor, ed.) (Paris: Karthala, 1989 [1793]).

Janzen, John. *Lemba, 1650-1930: A Drum of Affliction in Africa and the New World* (New York: Garland, 1982).

Jedrej, M. C., and Shaw, Rosalind. (eds.) *Dreaming, Religion and Society in Africa* (Leiden and New York: E. J. Brill, 1992).

Jewsiewicki, Bogumil, and Mumbanza, Bawele. "The Social Context of Slavery in Equatorial Africa during the Nineteenth and Twentieth Centuries," in Paul E. Lovejoy (ed.), *The Ideology of Slavery in Africa* (Beverly Hills: Sage, 1981), pp. 72-98.

Johnson, Howard. "The Liberated Africans in the Bahamas, 1811-1860," in Howard Johnson (ed.), *After the Crossing* (London: Frank Cass and Company, Ltd., 1988), pp. 16-40.

Joseph, E. L. *History of Trinidad* (London: Frank Cass, 1970 [1838]).

Jones, Adam. *Brandenburg Sources for West African History, 1680-1700* (Stuttgart: F. Steiner, Verlag and Wiesbaden, 1985).

Jones, Adam. "The Dark Continent: A Preliminary Study of the Geographical coverage in European Sources, 1400-1880," *Paideuma* 33 (1987): 19-26.

Jullien, Benoît, et al. *Île de La Réunion, Regards croisés sur l'esclavage 1794-1848* (Saint-Denis: CNH and Paris: Somogy éditions d'art, 1998).

Junod, Henri A. *The Life of a South African Tribe* 2 vols. (New Hyde Park, New York: University Books Inc.: 1962 [1926]).

Karasch, Mary C. *Slave Life in Rio de Janeiro 1808-1850* (Princeton: Princeton University Press, 1987).

Karasch, Mary C. "Zumbi of Palmares: Challenging the Portuguese Colonial Order," in Kenneth J. Andrien (ed.), *The Human Tradition in Colonial Latin America* (Wilmington, DE: Scholarly Resources, Inc., 2002), pp. 104-120.

Karl, Emmanuel. *Traditions Orales au Dahomey-Benin.* (Niamey, Niger: Centre Regional de Documentation pour la Tradition Orale, 1974).

Kempadoo, Peter. "Recordings of Folklore, Drama and Music Made in Guyana, 1971-3," University Library, University of Guyana, 1974, K104.

Kent, Raymond K. "Palmares: An African State in Brazil," *Journal of African History* 6/2 (1965): 161-175.

Kidder, Daniel P. *Sketches of a Residence and Travels in Brazil* 2 vols. (Philadelphia: Sorin & Ball and London: Wiley & Putnam, 1845).

Kiddy, Elizabeth W. "Who is the King of Congo? A New Look at African and African-Brazilian Kings in Brazil," in Heywood, *Central Africans and Cultural Transformations*, pp. 153-182.

Kiddy, Elizabeth W. "Ethnic and Racial Identity in the Brotherhoods of the Rosary of Minas Gerais, 1700-1830," *The Americas* 56/2 (1999): 221-252.

Klein, Herbert S. *The Atlantic Slave Trade* (Cambridge and New York: Cambridge University Press, 1999).

Klein, Herbert S. *The Middle Passage: Comparative Studies in the Atlantic Slave Trade* (Princeton: Princeton University Press, 1978).

Klein, Herbert S. "A Demografia do Tráfico Atlântico de Escravos para o Brasil," *Estudos Econômicos* 17/2 (1987): 129-149.

Klein, Herbert S. "O Tráfico de Escravos Africanos para o Porto do Rio de Janeiro, 1825-1830," *Anais de História* 5 (1973): 85-101.

Klein, Herbert S. "The Portuguese Slave Trade from Angola in the Eighteenth Century," *Journal of Economic History* 32 (1972): 894-918.

Klein, Herbert S. "The Trade in African Slaves to Rio de Janeiro, 1795-1811: Estimates of Mortality and Patterns of Voyages," *Journal of African History* 10 (1969): 533-549.

Klooster, Wim. "Dutch Trade, Capital and Technology in the Atlantic World, 1595-1667," Unpublished paper presented to the American Historical Association Annual Meeting, 1998).

Knight, Franklin, and Liss, Peggy K. (eds.) *Atlantic Port Cities: Economy, Culture and Society in the Atlantic World, 1650-1850* (Knoxville: University of Tennessee Press, 1991).

Kopytoff, Igor. "The Internal African Frontier: The Making of African Political Culture," in Igor Kopytoff (ed.), *The African Frontier: The Reproduction of Traditional African Societies* (Bloomington: Indiana University Press, 1987), pp. 3-83.

Kopytoff, Igor. "Revitalization and the Genesis of Cults in Pragmatic Religion: The Kita Rite of Passage among the Suku," in Ivan Karp and Charles S. Bird (eds.), *Explorations in African Systems of Thought* (Washington, D.C.: Smithsonian Institution Press, 1987), pp. 183-212.

Kopytoff, Jean Herskovits. *A Preface to Modern Nigeria: The 'Sierra Leonians' in Yoruba, 1830-1890* (Madison: University of Wisconsin Press, 1965).

Kriger, Colleen E. *Pride of Men: Ironworking in 19th century West Central Africa* (Portsmouth, NH: Heinemann, 1999).

Kriger, Colleen E. "Museum Collections as Sources for African History," *History in Africa* 23 (1996): 129-154.

Koster, Henry. *Travels in Brazil* (London: Longman, Hurst, Rees, Orme, and Brown, 1816).

Kovarik, Lúcio. *Trabalho e vadiagem* (São Paulo: Brasiliense, 1987).

Kubik, Gerhard. *Angolan Traits in Black Music, Games and Dances of Brazil: A study of African cultural extensions overseas* (Lisboa: Junta de Investigações Científicas do Ultramar, Centro de Estudos de Antropologia Cultural, 1979).

Kuper, Adam. *The Invention of Primitive Society: Transformations of an Illusion* (London: Routledge, 1988).

Lacroix, François-Joseph-Pamphile de. *Mémoires pour servir a l'histoire de la revolution de Saint-Domingue* (Paris: Chez Billet Ainé, 1819).

La Fosse, Alexandre. "Mémoire fait par un habitant d'Ouanaminthe sur les evénements arrivés a cette paroisse jusqu'au 15 janvier 1792, certifié par Alexandre la Fosse, le Cap, 22 sept. 1792," as cited in Fick, *The Making of Haiti*, p. 291, ft. 70.

Lamounier, Maria Lúcia. *Da escravidão ao trabalho livre* (Campinas: Papirus, 1988).

Landers, Jane. *Black Society in Spanish Florida* (Urbana: University of Illinois Press, 1999).

Landers, Jane. "Cimarrón Ethnicity and Cultural Adaptation in the Spanish Domains of the Circum-Caribbean, 1503-1763," in Paul E. Lovejoy (ed.), *Identity in the Shadow of Slavery* (London: Continuum, 2000), pp. 30-54.

Landers, Jane "Gracia Real de Santa Teresa de Mose: A Free Black Town In Spanish Florida," *American Historical Review* 95 (1990): 9-30.

Landes, David. *The Wealth and Poverty of Nations: Why Some are so Rich and Some so Poor* (New York: W. W. Norton, 1998).

Lane, Kris E. *Quito 1599: City and Colony in Transition* (Albuquerque: University of New Mexico Press, 2002).

Laotan, Anthony B. "Brazilian Influence on Lagos," *Nigerian Magazine* 69 (1964): 156-165.

Law, Robin. *The Kingdom of Allada* (Leiden: Research School CNWS, CNWS publications, 1997).

Law, Robin. *The Slave Coast of West Africa 1550-1750: The impact of the Atlantic Slave Trade on an African society* (Oxford: Oxford University Press, 1991).

Law, Robin. (ed.) *Source Material for studying the Slave Trade and the African Diaspora* (Stirling: Centre of Commonwealth Studies, University of Stirling: Occasional Paper No. 5, 1997).

Law, Robin, and Lovejoy, Paul E. (eds.) *The Biography of Mahommah Gardo Baquaqua: His Passage from Slavery to Freedom in Africa and America* (Princeton: Markus Wiener, Publisher, 2001).

Law, Robin, and Strickrodt, Silke. (eds.) *Ports of the Slave Trade (Bights of Benin and Biafra)* (Stirling: Centre of Commonwealth Studies, University of Stirling, 1999).

Law, Robin. "Francisco Felix de Souza in West Africa, 1800-1849," in Curto and Lovejoy, *Enslaving Connections*, pp. 189-213.

Law, Robin. "The Evolution of the Brazilian Community in Ouidah," *Slavery and Abolition* 22 (2001): 22-41 [Special Issue *Rethinking the African Diaspora: The Making of a Black Atlantic World in the Bight of Benin and Brazil*, Kristin Mann and Edna G. Bay (eds.)].

Law, Robin. "La cérémonie du Bois Caiman et le 'pacte du sang' dahoméen," in Laënnec Hurbon (ed.), *l'Insurrection des esclaves de Saint-Domingue* (Paris: Karthala, 2000), pp. 131-147.

Law, Robin. "Ethnicity and the slave trade: 'Lucumi' and 'Nago' as ethnonyms in West Africa," *History in Africa* 24 (1997): 205-219.

Law, Robin. "'My Head Belongs to the King': On the Political and Ritual Significance of Decapitation in Pre-Colonial Dahomey," *Journal of African History* 30 (1989): 399-415.

Law, Robin, and Mann, Kristin. "West Africa in the Atlantic Community," *William and Mary Quarterly* 3rd Series 56/2 (1999): 307-334.

Lawal, Babatunde. "The Living Dead: Art and Immortality among the Yoruba of Nigeria," *Africa* 47/1 (1977): 50-61.

Legislação da Província da Bahia sobre o negro: 1835-1888 (Salvador: Fundação Cultural do Estado da Bahia, 1996).

Le Herissé, A. *L'Anciên Royaume du Dahomey: Moeurs, Religion, Histoire* (Paris: Emile Larose Ed., 1911).

Leite, Paulo Gomes. "A Maçonaria, o Iluminismo e a Inconfidência Mineira," *Revista Minas Gerais* 33 (1991): 18-23.

"Letter of Mr. Samuel Crowther to the Rev. William Jowett, in 1837 . . . Detailing the Circumstances Connected with his Being Sold as a Slave," in *Journals of the Rev. James Frederick Schön and Mr. Samuel Crowther Who Accompanied the Expedition up the Niger in 1841* (London: Frank Cass, 1970), pp. 371-385.

Lienhard, Martin. *O Mare e o Mato: Histórias da Escravidão (Congo-Angola, Brasil, Caribe)* (Bahia: EDUFBA, 1998).

Liesegang, Gerhard. *Ngungunyane: A figura de Ngungunyane Nqumayo, Rei de Gaza 1884-1895 e o desaparecimento do seu Estado* Colecção Embondeiro Nº.8 (Maputo: ARPAC, 1986).

Lima, Vivaldo da Costa. "A família-de-santo nos Candomblés Jeje-Nagôs da Bahia: um estudo de relações intra-grupais," M. A. thesis, Universidade Federal da Bahia, 1977.

Lindsay, Lisa A. "To Return to the Bosom of their Fatherland: Brazilian Immigrants in Nineteenth-Century Lagos," *Slavery and Abolition* 15 (1994): 22-50.

Lobato, Alexandre. *Evolução Administrativa e Economica de Moçambique, 1752-1763* (Lisbon: Agência-Geral do Ultramar, 1957).

Lobato, Alexandre. *História do Presídio de Lourenço Marques, II (1737-1799)* (Lisbon: Junta de Investigações do Ultramar, 1960).

Long, Edward. *The History of Jamaica* 3 vols. (Frank Cass and Co., Ltd., 1970 [1774]).

Lopes, Edmundo Armenío Correia. *A escravatura (subsídios para a sua história)* (Lisbon: Agencia Geral das Colónias, 1944).

Lopes, Nei. *Bantos, Malês e Identidade Negra* (Rio de Janeiro: Forense Universitária, 1988).

Lourenço, Eunice. "III Cimeira da CPLP terminou ontem em Maputo" in *O Público* (Lisboa), 19 July, 2000, distributed electronically by António Teixeira to curry-lusoafrica@virginia.edu, 19 July, 2000.

Lovejoy, Paul E. (ed.) *Identity in the Shadow of Slavery* (London: Continuum, 2000).

Lovejoy, Paul E. "Methodology through the Ethnic Lens: The Study of Atlantic Africa," in Toyin Falola and Christian Jennings (eds.), *African Historical Research: Sources and Methods* (Rochester: University of Rochester Press, 2004), pp. 105-117.

Lovejoy, Paul E. "The Black Atlantic in the Development of the 'Western' World: Alternative Approaches to the 'Europeanization' of the Americas," in Dirk Hoerder (ed.), *Diversity in History: Transcultural Interactions from the Early Modern Mediterranean World to the Twentieth-Century Postcolonial World* (New York: Berghahn Books, 2003), pp. 109-133.

Lovejoy, Paul E. "Revisionist Interpretations of Ethnicity, Culture and Religion under Slavery," *Studies in the World history of Slavery, Abolition and Emancipation* II/1 (1997): 1-21 http://www2.h-net.msu.edu/~slavery/essays/esy9701love.html, 1/18/01.

Lovejoy, Paul E. "Background to Rebellion: The Origins of Muslim Slaves in Bahia," in Paul E. Lovejoy and Nicholas Rogers (eds.), *Unfree Labour in the Development of the Atlantic World* (London: Frank Cass, 1994), pp. 151-180.

Lovejoy, Paul E. "The Impact of the Atlantic Slave Trade on Africa: A Review of the Literature," *Journal of African History* 30 (1989): 365-394.

Lovejoy, Paul E. "The Volume of the Atlantic Slave Trade: A Synthesis," *Journal of African History* 23 (1982): 473-501.

Lovejoy Paul E., and Trotman David V. (eds.) *Trans-Atlantic Dimensions of Ethnicity in the African Diaspora* (London: Continuum Press, 2003).

Lovejoy, Paul E., and Richardson, David. "Letters of the Old Calabar Slave Trade, 1760-89," in Vincent Carretta and Philip Gould (eds.), *Genius in Bondage Literature of the Early Black Atlantic* (Louisville: University of Kentucky Press, 2000), pp. 89-115.

Lovejoy, Paul E., and Richardson, David. "Trust, Pawnship and Atlantic History: The Institutional Foundations of the Old Calabar Slave Trade," *American Historical Review* 104/2 (1999): 332-355.

Lupi, Eduardo do Couto. *Angoche* (Lisboa: Typographia do Annuario Commercial, 1907).

Lupi, João Eduardo Pinto Basto. *Moçambique, moçambiques: Itinerario de um povo afro-brasileiro* (Santa Maria: Edições UFSM, 1988).

MacCord, Marcelo. "O Rosário dos Homens Pretos de Santo Antônio: alianças e conflitos na história social do Recife, 1848-1872," M. A. thesis, Universidade Estadual de São Paulo, UNICAMP, 2001.

MacGaffey, Wyatt. *Kongo Political Culture: The Conceptual Challenge of the Particular* (Bloomington: Indiana University Press, 2000).

MacGaffey, Wyatt. *Art and Healing of the BaKongo commented by themselves* (Stockholm: Fokens Museum - Etnografiska, 1991).

MacGaffey, Wyatt. *Religion and Society in Central Africa: The BaKongo of Lower Zaire* (Chicago: University of Chicago Press, 1986).

MacGaffey, Wyatt. *Modern Kongo Prophets: Religion in a Plural Society* (Bloomington: Indiana University Press, 1983).

MacGaffey, Wyatt. *Custom and Government in the Lower Congo* (Berkeley: University of California Press, 1970).

MacGaffey, Wyatt. "Dialogues with the Deaf: Europeans on the Atlantic Coast of Africa," in Stuart Schwartz (ed.), *Implicit Understandings* (New York: Cambridge University Press, 1994), pp. 249-267.

MacGaffey, Wyatt. "Kimbanguism and the Question of Syncretism in Zaire," in Blakelely, van Beek, and Thomson, *Religion in Africa*, pp. 241-256.

MacGaffey, Wyatt. "Cultural Roots of Kongo Prophetism," *History of Religions* 17 (1977): 177-193.

MacGaffey, Wyatt. "Oral Tradition in Central Africa," *International Journal of African Historical Studies* 7/3 (1975): 417-426.

MacGaffey, Wyatt. "The West In Congolese Experience," in Philip D. Curtin (ed.), *Africa and the West: Intellectual Responses to Western Culture* (Madison: University of Wisconsin Press, 1972), pp. 49-74.

MacGaffey, Wyatt. "Kongo and the King of the Americans," *Journal of Modern African Studies* 6/2 (1968): 171-181.

MacLachlan, Colin M. "African Slave Trade and Economic Development in Amazonia, 1700-1800," in Robert B. Toplin (ed.), *Slavery and Race Relations in Latin America* (Westport: Greenwood Press, 1974), pp. 112-145.

Madan, A. C. *Kiungani* (London: George Bell and Sons, 1887).

Madiou, Thomas. *Histoire d'Haïti, tome 1* (Port-au-Prince: Deschamps, 1989 [1847]).

Maggie, Yvonne. "Introdução: cor, hierarquia e sistema de classificação," in *Catálogo: Centenário da Abolição* (Rio de Janeiro: CIEC/Núcleo da Cor/UFRJ, 1989): 1-29.

Mamigonian, Beatriz Galloti. "Do que 'o preto mina' é capaz: Etnia e resistência entre Africanos livres," *Afro-Ásia* 24 (2000): 71-95.

Mann, Kristin, and Edna G. Bay. (eds.) *Rethinking the African Diaspora: The Making of a Black Atlantic World in the Bight of Benin and Brazil* (London: Frank Cass, 2001).

Maret, Pierre de. "Archeological and Other Prehistoric Evidence of Traditional African Religious Expression," Blakeley, van Beek, and Thomson, *Religion in Africa*, pp. 183-195.

Marinho, Joaquim Pereira. *Memória de Combinações sobre as ordens de Sua Magestade a Senhora D. Maria II. Passados pelo Ministerio da Marinha e Ultramar, por diferentes Ministros da mesma repartição ao Brigadeiro Pereira Marinho como Governador Geral de Moçambique* (Lisbon: Typographia de Gouveia, 1842).

Marks, Morton. "Uncovering Ritual Structures in Afro-American Music," in Irving I. Zaretsky and Mark P. Leone (eds.), *Religious Movements in Contemporary America* (Princeton: Princeton University Press, 1974), pp. 60-134.

Mathias, Herculano Gomes. *Autos da Devassa da Inconfidência Mineira: Complementação Documental (Belo Horizonte: Editora UFMG, 2002).*

Matory, J. Lorand. *Sex and the Empire that is No More: Gender and the Politics of Metaphor in Ọ̀yọ́ Yoruba Religion* (Minneapolis: University of Minnesota Press, 1994).

Matory, J. Lorand. "The English Professors of Brazil: On the Diasporic Roots of the Yorùbá Nation," *Comparative Studies in Society and History* 41/1 (1999): 72-103.

Mattoso, Katia M. de Queirós. *Bahia século xix: Uma província do império* trans. Yedda de Macedo Soares (Rio de Janeiro: Editora Nova Fronteira, 1992).

Mattoso, Kátia M. de Queirós. *Être esclave au Brésil, XVIe-XIXe siècle* (Paris: Hachette, 1979).

Mattoso, Kátia M. de Queirós. *Bahia: a cidade do Salvador e seu mercado no século XIX* (São Paulo: HUCITEC, 1978).

Maupoil, Bernard. *La Géomancie a l'Ancienne Côte des Esclaves* (Paris: Institut d'Ethnologie, 1988 [1946]).

Mauro, Frédéric. *Le Portugal, le Brésil, et l'Atlantique au XVII Siècle (1570-1670)* (Paris: Fondation Calouste Gulbenkian / Centre Culturel Portugais, 1983).

Maxwell, Kenneth. *A Devassa da Devassa: A Inconfidência Mineira, 1750-1808* (Rio de Janeiro: Paz e Terra, 1985).

McAlister, Elizabeth. *Rara! Vodou, Power and Performance in Haiti and Its Diaspora* (Berkeley: University of California Press, 2002).

McAlister, Elizabeth. "Love, Sex, and Gender Embodied: The Spirits of Haitian Vodou," in Joseph Runzo and Nancy M. Martin (eds.), *Love, Sex and Gender in the World Religions* (Oxford: One World, 2000), pp. 129-145.

McAlister, Elizabeth. "A Sorcerer's Bottle: The Visual Art of Magic in Haiti," in Donald J. Cosentino (ed.), *Sacred Arts of Haitian Vodou* (Los Angeles: UCLA Fowler Museum of Cultural History, 1995), pp. 305-321.

McCusker, John J. *Rum and the American Revolution: The Rum Trade and the Balance of Payments of the Thirteen Continental Colonies, 1650-1775* (New York: Arno Press, 1989).

McDaniel, Lorna. *The Big Drum Ritual of Carriacou* (Gainesville: University of Florida Press, 1998).

McDougall, E. Ann. "Salt, Saharans and the trans-Saharan slave trade: Nineteenth-century developments," *Slavery and Abolition* 13/1 (1992): 61-80.

McDougall, E. Ann. "Salts of the Western Sahara: Myths, Mysteries and Historical Significance," *International Journal of African Historical Studies* 23/2 (1990): 231-257.

McFarlane, Anthony. "Cimarrones and Palenques: Runaways and Resistance in Colonial Colombia," *Slavery and Abolition* 6/3 (1985): 131-151.

Mckenzie, P. R. "O culto aos òrisà entre os yoruba: algumas notas marginais relativas a sua cosmologia e seus conceitos de divindade," in C. E. M. de Moura (ed.), *Candomblé, Desvendando Identidades* (São Paulo: EMW Editores, 1987), pp. 129-148.

Medeiros, Eduardo. "The 'Mozambiqueanisation' of Slaves Embarking at Mozambiquean Ports," *Portuguese Studies Review* 12/2 (2004, forthcoming).

Medeiros, Eduardo. "Moçambicanização dos escravos saídos pelos portos de Moçambique," Unpublished paper presented at the conference Enslaving Connections: Africa and Brazil during the Age of the Slave Trade, York University, Toronto, 12-15 October 2000.

Meek, C. K. *The Northern Tribes of Nigeria* 2 vols. (London: Frank Cass, 1971 [1921]).

Megenney, William W. *A Bahian Heritage: An Ethnolinguistic Study of African Influences on Bahian Portuguese* (Chapel Hill: North Carolina Studies in the Romance Languages and Linguistics, 1978).

"Memorias dos feitos que se deram durante os primeiros annos da guerra com os negros quilombolas dos Palmares, seu destroço e paz aceita em Junho de 1678," *Revista do Instituto Histórico e Geográfico Brasileiro* 39/1 (1876): 293-321, reproduced in Robert Conrad (ed.), *Children of God's Fire: A Documentary History of Black Slavery in Brazil* (Princeton: Princeton University Press, 1983), pp. 369-377.

Mendonça, Joseli Maria Nunes. *Entre a mão e os anéis* (Campinas: Ed. da UNICAMP/ CECULT, 1999).

Mendoça, Renato. *A Influência Africana no Português do Brasil* 3rd ed. (Porto: Livraria Figueirinhas, 1948).

Mello, José Antonio Gonçalves de. "Aditamentos e correções," in F. A. Pereira da Costa (ed.), *Anais Pernambucanos* 10 vols. (Recife: Fundarpe, 1983-1985).

Merlo, Christian. "Hiérarchie fétichiste de Ouidah," *Bulletin de l'IFAN* 2/1-2 (1940): 1-84.

Métraux, Alfred. *Voodoo in Haiti* (New York: Schocken Books, 1972 [1959]).

Mettas, Jean. *Répertoire des Expéditions Nègriers Françaises au XVIIIe Siècle* 2 vols. (Paris, Société française d'histoire d'outre-mer, 1978-84).

Mettas, Jean. "La traite Portugaise en Haute-Guinée, 1758-1797," *Journal of African History* 16 (1975): 343-363.

Miller, Joseph C. *Way of Death: Merchant Capitalism and the Angolan Slave Trade, 1730-1830* (Madison: University of Wisconsin Press, 1988).

Miller, Joseph C. *Kings and Kinsmen: Early Mbundu States in Angola* (Oxford: Clarendon, 1976).

Miller, Joseph C. "Retention, Reinvention, and Remembering: Restoring Identities Through Enslavement in Africa and Under Slavery in Brazil," in Curto and Lovejoy, *Enslaving Connections*, pp. 81-121.

Miller, Joseph C. "Central Africa During the Era of the Slave Trade, c. 1490s-1850s," in Heywood, *Central Africans and Cultural Transformations*, pp. 21-69.

Miller, Joseph C. "The Numbers, Destinations and Origins of Slaves in the Eighteenth-Century Angolan Slave Trade," in Joseph E. Inikori and Stanley L. Engerman (eds.), *The Atlantic Slave Trade: Effects on Economies, Societies and Peoples in Africa, the Americas, and Europe* (Durham, NC: Duke University Press. 1992), pp. 78-89.

Miller, Joseph C. "Introduction," in Joseph C. Miller (ed.), *The African Past Speaks* (Hamden, Conn.: Archon Books, 1980), pp. 1-59.

Miller, Joseph C. "Legal Portuguese Slave Trading from Angola: Some Preliminary Indications of Volume and Direction," *Revue française d'histoire d'outre-mer* 62 (1975): 135-176.

Mills, Kenneth, and Taylor, William B. *Spanish America, A Documentary History* (Wilmington, DE: Scholarly Resources Press, 1998).

Mintz, Sidney W. "Africa of Latin America: An Unguarded Reflection," in Manuel Moreno Fraginals (ed.), *Africa in Latin America: Essays on History, Culture, and Socialization* trans. Leonor Blum (New York: Holmes & Meier Publishers, Inc., 1984), pp. 286-305.

Mintz, Sidney W., and Price, Richard. *An Anthropological Approach to the Afro-American Past: A Caribbean Perspective* (Philadelphia: ISHI, 1976).

Mintz, Sidney W., and Price, Richard. *The Birth of African-American Culture: An Anthropological Perspective* (Boston: Beacon Press, 1992 ["An Anthropological Approach to the Afro-American Past: A Caribbean Perspective," *ISHI Occasional Papers in Social Change* 2 (1976)]).

Mintz, Sidney W., and Trouillot, Michel-Rolph. "The Social Character of Haitian Vodou," in Donald J. Cosentino (ed.), *Sacred Arts of Haitian Vodou* (Hong Kong: South Sea Press, 1995), pp. 123-147.

Monroy, Padre Joel. *Los religiosos de la Merced en el Antiguo Reino de Quito* 2 vols. (Quito: Editorial Labor, 1943).

Montaury, João Baptista de. "Moçambique, Ilhas Querimba, Rios de Sena, Vila de Tete, Vila de Zumbo, Manica, Vila de Luabo, Inhambane, c. 1778," in António Alberto Banha de Andrade (ed.), *Relações de Moçambique Setecentista* (Lisbon: Agência-Geral do Ultramar, 1955), pp. 339-373.

Montejo, Esteban. *The Autobiography of a Runaway Slave* (New York: Vintage Books, 1973 [1968]).

Moore, Brian L. *Cultural Power, Resistance and Pluralism: Colonial Guyana 1838-1900* (Jamaica: University of the West Indies Press, 1995).

Morgan, Philip. "The Cultural Implications of the Atlantic Slave Trade: African Regional Origins, American Destinations and New World Developments," *Slavery and Abolition* 18/1 (1997): 122-145.

Moses, Wilson Jeremiah. *Afrotopia: The Roots of African American Popular History* (New York: Cambridge University Press, 1998).

Moses, Wilson Jeremiah. *Classical Black Nationalism* (New York: New York University Press, 1996).

Mott, Luiz. "Acotundá - raízes setecentistas do sincretismo religioso afro-brasileiro," *Revista do Museu Paulista* New Series 3 (1986): 124-147.

Mouléro, Thomas. "Histoire et légendes des Djêkens," in *Études Dahoméennes* New Series 3 (1964): 51-76.

Moura, Clovis. *Rebeliões da Senzala: Quilombos-Insurreições-Guerrilhas* (Rio de Janeiro: Conquista, 1972).

Mulvey, Patricia. "The Black Lay Brotherhoods of Colonial Brazil: A History," Ph. D. dissertation, City College of New York, 1976.

Munford, Clarence J. *The Black Ordeal of Slavery and Slave Trading in the French West Indies, 1625-1715* (Lewiston: Edward Mellen Press, 1991).

Newitt, M.D.D. *Portuguese Settlement on the Zambesi* (London: Longman, 1973).

Niehoff, Arthur and Juanita. *East Indians in the West Indies* (Milwaukee: Olsen Publishing Company, 1960).

Nishida, Mieko. "From Ethnicity to Race and Gender: Transformations of Black Lay Sodalities in Salvador, Brazil," *Journal of Social History* Winter 1998: 329-348.

Northrup, David. "Igbo and Myth Igbo: Culture and Ethnicity in the Atlantic World, 1600-1850," *Slavery and Abolition* 21/3 (2000): 1-20.

Norton, Manuel Artur. *D. Pedro Miguel Almeida Portugal* (Lisbon: Agência-Geral do Ultramar, 1967).

Oldendorp, C. G. A. *History of the Mission of the Evangelical Brethren on the Caribbean Islands of St. Thomas, St. Croix, and St. John* Johann Jakob Bossar (ed.) (Ann Arbor: Karoma Publishers, 1987 [1877]).

Orlando Patterson, *Sociology of Slavery* (Rutherford, NJ: Fairleigh Dickinson University, 1969).

Osgood, Joseph B. F. *Notes of Travel or Recollections of Majunga, Zanzibar, Muscat, Aden, Mocha, and other Eastern Ports* (Salem: G. Creamer, 1854).

Orser, Jr., Charles E. "Toward a Global Historical Archaeology: An Example from Brazil," *Historical Archaeology* 28 (1994): 5-22.

Orser, Jr., Charles E. *In Search of Zumbi: Preliminary Archaeological Research in the Serra da Barriga, State of Alagoas, Brazil* (Normal, IL: Midwestern Archaeological Research Center, 1992).

Ott, Carlos. "O Negro Bahiano," in *Les Afro-Américains* (Mémoire de l'Institut Français d'Afrique Noire, No. 27 (Dakar: IFAN, 1952), pp. 141-153.

Palmer, Colin A. *Slaves of the White Gods: Blacks in Mexico, 1570-1650* (Harvard University Press, Cambridge: 1976).

Pantoja, Selma, and Saraiva, José Flávio Sombra. (eds.) *Angola e Brasil nas Rotas do Atlântico Sul* (Rio de Janeiro: Bertrand Brasil, 1999).

Parés, Luis Nicolau. *Do Lado do Jeje: História e Ritual do Vodun na Bahia* (Rio de Janeiro: Pallas, forthcoming 2005).

Parés, Luis Nicolau. "The phenomenology of spirit possession in the Tambor de Mina: An ethnographic and audiovisual study," Ph. D. dissertation, School of Oriental and African Studies (London), 1997.

Parish, John, and Robertson, William Parish. *Letters on Paraguay: Comprising an Account of a Four Years's Residence in that Republic under the Government of the Dictator Francia* (London: J. Murray, 1838).

Parsons, Talcott. "Introduction," in Max Weber, *The Sociology of Religion* (Boston: Beacon, 1963 [1922]), pp. xix-lxvii.

Pazzi, Roberto. "Aperçu sur l'implantation actuelle et les migrations anciennes des peuples de l'aire culturelle Aja-Tado," in François de Medeiros (ed.), *Peuples du Golfe du Bénin (Aja-Ewé)* (Paris: Éditions Karthala, 1984), pp. 10-19.

Pazzi, Roberto. *Introduction à l'histoire de l'aïre culturelle ajatado* (Lomé: Université du Benin, Institut National des Sciences Humaines, 1979).

Peel, John. "A comparative Analysis of Ogun in Precolonial Yorubaland," in Barnes, *Africa's Ogun*, pp. 263-289.

Peel, J. D. Y. *Religious Encounter and the Making of the Yoruba* (Bloomington: Indiana University Press, 2000).

Peel, J. D. Y. "For Who Hath Despised The Day of Small Things? Missionary Narratives And Historical Anthropology," *Comparative Studies in Society and History* 37/3 (1995): 581-607.

Perani, Judith, and Smith, Fred. *The Visual Arts of Africa* (Upper Saddle River, NJ: Prentice-Hall, 1998).

Perdue, Charles L., and Phillips, Robert K. (eds.) *Weevils in the Wheat* (Charlottesville: University of Virginia Press, 1997 [1976]).

Peytraud, L. *L'esclavage aux Antilles françaises avant 1789, d'après des documents inédits des archives coloniales* (Paris: Hachette et cie, 1897).

Piersen, William D. *Black Legacy: America's Hidden Heritage* (Amherst, MA: University of Massachusetts Press, 1993).

Piersen, William D. "White Cannibals, Black Martyrs: Fear, Depression, and Religious Faith as Causes of Suicide Among New Slaves," *Journal of Negro History* 62/2 (1977): 147-159.

Pitts, Walter F. *The Old Ship of Zion: The Afro-Baptist Ritual in the African Diaspora* (New York: Oxford University Press, 1993).

Planson, Claude. *Un initié parle* (Paris: Dulles, 1978).

Postma, Johannes. *The Dutch in the Atlantic Slave Trade: 1600-1815* (New York: Cambridge University Press, 1990).

Prado, J. F. de Almeida. "Les Relations de Bahia (Brésil) avec le Dahomey," *Revue d'Histoire des Colonies* 16 (1954): 167-226.

Prata, P. *Dicionário Português-Macua* (Cucujães: Edição da Sociedade Missionária Portuguesa [1986]).

Price, Richard. *Maroon Societies: Rebel Slave Communities in the Americas* (Baltimore: Johns Hopkins University Press, 1996).

Price, Richard. *Alabi's World* (Baltimore: Johns Hopkins University Press, 1990).

Price, Richard. *First Time: The Historical Vision of an Afro-American People* (Baltimore: Johns Hopkins University Press, 1983).

Price-Mars, Jean. "Lemba-Pétro: un culte secret, son histoire, sa localisation géographique, son symbolisme," *Revue de la Societé d'Histoire et de Géographie d'Haïti* 9/28 (1938): 12-31.

Puckett, Newbell Niles. *Folk Beliefs of the Southern Negro* (New York: Dover Publications, 1969).

Querino, Manoel. *Costumes Africanos no Brasil* (Recife: Fundação Joaquim Nabuco, Editora Massangana, 1988 [1938]).

Querino, Manoel. *A raça africana e seus costumes* (Salvador: Progresso, 1955).

Raboteau, Albert. *Slave Religion* (New York: Oxford University Press, 1978).

Ralston, Richard D. "The Return of Brazilian Freedmen to West Africa in the 18th and 19th Centuries," *Canadian Journal of African Studies* 3/3 (1969): 577-592.

Ramos, Artur *As Culturas Negras no Novo Mundo* (São Paulo: Ed. Nacional-INL-MEC, 1979 [1937]).

Ramos, Artur. *The Negro in Brazil* trans. Richard Pattee (Washington, DC: The Associated Publishers, Inc., 1951).

Ramos, Miguel "Willie". "Afro-Cuban Orisha Worship," in Lindsay, *Santeria Aesthetics in Contemporary Latin American Art*, pp. 51-76.

Raposo, Luciano. *Marcas de Escravos – Listas de escravos emancipados vindos a bordo de navios negreiros (1839-1841)* (Rio de Janeiro: Arquivo Nacional, Publicações Históricas 90, 1989/1990).

Rattray, Captain R. S. *Ashanti* (New York: Negro Universities Press, 1969 [1923]).

Rebelo, Manuel dos Anjos da Silva. *Relações entre Angola e Brasil (1808-1830)* (Lisbon: Agencia Geral do Ultramar, 1970).

"Relação das guerras feitas aos Palmares de Pernambuco no tempo do governador D. Pedro de Almeida, de 1675 a 1678," in Edison Carneiro, *O Quilombo dos Palmares* 4th ed. (São Paulo: Cia. Editora Nacional, 1988), pp. 201-222.

"Relación de la misión á que fué enviado el P. Juan Laurencio, acompañando a una escuadra de soldados que salía á la reducción de negros foragidos y salteadores," in Andrés Pérez de Ribes, *Crónica y historia religiosa de la Provincia de la Compañía de Jesús de México en Nueva España* 2 vols. (Mexico: Impr. Del Sagrado corazon de Jesús, 1896), I, 282-294.

Ribeiro, Joaquim António. *Memoria* (Lisbon: Typographia Patriotica, 1822).

Reis, João José. *Slave Rebellion in Brazil: The Muslim Uprising of 1835 in Bahia* trans. Arthur Brakel (Baltimore: Johns Hopkins Press, 1993).

Reis, João José. "Identidade e Diversidade Étnicas nas Irmandades Negras no Tempo da Escravidão," *Tempo* 2/3 (1997): 7-33.

Reis, João José. "'The Revolution of the *Ganhadores*': Urban Labour, Ethnicity and the African Strike of 1857 in Bahia, Brazil," *Journal of Latin American Studies* 29 (1997): 355-393.

Reis, João José. "Quilombos e revoltas escravas no Brasil," *Revista USP* 28 (1995-1996): 14-39.

Reis, João José. "Nas Malhas do Poder Escravista: A Invasão do Candomblé do Accú," in João José Reis and Eduardo Silva (eds.), *Negociação e Conflito. A resistência negra no Brasil escravista* (São Paulo: Companhia das Letras, 1989), pp. 32-61.

Reis, Meire Lúcia dos. "A cor da notícia: discursos sobre o negro na imprensa baiana," M. A. thesis, Universidade Federal da Bahia, 2000.

Rey, Terry. "A Consideration of Kongolese Catholic Influences on Haitian Popular Catholicism: A Sociohistorical Exploration," in Heywood, *Central Africans and Cultural Transformations*, pp. 265-285.

Rey, Terry. "The Virgin Mary and Revolution in Saint-Domingue: The Charisma of Romaine-la-Prophétesse," *Journal of Historical Sociology* 11 (1998): 341-369.

Reynier, "Eléments sur la reorganisation du commandement indigène à Ouidah (1917)," *Mémoire du Bénin*(matériaux d'histoire) 2 (1993): 29-73.

Richardson, David. "Slave Exports From West and West-Central Africa, 1700-1810: New Estimates of Volume and Distribution," *Journal of African History* 30 (1989): 1-22.

Richardson, David. "The Eighteenth-Century British Slave Trade: Estimates of its Volume and Coastal Distribution in Africa," *Research in Economic History* 12 (1989): 151-195.

Roback, Judith. "The White-Robed Army: Cultural Nationalism and a Religious Movement in Guyana," Ph. D. dissertation, McGill University, 1973.

Roback, Judith. "The White-Robed Army: An Afro-Guyanese Religious Movement," *Anthropologica* New Series 16/2 (1974): 233-268.

Robertson, Claire. "Africa into the Americas? Slavery and Women, the Family, and the Gender Division of Labor," in David Barry Gaspar and Darlene Clark Hine (eds.), *More Than Chattel: Black Women and Slavery in the Americas* (Bloomington: Indiana University Press, 1996), pp. 3-40.

Rocha, Aurélio. "Contribuição para o estudo das relações entre Moçambique e Brasil no séc. XIX (Tráfico de escravos e relações políticas e culturais)," *Estudos Afro-Asiáticos* 21 (1991): 200-204.

Rodrigues, José Honório. *Brasil e África: Outro Horizonte* (Rio de Janeiro: Civilização Brasileira, 1961).

Rodrigues, José H. "The Influence of Africa on Brazil and of Brazil on Africa," *Journal of African History* 3 (1962): 49-67.

Rodrigues, Raymundo Nina. *Os Africanos no Brasil* (São Paulo: Companhia Editora Nacional, 1977 [1906]).

Rodrigues, Raymundo Nina. *O animismo fetichista dos negros bahianos* (Rio de Janeiro: Civilização Brasileira, 1935 [1896-1897]).

Rosenthal, Judy. *Possession, Ecstasy, & Law in Ewe Voodoo* (Charlottesville: University of Virginia Press, 1998).

Ross, David A. "The Career of Domingo Martinez in the Bight of Benin 1833-64," *Journal of African History* 6 (1965): 79-90.

Ross, David. "The First Chacha of Whydah: Francisco Felix de Souza," *Odu* New Series 2 (1969): 19-28.

Rugendas, João Mauricio. *Viagem Pitoresca Através do Brasil* (Rio de Janeiro/São Paulo/Brasília: A Casa do Livro, 1972 [1835]).

Russell-Wood, A.J.R. *Fidalgos and Philanthropists: The Santa Casa da Misericórdia of Bahia, 1550-1755* (Berkeley: University of California Press, 1968).

Russell-Wood, A. J. R. "Ambivalent Authorities: The African and Afro-Brazilian Contribution to Local Governance in Colonial Brazil," *The Americas* 57/1 (2000): 13-36.

Rush, Dana. "Afro-Brazilian and Afro-Portuguese Arts and Cultures along Coastal Benin," Unpublished paper presented at the symposium on Rethinking the African Diaspora:

The Making of a Black Atlantic World in the Bight of Benin and Brazil, Emory University, Atlanta, April 1998.

Saint-Mery, M.E.L. *Déscription topographique, physique, civil, et historique de la partie française de l'isle de Saint-Domingue* 3 vols. (Paris: Societé de l'histoire des colonies française, 1959 [1797]).

Salles, Fritz Teixeira. *Associações religiosas no ciclo do ouro* (Belo Horizonte: Universidade Federal de Minas Gerais, 1963).

Sanderson, G. Meredith. *A Dictionary of the Yao Language* (Zomba: The Government Printer, 1954).

Santana, Francisco José Gingeira. *Documentação Avulsa Moçambicana do Arquivo Histórico Ultramarino* 3 Vols. (Lisbon: Centro de Estudos Históricos Ultramarinos, 1960).

Santos, Corcino M. dos. *O Rio de Janeiro e a Conjuntura Atlântica* (Rio de Janeiro: Expressão e Cultura, 1993).

Santos, Corcino M. dos. *Relações Comerciais do Rio de Janeiro com Lisboa (1763-1808)* (Rio de Janeiro: Tempo Brasileiro, 1980).

Santos, Corcino M. dos. "Relações de Angola com o Rio de Janeiro (1736-1808)," *Estudos Históricos* 12 (1973): 7-68.

Santos, Jocélio Teles dos. *O dono da terra (o caboclo nos candomblés da Bahia)* (Salvador: Editora Sarah Letras, 1995).

Sanvi (da Matha), Anne-Marie C. "Les Métis et les Brésiliens dans la Colonie du Dahomey," M. A. thesis, Université Nationale du Bénin, 1977.

Saugera, Eric. "Pour une histoire de la traite française sous le Consulat et l'Empire," *Revue française d'histoire d'outre-mer* 56 (1989): 203-229.

Savoia, P. Rafael. "El negro Alonso de Illescas y sus descendientes (entre 1553-1867)," in P. Rafael Savoia (ed.), *Actas del primer congreso de historia del negro en el Ecuador y el sur de Colombia* (Quito: Centro Cultural Afro-ecuatoriano, 1988), pp. 29-61.

Scelle, Georges. "The Slave Trade in the Spanish Colonies of America: The Asiento," *American Journal of International Law* 4 (1910): 614-661.

Schlichthorst, C. *O Rio de Janeiro como é 1824-1826 (Huma vez e nunca mais)* (Rio de Janeiro: Editora Getulio Costa, 1943).

Schmidt, Leigh E. "Time, Celebration and the Christian Year," in Mark A. Noll, et al (eds.), *Evangelicalism* (New York: Oxford Unversity Press, 1994), pp. 90-112.

Schneider, John T. *Dictionary of African Borrowings in Brazilian Portuguese* (Hamburg: Helmut Buske Verlag, 1991).

Schoenbrun, David Lee. *A Green Place, A Good Place: Agrarian Change, Gender, and Social Identity in the Great Lakes Region to the 15th century* (Portsmouth, NH: Heinemann, 1998).

Schuler, Monica. *"Alas, Alas, Kongo": A Social History of Indentured African Immigration into Jamaica, 1841-1865* (Baltimore: The Johns Hopkins University Press, 1980).

Schuler, Monica. "Liberated Central Africans in 19th Century Guyana," in Heywood, *Central Africans and Cultural Transformations*, pp. 319-352.

Schuler, Monica. "Liberated Africans in Nineteenth-Century Guyana," in Brian L. Moore, et al., (eds.), *Slavery, Freedom and Gender: The Dynamics of Caribbean Society* (Kingston, Jamaica: University of the West Indies Press, 2001), pp. 133-157.

Schuler, Monica. "Kru Emigration to British and French Guiana, 1838-1870," in Paul E. Lovejoy (ed.), *Africans in Bondage: Studies in Slavery and the Slave Trade* (Madison: University of Wisconsin, 1986), pp. 155-201.

Schuler, Monica. "The Recruitment of African Indentured Labourers for European Colonies in the Nineteenth Century," in P. C. Emmer (ed.), *Colonialism and Migration: Indentured Labour before and after Slavery* (Dordrecht: Martinus Nijhoff Publishers, 1986), pp. 125-161.

Schuler, Monica. "Myalism and the African Religious Tradition in Jamaica," in Margaret E. Crahan and Franklin W. Knight (eds.), *Africa and the Caribbean: The Legacies of A Link* (Baltimore: Johns Hopkins University Press, 1979), pp. 65-79.

Schuyler, George Samuel. *Black Empire* Robert A. Hill and R. Kent Rasmussen (eds.) (Boston: Northeastern University Press, 1991).

Schwarcz, Lilia Moritz. *O espetáculo das raças* (São Paulo: Companhia das Letras, 1993).

Schwarcz, Lilia Moritz. *Retrato em branco e negro: Jornais, escravos e cidadãos em São Paulo no final do século xix* (São Paulo: Companhia das Letras, 1987).

Schwartz, Stuart. *Slaves Peasants and Rebels: Reconsidering Brazilian Slavery* (Urbana: University of Illinois Press, 1992).

Scisínio, Alaôr Eduardo. *Dicionário da Escravidão* (Rio de Janeiro: Léo Christiano Editorial Ltda., 1997).

Scott, David Clement. *A Cyclopaedic Dictionary of the Mang'anja Language spoken in British Central Africa* (Farnsborough: Gregg International Publishers Limited, 1968 [1892]).

Segal, Daniel A. "'Western Civ' and the Staging of History in American Higher Education," *American Historical Review* 105/3 (2000): 770-805.

Segurola, R. P. B. *Dictionnaire Fon-Français* 2 vols. (Cotonou: Procure de l'Archidiocèse, 1963).

Seidler, Carlos. *Dez Anos de Brasil* (São Paulo: Livraria Martins, 1941).

Shaw, Rosalind. Memories *of the Slave Trade: Ritual and the Historical Imagination in Sierra Leone* (Chicago: University of Chicago Press, 2002).

Shaw, Rosalind. "The Production of Witchcraft/Witchcraft as Production: Memory, Modernity and the Slave Trade in Sierra Leone," *American Ethnologist* 24/4 (1997): 856-876.

Shaw, Rosalind. "Splitting Truths from Darkness: Epistemological Aspects of Temne Divination," in Peek, *African Divination Systems*, pp. 137-152.

Silva, Alberto da Costa e. "Os Estudos de História de África e sua importância para o Brasil," in *A dimensão atlântica da África: II Reunião Internacional de História de África* (São Paulo: CEA-USP/SDG-Marinha/CAPES, 1997), pp. 13-20.

Silva, Luiz Geraldo. "'Sementes da Sedição': Etnia, Revolta Escrava e Controle Social na América Portuguesa (1808-1817)," *Afro-Ásia* 25-26 (2001): 9-60.

Silva, Marilene Rosa Nogueira da. *Negro na rua: A nova face da escravidão* (São Paulo: Editora Hucitec, 1988).

Silva Rebelo, Manuel dos Anjos da. *Relações entre Angola e Brasil, 1808-1830* (Lisbon: Agência-Geral do Ultramar, 1970).

Simpson, George Eaton. *Black Religions in the New World* (New York: Columbia University Press, 1978).

Simpson, George Eaton. "The Ras Tafari Movement: Political Cultism in West Kingston, Jamaica," in George Eaton Simpson (ed.), *Religious Cults of the Caribbean: Trinidad. Jamaica and Haiti* 3rd ed. (Rio Pedras, Puerto Rico: Institute of Caribbean Studies, University of Puerto Rico, 1980), pp. 208-223.

Simpson, George Eaton. 'The Shango Cult in Trinidad," in Simpson, *Religious Cults of the Caribbean*, pp. 11-111.

Simpson, George Eaton, and Moore, Joseph G. "A Comparative Study of Acculturation in Morant Bay and West Kingston, Jamaica," *Zaïre* 11 (1957): 979-1019.

Sinou, Alain. (ed.) *Ouidah et son patrimoine* (Paris: ORSTOM/PUB, 1991), p. 249.

Skinner, Elliott P. "Ethnic Interaction in a British Guiana Rural Community: A Study in Secondary Acculturation and Group Dynamics," Ph. D. dissertation, Columbia University, 1955.

Slenes, Robert W. "Malungu, Ngoma's Coming!" Africa Hidden and Discovered in Brazil," in Nelson Aguilar (ed.), *Mostra de redescobrimento: Negro de Corpo e Alma, Black in Body and Soul* (São Paulo: Associação Brasil 500 Anos Artes Visuais, 2000), pp. 221-229.

Smith, E. Valerie. "The Sisterhood of Nossa Senhora da Boa Morte and the Brotherhood of Nossa Senhora do Rosário: African Brazilian Cultural Adaptations to Antebellum Restrictions," *Afro-Hispanic Review* 11/1-3 (1992): 58-69.

Smith, M. G., Augier, Roy, and Nettleford, Rex. *Report on the Rastafari Movement in Kingston, Jamaica* (Kingston: Institute of Social and Economic Research, U. W. I., 1968 [1960]).

Smith, Robert S. *The Lagos Consulate: 1851-1861* (London: The Macmillan Press, 1978).

Snelgrave, William. *A New Account of Some Parts of Guinea and the Slave Trade* (London: Frank Cass & Co. Ltd., 1971 [1734]).

Soares, Carlos Eugênio Líbano. *Zungú: rumor de muitas vozes* (Rio de Janeiro: Arquivo Público do Estado, 1998).

Soares, Carlos Eugênio Libano Soares, and Gomes, Flávio. "Sedições, *Haitianismo* e conexões no Brasil: Outras margens do Atlântico Negro," *Novos Estudos CEBRAP* 63 (2002): 131-144.

Soares, Mariza de Carvalho. *Devotos da cor: Identidade étnica, religiosidade e escravidão no Rio de Janeiro, século XVIII* (Rio de Janeiro: Civilização Brasileira, 2000).

Soares, Mariza de Carvalho. "Descobrindo a Guiné no Brasil Colonial," *Revista do Instituto Histórico e Geográfico Brasileiro* 161/407 (2002): 71-94.

Sobel, Mechal. *Teach Me Dreams: The Search for Self in the Revolutionary Era* (New York: Oxford University Press, 2000).

Sobel, Mechal. *Trabelin' On* (Princeton, N. J.: Princeton University Press, 1988 [1979]).

Soulodre-La France, Renée, and Lovejoy, Paul E. "Intercambios transatlánticos, sociedad esclavista e inquisición en la Cartagena del siglo XVII," in Claudia Mosquera, Mauricio Pardo and Odile Hoffmann (eds.), *Afrodescendientes en las Américas. Trayectorias sociales e identitarias. 150 años de la abolición de la esclavitud en Colombia* (Bogotá: Universidad Nacional de Colombia, ICANH, IRD, ILSA, 2002), pp. 195-211.

Soumonni, Elisée. "Afro-Brazilian Communities of the Bight of Benin in the Nineteenth Century," in Paul E. Lovejoy and David V. Trotman (eds.), *Trans-Atlantic Dimensions of Ethnicity in the African Diaspora* (London: Continuum, 2003), pp. 181-194.

Soumonni, Elisée. "Some Reflections on the Brazilian Legacy in Dahomey," *Slavery and Abolition* 22 (2001): 61-71 [Special Issue*Rethinking the African Diaspora: The Making of a Black Atlantic World in the Bight of Benin and Brazil*, Kristin Mann and Edna G. Bay (eds.)].

Soumonni, Elisée. "The compatibility of the slave and palm oil trades in Dahomey, 1818-1859," in Robin Law (ed.), *From Slave Trade to 'Legitimate' Commerce: The Commercial Transition in Nineteenth Century West Africa* (Cambridge: Cambridge University Press, 1995), pp. 78-92.

Souza, Norberto Francisco de. "Contribution a l'histoire de la famille de Souza," *Études Dahoméennes* 15 (1955): 17-21.

Sowell, Thomas. *Conquests and Cultures: An International History* (New York: Basic Books, 1998).

Sparks, Randy J. *The Two Princes of Calabar: An Eighteenth-Century Atlantic Odyssey* (Cambridge, Mass.: Harvard University Press, 2004).

Spieth, Jacob. *Die Religion der Eweer in Süd-Togo* (Leipzig: Dieterich'sche, 1911).

Strickrodt, Silke. "Afro-Brazilians of the Western Slave Coast in the Nineteenth Century," in Curto and Lovejoy, *Enslaving Connections*, pp. 215-247.

Sweet, James H. *Recreating Africa: Culture, Kinship and Religion in the African-Portuguese World, 1441-1770* (Chapel Hill: University of North Carolina Press, 2003).

Sweet, James H. "Male Homosexuality and Spiritism in the African Diaspora: The Legacies of a Link," *Journal of the History of Sexuality* 7 (1996): 184-202.

Taylor, William B. "The Foundation of Nuestra Señora de Guadalupe de los Morenos de Amapa," *The Americas* 26 (1970): 439-446.

The Americas 57/2 (2000) [Special Issue *The African Experience in Early Spanish America*, Matthew Restall and Jane Landers (eds.)].

Thompson, Robert Farris. *Face of the Gods: Art and Altars of Africa and the African Americas* (Prestel, Munich and New York: The Museum for African Art, 1993).

Thompson, Robert Farris. *Flash of the Spirit: African and Afro-American Art and Philosophy* (New York: Random House, 1983).

Thompson, Robert Farris. "Kongo Influences on African-American Culture," in Joseph E. Holloway (ed.), *Africanisms in American Culture* (Bloomington: Indiana University Press, 1990), pp. 148-184.

Thompson, Robert Farris, and Cornet, Joseph. *The Four Moments of the Sun: Kongo Art in Two Worlds* (Washington, D.C.: National Gallery of Art, 1981).

Thornton, John K. *Warfare in Atlantic Africa, 1500-1800* (London: University College London Press, 1999).

Thornton, John K. *Africa and Africans in the Making of the Atlantic World, 1400-1800* (Cambridge: Cambridge University Press, 1998, [1992]).

Thornton, John K. *The Kongolese Saint Anthony: Dona Beatriz Kimpa Vita and the Antonian Movement, 1684-1706* (New York: Cambridge University Press, 1998).

Thornton, John K. *The Kingdom of the Kongo: Civil War and Transistion, 1641-1718* (Madison: The University of Wisconsin Press, 1983).

Thornton, John K. "Cannibals, Witches, and Slave Traders in the Atlantic World." *The William and Mary Quarterly* 60/2 (2003): 273-297.

Thornton, John K. "Religion and Cultural Life in the Kongo and Mbundu Areas, 1500-1800," in Heywood, *Central Africans and Cultural Transformations*, pp. 71-90.

Thornton, John K. "The Origins and Early History of the Kingdom of Kongo, c. 1350-1550," *International Journal of African Historical Studies* 34/1 (2001): pp. 1-31.

Thornton, John K. "The Coromantees: An African Cultural Group in Colonial North America and the Caribbean," *Journal of Caribbean History* 32/1-2 (1998): 161-178.

Thornton, John K. "Perspectives on African Christianity," in Vera Lawrence Hyatt and Rex Nettleford (eds.), *Race, Discourse, and the Origins of the Americas* (Washington: Smithsonian Institution, 1995), pp. 169-198.

Thornton, John K. "'I Am the Subject of the King of Congo': African Political Ideology and the Haitian Revolution," *Journal of World History* 4 (1993): 181-214.

Thornton, John K. "African Dimensions of the Stono Rebellion," *American Historical Review* 96/4 (1991): 1101-1113.

Thornton, John K. "African Soldiers in the Haitian Revolution," *Journal of Caribbean History* 25/1-2 (1991): 58-80.

Thornton, John K. "The African Experience of '20. and Odd Negroes' Arriving in Virginia in 1619," *William and Mary Quarterly* 3rd Series 55/3 (1988): 421-434.

Thornton, John K. "On the Trail of Voodoo: African Christianity in Africa and the Americas," *The Americas* 44 (1988): 261-278.

Thornton, Robert. "Narrative Ethnography in Africa, 1850-1920: The Creation and Capture of an Appropriate Domain for Anthropology," *Man* New Series. 18/3 (1983): 502-520.

Tidjani, Serpos. "Notes sur le marriage au Dahomey," *Études Dahoméennes* 6 (1951): 27-107.

Toussaint-Samson, Adèle. *A Parisian in Brazil* (Boston: James H. Earle, 1891).

Turner, Jerry Michael "Les Brésiliens: The Impact of Former Brazilian Slaves upon Dahomey," Ph. D. dissertation, Boston University, 1975.

Turner, Jerry Michael. "Identidade étnica na África Ocidental: o caso especial dos afro-brasileiros no Benin, na Nigéria, no Togo e em Ghana nos séculos XIX e XX," *Estudos Afro-Asiáticos* 28 (1995): 85-99.

Turner, Jerry Michael. "Africans, Afro-Brazilians and Europeans: 19th Century Politics on the Benin Gulf," *África* (Universidade de São Paulo) 4 (1981): 3-31.

Turner, Jerry Michael. "Cultura afro-brasileira na África Ocidental," *Estudos Afro-Asiáticos* 1 (1978): 19-25.

Turner, Lorenzo D. "Some Contacts of Brazilian ex-slaves with Nigeria, West Africa," *Journal of Negro History* 27 (1942): 55-67.

Vanhee, Hein. "Central African Popular Christianity and the Making of Haitian Vodou Religion," in Heywood, *Central Africans and Cultural Transformations*, pp. 243-264.

Vansina, Jan. *Paths in the Rainforests: Toward a History of Political Tradition in Equatorial Africa* (Madison: University of Wisconsin Press, 1990).

Vansina, Jan. *Oral Tradition as History* (Madison: University of Wisconsin Press, 1985).

Vansina, Jan. *Art History in Africa* (London: Longman, 1984).

Vansina, Jan. *Children of Woot* (Madison: University of Wisconsin Press, 1978).

Vansina, Jan. "The Doom of Early African History?," *History in Africa* 24 (1997): 337-343.

Vansina, Jan. "New Linguistic Evidence and 'The Bantu Expansion,'" *Journal of African History* 36 (1995): 173-195.

Vansina, Jan. "The Ethnographic Account as a Genre in Central Africa," *Paideuma* 33 (1987): 433-444.

Velasco e Cruz, Maria Cecília. "Tradições negras na formação de um sindicato: Sociedade de Resistência dos Trabalhadores em Trapiche e Café, Rio de Janeiro, 1905-1930," *Afro-Ásia* 24 (2000): 271-273.

Verger, Pierre. *Notas sobre o culto aos Orixás e Voduns na Bahia de Todos os Santos, no Brasil, e na antiga Costa dos Escravos, na África* trans. Carlos Eugenio Marcondes de Moura (São Paulo: Edusp, 1999 [1957]).

Verger, Pierre. *Notícias da Bahia-1850* (Salvador: Corrupio, 1981).

Verger, Pierre. *Trade Relations between the Bight of Benin and Bahia, 17th -19th Century* trans. by Evelyn Crawford (Ibadan: Ibadan University Press, 1976).

Verger, Pierre. *Fluxo e Refluxo do Tráfico de Escravos entre o Golfo de Benin e a Bahia de Todos os Santos, dos Séculos XVII ao XIX* trans. by Tasso Gadzanis (São Paulo: Corrupio, 1987).

Verger, Pierre. *Flux et Reflux de la traite des Nègres entre le Golfe de Bénin et Bahia de Todos os Santos, du XVIIe au XIXe siècle* (Paris: Mouton, 1968).

Verger, Pierre. "Mouvement des navires entre Bahia et le Golfe du Bénin (XVIIe-XIXe siècle)," *Revue française d'histoire d'outre-mer* 55 (1968): 5-36.

Verger, Pierre. "The Yoruba high god – a review of the sources," *Odu* 2 (1966): 19-40.

Verger, Pierre. "Retour des 'Bresiliens' au Golfe du Benin au XIXeme Siecle," *Études Dahoméennes* 8 (1966): 5-28.

Verger, Pierre. "Influence du Brésil au Golfe du Bénin," *Les Afro-Americains, Memoires de l'IFAN* 27 (1953): 11-101.

Vergolino, José Raimundo Oliveira. "A Demografia escrava no nordeste do Brasil: O caso de Pernambuco – 1800/1888," Texto para Discussão N°. 383, Departamento de Economia, Universidade Federal de Pernambuco, March 1997.

Viana, Antonio. *Quintal de nagô e outras crônicas, Cadernos do Centro de Estudos Baianos* N°. 84 (Salvador: UFBa, n/d).

Vilar, Enriqueta Vila. *Hispanoamerica y el comercio de esclavos: Los Asientos Portugueses* (Sevilla: Escuela de Estudios Hispano-Americanos, 1977).

Vogt, Carlos, and Fry, Peter. *Cafundó - A África no Brasil: Linguagem e sociedade* (São Paulo: Editora da UNICAMP, 1996).

Wadell, Rev. Hope Masterton. *Twenty-Nine Years in the West Indies and Central Africa: A Review of Missionary Work and Adventure 1829-1858* (London: Frank Cass, 1970 [1863]).

Wafer, Jim. *The Taste Of Blood: Spirit Possession In Brazilian Candomblé* (Philadelphia: University of Pennsylvania Press, 1991).

Walsh, R. *Notices of Brazil in 1828 and 1829* 2 vols. (London: Frederick Westley and A.H. Davis, 1830).

Warner-Lewis, Maureen. *Central Africa in the Caribbean: Transcending Time, Transforming Cultures* (Jamaica: University of the West Indies Press, 2003).

Warner-Lewis, Maureen. *Guinea's Other Suns* (Dover, MA: The Majority Press, 1991).

Weber, Max. *The Sociology of Religion* (Boston: Beacon, 1963 [1922]).

Weeks, John H. *Among the Primitive Bakongo* (New York: Negro Universities Press, 1969 [1914]).

White, Luise. "Vampire Priests of Central Africa: African Debates About Labor and Religion in Colonial Northern Zambia," *Comparative Studies in Society and History* 35/4 (1993): 746-72.

Wilks, Ivor. *Forests of Gold* (Athens: Ohio University Press, 1993).

Williams, Brackette. "Dutchman Ghosts and the History Mystery: Ritual, Colonizer, and Colonized: Interpretations of the 1763 Berbice Slave Rebellion," *Journal of Historical Sociology* 3/3 (1990): 133-165.

Williams, George Washington. *A History of the Negro Race in America from 1619 to 1880: Negroes as Slaves, as Soldiers, and as Citizens* (New York: G. P. Putnam's, 1882)

Wilson Thomas W., and Grim, Clarence E. "The Possible Relationship between the Transatlantic Slave Trade and Hypertension in Blacks Today," in Joseph E. Inikori and

Stanley Engerman (eds.), *The Atlantic Slave Trade* (Durham, NC: Duke University Press, 1992), pp. 339-359.

Winsnes, Selena Axelrod. (ed.) *Letters on West Africa and the Slave Trade: Paul Erdmann Isert's Journey to Guinea and the Caribbean Islands in Columbia (1788)* (New York: Oxford University Press, 1992).

Wissenbach, Maria Cristina Cortez. *Sonhos africanos, vivências ladinas: Escravos e forros em São Paulo (1850-1880)* (São Paulo: Editora Hucitec, 1998).

Work, John. (ed.) *American Negro Songs and Spirituals* (New York: Bonanza Books, 1940).

Worsley, Peter. *The Trumpet Shall Sound: A Study of "Cargo" Cults in Melanesia* (New York: Schocken Books, 1968).

Xavier, Regina Célia. *A conquista da liberdade* (Campinas: Centro de memória da UNICAMP, 1996).

Yai, Olabiyi B. "The Identity, Contributions, and Ideology of the Aguda (Afro-Brazilians) of the Gulf of Benin: A Reinterpretation," *Slavery and Abolition* 22 (2001): 72-82.

Yai, Olabiyi B. "From Vodun to Mahu: Monotheism and history in the Fon cultural area," in Jean-Pierre Chrétien (ed.), *L'invention religieuse en Afrique: histoire et religion en Afrique Noire* (Paris: Karthala, 1992), pp. 242-263.

Zahan, Dominique. *The Religion, Spirituality, And Thought Of Traditional Africa* (Chicago: University of Chicago Press, 1983).

Zane, Wallace W. *Journeys to the Spiritual Lands: The Natural History of a West Indian Religion* (New York: Oxford University Press, 1999).

Contributors' Biographies

EDITORS

José C. Curto is Assistant Professor in History at York University, Toronto, Canada. A member of the Harriet Tubman Research Centre on the African Diaspora, York University, he specializes on the alcohol-slave trades in, the historical demography of, and slavery in Angola, with publications in periodicals such as *Topoí* (Universidade Federal do Rio de Janeiro), *Portuguese Studies Review*, *Africana Studia* (Centro de Estudos Africanos, Universidade do Porto), *International Journal of African Historical Studies*, *Annales de démographie historique*, *África* (Centro de Estudos Africanos, Universidade de São Paulo), *African Economic History*, *Revista Internacional de Estudos Africanos*, and *History in Africa*. He is the author of *Enslaving Spirits: The Portuguese-Brazilian Alcohol Trade at Luanda and its Hinterland, c. 1550-1830* (Leiden, 2004), and *Álcool e Escravos: O comércio luso-brasileiro do álcool em Mpinda, Luanda e Benguela durante o tráfico de escravos (c. 1480-1830) e o seu impacto nas sociedades da África Central Ocidental* (Lisbon, 2002). He has also co-edited, with Paul E. Lovejoy, *Enslaving Connections: Changing Cultures of Africa and Brazil during the Era of Slavery* (Amherst, NY, 2004).

Renée Soulodre-La France is Assistant Professor at King's University College at the University of Western Ontario, Canada. She received her Ph. D. from the University of California, San Diego in 1999. She has taught Latin American and British history at the University of Alberta and the University of Lethbridge, and has been the Coordinator of Research at the York University/UNESCO/SSHRC Nigerian Hinterland Project, York University. The focus of her research is on enslaved Africans in eighteenth-century New Granada (Colombia), especially questions of identity, slavery and religion, infanticide and resistance. She has published in *Colonial Latin American Review*, *Slavery and Abolition*, in Paul E. Lovejoy and David V. Trotman (eds.), *Trans-Atlantic Dimensions of Ethnicity in the African Diaspora* (London, 2003), and [with Paul E. Lovejoy] in Claudia Mosquera, Mauricio Pardo and Odile Hoffmann (eds.), *Afrodescendientes en las Américas: Trayectorias sociales e identitarias. 150 años de la abolición de la* *esclavitud en Colombia* (Bogotá, 2002). Her first monograph, *Región y Imperio: El Tolima Grande y las Reformas Borbónicas en el siglo XVIII,* has just been published by the Instituto Colombiano de Antropologia y Historia, ICANH, Santafe de Bogotá.

CONTRIBUTORS

Edward A. Alpers is Professor of History at the University of California, Los Angeles, where he has chaired over forty Ph. D. dissertations. He also taught at the University of Dar es Salaam, Tanzania (1966-1968), and the Somali National University, Lafoole (1980). In 1994 he served as President of the African Studies Association. He has published widely on the history of East Africa and the Indian Ocean and is currently engaged in research on the African Diaspora in the Indian Ocean. His major publications include *Ivory and Slaves in East Central Africa* (Berkeley, 1975) and co-edited volumes *Walter Rodney: Revolutionary and Scholar* (Los Angeles,1982), *History, Memory and Identity* (Mauritius, 2001), *Africa and the West: A Documentary History* (Phoenix, 2001) and *Sidis and Scholars: Essays on African Indians* (Trenton, NJ, 2004).

Stephen D. Behrendt is Senior Lecturer in History at Victoria University of Wellington, where he has taught since 1999. Steve is co-author of *The Trans-Atlantic Slave Trade: A Database on CD-ROM* (Cambridge, 1999) and numerous articles on the eighteenth century British slave trade. He currently is working on a revised edition of Antera Duke's diary (published first in 1956), a study of surgeons in the British slave trade, and a general study of Africans in the Atlantic World. He may be contacted at steve.behrendt@vuw.ac.nz.

José Capela was born in northern Portugal and undertook his studies at the Seminary of Porto. In 1956 he became the chief editor of the daily «Diário de Moçambique» and in 1959 he became the director of the same. In 1962 he founded the «Voz Africana» and in 1963 the journal «Economia de Moçambique». In 1970 he returned to Portugal, where he founded the «Voz Portucalense» and served as its editor. Between 1978 and 1996 he was the Cultural Attaché for the Embassy of Portugal in Maputo. He has published more than a dozen major works focusing upon colonial relations and the history of Mozambique. He is a researcher at the Centro de Estudos Africanos at the University of Porto.

David Eltis is Robert W. Woodruff Professor of History, Emory University, editor of *Free and Coerced Migrations: A Global Perspective* (Stanford, 2002), co-editor of *Slavery in the Development of the Americas* (Cambridge, 2004) author of *The Rise of African Slavery in the Americas* (Cambridge, 2000), and co-author of *The Transatlantic Slave Trade: A Database on CD-ROM* (Cambridge, 1999).

Dale T. Graden received his Ph. D. from the University of Connecticut. He is Associate Professor of History and director of Latin American Studies at the University of Idaho. His research focuses upon slavery, emancipation and race in Brazil during the 19th and 20th centuries. He has published several articles on these themes. His forthcoming monograph is entitled *From Slavery to Freedom in Brazil: Bahia, 1835-1900.*

Jane Landers (Ph. D., University of Florida) is Associate Dean of the College of Arts & Science, Associate Professor of History and Director of the Center for Latin American and Iberian Studies at Vanderbilt University. She has also served as a historical consultant on museum exhibits, documentary films, and archaeological projects related to her research interests. Her major publications are *Black Society in Spanish Florida* (Urbana, 1999), editor of *Colonial Plantations and Economy of Florida* (Gainesville, 2000) and *Against the Odds: Free Blacks in the Slave Societies of the Americas* (London, 1996) and co-editor of *The African American Heritage of Florida* (Gainesville, 1995). Landers has also published essays on the African history of the Hispanic Southeast and of the circum-Caribbean in *The American Historical Review, Slavery and Abolition, The New West Indian Guide, The Americas, Colonial Latin American Historical Review* and *Historical Archaeology*, with other work appearing in a variety of anthologies and edited volumes. She is currently working on two new books based on archival research in Spain, Mexico, Cuba, the Dominican Republic and Ecuador ("Juan Bautista Witten, Formerly Known as Big Prince: An African in the Atlantic World" and "Black Kingdoms, Black Republics: Free African Towns in the Spanish Americas"), editing a volume entitled *Slaves, Subjects, and Subversives: Blacks in Colonial Latin America*, and co-authoring a textbook on Atlantic world history. Landers is former president of the Forum on European Expansion and Global Interaction and a member of the International Advisory Board of the Nigerian Hinterland Project sponsored by UNESCO and York University, Canada.

Elizabeth W. Kiddy is an Assistant Professor of history and the Director of the Latin American Studies Program at Albright College in Reading, Pennsylvania. She received her doctorate from the University of New Mexico in 1998. She has published several articles and book chapters, and her first monograph, *Blacks of the Rosary, Memory and History in Minas Gerais, Brazil*, is to be published by Penn State Press. In addition to her academic work, she has been a practitioner of the Afro-Brazilian art form, *capoeira*, since 1984, and has been teaching the art since 1992.

Colleen Kriger Colleen Kriger received her Ph. D. from York University in 1993. She is Associate Professor of History at the University of North Carolina at Greensboro. Her recent publications include *Pride of Men: Ironworking in*

19th century West Central Africa (Portsmouth, NH, 1999) as well as articles on economic history and material culture. She is currently completing a book on textile production and trade in West Africa for the African Archaeology Series published by AltaMira Press.

Luis Nicolau Parés received his Ph. D. at SOAS in 1997. He is an Assistant Professor at the Universidade Federal de Bahia, where he teaches and conducts research on Afro-Brazilian religion and culture. His most recent publications include: "The Jeje in the Bahian Condomblé and in the Tambor de Mina of Maranhão," in K. Mann and E. Bay, eds., *Rethinking the African Diaspora: The Making of a Black Atlantic World in the Bight of Benin and Brazil* (London, 2001), pp. 91-115; and "The Nagôization process in Bahian Candomblé," in Toyin Falola and Matt D. Childs, eds., *The Yoruba Diaspora in the Atlantic World* (Bloomington, 2005), pp. 300-341. His monograph *The Jeje Candomblé: History and Ritual of the Vodun in Bahia* is forthcoming.

David Richardson is Professor of Economic History and Director-Designate of the newly established Wilberforce Institute for the study of Slavery and Emancipation (WISE) at the University of Hull, United Kingdom. He has published extensively on the Atlantic slave trade, and is co-editor (with David Eltis) of *Routes to Slavery: Direction, Ethnicity and Mortality in the Transatlantic Slave Trade* (London, 1997), and co-author (with David Eltis, Stephen D. Behrendt, and Herbert S. Klein) of *The Transatlantic Slave Trade 1527-1867: A Database on CD-Rom* (Cambridge, 1998). An enlarged and online version of this dataset is currently in preparation.

João José Reis is Professor of History at the Universidade Federal da Bahia, Brazil. His major research interest is the history of slavery and slave resistance in Brazil. He is the author of *Slave Rebellion in Brazil: The 1835 Muslim Uprising in Bahia* (Baltimore, 1993), and *A Morte é uma Festa: Ritos Fúnebres e Revolta popular no Brasil no Século XIX* (São Paulo, 1992), among other works.

Terry Rey, formerly Professeur de Sociologie des Religions at l'Université d'État d'Haïti, is Associate Professor of African and Caribbean Religions at Florida International University. He has published "The Virgin Mary and Revolution in Saint-Domingue: The Charisma of Romaine-la-Prophétesse," *Journal of Historical Sociology* 11 (1998); and "A Consideration of Kongolese Catholic Influences on Haitian Popular Catholicism: A Sociohistorical Exploration," in Linda M. Heywood (ed.), *Central Africans and Cultural Transformations in the American Diaspora* (New York, 2002). His first monograph was *Our Lady of Class Struggle: The Cult of the Virgin Mary in Haiti* (Trenton, NJ, 1999). He received his Ph. D. from Temple University in 1996.

Monica Schuler was born in Guyana. She was a Research Assistant in the Caribbean History Project at the University of the West Indies, Mona, from 1965 to 1966 and obtained a Ph.D. in history from the University of Wisconsin-Madison in 1977. In 1973, she began teaching at Wayne State University from which she retired with the rank of Professor in 2001. She has published extensively on Caribbean slave resistance and religion and also post-emancipation African laborers in Jamaica, Guyane française and Guyana, including *"Alas, Alas, Kongo": A Social History of Indentured African Immigration into Jamaica, 1841-1865* (Baltimore, 1980). She is currently finishing a biography of the Jamaican religious leader and healer Alexander Bedward.

Elisée Soumonni has been teaching and conducting research in West Africa since the 1960s, first at the University of Ile-Ife (now Awolowo University), where he received his Ph. D., then at Ahmadu Bello University, in Zaria, and since 1984 at the Université Nationale du Bénin in Cotonou. He currently is Coordinator of the *Institut Béninois d'études et de recherche sur la diaspora africaine* (IBERDA), member of the International Scientific Committee of the UNESCO "Slave Route" Project, and also sits on the Steering Committee of the UNESCO ASPnet Transatlantic Slave Trade (TST) Education Project. His research focuses on the slave ports of the Bight of Benin, including a biography of Pierre Tamata, the leading merchant at Porto-Novo at the end of the 1700s, and biographies of Afro-Brazilian and Afro-Cuban families in coastal towns; and the specific history of Dahomey and the various Yoruba states. His publications (in English) have appeared in Robin Law (ed.), *From Slave Trade to 'Legitimate' Commerce: The Commercial Transition in Nineteenth Century West Africa* (Cambridge, 1995), *Slavery and Abolition*, and in Paul E. Lovejoy and David V. Trotman (eds.), *Trans-Atlantic Dimensions of Ethnicity in the African Diaspora* (London, 2003). He is currently writing a book with Paul E. Lovejoy on the history of Atlantic Africa.

Index